TECHNICAL WRITING

FOR SUCCESS

A SCHOOL-TO-WORK APPROACH

Sue Mehlich

Pitt Community College
Greenville, North Carolina

Darlene Smith-Worthington

Pitt Community College
Greenville, North Carolina

SOUTH-WESTERN EDUCATIONAL PUBLISHING

Editor-In-Chief: Peter McBride
Project Manager: Penny Shank
Production Coordinator: Tricia Boies
Editor: Timothy Bailey
Design: Rosa + Wesley Design Associates
Production Services: Navta Associates
Cover Design: Joe Pagliaro
Photo Editor: Connie Springer
Marketing Manager: Carolyn Love

ISBN: 0-538-68296-5

Page 3, "Rebuilding Your Engine" and Page 165, "Header Comparison: Horsepower vs. Engine Speed" reprinted with permission of Summit Racing Equipment, Akron, Ohio.

Page 5, "she being Brand" is reprinted from COMPLETE POEMS: 1904–1962 by E.E. Cummings, Edited by George J. Firmage, by permission of Liveright Publishing Corporation. Copyright © 1926, 1954, 1991 by the Trustees for the E. E. Cummings Trust. Copyright © 1985 by George James Firmage.

Page 60, Figure 4.2, letter reprinted with permission of Garrie W. Moore, Pitt Community College, Greenville, NC.

Page 121, reprinted by permission of Atlanta Committee for the Olympic Games.

Page 171, VCR instructions courtesy of Thomson Consumer Electronics.

Page 191, "Printers for the Road" reprinted by permission of Macworld Communications, Inc. Copyright © 1995. All rights reserved.

Page 294, excerpt from AN INCOMPLETE EDUCATION by Judy Jones and William Wilson. Copyright © 1987 by Judy Jones and William Wilson. Reprinted by permission of Ballantine Books, a Division of Random House Inc.

Page 373, Figure 18.5; Page 375, Figure 18.7; and Pages 383–384, "Apply What You Have Learned" Passage 2, from *Nelson Biology* by Ritter, Coombs, Drysdale and Gardner. Reprinted with permission of Nelson Canada, A Division of Thomson Canada Limited.

I(T)P
International Thomson Publishing

South-Western Educational Publishing is a division of International Thomson Publishing Inc. The ITP trademark is used under license.

7 8 9   BAW 04 03

Printed in the United States of America

Preface

Welcome to *Technical Writing for Success: A School-to-Work Approach*! If developing skills for a successful future is important to you, this textbook was designed for you. We believe there is a need for a report-writing textbook that is lively and relevant for students and easy and effective for teachers.

Technical Writing for Success: A School-to-Work Approach offers a usable, relevant, comprehensive, and appropriate text. This highly readable book will motivate you to use **the thinking, listening, composing, revising, editing, and speaking skills employers demand in the workplace.**

Skills for Future Success

Technology is changing our world almost daily, and successful employees (and students) will be those who

- communicate effectively with others at all levels, both inside and outside the organization,
- learn and change as the demands of the workplace change,
- work in teams,
- use technology to get the job done efficiently and economically,
- think critically and solve problems, and
- make important decisions.

Success in the workplace begins in the classroom as students develop the skills they will need to compete in a global economy.

Philosophy

Technical Writing for Success: A School-to-Work Approach supports these beliefs about the teaching of technical communication:

- Students learn more readily when they have a need for the knowledge or the skill being taught and when they perceive the learning as relevant.
- Technical communication complements, rather than conflicts with, traditional English and literature instruction.
- Students must take responsibility for their learning.
- Technical communication classrooms should be active and sometimes interactive places as students apply communication skills they are learning.

- Students develop critical thinking skills through discovery learning.
- Students benefit from collaborative learning activities.
- Students are especially motivated to improve communication skills when the topic relates to their area of career interest and when the skills are taught in that technical context.
- Writing is a process, not a product.
- Everyone in the class has something valuable to contribute.
- Effective teaching starts with the familiar and moves toward new concepts and skills.

Tools for Developing Skills

Technical Writing for Success was designed to encourage students to acquire many workplace skills through integrated and applied instruction. It features

- an engaging writing style
- student and real-world models
- writing process instruction
- editing and revision checklists
- technical reading guidelines
- journal and write-to-learn activities
- employment communications
- terms and definitions
- case studies
- collaborative activities
- technical writing style tips
- audience analysis instruction
- discovery learning opportunities
- primary and secondary research
- anecdotes and examples including
  Focus on Ethics
  Writers on the Job
  The Professional Speaks
  Technology Update

Organization for Ease of Use, Flexibility, and Integration

Chapters are organized to move from basic, simple skills progressively through more complex, difficult activities. However, each chapter has been written to be independent of other chapters, thus making the book flexible to meet the needs of your course.

   This textbook is divided into the following six parts:

- **Part 1** includes an overview of technical writing—what it is and how it relates to other types of writing. Audience analysis is then addressed before instruction on writing principles begins.
- **Part 2** quickly moves students into writing. We believe that communication skills improve most rapidly when students can practice writing.

Students learn to write brief communications—including memorandums, letters, employment communications, and news releases—as well as to make oral presentations.

- **Part 3** guides students through informative reports including instructions summaries, mechanism descriptions, and incident reports. Document design and visual aids are also presented.

- **Part 4** covers a variety of analytical reports—science lab reports, progress reports, and periodic reports—as well as a persuasive report—the recommendation report.

- **Part 5** includes four chapters related to researched reports. Problem solving and data collection are presented before the introduction of informal and formal proposals.

- **Part 6** provides guidelines to improve technical reading skills. Excerpts from various types of technical writing are provided for discussion and reinforcement.

The textbook's design also supports integration. First, the thinking, problem-solving, reading, writing, and speaking of technical and scientific subjects are integrated throughout the text. Second, classes using the text may integrate the technical communication course with materials from technical or core academic classes. In fact, teachers should consider coordinating assignments or team teaching some reports with technical or other academic teachers and using authentic, real-world problems for reporting.

Features to Enhance Writing

Writing chapters emphasize the writing process and enhance learning by moving from the familiar to the unfamiliar. Each writing chapter includes the following features:

- Opening **real-world model** to add relevance to the chapter
- **Glossary of definitions** to expand technical communication vocabulary
- **Write-to-Learn activity** to prepare students for the chapter's detailed instruction
- **Prewriting section** to aid students in their planning
- **Warm Up activity** in every section (except prewriting) to focus students on what they already know about the subject
- **Stop and Think exercises** concluding each section to check comprehension or to prepare students for the next section
- **Editing and Revision Checklist** to encourage students to be responsible for their own writing success
- **End-of-Chapter exercises and activities** including practice exercises, case studies, and suggestions for writing to reinforce and assess learning
- **The Inside Track** to provide suggestions for improving technical writing style

● Icons are used for your convenience in identifying special activities. These symbols specify the following:

 Collaborative Activity

 Template Disk Application

Supplements

The following instructional supplements are available to accompany the textbook.

● **Computer Diskette.** This optional diskette provides activities and exercises that are correlated with the organization and content of the textbook.

● **Blackline Masters.** A set of reproducible blackline masters duplicates many of the most important teaching materials from the textbook and includes new materials to supplement the text.

● **Teacher's Manual.** The comprehensive teacher's manual contains general suggestions for the course; SCANS, Tech Prep, and Goals 2000 correlations; teaching suggestions for each chapter including objectives, additional resources, supplemental acitivies, and suggested answers to activities and exercises; and one-page chapter quizzes.

Message to the Student

How important is technical communication for you? If you aren't certain, read advertisements for jobs or ask employers what skills are necessary. In the employment and academic world, you can be only as effective as your communication skills will allow you to be. No matter how proficient your technical skills, if you cannot communicate your ideas to others you cannot function successfully.

While technical communication skills are essential, gaining those skills should not be a painful process. In fact, one of the aims of this textbook is to be lively and connected to your interests. You may even be surprised that technical communication builds on your composition skills but is not like English or writing classes you have had before.

About the Authors

Sue Mehlich and Darlene Smith-Worthington are full-time teachers who are enthusiastic and earnest supporters of education that prepares people for the world of work. Sue Mehlich has taught in middle and high school, and currently teaches community college students; she also has owned and managed several businesses. Darlene Smith-Worthington is a community college instructor who also has experience in editing a weekly newspaper, directing public relations for a junior college, and managing small businesses, including a farming operation. Both have taught technical writing for more than 10 years. Using their business backgrounds and their combined 29 years' teaching experience, the authors present real-world-based reporting materials and sensible, useful teaching suggestions.

Acknowledgements

We thank the many people who helped us create this book. The talents and contributions of these individuals have been essential in developing a text that will be valued by students, faculty, and business and industry. We are particularly grateful to the following professionals for their advice and generous support: John Hutchens, Dr. Edgar Boyd, our English and Humanities family, the Arts and Sciences Division, and all our colleagues at Pitt Community College and Pitt County Public Schools, Greenville, North Carolina.

We specifically acknowledge the help of the following people: Hilda Barrow for advice on technical reading; Judith Kasperek and Linwood Woodard for suggestions on the graphics used in Chapter 8; Linda Leighty for information and advice on Data Collection; Jane Smith for help with research; Matthew Mehlich and Ashley Respess for the use of their lab reports in Chapter 11; Susan Nobles and Kim Dale for news release information and anecdotes; and Worth Worthington for advice on proposals.

We also appreciate the following educators who reviewed our manuscript and made suggestions for improvement:

Linda Barr, Otterbein College, Westerville, Ohio

Sally Becker, Oldebolt-Arthur High School, Oldebolt, Iowa

Gaynell Deans, D.H. Conley High School, Greenville, North Carolina

Andy Foster, Monticello Community High School, Monticello, Iowa

Jan Kakela, Ingram Intermediate School District, Mason, Michigan

Mary J. Kisner, The Pennsylvania State University, University Park, Pennsylvania

Elaine Langlois, technical consultant, Cincinnati, Ohio

Mary Poremba, Wyoming Valley West High School, Plymouth, Pennsylvania

Also, thanks to all our students for their compliments and criticism, for their honesty, and for their willingness to share their writing experiences with us.

Finally, the greatest appreciation must go to our families—Mark and Frankie; Worth and David; and Mamie, Patsy, and David. Without their support, this book would still be a dream.

Brief Contents

Table of Contents

PART 3 Informative Reports

PART 4 Analytical and Persuasive Reports

Background

CHAPTER 1

What is Technical Writing?

Write-to-Learn

Read each of the four models presented at the beginning of the chapter. Think about the type of writing each one represents. In a one-page journal entry, write the answers to these questions: Which type represents the kind of assignment you are accustomed to writing? Describe the circumstances under which you were writing. Which of the four types would you prefer to write? Why? Which do you prefer to read? Why?

DEFINITIONS

ambiguous more than one interpretation is possible; describes writing that can mean different things to different people

academic writing the expository and persuasive writing done in academic circles; examples include personal essays, research papers, analyses, arguments

expository writing writing to explain or inform

expressive writing writing to express or portray personal observation or feeling

field research research done in the field, especially through surveys and interviews

inferences making judgments about reading that the author does not make for you

jargon the highly specialized language of a particular discipline or technical field

literary writing writing such as novels, short stories, drama, and poetry created as an art form

imaginative writing writing such as novels, short stories, drama, and poetry whose situations grow out of fantasy or imagination; events and people are fictional although the themes may reveal universal truths

persuasive writing writing to convince others

rights-based ethics acts assume that human beings have certain *rights* that cannot be taken away

rule-based ethics acts are judged against the *rules* of the group

style the way an author uses words and sentences

syntax the order of words in a sentence

technical writing writing done in the workplace; subject is usually technical, written carefully for a specific audience; organization is predictable and apparent; style is concise; tone is objective and business-like; and special features include visual elements

tone emotional overtones; the way words make readers feel

utilitarian useful in a practical way

utility-based ethics acts are judged by what is best for the *general good* of the group

Rebuilding Your Engine

TECHNICAL WRITING
Excerpt

Excessive **smoking** or **knocking** could mean it's time to rebuild your engine. When it comes time to rebuild, consider Summit's 1) Engine Kits or 2) Re-Ring Kits.

Engine Kits

Engine kits can be purchased with one of the following combinations:
- premium forged TRW pistons and moly rings,
- premium cast TRW pistons with moly rings, or
- cast TRW pistons with regular rings.

The kits also come with TRW main, cam and rod bearings; a TRW high volume oil pump; top quality Fel-Pro Blue Perma Torque gaskets; a set of oil and freeze plugs; and Clevite assembly lube. See Table 1 for a cost breakdown.

Re-Ring Kits

If your present pistons are in good shape and you don't need main and cam bearings or an oil pump, Re-Rings Kits may work. They include regular or moly rings, rod bearings, and a Fel-Pro Blue Perma Torque gasket set. See Table 2 for . . . .

Table 1 Engine Kits

Engine	Our Good Kit: Cast Pistons Regular Rings	Our Better Kit: Cast Pistons Moly Rings	Our Best Kit: Forged Pistons Moly Rings
Chevy 327 '62–'66	$214.95	$219.95	$308.95
Chevy 350 '67–'80	$172.95	$184.95	$298.95
Chevy 350 '81	$181.95	$189.95	$291.95

The Evolution of the Automobile

. . . The history of the automobile engine is a history of change, changes in technology accompanied by changes in attitude.

In 1801, Englishman Richard Trevithick designed the first steampowered carriage for transporting passengers, but England was not ready for speed. The Red Flag Law, passed by Parliament in 1865, slowed down the production of the steampowered vehicle by limiting its speed to 3 miles per hour. The law required a man to walk in front of the vehicle and hold a red flag by day and a red lantern by night to warn others of its arrival (Roland 367). By the mid 19th century, however, ...

Owning a Car

Owning a car is not all it's cracked up to be. My parents offered to make the down payment on a used Ford Mustang, but I was responsible for the monthly payments, half the insurance premium, and the cost of maintenance. Sure, a job waiting tables at Schooner's promised to cover all my expenses—that is, until the restaurant closed for repairs. And then my "maintenance-free" Ford sprung a leak when the radiator rusted out. Oil changes, inspection stickers, a headlight out, a fuse blown—I began to wish I lived in a big city with public transportation, or maybe in a very small town where my bike . . . .

she being Brand

by e.e.cummings

she being Brand

-new;and you
know consequently a
little stiff i was
careful of her and(having

thoroughly oiled the universal
joint tested my gas felt of
her radiator made sure her springs were O.

K.)i went right to it flooded-the-carburetor cranked her

up,slipped the
clutch(and then somehow got into reverse she
kicked what
the hell)next
minute i was back in neutral tried and

again slo-wly;bare,ly nudg. ing(my

lev-er Right–
oh and her gears being in
A 1 shape passed
from low through
second-in-to-high like
greasedlightning)just as we turned the corner of Divinity

avenue i touched the accelerator and give

her the juice, good

               (it

was the first ride and believe i we was
happy to see how nice she acted right up to
the last minute coming back down by the Public
Gardens i slammed on

the
internalexpanding
&
externalcontracting
brakes Bothatonce and

brought allofher tremB
-ling
to a:dead.

stand–
;Still)

After completing this chapter, you will be able to

- Discuss the importance of technical writing in the workplace

- Define technical writing

- Compare technical writing to other types of writing

- Discuss solutions to ethical dilemmas in the workplace

S–S–S–S–S–S–S–S–S KABOOM! Information explosion! Everywhere you look: print media including books, magazines, pamphlets, reports, manuals; electronic media including electronic mailboxes, CD-ROMS, computer networks, satellite dishes. Never before has there been so much technical information to disperse to so many people.

But don't run for cover. Enjoy the blasts of color and light, the sending and receiving of new information. We even dare you to set off your own information explosion!

Writing in the Workplace

WARM UP

Think about your chosen profession. What kind of documents do you think you will write in that profession?

Regardless of the career you choose, you will write in the workplace. Conservative estimates suggest that you will spend at least 20% of your time writing in a technical or business occupation. If you plan to move up, your chances of promotion will most assuredly depend on how well you communicate. One chief engineer said competent engineers could be "hired by the dozen, but there's a shortage of those who can put their ideas on paper clearly." In a series of interviews with business and technical managers, all agreed that clear and effective writing "is a skill crucial to achievement in the corporate world" (Hamermesh 22).

For work to be productive, employees must write down what they do on the job. Nurses chart a patient's medical condition so that the nurses on the next shift can carry on. Police accident reports record facts for later use in court. Chemists and engineers document procedures for the government; accountants prepare annual reports for their clients. The kind of writing these people engage in is called **technical writing**, the writing done in the work-place.

Technical writing can be anything from a short memo in an office to a researched grant proposal for a major firm. Sales catalogs, business letters, financial reports, standard operating procedures, medical studies, lab reports—all these and more fall under the heading of technical writing, the focus of this book.

STOP AND THINK

Discuss the importance of technical writing in the workplace. Why do you think writing affects your chances of advancement?

Characteristics of Technical Writing

WARM UP

Review the four models at the beginning of this chapter. (Remember the models are excerpts from longer documents.) Divide a sheet of notebook paper into four columns. It may help to turn your paper sideways. Label column 1 as technical document, column 2 as research paper, column 3 as personal essay, and column 4 as poem. Using your columns as a chart, answer the following questions for the four models.

1. What is the subject of each? How does the treatment of each subject differ? Describe the research required for each document.

2. What does each writer want from his or her audience? What has the writer done to consider the needs of the reader?

3. Describe the organization of each document. In which one is the organi-zation of the document apparent at one glance?

4. Describe the style (author's use of word and sentences) of each document.

5. Describe the tone (the emotional flavor—the way the words make you feel) of each document.

6. Which document uses special features such as underlining, boldfacing, and visuals to enhance the writing?

Subject

The subject of each model on pages 3–5 is cars, but the approach to this subject is different for each document. The poem humorously describes the stops and starts of learning to drive a manual transmission, an experience with which many of us can identify. Such writing is **literary writing**, an art form represented by short stories, novels, and poetry. Often a poet relies on personal experience for research, as Cummings did here.

The personal essay expresses a young woman's frustration at the cost of owning an automobile, another experience with which many of us can identify. **Expressive writing** is created to convey personal observations and, like literary writing, relies on personal experience for research.

The treatment of cars in the research paper is factual. The research paper's purpose is not to relate personal experience but to explain facts gained from library research. Writing to explain or inform is **expository writing.**

While most academic research papers are factual papers written on topics of interest to the reader, the technical document (even a technical research document) is written to fulfill a need. Often the need is for information. Here, someone with serious engine trouble may need to rebuild an engine; hence, the technical document fulfills the special needs of a specific reader. The writer of this technical document also hopes to persuade the reader to buy the kits from the Summit catalog instead of somewhere else. **Persuasive writing** may require library research, scientific observation, or **field research** (use of surveys and interviews). Whether to inform or persuade, technical writing relies on data presented with precision and accuracy.

Audience

The writer of the poem and the essay expect some understanding from their readers as they share experiences. Cummings might also want his reader to have some fun with the words, but he probably didn't think seriously of meeting his readers' needs. Certainly, if he had, he would have written in a more conventional style. The student writing the personal essay seeks some understanding from the reader but is more likely interested in expressing her point of view. The writer of the research paper may be very interested in the subject and hopes an interested reader will read it for the facts.

The technical writer, however, expects more from a very specific reader—one needing information on engine kits. The technical writer not only expects the reader to understand the writing but also wants the reader to do something after reading—order an engine kit. When you want more from a reader, you have to work harder as a writer to meet the reader's needs.

In technical writing the needs of the reader dictate every decision the writer makes. In our model the writer has worked hard to present the information the reader needs in a format that is easy to read. The headings, bold-facing, special table and no-frills language show that the writer is extremely conscious of his or her reader.

Lynette Thomas is a Legal Assistant with the firm Thomas and Farris. On the job, she spends approximately one third of her time writing. Among her writing tasks are letters of transmittal to accompany estate information. She also transcribes lawyers' notes and drafts wills, legal complaints, and accident reports. Thomas is an asset to the firm because she is a good grammarian with an understanding of legal terms. In particular, her job demands that her writing be clear and accurate.

Organization

It's impossible to detect the organization of the poem at one glance. In fact, the liberties the author takes with spacing and line lengths make the poem appear confusing until you've read it several times. The personal essay and research paper make standard use of a topic sentence, thesis, and transitional expressions, but you still have to read each paper before the organization becomes apparent.

The technical writing model, however, uses headings to help you perceive the organization at a single glance *before* you read. The use of **1)** and **2)** in the first sentence also helps draw your eye to the thesis of this document before you read. Also, use of headings gives a reader an opportunity to read only what he or she wants or needs to read. If the customer interested in rebuilding an engine wants to price only the re-ring kits, the heading "Re-ring Kits" allows the eye to travel quickly to the information needed.

Style

The poem has the most unusual **style**—as poems often do. Cummings breaks the conventional rules of punctuation and **syntax** (sentence order) for poetic effect. The style mirrors the stops and starts of a car. Readers must read the poem several times to understand how the punctuation fits his message.

The personal essay is casual, almost conversational, but more conventional than the poem. We are comfortable with this style, having written personal essays in school. The writer uses examples and some description. The research paper's style is also conventional.

The technical document uses a simple, concise, straightforward style that is easily understood. The long sentences are simply lists. The other sentences are short, and the sentence order is predictable. There are no surprises for the reader. The vocabulary is highly specialized, the **jargon** of the automotive technician.

Tone

The **tone** of the poem is humorous, the tone of the personal essay is casual, and the tone of the research paper is objective.

Emotion creates tone. The expressive nature of a poem or a personal essay can run the gamut of emotion—sadness, excitement, irony, humor. However, we don't expect research papers or technical documents to convey emotion. In fact, emotion can get in the way of a technical document. Readers of technical documents read for information, not for entertainment. Some say technical writing is boring because of its lack of emotion. However, for the person needing or wanting that information, the topic is not boring. The tone in technical writing is best described as objective or businesslike.

Special Features

The only document to rely on special features is the technical document. Technical writing uses special features such as boldfacing, underlining, and bulleted lists to draw attention to certain words. Also, the use of visual aids—such as tables, graphs, and diagrams—helps to relay complex information instantaneously.

S T O P   A N D   T H I N K   1.2

From your analysis in Warm Up 1.2 activity, write your own definition of technical writing.

How Technical Writing Differs from Other Writing

W A R M   U P   1.3

From your experience with writing, what characteristics does good writing share? In other words, how would you describe good writing?

Technical writing shares much in common with the academic writing you have experienced so far in school. It also shares much in common with the literature you have read. The differences, however, set technical writing apart.

Technical Writing Vs. Academic Writing

Academic writing—such as the personal essay, research paper, analysis, and argument—must be unified, coherent, and well organized. Technical writing must also be unified, coherent, and well organized. Matters of style and standard usage are important to both academic and technical writing. Certainly both types rely on a complex writing process. They are written in stages from prewriting to writing to editing and revising. The purpose is often the same—to inform or persuade.

The difference between the two is in the presentation, audience, and approach. Academic writing presents itself in a succession of paragraphs—usually an introductory paragraph, a number of paragraphs that develop a thesis, and a concluding paragraph. Academic writing is written for an academic audience—a teacher, your classmates, or a group of interested scholars. Its approach is to expand on thought or make observations about human experience. As a result, the subject matter, style, and tone are more varied.

Technical writing also presents itself in paragraphs and often begins with an introduction and closes with a conclusion, but technical writing (with its headings, itemized lists, boldfacing, and visual aids) looks different from academic writing. Written for a specific audience, the subject is treated in a more technical, business, or scientific way. Generally, the approach is more **utilitarian**, and there is less flexibility in the subject matter, style, and tone.

Technical Writing Vs. Imaginative Writing

Imaginative writing also holds to principles of unity, coherence, and standard usage and develops according to a complex process. Such writing, however, is less academic and more artistic.

Imaginative writing can be **ambiguous**, meaning different things to different people. Imaginative writing also requires the reader to draw **inferences**, to make judgments that the writer does not state.

Technical writing should be unambiguous and direct. A work of literature may be especially good because it means different things to different readers. It is thought-provoking to ponder the different meanings of the old man's voyage in Hemingway's *The Old Man and the Sea*, but W. Earl Britton says "that the primary, though not the sole, characteristic of technical and scientific writing lies in the effort of the author to convey one and only one meaning in what he says" (114).

There must be no doubt about the meaning of a sentence in technical writing. "Turn *there*," the man said, and the woman turned left when he meant for her to turn right. The word "there" is subject to interpretation. However, "Turn right at the next paved road" has only one meaning.

Imaginative writing requires us to make inferences. When Emily Dickinson writes: "Because I could not stop for Death—/He kindly stopped for me—/The Carriage held but just Ourselves—/and Immortality," we have more questions at first than answers. Why is death being personified? Why does Dickinson capitalize *Death, Carriage, Ourselves,* and *Immortality?*

We expect to make inferences about poetry. We do not expect to make inferences about technical writing.

On the other hand, if a doctor gave instructions like the following to his nurse, what would happen? *Because I could not remember the name of Ms. Dickinson's medication, would you kindly call the pharmacy and ask for the bottle that holds the blue pills and the red?* Poor Ms. Dickinson. She'd find more comfort in the words of her poem than in the advice of her doctor.

Exposure to both imaginative literature and technical writing can broaden your understanding of writing in all areas. As a result, you can become a more versatile and capable reader and writer, no matter what the subject.

S T O P   A N D   T H I N K   1.3

Write a paragraph comparing technical writing to academic and imaginative writing.

Ethics and Technical Writing

W A R M   U P   1.4

What would be the right thing to do if a person you don't know becomes intoxicated at a party and insists on driving home? Suppose your best friend becomes intoxicated at a party and insists on driving home?

Ethics is a code of morality that determines how human beings should treat each other. Ethical codes can vary from one culture to another and from one individual to another. Where there is a spirit of mutual respect and responsible behavior, a framework for acceptable ethical conduct exists.

Ethical conduct is important in the workplace—so important that ethical standards are protected by our legal system. Companies can be sued for ethical infractions such as endangering the environment, selling a product that hurts customers, or failing to hire workers fairly. Tobacco companies have been sued for endangering an individual's health. Accident victims claim negligence by car manufacturers. At any given time, you can find examples such as these in news reports of companies whose ethics have been called into question.

Our Society and Ethics

Although much ethical behavior grows out of religious beliefs, ethical behavior does not necessarily mean religious behavior. Hoop and Pearsall summarize three types of ethical systems as "utility-based," "rule-based," and "rights-based." **Utility-based ethics** do what is best for the *general good* of the group. In **rule-based ethics**, acts are judged against the *rules* the group has set up. **Rights-based ethics** assume that human beings have certain *rights* that cannot be taken away (20).

In the Warm Up, you were asked what would be the right thing to do if someone you knew were intoxicated at a party and insisted on driving home. Applying utility-based ethics to this situation, we might ask: Is it good for the group if the individual drives home? The answer here is no. If the individual poses a threat to others on the road, his or her driving is not an action that is good for the group.

Applying rule-based ethics, we might ask: Would this person's driving break any rules? Yes, driving under the influence breaks the law. If the driver has a wreck and kills someone, then a law has been broken. Applying rights-based ethics, we might ask: Does this person have the right to drive? No. Driving in itself is a privilege, not a right. This person may be depriving someone else of his or her right to a safe highway.

No matter what the ethics are based on, ethical systems assume that people are responsible, that they will weigh the consequences of their actions, that they are aware of others, and that they are aware of self. People have a choice—they can choose to act ethically, or they can choose to act unethically.

Sometimes an individual's ethical code may come into conflict with the codes of others. If your personal ethics come into conflict with workplace practices, then you can define yourself by how well you stand up for your own ethics. It's not easy, however. If you discover that the company that pays your salary is doing something wrong, it can be difficult to criticize.

> *Writing is manual labor of the mind: a job, like laying pipe.*
>
> JOHN GREGORY DUNNE

FOCUS ON ETHICS

At the turn of the century, children of all ages were orphaned on the streets of New York. Most were the sons and daughters of immigrants who had died enroute to the New World or shortly thereafter. These children roamed the streets begging for and stealing food. The penalty for stealing was death by hanging, and some children were actually hanged for such crimes. Suppose you had been a store owner at the turn of the century in New York and had seen a young boy take three apples off a cart. What would you have done?

Ethics for Technical Communicators

The Society for Technical Communicators has adopted a code of ethics for its members. Read the code in Figure 1.1, written specifically for technical writers and speakers.

Figure 1.1 Code for Communicators

Code for Communicators

As a technical communicator, I am the bridge between those who create ideas and those who use them. Because I recognize that the quality of my services directly affects how well ideas are understood, I am committed to excellence in performance and the highest standards of ethical behavior.

I value the worth of the ideas I am transmitting and the cost of developing and communicating those ideas. I also value the time and effort spent by those who read or see or hear my communication.

I therefore recognize my responsibility to communicate technical information truthfully, clearly, and economically.

My commitment to professional excellence and ethical behavior means that I will

- Use language and visuals with precision.

- Prefer simple, direct expression of ideas.

- Satisfy the audience's need for information, not my own need for self-expression.

- Hold myself responsible for how well my audience understands my message.

- Respect the work of colleagues, knowing that seldom is only one communications solution right and all others wrong.

- Strive continually to improve my professional competence.

- Promote a climate that encourages the exercise of professional judgement and that attracts talented individuals to careers in technical communication.

 SOCIETY FOR TECHNICAL COMMUNICATION

1. How does the "Code" define a technical communicator?

2. What does the "Code" value?

3. What does the "Code" claim reponsibility for?

4. What does the "Code" require a writer or speaker to do?

5. In what way is "use language and visuals with precision" an ethical concern?

6. In what way is "simple, direct expression of ideas" an ethical concern?

7. The "Code" says, "I will...satisfy the audience's need for information, not my own need for self-expression." Why is this statement important?

8. The "Code" says, "I will...hold myself reponsible for how well my audience understands my message." What implications does this statement hold for you as a writer?

9. How does the "Code" apply to the discussion of ethics above?

SUMMARY

1. Technical writing is critical in the workplace and improves your chances of being hired and promoted.

2 Technical writing, writing done in the workplace, exhibits the following characteristics: subject – technical, factual; audience – carefully considered; organization – predictable, apparent; style – concise, direct, specialized vocabulary; tone – objective, businesslike; special features – visual elements

3. Technical writing differs from traditional academic writing in its presentation, approach to subject matter, and audience. Technical writing differs from imaginative writing in its "one-meaning-and-one-meaning only" presentation and in its explicit meaning.

4. Utility-based ethics do what is best for the *general good* of the group. In rule-based ethics, acts are judged against the *rules* the group has set up. Rights-based ethics assume that human beings have certain *rights* that cannot be taken away. The "Code for Communicators" provides ethical guidelines for writers.

BUILD ON WHAT YOU KNOW

1. What characteristics does technical writing share with other types of writing?
2. Do you think you will make a good technical writer? Why or why not?
3. What are your ethical values?

CONDUCT YOUR OWN RESEARCH

1. Interview a businessperson to ask about his or her technical writing on the job. What types of documents does this person write most often? Ask if you can bring a sample of the writing to your class.
2. Interview a technician or scientist to ask about his or her technical writing on the job. Ask if a mistake has ever been made as a result of imprecise reporting.
3. Johnny doesn't know the answer to a test question. He is sure the person next to him has marked it correctly. He is tempted to look. List possible consequences if he chooses to look at someone else's test.

4. Watch the news closely. Skim your local newspapers. Find a news story that reports some breach of ethics—by a company, an employee, a sports figure, or a politician. Bring the story to class. In small groups, discuss the consequences of the company or individual under scrutiny.

APPLY WHAT YOU HAVE LEARNED

1. Read your favorite magazine or your favorite textbook. Pick out three technical writing features. How do those features make the writing easier to read?
2. Which of these subjects would most likely be written about in a technical style? Which of these subjects would most likely be written about in an academic style?

sunset	homelessness	first car
electrical circuits	high school graduation	prom
computer screen	a close friend	flowers

3. Supply a technical writing context and an academic writing context for each of the topics in exercise **#2.**
4. Which of the statements below would you expect to come from a technical writing document? Which come from imaginative literature? How can you tell? What are your clues?

   a. My memory of her will never fade; she brought music into my life.

   b. There are two types of computer RAM (Random Access Memory): static RAM and dynamic RAM.

c. Most intriguing is the adaptation of Corvette Z52 calipers to the car.

d. The mist peeked over the marshland.

e. Once upon a time there was a princess who ruled a great country.

f. The video output stage simply provides the voltage amplification and driving power for the cathode-ray tube and accepts the vertical and horizontal blanking signals.

5. In small groups, discuss the ethical dilemma presented by the following situations.

a. The air conditioner repairperson lets freon escape into the air (an illegal activity).

b. You are making $60,000 a year at Weller Pharmaceuticals. You have just heard a rumor that an expensive anti-cancer drug produced by the company does no good at all; in fact, it lowers the immune system in some of the patients who have used the drug. Your company has invested 2 million dollars in developing the drug and needs to continue sales for another year to recover the costs.

WORKS CITED

Britton, W. Earl. "What is Technical Writing?" *College Composition and Communication.* May 1965: 113–116.

Hamermesh, Madeline. "Speaking of Writing—Interviews with People on the Job." *The Bulletin.* Mar. 1986: 20–22.

Hoop and Pearsall. "The Process of Transactional Writing." *How to Write for the World of Work.* 5th ed. New York: Harcourt Brace, 1994, 3–24.

Tenner, Edward. "The Impending Information Explosion." *Harvard Magazine* Nov./Dec. 1991: 31–34.

Audience

Write-to-Learn

Make a list of four people you talked to in the last week. Write one page describing how your subject matter, your manner, your tone, and your expression changed according to the person to whom you were speaking. What is responsible for the change?

DEFINITIONS

jargon the highly specialized language of a particular discipline or technical field

accommodate to adjust; to change circumstances so that others will like a situation better

culture the special beliefs, customs, or manners that are specific to a particular group of people or a particular region

select audience a single person or group whose point of view is singular and the same

multiple audience an audience that includes more than one person or group whose point of view is singular; an audience that includes readers whose points of view differ

CHAPTER 2 OBJECTIVES

After completing this chapter, you will be able to

● Determine how knowledge level, interest, role, cultural background, personality, and format can affect communication with a select audience

● Determine how a multiple audience affects communication

● Analyze the particular needs of select and multiple audiences for written communication

● Accommodate the needs of select and multiple audiences

Do you understand the message above? It is written in Morse code—letters as a series of dots and dashes. Many people have no need or desire to know Morse code. They are the wrong audience for Morse code; therefore, the message fails to communicate.

A Navy radio operator during World War I understood this code. The operator's audience shared a common mission: to receive important military messages over long distances. In short, the Navy radio operator used Morse code to meet the highly specific *needs* of a particular audience.

To communicate successfully, you must speak the "language" of your audience. Failure to speak in terms your reader expects will slow down or inhibit communication. Whether your audience is a **select audience** (one person or one limited group) or a **multiple audience** (a variety of people), you must understand what your audience needs and wants. Understanding your audience's knowledge level, role, interests, cultural background, personality, and expected format is the first step to successful communication.

Attending to the needs and wants of your audience is much like attending to a special guest. You are very conscious of this person and make every effort to please. You may choose food, entertainment, and clothing with this person in mind. As with your special guest, you should be equally aware of your audience, making every effort to accommodate his or her needs.

In technical writing, one rule dominates: *the needs and wants of your audience dictate every decision you make as a writer.*

Meeting the Needs of a Select Audience

W A R M   U P   2.1

Suppose your younger brother or sister did something you didn't like. How would you talk to your brother or sister about the problem? Now suppose the person who offended you was a co-worker? How would your audience affect what you said?

Sometimes your audience will be a specific person or a select group of persons with a similar perspective. After you have identified your readers, consider how their knowledge level, role(s), interests, cultural background, and personality may influence what you write and how you write it. Age, experience, attitude, organizational distance, income, and politics may sometimes affect the language you choose to communicate successfully. As Figure 2.1 illustrates, trying to target the special needs of your audience can become quite a challenge!

Figure 2.1 Targeting Your Audience's Needs

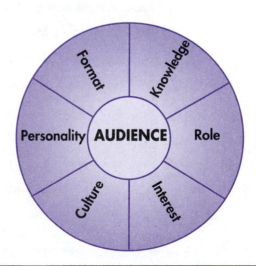

Knowledge Level

Ask yourself what your readers know or do not know about your subject. If you tell them what they *already* know, you risk wasting their time. But make sure thay have the necessary information.

After falling down a flight of stairs, two-year-old Christopher was taken to the emergency room by his distraught parents. Christopher's emergency room report read: "The child suffered from contusions and lacerations." "Contusions" and "lacerations" are familiar terms to doctors and nurses. For Christopher's parents, however, the medical jargon did not communicate as well as the everyday equivalent: "The child suffered from cuts and bruises." The medical jargon was confusing and frightening.

Experience, age, and role can affect how much someone knows. Christopher's parents lacked the experience and background of a doctor or nurse. Because of his age, Christopher would not understand medical terms either. The technician who X-rayed Christopher's finger would not know which medication to prescribe for the child's pain; however, the doctor would. The X-ray technician has one role; the doctor has another.

Role

Consider your reader's role before writing. Not only does role affect knowledge level, but it also affects what your reader thinks is important. Understand that role and accommodate it. An accountant, for example, is concerned about the company's money. If you write a memo to the accounting office about a planned purchase, you should accommodate the accountant's role by including information about cost. The technician who reads the same memo may be more interested in the equipment being purchased and have no concern about the cost. For the technician, you should include sufficient information about the equipment.

> *I can't write without a reader. It's precisely like a kiss—you can't do it alone.*
>
> JOHN CHEEVER

TECHNOLOGY UPDATE

Being on the right electronic bulletin board at the right time may help job hunters find jobs. Advanced Technology Materials, a Connecticut developer of diamond semiconductors, uses electronic mail on the Internet to advertise positions. The Internet, an international computer network, is used by scientists who might see the ad and answer it. Here the employer has found the perfect medium in which to advertise, a medium readily used by the very people most likely qualified for the job.

Interest

If you can pique your reader's interest, then he or she is apt to read with greater acceptance. Where you find interest, capitalize on it. Where there is none, try to create it. Some readers, however, will never have an interest in your subject. For those readers, be aware of their lack of interest.

Interest can be affected by such factors as age, experience, cultural background, and role. For example, your interests now are different from what they were 10 years ago. Your interests have changed as you have grown older. After going camping and riding a bicycle a few times, you might decide that you like camping, but not riding a bicycle. Experience has helped you determine your interests. Perhaps everyone in your family reads a lot; maybe you enjoy reading because your cultural background values reading. Right now, your role is to be a student. When you join the work force, your interests will be determined in part by your professional role.

Cultural Background

Culture, a person's family and community background, can have a deciding effect on what an audience believes. Many beliefs about right and wrong and religious beliefs are affected by an individual's cultural background. By failing to consider someone's cultural background, you may offend. When you understand the cultural background of your audience, your writing will have greater depth and appeal.

In the South, many parents insist that their children say, "Yes, m'am," "No, m'am," "Yes, sir," and "No, sir" to their elders. To them, these terms signify respect and proper etiquette. Other regions of the country don't rely as heavily on these endearments. Why? Regional differences in culture create differences in etiquette. Such differences in etiquette affect the way someone receives a message. While "yes, m'am" or "yes, sir" is expected as a gesture of politeness in one region, the expression may sound out of place in another region.

Personality

Personality can be affected by culture, heredity, age, experience, and role. Personality can also affect attitude. In communicating, you will not always know your reader well enough to make judgments about his or her personality. If you do know, you can tailor your language appropriately.

Parham is a successful manager. Part of his success comes from analyzing the personalities of his subordinates and his supervisors. He knows his supervisor is a busy woman who likes to make decisions based on sufficient facts. When Parham talks to her, he is direct and presents only the facts. When Parham writes reports to her, his tone is objective and he includes ample statistical data. In fact, the company's new medical plan is the result of Parham's very detailed proposal. Parham's line manager, on the other hand, is laid back and wants to know only the bottom line. Memos to him are short,

Theodore Roosevelt was the first president to ride in an automobile in 1902.

infrequent, and friendly. The line manager is not interested in details, would prefer a visit to a memo, and would be hurt if the tone were too formal. Parham has a good working relationship with this line manager, who might otherwise be suspicious of a superior.

Format

Format deals with practical matters of design: type of document, length, preferred style manual, and organization. Just as your English teacher may prefer that your English essays be written in a particular way, your employer may prefer that your report be written in a particular way. Your English teacher may require papers to be written in ink or typed, double-spaced, using the *MLA Handbook for Writers of Research Papers* style sheet. Your employer may require company letterhead and may have already developed a company style sheet to follow. Sometimes audience determines the format: Outside correspondence usually requires letters; in-house correspondence usually requires memos. For reports, format (business report, memo report, etc.) and level of formality may depend on the subject matter, the audience, and company standards.

STOP AND THINK 2.1

1. Explain how knowledge level, role, interests, cultural background, personality, and format can affect communication.

2. How do organizational distance and personality affect the following communication dilemma? How would you write this memo, if you were Jack?

   Jack, a security officer, must write a memo to a new executive explaining that he can no longer allow her into the building without her security pass. She's been forgetting her security card ID, and Jack has been letting her into the building without it. His supervisor has told Jack he can't continue to let her into the building without her ID. This is Jack's first job out of high school, and he likes it. He doesn't know the new executive very well, but he has observed that she's often in a hurry and impatient of routine.

Meeting the Needs of a Multiple Audience

WARM UP 2.2

Think about the last Shakespearean play you read. How did Shakespeare appeal to more than one type of person in this play?

It could be argued that Shakespeare was the greatest writer that ever lived. Shakespeare's success depended on his wit, his knowledge of theater, and his understanding of audience. The businessperson in Shakespeare knew he had to please England's royal family as well as the peasants who came to see his plays. He had to appeal to young and old, to men and women, to the educated and the uneducated. In the 16th century, Shakespeare wrote successfully to a multiple audience, a task still difficult for writers today.

Mark, a computer programmer for a local school system, faced the difficult task of writing a manual for a multiple audience. The manual would be used by assistants to encode data, the new programmer to modify the program, and the Director of Administrative Services to gain an overview of the program. Also, the Superintendent, not very computer-literate, would look at the manual to try to understand of the role of computers in administration.

So Mark's audience was varied. His audience ranged from readers with no knowledge of computers to readers with extensive knowledge of computers. How was he to **accommodate** all their needs? He wrote different parts for different people:

Cover memo	*written for the Superintendent*
Executive summary	*written for the Director*
Introduction	*written for everyone*
Discussion	*written for the assistants*
Appendix	*written for the programmer*

Figure 2.2 on page 24 reveals the complexity of Mark's assignment and the adjustments he had to make.

WRITERS ON THE JOB

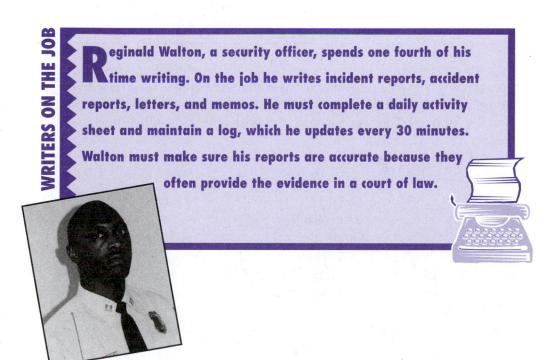

Reginald Walton, a security officer, spends one fourth of his time writing. On the job he writes incident reports, accident reports, letters, and memos. He must complete a daily activity sheet and maintain a log, which he updates every 30 minutes. Walton must make sure his reports are accurate because they often provide the evidence in a court of law.

Figure 2.2 Mark's Adjustment to a Multiple Audience

READER'S ROLE	READER'S NEEDS	MARK'S ADJUSTMENT TO READER
Superintendent *Decision Maker*	To understand the advantages of using computer applications	Writes a **cover memo** briefly summarizing the report and outlining advantages to the school system. Uses little or no technical language. Carefully defines any technical terms.
Director *Manager*	To gain an overview of the program; to convince Superintendent that computer applications can simplify inventory control	Writes the **Executive Summary**, which presents a summary of most important information in the report. Includes some technical language. Realizes the Director will use the manual to convince others to use more computer applications.
All *Roles Varied*	To understand the purpose of the manual and which parts will help each one	Explains the purpose of the manual and its organization in the **Introduction**. Uses little or no technical language.
Programmer *Technician*	To understand programming	Writes in Fox Base Programming language commands. Places information in the **Appendix** at the end.
Assistants *Users*	To understand how to encode and find data	Writes the main **Discussion** that tells how to use the program. Uses short commands with occasional explanation. Uses screen shots as visual aids.

How do technical writers appeal to a general audience or a multiple audience? They write different parts for different people. Then they label those parts with headings so that people can easily find which parts were written for them. This way writers can adjust style and content to match each reader's needs and wants.

STOP AND THINK 2.2

1. How does a technical document appeal to a multiple audience?

2. Look at a recent newspaper. Does every section, every ad, and every article appeal to the same select audience? How do newspapers appeal to a variety of audiences?

3. Look through your local phone book. Does every section appeal to the same select audience? How do phone books appeal to a variety of audiences?

Analyzing Your Audience

W A R M   U P   2.3

Choose a topic you like and one you don't like (for example, your favorite school subject and your least favorite). Analyze yourself as an audience for each of these topics. Consider knowledge level, interest, and personality.

Before you work on technical reports in this book, always analyze your audience to determine their special needs. Use this list of questions to help you decide what is important to remember about your reader(s). When you have answered all the questions, place an asterisk next to the three most important things to remember about your audience.

Audience Identification
- Is my audience a select audience (a single group or a single person)?
- Is my audience a multiple audience (several groups with different interests or several readers with different roles)?

Knowledge Level
- What does my reader already know about the topic?
- What does my reader need to know?
- What does my reader want to know?

Role
- Is my reader's role to make decisions, make suggestions, or implement action?
- What is my reader's job? Administrative? Technical? Clerical? Other?
- Is my communication going up to management, across to a peer, or down to a subordinate?

Interest
- How strong is my reader's interest in my topic?
- Are my reader's priorities different from mine or the same as mine?

Cultural Background
- What is my reader's cultural background? What are my reader's beliefs?
- Are my reader's beliefs different from mine or the same as mine?

Personality
- What kind of personality does my reader have?

Format
- What format (type of document, length, organization, style manual) does my reader expect?

FOCUS ON ETHICS

Seventeen-year-old Tammi is baby-sitting her eight-year-old brother. A friend calls and invites her to a movie, a movie Tammi really wants to see. The movie is rated R. If she goes, she will have to take her younger brother. What should she do?

Accommodating Your Audience's Needs

Now that you've analyzed your audience, you must decide how to accommodate your reader's needs. Figure 2.3 summarizes some ways you can adjust to your audience's needs.

Figure 2.3 Adjusting to Your Audience's Needs

TO ACCOMMODATE	MAKE THE FOLLOWING ADJUSTMENTS
Knowledge Level	Add particular knowledge your audience doesn't have. Leave out or quickly summarize knowledge your audience already has. Decide how much technical language to include. Use informal definitions or glossary, if necessary. Present complex information visually.
Interests	Appeal to known interests; try to create interest where there is none.
Role	Include knowledge that the role requires. Write different parts for different roles.
Cultural Background	Understand how culture affects someone's beliefs and decisions. Learn about the cultural background of your audience.
Personality	Adjust tone to personality.
Format	Write letters to readers outside the company and memos to readers inside the company. In choosing a report format, consider subject matter, audience, and employer standards. Follow established company format.

Figure 2.3 can help you make decisions about the accommodations you need to make. When you have analyzed your audience's needs, use the suggestions in Figure 2.3 to help you complete the chart in Figure 2.4 for your specific writing task.

Figure 2.4 Accommodate Your Reader

Accommodate Your Reader

Identify audience
    Describe your Select audience_____
    OR
    List your Multiple audiences_____

Complete one chart for each select audience, or complete one chart for each audience listed under multiple audiences.

Notes about audience	Plans to adjust to my audience
Knowledge Level	
Role	
Interest	
Cultural Background	
Personality	
Format	

REAL-LIFE CRISIS

Your friend Steve, who works with you evenings as a cashier at the supermarket, has an internship at the local paper. To him, it's the chance of a lifetime: he's always wanted to be a journalist, but he can't afford college on his own. The paper offers scholarships and jobs to promising interns.

Since he accepted the internship, Steve's work at the supermarket has suffered. He's been late several times, has been impatient with customers, and has made some errors in sales. You overhear your supervisor making an appointment with the school counselor who runs the internship program to discuss Steve's "poor attitude and poor work habits."

You don't want Steve to lose the internship, so you decide to help. Whom do you talk to, and what do you say?

STOP AND THINK 2.4

1. What can you do to accommodate knowledge level, role(s), interest(s), cultural background, personality, and format?

2. Think of an issue you feel passionately about. It may be a political, social, or moral issue. Suppose you had to convince the entire student body to agree with you. Use Figure 2.4, Accommodate Your Reader, to analyze your multiple audience. What kind of adjustments would you make to appeal to your multiple audience?

SUMMARY

1. The needs and wants of your audience should dictate every decision you make as a writer.

2. A select audience is a specific single reader or a specific group of readers with a common purpose. Knowledge level, role(s), interests, cultural background, personality, and format affect communication with a select audience.

3. Multiple audiences are readers with different points of view. Analyzing knowledge level, role(s), interests, cultural background, personality, and format are still important when communicating with a multiple audience. Adjustments can be made by writing different parts of a report for different readers.

4. Always analyze your audience.

5. After you have analyzed your audience, decide how you will accommodate your readers' needs and wants.

BUILD ON WHAT YOU KNOW

1. To make you more aware of audience, answer the following questions: Who might be the target audience for these TV shows or networks? What groups of people might they appeal to? Why?

Home Shopping Channel	Monday Night Football	Sesame Street
Sixty Minutes	Jeopardy	Nickelodeon
MTV	Star Trek: Voyager	Masterpiece Theatre

2. Consider the following terms. If you are not familiar with some of them, look them up in a dictionary or ask your family and friends. Which audience(s) would understand these terms?

blitz	RAM	curl	sauté
goalie	handle	dunk	V-8
rap	10-20	angioplasty	starboard

3. Name some slang terms that are used by your friends or that are popular with your generation. Why do these terms appeal to your age group? Ask your parents or grandparents for slang terms popular when they were growing up. What do you think about their slang terms? Would you use them? Why or why not?

CONDUCT YOUR OWN RESEARCH

1. Go to your nearest newsstand, perhaps as close as your local grocery store. Notice which magazines appeal to specific interests and which magazines appeal to a general audience. In particular, look for these targeted groups: women, teens, sports lovers, craft lovers, technicians, parents, children, and a general audience.

   a. For each of these targeted groups, list several magazines that are obviously written for the target group.

   b. For each group, select one of the magazines you identified and look through it more closely. List at least four adjustments the editors have made to accommodate the needs of their readers.

2. Bring your favorite magazine to class. Spend 15–20 minutes looking at the table of contents and browsing through the pages. Who is the intended audience? List four things the editors have done to appeal to the reader. Test their strategy. Do you like what the editors have done to appeal to you? Do you have suggestions for improving their appeal?

3. Look through the comic section of a major Sunday newspaper. Which comic strips appeal to which audiences? How do you know?

APPLY WHAT YOU HAVE LEARNED

1. Write a letter to the President of the United States telling him you like (or don't like) a particular policy of his. Tell your friend you like (or don't like) the same policy. How does your language change from audience to audience?

2. Write a letter to your employer requesting time off for a special event such as the prom, homecoming, or a family vacation. Then switch roles. Write a letter from the employer denying the time off. How are your letters different? How are they alike?

3. Divide into teams of three or four students. Use the following scenario to answer questions **a–f**.

Sam, John, and Susan have just started publishing <u>TV Highlights</u>, a weekly magazine. Sam sells the advertising. John, a graphic designer, is responsible for the artwork. John's uncle is the owner. He makes most of the decisions but often defers to John's opinions. Susan is the accountant.

Think about the role each person performs in this small company. How do each one's responsibilities affect decisions? How does each one's role affect how he or she communicates with others in the company? Think also about the readers *TV Highlights* will serve. Who could be the target audience?

a. John wants a four-color cover for the first issue because he thinks the first issue should look impressive, but Susan thinks a four-color cover is too expensive. Sam says the advertisers don't care how many colors are on the cover; they want only to make sure the local high school's blue and red colors are represented. Susan decides to write a report to John's uncle recommending a two-color cover for the first few issues. What should she remember about her audience? What kind of information might she include to convince John's uncle (and John)? Should she include information about Sam's concerns?

b. Ulrike Bohm, a free-lance writer, has written to John asking what topics interest the magazine's readers. The magazine is written for a rural audience in the southeastern part of the United States. The average reader is a middle-aged woman. What do you think *TV Highlights'* readers are interested in?

c. John's uncle writes a news release announcing the new magazine. What kind of information should he include for the public?

d. John writes a memo to Susan and Sam about the progress of the design of the holiday issue. The design is a little behind schedule. What does John need to remember about Sam's role and Susan's role within the company? What kind of information should he include for both Susan and Sam?

e. When Susan works on the accounts, she has a difficult time deciding which of John's and Sam's business expenses are tax deductible. She suspects that John and Sam are not recording some of their legitimate business expenses. Neither one seems to understand the importance of accurate record keeping; plus they are also busy with other tasks. John has never even had an accounting course. Susan is devising an SOP (standard operating procedure) for reporting business expenses and a new form for recording information. What does she need to remember about John and Sam when she writes the SOP and designs the form?

f. Susan, Sam, and John can no longer depend on local printers to print the magazine. They decide to consider printing it themselves. Susan writes a proposal to a bank asking for a special loan with which to purchase a new press. What should she remember about the bank when writing this report? What kind of information will the bank need?

PART

2

Brief Communications

Memorandums

Write-to-Learn

Consider how you try to keep things operating smoothly in your life as a student. To what degree do you rely on your memory and to what degree do you need to put information in writing? For instance, how do you keep track of your homework assignments or club meetings? What happens when you don't make a written record? Write several paragraphs concerning how necessary putting things in writing is to your school life.

DEFINITIONS

document a handwritten or typed paper

format the layout of a publication, standard elements of a document's presentation

hierarchy people in an organization arranged by rank, authority, or ability

hook an attention-getter; words or sentences designed to engage the reader

internal audience a receiver inside the sender's organization

memo/memorandum a brief, written internal communication

Ayden-Grifton High School

Route 3, Box 172
AYDEN, NORTH CAROLINA 28513

Telephone:
555-0183

MEMORANDUM

To: Mrs. Lawrence, Ms. Parham, and Members of FHA/HERO

From: Mr. James D. Gray, Principal

Date: February 6, 1995

Subject: CONGRATULATIONS ON HOMELESS SHELTER PROJECT SUCCESS

Congratulations, students, on the outstanding contributions made to the Pitt County Homeless Shelter by the members of FHA/HERO and compliments, Mrs. Lawrence and Ms. Parham, for the leadership you provided.

This project involving the entire school and community helped make us all more aware of the difficult conditions faced by many members of our community. I was especially pleased that so many of our students and parents participated in donating food, money, and consumable items for this worthwhile program.

I thank you for organizing and seeing this project to completion. This is a great example of teaching and learning.

Member of Southern Association of Colleges and Schools

It is the Purpose of Pitt County Schools to Provide
Equal Opportunity Regardless of Race, Color,
National Origin, Sex or Handicap.

After completing this chapter, you will be able to

- Recognize and plan a simple-message memo

- Analyze an audience

- Use memo formats

- Organize information effectively in the body of a memo

- Compose an effective memo message appropriate for the audience

Memorandums, commonly called memos, are brief written messages sent within an organization. Sharing information between people and divisions is essential to smooth and effective operations in business and industry. Memos are designed to meet this internal communication need.

In fact, the following four characteristics have made memos one of the most frequently used business communication tools today:

1. *Memos are economical.* A simple format and concise message can assure that words and time are not wasted by the writer or the reader. In fact, some writers use preprinted memo forms.

2. *Memos are efficient.* Since the format is standard, the writer and the reader know what data to include and where to look for it. Memos, being internal documents, may also be delivered very quickly to the reader(s). They encourage a rapid response. Sometimes a reader will choose an answer from a list of options or write an answer in the margin and return the original memo to the sender. This flow of ideas is much faster than writing a letter, mailing it, and waiting for the receiver to write and mail an answering letter.

3. *Memos are inexpensive.* Because the audience is internal, the document may be typed on less expensive paper than that used for external correspondence. In fact, some organizations use plain paper or a simple form rather than letterhead stationery for memos. Moreover, memos usually do not require an envelope or postage.

4. *Memos provide a permanent record.* If a memo is filed, it may be used for reference to check all sorts of data, such as the date on which an employee is scheduled to have a performance evaluation meeting or the number of bolts ordered for a machine repair.

The model memorandum on the preceding page illustrates this simple and efficient way to share information within an organization. Employees at all levels of almost all organizations have a need to write memos. Since it is not always practical to speak person-to-person, workers usually "put it in writing." For instance, Mr. Gray, the writer of the model memo, could have tried to talk with or write to each student and teacher. However, that isn't always practical. Instead, the memo can convey the message to everyone. Anyone in an organization who needs to communicate may need memo-writing skills.

Reading maketh a full man, conference a ready man, and writing an exact man.

FRANCIS BACON, "OF STUDIES," *ESSAYS*

Technology offers much to make life easier for writers. One of these aids is the template for memos. Many word-processing programs include a stationery feature. For example, WordPerfect 3.0 provides a memo template in its stationery package. This template may save typing and time for the writer by giving the caption MEMORANDUM and the four headings TO, FROM, DATE, and SUBJECT. For the inexperienced writer, the template even directs the writer where to place the body of the memo.

Audience: Who Reads Memos?

WARM UP 3.1

Think of notes you leave for other family members at home. Then remember a note you have left for a teacher or an employer. Compare the two. Consider elements such as word choice, sentence structure, content, and even handwriting. Do the differences you discover, if any, relate to the different audiences?

Remember that memos are used only to correspond inside an organization. Therefore, the reader will always be a member of the writer's own organization, an **internal audience**.

Within an organization everyone, from the lowest person on the company ladder to the highest, is likely to receive and read memos. For example, an employee might get a memo from a co-worker reminding him or her of a meeting date. A memo outlining the facts—time, date, location—provides a written record so the person receiving the reminder doesn't become confused.

Even though memos are addressed to people inside the same company, the writer must consider the audience carefully. The audience may consist of people with a variety of outlooks, backgrounds, opinions, and interests. Once identified, each audience must be thoroughly studied to ensure that its needs are met. Sometimes it helps to make a list of the audience's characteristics.

Some audiences will be made up of single readers; others will have several readers who may have the same or different levels of interest. If the reader will be only one person, try to meet the needs of that person. Use language and information he or she will be able to understand, and answer questions that reader would ask if he or she were present. If an audience is made up of a group of readers, consider the needs of all the readers.

S T O P   A N D   T H I N K   3.1

1. Do the presidents and CEO's of large companies receive memos?

2. Does the night cleaning staff receive memos?

3. If you were asked to make an announcement at a school assembly with an audience of students, teachers, staff, and administrators, to whom would you address your message?

Prewriting

Carefully planning a memo is important. People sometimes think of memos as second-class letters or fast-and-easy notes. Such thinking is a mistake. Memos not only help to get the job done but also serve as a means of evaluating the writer's performance. Since memos are so important, learning to compose effective ones makes sense.

Once you have analyzed your audience, you have a number of decisions to make based on what you have learned. Here are several questions you might ask yourself before beginning to write:

- What do I want to accomplish with this message?
- What do I want to have happen after the receiver reads this memo?
- What is the main point?
- Does my reader need background? How much?
- Do I need to make the idea simpler for this audience?
- Is this reader familiar with the subject matter?

Using these questions, you should try putting some ideas on paper. Some writers prefer a list, like the kind you would make for grocery shopping. Other writers like to use freewriting. As you probably already know, freewriting is writing everything that comes to mind as you think of it. Remember that this is the creative part of writing, so don't be judgmental. Get all of the ideas, brilliant or otherwise, on paper.

Whichever technique you use will generate a collection of ideas you want to cover in the memo message or body. With all of the ideas before you, you can begin to be critical—cutting out the ones that don't relate or are unnecessary and changing those that don't say exactly what you want to say. Prewriting is also the time to begin prioritizing ideas by importance. Consider what you will place first, second, third, and so on. You will read more about **organization** later in this chapter in the Composing the Message section.

Answering the questions from the beginning of this section will help you to analyze your audience and determine your goals. Having completed that and used freewriting or listing to work with the ideas you want to cover, you are ready to begin composing a rough draft of your memo. The rough **draft** begins with a standard format of headings and is followed by the body or message.

Formatting

Like the addresses and salutation (Dear Mr. Roberio:) in a letter, headings make a **document** recognizable as a memo. Five elements almost always appear at the top of a memo:

> M E M O
>
> TO:
> FROM:
> DATE:
> SUBJECT:

However, the headings do not always appear in this order. This is a popular arrangement, but several other patterns are frequently used as well. When you begin work, your new employer will probably give you a style manual that will show you the format the company prefers. If the company does not have a preferred **format**, then you are free to choose one you like.

Caption

The word "MEMO" or "Memorandum" should be placed at the top of the page. Some preprinted memo forms and computer software packages provide the caption for writers.

TO Line

In the TO section, name your audience. You can name one person, such as John James, or you can name a group, such as the Junior-Senior Prom Committee. On occasion you may need to name several readers who are not connected by a unit or committee. In this case, you may simply list their names.

Three of the first five presidents died on the 4th of July: John Adams, Thomas Jefferson, and James Monroe.

The list of receivers' names could be presented in several different ways. For example, you could place all names on one or two lines and connect them with commas, as in the model memo at the beginning of this chapter on page 33. Another option is to place the names in one or several columns, as in Figure 3.1 below. The number of columns you choose depends on how many names you list.

Figure 3.1 Receivers' Names Listed in Columns

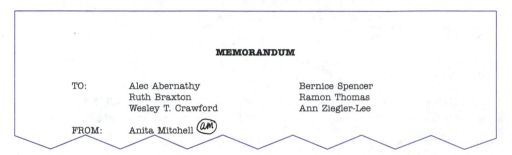

If you list several persons' names, enter them either in alphabetical or hierarchical order. In **hierarchical** order, the people of greatest importance or recognition in the organization, such as the president and vice-president, are listed first. Then others are listed in decreasing order of importance.

FROM Line

After the FROM heading, list the name or names of the sender of the message. If you are the only person responsible for the message, your name appears. If the memo comes from a group, then the group or unit name is listed, such as *FROM: Jefferson Jazz Band.*

Some memos are from several people not tied to a group. In this case, list names of the individual senders in a line joined by commas or in columns, again in alphabetical or hierarchical order. Also remember to write your initials or sign your full name after the typed name in the FROM section, as in Figure 3.1 above.

Initialing or signing is especially important on memos that may deal with important legal or organizational matters. Memos become legal documents that can be used in a court of law if they are signed and dated. In addition, your initials or signature tells your reader that you accept responsibility for this message, especially if someone else typed the document.

DATE Line

The DATE line usually appears after TO and FROM and before the SUBJECT line or in the upper right corner across from the TO line. You can choose between two styles for writing the date: international (also called military in the United States) or traditional.

International date style is becoming increasingly popular in technical documents because of economy. International style requires no commas. In this style, the writer gives the day first, the month next, and the year last, as in 12 December 1996.

Traditional-style dates, as in June 4, 1955, or April 1, 1985, give the month, the date, *a comma,* and then the year.

SUBJECT Line

You may see terms such as "Reference," "Regarding," or "Re" (which comes from the Latin "res" meaning "thing" or "matter") used in the same way as the word SUBJECT. The SUBJECT line logically appears as the last of the headings. Its purpose is to announce the point or main idea of the memo immediately before you begin to develop or prove this point. In addition to helping the reader predict the topic, the SUBJECT line distinguishes one message from another and focuses the writer on one point.

Predict. The SUBJECT line should allow readers to predict what the memo will say; in other words, it reflects the main idea discussed in the body. Be as specific as you can when composing the SUBJECT line. This line should not be a complete sentence, but a phrase or clause, more like a newspaper headline.

Distinguish. In addition to helping the reader predict, the SUBJECT line should make clear the difference between one memo and many others. For instance, waiters and waitresses at a restaurant may read numerous memos that deal with menu items during one year. Therefore, if the SUBJECT line says only "Menu Changes," the server reading it will not immediately know that this is not the same memo he or she read last week. Instead, specific SUBJECT lines, such as "Italian Items Added to Menu for June" or "Lobster Price Increase" or "Salmon Unavailable Until 20 April" would tell the server exactly what to expect the message to cover. It should also convince him or her that this is indeed a new message and not last week's.

Focus. The SUBJECT line also aids the writer. Writing a SUBJECT line forces the writer to focus on the most important idea. It further allows the writer to check the message of the memo against the SUBJECT line. The opening lines of the message should cover the same idea that the SUBJECT line announces.

TECHNOLOGY UPDATE

E-mail (electronic mail or messages transmitted from computer to computer) has made changes in the way readers use memos. First, e-mail means that employees' desks are not cluttered by sheets of correspondence. Instead, the reader may return from lunch to find a memo on the computer screen. Second, transmission by computer network is almost immediate, much faster than having a messenger deliver interoffice correspondence.

Review the memo headings given for the writing situation described below. Decide how you might improve them. Then revise the headings to make them as effective as possible for the reader.

A professional baker, Rose Marie Kestler sells birthday, wedding, and other-occasion cakes. Approximately 55 people have now joined Kestler's Cake Club, made up of patrons who buy three or more cakes a year and receive a discount for their loyalty. Because Kestler's business is thriving, she decides to increase the Cake Club discount from 5% to 10%. Kestler writes a memo to the participating customers announcing the increased discount.

MEMO

SUBJECT: Cake Club Benefit
TO: CAKE CLUB MEMBERS
FROM: Owner, Kestler's
DATE: June 15

Composing the Message

If you were going into an ice cream shop to buy two gallons of cherry ice cream, with which comment would you begin? Why?

a. May I have two gallons of cherry ice cream, please.

b. Cherry is my stepfather's favorite flavor, and this is for his birthday celebration.

While formatting the memo is important, the headings are only a means for conveying the ideas you want to share. The message or the body of the memo is the heart of this document. When composing a memo, consider organizing ideas according to the message, limiting to one main point, creating a suitable tone, and using humor appropriately and effectively.

Organizing Ideas According to the Message

The message section of a memo should be organized for the reader, not for the writer. Employees who read memos are usually busy and do not have time to waste. Planning what to say and in what order to say it is one of the most challenging aspects of writing a memo.

Informative and Good News Messages. Memos usually involve giving the audience information that will be pleasant or at least acceptable. The strategy is direct—present the main idea first. In this way, the reader does not have to search through the entire document to discover the idea he or she needs. The model memo at the beginning of the chapter (page 33) and the memo message from the Imperial Waters, Inc. Production Manager below are examples of the direct approach to organizing a message.

> Please turn in all leased Chemical Lab garments checked out to you by December 7, 19--.

Main Idea— what the writer wants the reader to do

> We signed a contract and will receive service from a new cleaning company, D & W Garment Care Center, effective December 8, 19--. Benefits of the change you should notice are
> - perfume and starch-free garments
> - an additional coat each week
> - immediate replacement of worn or damaged garments

Explanation and Supplementary Ideas—why the writer is requesting this action and what effect it will have on the reader

Explanations, background information, and supplementary ideas follow the main or most important idea. A good technical writer does not make the reader work for understanding. Although it may be easier for writers to work their way slowly toward a main idea at the end, it is easier for readers to get the essential information at the beginning.

Bad News Messages. Occasionally the purpose of a memo is to share negative news, ideas readers will not be pleased to see, such as employee layoffs or unpopular policy changes. In this case, the direct approach probably is not the best choice. If readers find the bad news immediately, the disappointment might be so great that they miss the explanation entirely.

Therefore, the strategy of bad news messages is indirect. The bad news is softened by surrounding it with pleasant ideas in this way:

1. Open with a positive statement, generally some idea about which both writer and reader can agree.
2. In the next section of the message, clearly announce the bad news, but place it in the middle or end of the section, not at the beginning.
3. Close the message on a pleasant note, perhaps offering an alternative solution or a different perspective.

The following memo message written by the owner of Precision Cuts Hair Studio shows how the bad news in the middle is buffered by pleasant ideas in the opening and closing:

> Being creative folks, we enjoy expressing our individuality in the way we dress. We have been quite stylish and unique of late.

Positive Statement— creativity, something about which reader and writer agree

Some of us have been talking about ways to improve our professional image. Toward this end, the shop will adopt a uniform dress policy beginning on the first working day of next month. You may choose from solid navy and solid white outfits or outfits combining the two colors.

Besides enhancing the shop's professional image, the new policy will save you money because your personal clothes will not be subjected to the chemicals we use every day. Any creative energy you have left can be spent on clients to make ours the most popular shop in town!

Persuasive Messages. A routine request for a design from a commercial art department might use the direct approach, presenting the main idea first. However, a design request on short notice, such as "I need it by 2 p.m. today," should use this plan for convincing readers:

1. HOOK—Open with a **hook** to introduce the topic.
2. SELL—Convince your audience with concrete, specific evidence.
3. MOTIVATE—Get your audience to respond to your ideas; ask for action.

The memo body below written by a sales director shows this persuasive strategy at work:

Would you like the IRS to be able to find you in order to deliver your tax refund check? Would you like customers to be able to find you when they want to place an order?

If these possibilities are important to you, then please help me to help you. Just today I have had five calls for sales representatives I could not locate. That could be five orders that will never be placed as well as commissions that will not go into your paycheck. To avoid this problem, check in and out on the board. It is still on my office door, and a brand-new marker is attached for your use.

Please remember to sign in when you arrive at work and out when you leave for the day, but especially mark times when you leave the building for lunch or sales calls. If you do, I can tell your callers when to call again or to expect your return call. And I'll even hold your refund check until you return!

In addition to organizing ideas to suit the message and purpose, several other elements of memos need to be considered.

Limiting to One Main Point

A memo should cover only one main point. Writers who have two messages for the same audience need to write two memos. Why do you think this is true?

First, if a memo has more than one message, the reader cannot determine what is truly important. Second, the very busy reader may find the first idea, assume it is the only important information, and quit reading. Third, the memo might be so lengthened that it will intimidate readers. Readers generally expect memos to be one to four paragraphs. Finally, it is inappropriate to combine some messages, as in Figure 3.2 below.

Figure 3.2 Ineffective Memo with Two Main Ideas

MEMORANDUM

TO: Dr. Joyner   Ms. Shankowski
           Mr. Everest   Mr. Henderson

FROM: Harry Smith, Personnel Officer (HS)

DATE: June 10, 19--

SUBJECT: 1. Vacation and Sick Leave Slips
           2. Death of Mr. Martin's Mother-in-law

1.   Please ensure that <u>all</u> vacation and sick leave slips for this fiscal year
      (July 1996 through June 1997) are turned in to Tammie by June 27,
      19--.

2.   Dan Martin's mother-in-law and Susan Hale's grandmother, Mrs. Sudie
      Harper, passed away on Sunday, June 9, 19--. Funeral arrangements
      are being handled by Belevedere's Funeral Home. Services will be held
      at Belevedere's Funeral Home at 2 p.m. on Tuesday, June 11.
      Expressions of sympathy may be sent to

      Dan at: PO Box 326   Susan at: Route 1, Box 32
               811 E. Cooper Street   Tylerville, SD 47934
               Tylerville, SD 47934

S T O P   A N D   T H I N K   3.3

Read the ineffective memo in Figure 3.2 and try to determine how the readers might have reacted.

Creating a Suitable Tone

Memos usually have a conversational, informal tone. In fact, it is appropriate in this type of correspondence to use "I," the first person pronoun. Readers are more likely to cooperate when the memo sounds as if it were written by a person rather than a machine. This informal writing style is a great deal like conversation you might have with a friend or acquaintance if that conversation were polished slightly.

Using Humor Effectively

Humor can be very effective in creating goodwill and in dealing with difficult situations or uncooperative audiences. For example, in Figure 3.3, McIntrye uses humor to convince students to do something she wants them to do.

Figure 3.3 Memo Using Humor to Persuade

MEMORANDUM

23 October 1996

TO: All Students

FROM: Marissa McIntrye, Volunteer Club Chair

REFERENCE: Giving up your blood!

The Volunteer Club again this fall invites you to give blood when we host the American Red Cross Bloodmobile on campus 28 October 1996. See Mrs. Wilkerson in the main office to schedule an appointment for any free period on Bloodmobile day. Please show your pride and sign up today!

Mrs. DeLeone, the Volunteer Club sponsor, says not to worry if you are afraid of the sight of blood—especially your own. This year she offers blindfolds for the faint-hearted and a shoulder to lean on for those who just plain faint!

STOP AND THINK 3.4

1. The main idea should be buffered or surrounded by something else in which type of message?

2. Should memos contain sentences such as "This writer believes...?"

3. In a memo announcing a 10% pay increase to all employees, should the main idea be presented at the beginning, middle, or end?

REAL-LIFE CRISIS

Dr. Frank Pai, a researcher in the Research and Development Division of a major textiles corporation, faced this dilemma with the employment of a graduate student who would work as his research assistant for the summer. After writing a job description, determining a fair salary, evaluating 23 resumes, and interviewing five candidates, Dr. Pai hired an assistant and confirmed the details in a letter to the new employee. However, when Dr. Pai submitted a report of the assistant's hours worked during the first month along with a request that she be paid accordingly, he received a note from the comptroller, the financial officer of the company. The note politely but clearly explained that the company had no system for paying graduate students. Employees could be hired as full-time, part-time, or temporary; and temporary employees could not be paid at the level of salary requested for this research assistant. Since the assistant had already worked one month and had received written confirmation of her employment from Dr. Pai, and since the comptroller was not willing to pay her the salary Dr. Pai promised her, what could Dr. Pai do?

SUMMARY

1. Memos or memorandums are a brief, efficient, economical kind of internal correspondence.

2. Frequently written by anyone in an organization who has a message to share, memos are read by busy employees, at all levels of organizations. These memo readers want the message presented clearly and directly.

3. Analyzing audience, determining goals, and listing or freewriting are prewriting steps to successful memo writing.

4. Memos begin with the word "MEMO" and four standard headings that all memo readers expect to see. These headings—TO, FROM, DATE, and SUBJECT—also allow for quick reference so that the document may be filed and easily found again.

5. Following the headings at the top of the memo is the message or the body of the document. The body must be ordered with the type of message and the reader's needs in mind. Writers effectively share good news messages using a direct approach. However, bad news messages require an indirect approach to buffer the unpleasant news. Persuasive messages, on the other hand, are best presented with a "Hook, Sell, Motivate" strategy.

6. The body of the memo should cover only one main idea, create a suitable tone, and use humor appropriately.

Editing and Revision Checklist

✓ Have I identified and analyzed my audience? If I am addressing a multi-level audience, have I planned to meet the needs of each group or type of reader?

✓ Did I establish my purpose or goal in this memo?

✓ Did I use freewriting or listing to generate the information I wish to share with the audience?

✓ Have I decided what is to be the most important idea for my reader? (You could pretend to be the reader and then ask yourself, "What is it I most need or want to know?")

✓ Did I develop an organizational plan? Does it take into account a good news, bad news, or persuasive message?

✓ Have I announced to my audience what the document is by including the word "Memo" or "Memorandum" at the top of the document?

✓ Have I listed the sender, the receiver, the date, and the subject of the memo in the headings at the top of the correspondence and beneath the word "Memo"? Did I follow each heading with a colon and the appropriate information for that entry?

✓ Have I edited and revised the body of the memo to make it as effective as possible?

✓ Have I asked a respected peer to read my memo and give specific feedback on the impact and effectiveness of my message? (Be certain to ask this editor if he or she has questions after reading. Also ask if any part is unclear or inappropriate.)

✓ Did I proofread the headings for completeness and accuracy?

✓ Did I proofread the message for errors in spelling, typing, grammar, and punctuation?

✓ When everything else has proven acceptable, have I signed my name or written my initials to the right of my typed name?

APPLY WHAT YOU HAVE LEARNED

1. Read the following writing situations. Select the details you will need, and then write the headings for each memorandum.

   a. You are manager for your school's soccer team. Normally you coordinate the packing of equipment and supplies for traveling to *away* games. However, for the next conference game to be played at Midland you will be out-of-state attending your cousin's wedding. Therefore, you are writing a memo to Coach Marsh Rivers and your two assistant managers, Josh Abene and Deborah Jackson, to remind them of what needs to be done in your absence.

   b. You are Janice Faulkner, manager of A Helping Hand, a residential cleaning service in San Alto, New Mexico. Six full-time and fifteen part-time employees are under your supervision. To thank the entire staff for their contribution to the business' success, you have planned a company picnic to be held in your backyard. The event will take place on October 1, 19-- from 5 to 8 p.m. You are writing a memo today to invite all employees and their families to the picnic.

2. The following memos contain many problems. Read them carefully. Decide what needs to be improved, and then revise to make the correspondence more effective. You may reorganize, add, or delete material as you wish. These two memos are also available for editing and revising on the computer applications diskette as **TEXT3A** and **TEXT3B**.

a.

MEMORANDA

To,   All Students   August 5
From,   Yuan Ho
Re,   Parking Situation

  The painted lines in the parking lots have faded so much that they can barely be seen now. So Acme Paint Company has agreed to give us a fresh new look. The crew will be repainting the student parking lot on Thursday and Friday of next week, August 13–14. The supervisor of the paint crew informed us that the paint can sometimes drift if the breeze is strong enough, and the specks of paint can do serious damage to a vehicle's paint. For that reason, we plan for students to park in the Staff lot and the gravel lot behind the baseball field on those two days. Please remember not to park in the Student Parking Area on August 13–14.

b.

MEMO

To: John Hutchens, Cathy Galloway, Cathy Marsh,
         Mr. Charles Saunders, and Mrs. Jane Keller
From: Department Manager
Subject: Celebration
Date: June 27, 19--

  I am so thrilled that this fiscal year has been so successful, and I am sure you are too. We have all worked very hard to get this new product on the market. So I think we have earned a celebration. You will receive a paid holiday Friday, July 6, and a bonus check for 1% of your base salary at the end of this month.

CONSIDER THIS CASE

1. As assistant to your Quality Assurance Team at World Wide Insurance Association, it is your job to schedule meetings. The chair, Janine Leone, has asked you to call a meeting for Monday afternoon, April 24, 19--. She wants the group to discuss a recent employee concern regarding unsafe exercise equipment in the Employee Wellness Center. Janine would like the Quality Assurance Team to gather in Room 124–C at 4:15. She expects the meeting to end at 5 p.m. Write a memo announcing the meeting.

2. Write a memo from Cheryl Daniels, Chief of Installation Services for Fox Cablevision, to Eric Monroe, an employee under her supervision. Monroe has just completed 25 years of service with Fox Cablevision, and Daniels wants to show her support for his work. Monroe has had perfect attendance for the last three years, and his customer evaluations are consistently positive.

3. You are Chief Food Scientist for Leigh Bakery in Anderson, Wisconsin. Matthew Carlson, president of the Logan Dairy Cooperative, a farmer-owned and -operated sales organization under contract to sell all of its product to your company, has invited you to speak to his members regarding the effect of certain veterinary medicines on the taste of dairy products. On the date the Cooperative requested, Thursday, January 18, 19--, you already are scheduled to attend a meeting of the American Association of Bakers. Write a memo declining the invitation to speak to the Cooperative.

4. Write a memo to students, teachers, and administrators encouraging involvement and explaining why participation in the local Special Olympics is important. The event will take place 3–5 p.m. Friday, 9 June and 8–4 p.m., Saturday, 10 June 19--. You may write as a concerned individual or as the representative of a school group. Remember to consider each level of audience. Ask yourself what will appeal to students, what teachers will want to know, and what will concern administrators.

PURSUE AN IDEA

1. Many occasions in everyday life offer opportunities to write memos. Consider any group to which you belong, such as the class for which you are using this book. Are there ever times when you need to share information with others that you'd like them to be able to refer to later? To practice writing memos, you might choose as your topic a message you need to share with a group.

2. One way to determine what kind of memos you might need to write is to interview someone who is pursuing a career in your field of interest. Ask that person questions such as those below:

   ● How many memos do you *write* in a typical week?

   ● How many memos do you *read* in a typical week?

   ● How important are memos to your job?

- To what extent is your performance evaluation based on your memos?
- Do you judge the effectiveness of others by their memos?
- Do you think teachers should emphasize memo writing?
- Does your organization have a particular format all employees use for memos?

You might even ask this person or other memo writers you know for sample memorandums. Having collected this information, present your findings to your class.

3. In small groups, select any piece of literature you have studied recently. Assume the role of a character in the story, and write a memo to another character or characters based on an event in the story. For instance, as Shakespeare's Hamlet, you could write a memo to King Claudius inviting him to attend the play in which the murder of Hamlet's father will be reenacted. Working as a team, follow the steps in the process to compose a memo. Use word processing software if available. Exchange your memo with other teams, revise it using their feedback, and incorporate any worthwhile ideas from other teams' memos. Keep your revised memo to refer to in writing future memorandums.

Organizing with the Direct Approach

The way you organize ideas in conversation and the way you organize for writing can be quite different. To understand the difference, think of a recent exciting event in your life. Imagine yourself telling friends about this event in a casual conversation. Now write a one- or two-paragraph description as if you were speaking to friends. Include a sentence containing the main idea in your description. Compare the organization of the two messages. Where did you place the main idea?

In many technical reports and documents, the main idea should be placed first for the convenience of the reader. Use this strategy to organize good news or informative memos. This strategy calls for putting the most important idea, or the information the reader needs most, first and reserving explanatory and supplementary ideas for later in the memo. Figure 3.4 illustrates the direct approach to organizing a message.

Figure 3.4 **Model for Direct Approach to Organization**

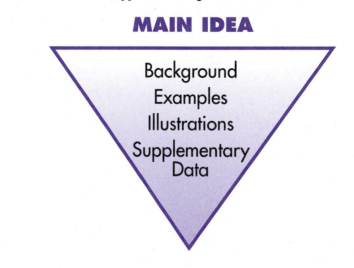

As Figure 3.4 shows, when you organize for your reader, you place the main idea first. Then, other statements are added in order of most important to least important. As the writer, you must decide how much information your reader needs and how far to continue with background and explanation.

1. Identify the most important idea for the employee (reader) from each grouping below.

   ☐ **a.** Sonja fell and broke her leg last night.
   ☐ **b.** You will need to operate the Ricoh 2086 in her place today.

   ☐ **a.** The electrician checked the thermostat by turning the power off and attaching VOM clips to the two leads from the thermostat to the motor.
   ☐ **b.** The thermostat failed the test and needs to be replaced.
   ☐ **c.** When the electrician turned the power on and moved the thermostat control button to the top of the scale, the reading was not 120 volts as it should have been.

   ☐ **a.** I took a calligraphy course last year and loved it.
   ☐ **b.** In overseeing most of the weddings here at Maui's Special Occasions, I have found calligraphy, the art of beautiful handwriting, to be a valuable skill.
   ☐ **c.** If you wish to study calligraphy, I will pay for your tuition and supplies.

2. Use main-idea-first or direct organization to arrange the following information. Write the rearranged version in a paragraph for an audience of professional chefs.

   Shalon cookware is made of heavy-duty anodized aluminum.

   It has nickel-plated cast iron and steel handles.

   Its dark surface absorbs and conducts heat evenly.

   Shalon is one of the most highly recommended cookware products on the market.

   It does not interact with foods.

   Shalon cleans easily.

Professional Letters

Write-to-Learn

Think about the flow of letters into your life. What kinds of letters do you receive? What kinds of letters do you write? What is the most important letter you have ever received or written? What kind of news did it contain?

DEFINITIONS

block style letter style that aligns the return address, dateline, and closing flush with the left margin

buffer in letters, something positive said to protect a reader from bad news to come

buyer involvement how much a consumer cares personally about a purchase; affects how much research a buyer will conduct before purchasing something

goodwill the feeling of friendship; doing things that create mutual admiration and respect

hook attention-getter designed to create interest in an idea

Maslow's Hierarchy of Needs division of human needs into basic needs (physiological, safety and belonging) and higher-order needs (esteem and self-actualization)

modified block style letter style that places the return address, dateline, and closing on the right side of the page

motivate encourage someone to take action

sell convince someone to buy or donate something

sociological influences social factors—such as culture, family, and class—that cause buyers to purchase certain goods and services

testimonial a personal story or a person's statement (often someone famous) endorsing a product or service

```
Jefferson Gas and Appli
HWY 17 South
Post Office Box 11
Washington, North Ca
13 July 199-

Ms. Ruth Tankard
Malloy's Manager
1023 West Main Street
Washington, North Car

Dear Ms. Tankard

Subject: Contract for
.

Xxxxx xxxx x xxx
xxxxxxxx xxxxxx xx
x xxx xx. Xxxx xxx :
xxxx xxxxxxxx xxxxx :
Xx xxxxx xxxxx xxxx:
Xxxx

Xxxxx xxx xxxx xx
xxx xxxxxx xxxxx xx
xxxxx xx. Xxxxxx xx:
xxxxxxx xxxxxx xxxx.
Xxx xxxxx xx xxxxx
xxx xxx xxxxxx xxx x
xxx xxxx.

Sincerely yours



W.B. (Jeff) Jefferson
President

pjm

Enclosures (3)

c:    Pat Morgan
      Jon Reardon
```

HEADING: complete address (no abbreviations) of the sender as a *return address* (personal business letter) or *letterhead* (company letter).

DATELINE: date the letter was dictated.

INSIDE ADDRESS: correct name (first name/first initial and last name), title, and address of the person to whom you are writing (no abbreviations). Name here should match the name used in the salutation.

SALUTATION: exact name of the person you want to read your letter. May be written with or without end punctuation.

SUBJECT LINE (optional): focuses on the topic of the letter.

BODY: usually 2–5 paragraphs long but can be several pages and may use headings similar to reports. The letter should look balanced on the page.

The BODY of most letters is single-spaced with a double space (or one blank line) between paragraphs. The organization depends on the type of letter you are writing.

CLOSING: friendly but businesslike ending. Common closings include Sincerely, Yours truly, and Cordially (*never* Thank you). Punctuate in *pairs:* Punctuate *both* the salutation *and* the closing OR punctuate *neither* the salutation *nor the* closing.

SIGNATURE LINE: handwritten signature along with the typed name and title.

REFERENCE INITIALS: initials of the person who dictated the letter followed by the initials of the person who typed the letter.

ENCLOSURE NOTATION: indicates additional pieces in the envelope.

COPY NOTATION: indicates copies have been sent to other people.

After completing this chapter, you will be able to

- Recognize characteristics of an effective letter
- Analyze the audience for a letter
- Recognize the parts of a business letter
- Write a positive news letter
- Write a negative news letter
- Write a persuasive letter

Fax machines, car phones, and computer bulletin boards have done much to speed up communication in today's business world. However, our send-it-right-away, needed-it-yesterday society has done little to eliminate one of the oldest forms of communication—the letter. Letters, whether sent by pony express or Federal Express, are still the mainstay of business life.

Business letters are written to inform or persuade. Informative letters typically fall into two categories: positive news letters (often called good news letters) and negative news letters (often called bad news letters). Persuasive letters try to convince readers to buy a product or service or to donate to a cause.

TECHNOLOGY UPDATE

AT&T predicts a Worldwide Intelligent Network that can do some amazing things. All communication tools we use today—faxes, phones, TV's—will be wireless and much smaller. AT&T's Personal Communicator 440 already allows users to exchange voice, fax, and electronic mail messages with anyone in the world. Soon the Personal Communicator will send video and graphic images. Because this device is wireless, it will be much more versatile and can go everywhere its owner goes.

Characteristics of Good Letters

W A R M   U P   4.1

How do you make and keep a friend?

All letters seek the **goodwill** of their readers and practice principles of good communication.

Goodwill

Goodwill is the act of making a friend and then keeping the friend. Goodwill is like good "vibes," a feeling of good intentions. Effective business correspondence tries to foster goodwill through its word choice and message. You can create goodwill in writing the same way you create the bonds of a friendship.

Friendship and goodwill are created by being honest, sincere, and polite. Business friendships grow in an atmosphere of mutual respect and trust. You also foster goodwill by attending to correspondence as quickly as you can. In short, you generate goodwill by treating your reader as you would like to be treated.

Principles of Good Communication

In addition to generating goodwill, letters should be concise, accurate, complete, and clearly worded. Writing that is not concise takes up the reader's time with details he or she does not need to know. Sending out inaccurate or incomplete information creates problems to be solved later. Unclear wording creates misunderstandings.

Letters should also be well written and look professional. Grammatical errors, misspelled words, and sloppy appearance in correspondence can make you and your organization look incompetent. Information should be carefully organized and coherent. Sentences should flow naturally from one to another. Following conventional letter format and using standard English help make a good impression on your reader. To ensure that the information in your correspondence is well organized, complete, and free of errors, always reread the document just before you send it. If you are unsure of the clarity of your message, have a colleague read your correspondence and provide feedback.

FOCUS ON ETHICS

The transmission in Randall Hauser's Pontiac Grand Am has been slipping a little. He decides to try to sell the car. Should he tell potential buyers that the transmission has been slipping?

S T O P   A N D   T H I N K   4.1

1. What is goodwill? How can you create goodwill?
2. What are the principles of good communication? Why are they important?

Audience: Who Reads Letters?

WARM UP **4.2**

How do you make a good impression on someone?

A letter is an extension of your organization. The letter will be in the presence of your reader when you are not. If the letter is well written, you will make a good impression and inspire confidence in your organization.

While memos are reserved for members inside an organization (internal communication), letters are for readers outside an organization (external communication). Although you may know a lot about members inside your organization, you may know very little about readers outside your company. Some letters are mailed to a multiple audience, and some are written with a very select audience in mind. Regardless of how well you know your readers, always use the questions and chart in Chapter 2 to help you focus on your audience.

If you do not know much about your audience, find out as much as you can. Ask others what they know about your audience, or read correspondence written by this person.

If you cannot find out much about your audience, assume a serious or neutral tone. Keep your language moderately simple and natural. Work especially hard to build goodwill.

Be guided by the type of letter you are writing. Readers of positive messages are easier to approach than readers of negative messages. Use tact with readers of negative messages. Know what the readers of sales letters need and want.

STOP AND THINK **4.2**

1. Which audience is more difficult to write for? Why do you think so?
2. What advice does the text give on writing to a reader you know little about?

Prewriting: Getting Started on Letters

To help you get started with your letters, follow these steps:

1. Decide what kind of letter you have to write: a positive letter, a negative letter, or a sales letter.
2. Determine what information you will need. What questions should your letter answer?
3. Take notes on the details you need for your letter. Gather the facts such as the background of the situation, events that occurred, problems created,

order/parts numbers, accurate description, or questions to ask. Find out the name, title, correct spelling, and correct address of the person(s) to whom you are writing.

4. Double-check to make sure the information you have gathered is accurate and complete.

5. Review the organizational plan for each letter.

6. Organize your notes according to the organizational plan for each letter.

Formatting Letters

**W A R M   U P   **

Look closely at the sample letters in this chapter. Notice how they are typed. How are they alike? How are they different?

Informative and persuasive letters differ in purpose but all share a similar format. They are constructed in basic parts and may be written in one of several styles. Two possible styles are **block style** and **modified block style.**

Letter Parts

The opening model illustrates the basic parts of a letter: heading, dateline, inside address, salutation, body, closing, signature, and reference initials. Note the description of each part. Your teacher can provide you with more detailed information on current letter format.

Letter Styles

Letter styles vary. Usually business letters are written on letterhead stationery in either block or modified block style. Personal letters include return addresses instead of letterheads and may be written in block or modified block style.

Block style letters are easier to key but may look off balance. Paragraphs are not indented and every part (except the letterhead, which may be centered) is flush with the left margin.

Modified block style is more difficult to key but looks more symmetrical on the page. Here the dateline, return address (if letterhead stationery is not used), closing, and signature line are keyed beginning at the horizontal center of the page. Paragraphs may be indented or kept flush with the left margin. Figure 4.1 illustrates basic differences in block and modified block design.

Two punctuation styles are commonly used in business letters: open and mixed. Open punctuation means no punctuation marks are used after the salutation and the complimentary close. Open punctuation is considered a time-saving style and is often used with a block format letter. When the mixed punctuation style is used, the salutation and complimentary close are followed by punctuation marks. The proper punctuation with this style is a comma after the complimentary close and a colon or a comma after the salutation.

Figure 4.1 Letter Styles

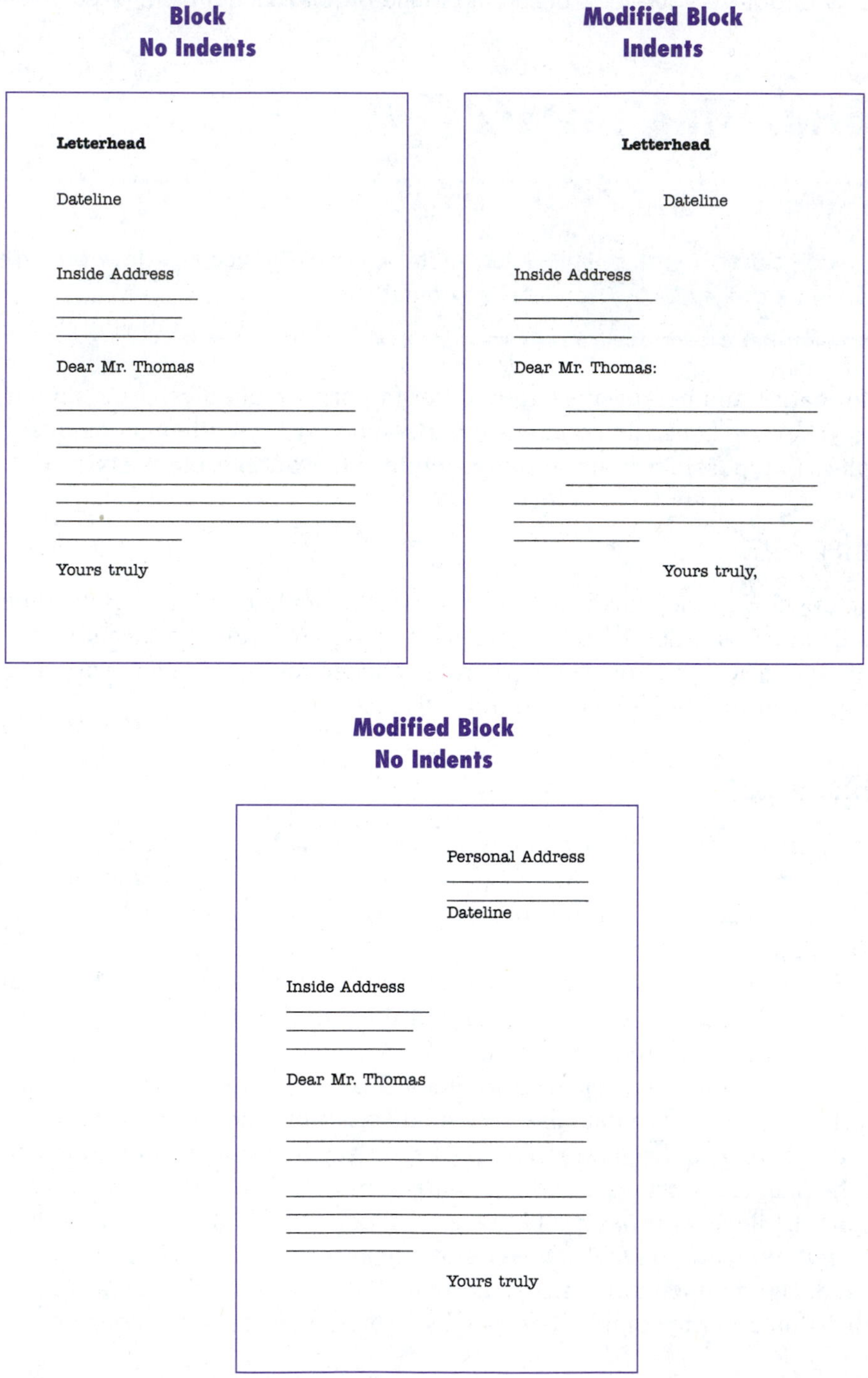

**Block
No Indents**

Letterhead

Dateline

Inside Address
_____
_____
_____

Dear Mr. Thomas
_____
_____
_____
_____
_____
_____

Yours truly

**Modified Block
Indents**

Letterhead

Dateline

Inside Address
_____
_____
_____

Dear Mr. Thomas:
_____
_____

_____
_____
_____

Yours truly,

**Modified Block
No Indents**

Personal Address
_____
_____
Dateline

Inside Address
_____
_____
_____

Dear Mr. Thomas
_____
_____
_____
_____
_____
_____

Yours truly

STOP AND THINK 4.3

1. What are the parts of a letter? What information is found under each part?
2. Which style do you prefer—block or modified block? Why?

Positive Messages

WARM UP 4.4

When was the last time you either gave or received good news? Describe what happened. Include the reaction of the receiver of the good news.

Many situations warrant the use of the positive message structure. Pronouncements of good news, routine letters of inquiry, responses to letters of inquiry, and letters of appreciation all use a similar organizational structure.

Audience: Who Reads Positive Messages?

You can expect the audience of a positive message letter to be in a receptive mood as he or she reads your letter. Picture a smile, a HOORAY, or at least an affirmative nod from this reader. Because your news is responsible for the pleasant mood, this reader is easy to approach.

Positive messages convey information a reader wants to hear. The pleasant news can be anything from winning the sweepstakes to expressing interest in a product. Each of these letters has a similar structure: the most important information is first and the least important information is last. Positive messages use a friendly (sometimes enthusiastic) tone.

Organizing and Composing Positive Messages

Use the same direct approach for positive messages in letters as you did for positive messages in memos:

- State the good news early
- Provide necessary details
- Close on a friendly note

Figures 4.2 and 4.3 are examples of positive news letters. Figure 4.2 conveys good news to Regina Williams, the recipient of an $800 scholarship to a local community college. Here the tone is enthusiastic.

Figure 4.3 shows the body of a letter of inquiry. Letters of inquiry, while employing a more neutral tone, still represent positive messages because they show an interest in a product or service. The writer of the Faulkner letter

In 1947, the American pilot Charles Yeager was the first to fly faster than the speed of sound (about 750 miles per hour at 32°F).

Figure 4.2 Positive Message: Good News Letter

PITT Community College

Office Of The Dean Of Students

Telephone   (919) 555-0139
Fax Number   (919) 555-0140

October 26, 1994

Ms. Regina Williams
P O Box 2453
Winterville, North Carolina 28590

Dear Ms. Williams:

I am pleased to award you an $800 PCC Student Government Association Scholarship to attend Pitt Community College for the 1994-95 academic year. The selection committee recognizes your achievements and your need for assistance in attaining your chosen goal.

The funds will be disbursed during the upcoming academic year. These monies will be available for you to use during pre-registration and registration for tuition and fees, as designated in the scholarship. Any remaining funds may be used to purchase books, supplies, or other school-related items in the PCC bookstore. Remaining funds will be given to you approximately four to eight weeks after registration.

I warmly congratulate you and wish you every possible success. We look forward to having you as a student at PCC. If you have any questions, feel free to contact Mr. Rudy Lloyd in our scholarship office in room 02 in the Vernon White Building, or call (919) 555-0164.

Sincerely,

Garrie Moore
Dean of Students

ta

P. O. Drawer 7007 ● Greenville ● North Carolina ● 27835-7007
An Equal Opportunity/Affirmative Action Institution

draws attention to questions in an itemized list that is numbered and set apart from the margin. Because the questions are so different from each other, the itemized list is a good choice. Questions that are more alike could be listed in one sentence like this: Please tell me where Faulkner attended grade school, what his teachers thought of him, and which activities attracted his interest.

Figure 4.3 **Positive Message: Letter of Inquiry**

I would appreciate any information you can send me on William Faulkner's life as a young man in Oxford, Mississippi.

Specifically, I am interested in knowing

1) Why did Faulkner join the Royal Air Force?

2) How old was Faulkner when he started to write?

3) Where did he get the idea for Benji in The Sound and the Fury?

In addition, I would appreciate any brochures you have that show pictures of his birthplace, family, and life as a young man. I am working on a research paper for English and need this information by 12 December if I am to complete my research in time.

Thank you for any information you can send.

STOP AND THINK **4.4**

1. How are the good news letter, the letter of inquiry, the response to inquiry, and the letter of appreciation alike in organization?

2. How do a good news letter and a letter of inquiry differ in tone?

Negative Messages

WARM UP **4.5**

When was the last time you either gave or received bad news? Describe what happened. Include the reaction of the receiver of the bad news.

Negative messages can range from serious to mildly disappointing. A letter with a negative message can refuse a request, delay an order, or register a complaint.

Audience: Who Reads Negative Messages?

The reader of a negative message will not like a portion of your letter. How much and to what degree he or she will not like your letter will depend on how

good a job you do presenting that bad news, how bad the news is, and how intense the reaction of your reader is. You have some control over your presentation, but you do not have much control over the bad news or your reader's reaction.

Ask yourself just how bad the news is. Readers receiving really bad news need a lot of sympathy. A customer may be disappointed to find out that the converter gaskets for the customer's Camaro are no longer in stock but will not lose sleep over the news. However, a businessperson whose stockbroker reports a $10,000 loss will need some consoling. Put yourself in the reader's place to determine what the emotional reaction is likely to be. Then remember that reaction and try to counter it as you write the letter.

Temperament may cause a reader to be angry, sad, or accepting. Whenever possible, try to gauge the temperament of your reader. Think about what would satisfy him or her. Will an apology work? Can you offer your reader something?

Organizing and Composing Negative Messages

Relaying negative news requires some strategy to make the negative news "go down" easier. A negative news letter must say "no" and try to maintain the goodwill of the reader. To make the negative news "go down" easier, use the indirect approach illustrated in Chapter 3:

- Open with a buffer
- Explain the reason for the negative news
- State the negative news (sometimes negative news can be implied, making it more easily accepted)
- Close in a friendly manner

    Make a constructive suggestion

    Look to the future

    Offer something, if possible

    Ask for something (complaint letters only)

The opening **buffer** protects the reader from the bad news, a friendly close ends on a positive note, and the bad news is strategically "sandwiched" in between.

Figure 4.4 shows the body of a negative news letter. Bizmark Jewelry writes the Junior Class President that the order for class rings will be delayed.

Figure 4.4 Negative Message: Bad News

Thank you for your recent order from Bizmark Jewelry. We know you and your classmates are looking forward to receiving your class rings.

> Buffer

However, the recent trucking strike has made it difficult for us to deliver customers' orders in the southwest region of the state. Therefore, your order for 256 class rings, which would normally reach you in 10 working days, will be delayed until the trucking crisis has been resolved.

> Explanation

> Bad News

We appreciate your understanding and apologize for any inconvenience. The trucking strike has caused similar delays with other businesses in the region.

Class rings are an important event in a student's life, so we will make sure your rings are on the very first truck out of Missoula as soon as the new trucking contracts are signed.

> Friendly Close

Letters of complaint are also negative news letters. When an individual has a legitimate complaint, the challenge is to present the complaint without alienating the reader. Most complaint letters also include a request to make things right, sometimes a refund, an exchange, extra service, or at least an assurance that the problem will not recur. Figure 4.5 shows the body of a complaint letter to Luigi's Restaurant.

Figure 4.5 Negative Message: Letter of Complaint

I have enjoyed dining at Luigi's for a number of years. My parents have used your restaurant to celebrate special occasions—birthdays, anniversaries, graduations—ever since I can remember.

> Buffer

Last Saturday night, I took my date to Luigi's for an elegant meal before our Senior Prom. However, instead of receiving the special treatment my date and I were expecting, we were treated unfairly.

> Explanation and Complaint

My 7:40 reservation, made well in advance three weeks ago, was not honored. Instead, I saw the host give the corner table I had requested to another couple. As a result, my date and I had to wait 45 minutes (a very long and hungry 45 minutes) before another table was ready. I was embarrassed, and our late dinner caused us to miss the opening toast at our Senior Prom.

Request for Action

I would like to know that I can look forward to other special dinners at Luigi's. Would you please talk to your host and convey my disappointment? Maybe the next time I bring a friend to eat at Luigi's, the service will be different.

STOP AND THINK

1. What is the indirect approach to delivering unpleasant news?
2. Why is the indirect approach psychologically sound advice?
3. Describe several effective ways to close a negative letter.

Persuasive Messages

WARM UP 4.6

Name several products or services you regularly buy. What do you look for in these products? What kinds of advertisements motivate you to buy one of these products?

In a market economy, someone is always trying to sell something. Sales letters are only one way companies compete for your dollar. Sales letters, even though they include information, are written primarily to persuade.

Audience: Who Reads Sales Letters?

Today's sophisticated marketing techniques make it possible to target very select audiences for certain products. Knowing your audience's needs and interests is vital to writing sales literature.

Consumers make buying decisions based on a number of psychological and sociological factors. Abraham Maslow, in his work on human motivation, said people try to satisfy the following basic needs and higher-order needs. His system is known as **Maslow's Hierarchy of Needs:**

Physiological. People must satisfy physical needs for food, water, and air. Included in this category are the need to be free from pain and the need to have a family.

Safety. People must feel safe, protected from the environment by adequate shelter.

Love and Belonging. People need to receive and to give affection. They need to feel accepted by others.

Esteem. People need to be respected by others and by themselves. Included here is the need for recognition, status, and prestige.

Self-Actualization. Self-actualization, the highest of needs, is attained by only a few people. After satisfying the first four needs, self-actualized people fulfill their potential.

The steps in Figure 4.6 illustrate that basic needs must be met before higher-order needs can be met. For example, individuals must have food and shelter and feel physically secure before they can seek love and belonging. They must feel love and belonging before they can seek esteem.

Figure 4.6 Maslow's Hierarchy of Needs

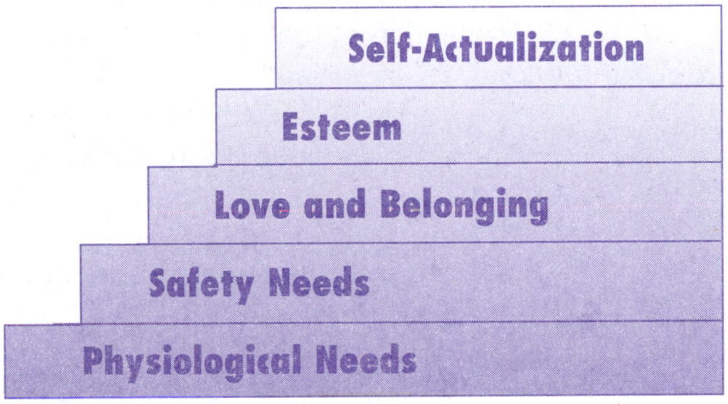

When writing a sales letter, ask which needs on Maslow's Hierarchy you are addressing. Always meet the lower needs first, and remember that people's buying decisions can be more complicated than they appear. Wanting a particular brand-name pair of shoes may have more to do with a need for acceptance than with a physical need for footwear.

Also take into consideration **sociological influences** and **buyer involvement.** Present circumstances, social class, culture, and family influence buying decisions. Also, some consumers may be more involved in buying decisions than others. Highly involved consumers will search for information and evaluate alternatives. Less involved consumers may be indifferent, buying what's on sale or what's convenient.

Know what your competition has to offer so you can counter with convincing proof of your product. Try to find out how much your reader is willing to spend.

Use these questions to analyze your sales audience:

- What psychological needs does my reader have? (Use Maslow's Hierarchy as a starting point.)
- What sociological factors may influence my reader's buying decision?
- How involved is my reader likely to be?
- What objections will my reader have to my product?
- How much is my reader willing to spend?

Organizing and Composing Sales Letters

Persuasion means you make your product or service look appealing. It would be unethical to present false information, but it's considered good business sense to present the strengths of a product in a sales letter. To present a good argument for a product or service, write sales letters according to the following organizational plan:

- HOOK your reader's attention.
- SELL your product or service.
- MOTIVATE your reader to action!

HOOK Your Reader's Attention. **Hooks** are attention-getters designed to make you open the letter and start to read. They often start on the envelope itself and continue once you open the letter.

Sometimes an announcement written in boldface precedes the letter itself. The first line of the body will sound inviting, exciting. Throughout the letter, the writer "pulls out all the stops": some information is boldfaced, underlined, bulleted, shadowed with color, set apart from the text. Some letters use headings and different fonts. Some have borders, pictures—anything to get your attention. Figure 4.7 illustrates some familiar attention-getters.

Figure 4.7 Hooks in Sales Letters

The appeals of the attention-getters vary. Some appeal to the desire to get something for nothing. Some appeal to our sense of compassion or our need for security or our desire for prestige. Some appeal to our curiosity.

SELL Your Product or Service. Advertisers describe their product (sometimes including pictures) to aid your understanding but also to give you a favorable impression of the product. It is unethical (and illegal) for an advertiser to lie, but the words are usually written to **sell**—to create a favorable impression and hence a desire for the product or service.

A sales letter should offer convincing evidence of the merits of the product or service. Facts, figures, and statistics can provide objective proof. **Testimonials,** endorsements from real people (often famous people), provide more personal stories that the product or service worked for them. Sometimes the advertisers try to compel the reader to try their product for free, for a limited time. This way, they hope the product itself will convince the reader to keep it and pay for it. Often enclosures are included—brochures with pictures, order forms, more testimonials. Sometimes a sales letter isn't just a letter; it's a whole packet of materials!

MOTIVATE Your Reader to Action. Finally, the writer must try to **motivate** you do something—to go to the phone and dial a number, to get into your car and drive to the store, to write a check or fill in a credit card number. In order to move you to action, advertisers make this part as convenient as they can. We've all heard motivators similar to the ones listed in Figure 4.8.

Figure 4.8 Motivating Statements in Sales Letter

An operator is waiting to take your call.

COME ON DOWN to Barton's Building Supplies.

Buy **now** and save **15% off** the cover price.

Send your tax-deductible contribution and help a homeless person find shelter from the cold.

Figure 4.9 on page 68 is a sales letter from West Winchester University trying to convince Jennifer Nelson to apply for admission.

S T O P   A N D   T H I N K   4.6

1. What are the three parts of a sales letter? What information is included in each part?
2. What motivates people to buy something?
3. What psychological appeals are in the letter to Jennifer from the university (Figure 4.9)?
4. How would you describe the attention-getter, the proof, and the motivator in the letter to Jennifer (Figure 4.9)?

Figure 4.9 Example of a Sales Letter

WEST WINCHESTER UNIVERSITY

1203 South Leming Road, Alexandria, Virginia 22314.
Phone 202-555-0171 • FAX 202-555-0190

April 17, 19--

Jennifer L. Nelson
764 Lord Fulford Drive
Boling, North Carolina 27878-7873

Dear Jennifer:

We've heard great things about you from the Student Search Office. Based on what we've heard, we thought you would be interested in West Winchester University, one of Virginia's most progressive universities specializing in technology, teaching, and public service.

Here is what others are saying about us:

"WWU trains its students to tackle the tough problems of a technological age."

    —EDUCATION WEEKLY

"WWU's academic program is impressive…. Its professors rank teaching as their number-one priority."

    —HOW TO GET A GOOD EDUCATION AT A STATE UNIVERSITY
      by Susan Straker

"One of the twenty best comprehensive universities in the East."

    —NATIONAL NEWS REPORT

WWU offers programs under the College of Arts and Sciences, and five professional colleges—Architecture, Business Administration, Engineering, Education and Allied Professions, and Nursing. Classes, averaging 33 students, encourage individual attention. Laboratories are equipped with the most up-to-date facilities. Our 940-acre campus is located in the largest urban area in Virginia.

Want to learn more? Send us the enclosed card and we will tell you more. Find out why WWU is the right decision for your education.

Sincerely,

Marilyn L. Richardson

Marilyn L. Richardson
Director of Admissions

SUMMARY

1. Letters generally fall into three categories: positive letters, negative letters, and persuasive letters. Letters should promote goodwill and follow principles of good communication.

2. Writers should realize that positive news is welcomed, whereas negative news is not. Writers should try to gauge the reaction of their reader to negative news. Writers of persuasive letters should know what the reader wants and needs, what the reader's objections to a product are likely to be, what the competition has to offer, and how much the reader is willing to pay.

3. Letters should be carefully planned to make sure details are accurate, complete, and organized according to the type of letter being written.

4. Letters use standard parts: heading, dateline, inside address, salutation, body, closing, signature, and reference initials. They may also be written in block and modified block styles.

5. Positive news letters follow this organization: positive news, necessary details, friendly close.

6. Negative news letters follow an organizational plan that "sandwiches" in the bad news: buffer, explanation, negative news, friendly close (make a constructive suggestion, look toward the future, and/or offer something). In a complaint letter, you may ask for something in the closing.

7. Consumers purchase products and services for psychological and sociological reasons. Some consumers are highly involved, while others are indifferent. Sales letters hook, sell, and motivate their readers.

Editing and Revision Checklist

✓ Does my letter follow the appropriate organizational strategy for the type of letter?

✓ Is my information accurate, clear, and concise?

✓ Does my letter promote goodwill?

✓ Is my tone positive—even in the bad news letters?

✓ Does my letter follow the correct format? Does it contain correct letter parts? Does it follow a consistent style?

1. Here are eight parts to a good news letter announcing that Tiffany Heilig has won a cruise to the Caribbean. The parts, however, are all mixed up. Rewrite the letter, putting the sentences in proper order. Several combinations may be possible.

   a. In order to claim your prize, you must call 1-800-CRUISES before April 18 and provide the operators with proof of your identity.

   b. You have just won an all-expense paid cruise to the Caribbean!!

   c. Congratulations, Tiffany. We look forward to helping you arrange the vacation of your life!

   d. Enjoy a variety of on-board recreational activities, delectable meals, and superb entertainment at our expense.

   e. Your name, Tiffany Heilig, was drawn out of 456,897 entries to be our top prize winner in the Colombo Publishers Sweepstakes.

   f. Colombo has reserved four nights and five days just for you and your guest.

   g. You must schedule your trip between 1 June 19-- and 21 September 19--.

   h. Pack your bags, Tiffany, and include lots of sunscreen!

2. The paragraphs in this letter denying a charitable contribution are in the wrong order for an effective bad news letter. Using modified block style, rewrite the letter putting the paragraphs in proper order. Add a return address, inside address, salutation, and proper closing. This activity is also on the computer application diskette as **TEXT4A**.

   a. In the meantime, keep up the good work.

   b. Your fight for the blue heron is a worthy one, and we understand it takes money to get things done. We encourage you to resubmit your request for a contribution by October 19-- in plenty of time to be considered for the next fiscal year.

   c. Each year we give up to $15,000 to various environmental projects. This year we have exceeded our annual contributions by $5,000 to help the Town Council finance its clean-water campaign. Under the circumstances, we will have to consider your request for a contribution at another time.

   d. We are delighted to hear of your interest in preserving the natural habitat of the blue heron in our region. We agree with you: we all have a responsibility to preserve what is beautiful on the earth.

3. Here is the body of a letter of inquiry that includes too much information. Work with two other people to decide what should be left out and rewrite the letter.

   We have really enjoyed our Macintosh Performa 575 computers. We have purchased quite a bit of equipment and several software programs.

Students enjoy working on computers in the lab. One of them the other day remarked on how professional her book report looked. She thanked me for helping her with the report and told me later that she received an A on it.

In the lab we have a CD-ROM manufactured by NEC that we purchased last year. I forgot to request the proper cable and you sent me cables for an IBM computer. Ms. Schroder, I called the NEC home office and found out that we need a OO1 M 4088 SCSI Interface cable in order to hook up our CD-ROM to our Mac. The NEC home office suggested that you might have the cable we need. Do you have one in stock? If not, can you tell me where I can get one? If so, how much does it cost? Please include shipping costs.

We can fax a purchase order from our business office if you'll just let me know if you have the cable. By the way, our fiscal year ends June 30, so you need to move quickly to get this order processed!

CONSIDER THIS CASE

1. Jake Erwin of the ABC Detective Agency has just located Nina Reddenberger's car, stolen three months ago from a shopping mall. Write a letter to Reddenberger from Erwin announcing the good news. Make up the addresses. Before writing the letter, use your imagination to answer these questions:

   How can Reddenberger get her car back? When can she get her car back?

   How did the detective find the car?

   How does Reddenberger feel?

2. Marshall Roberts has worked for Mr. Pate (manager) at the Dixie Diner (506 Glenwood Drive, Linville, North Dakota 58478) for six months. He has been a good worker and has enjoyed a good working relationship with everyone there. Yesterday, he was offered a job at McKnight's Restaurant as Crew Trainer earning $1.75 more an hour. He feels he must take the job. He has a monthly car payment and he's trying to save some money for college. Help Roberts write a bad news letter resigning his present position after a two-week notice. Make up the return address.

3. Write a letter of inquiry to YO-YO Snacks at 2445 Parkway Avenue, Finley, New York 90876, to ask questions about the nutritional value of YO-YO Granola Bars. The bars are delicious, but you'd like to know how many calories come from fat, protein, and sugar. You'd also like to know what vitamins the bars contain and if they contain any preservatives.

4. Design a sales letter for Robo-Clean, the revolutionary robot that cleans a house just like a human cleaning service can do. It vacuums, cleans bath-

rooms, washes dishes, and even takes out the trash. Robo-Clean costs only $15,999, plus shipping and handling. Ad lib additional details. Answer the questions that follow to help you make decisions about the letter:

Who is your buyer? (i.e., your audience)

What objections will you have to overcome from this buyer?

What sales appeal will you use? (i.e., why would anyone want to buy Robo-Clean?)

How will you convince your reader to buy Robo-Clean?

How will you motivate your reader to purchase Robo-Clean? What can you say or do to make the purchase convenient and easy?

5. Karen and George Smedley, two devoted, reliable, and influential customers of Fly With Us Airlines, are vowing to sue. The Smedleys have used Fly With Us Airlines for 15 years and have always been satisfied with the service. This time, though, a new Reservations Clerk at Fly With Us made a number of mistakes: **1)** the clerk erased the Smedleys' reservation and the Smedleys had to wait two hours for another flight; **2)** the clerk put the Smedleys' luggage on the wrong flight and it ended up in a remote airport; **3)** the clerk double-billed the Smedleys' credit card for the flight. To add insult to injury, the flight was unusually bumpy and a flight attendant spilled a drink in George Smedley's lap. Write a letter from the Smedleys complaining about their ordeal. Jot down answers to these questions:

How do the Smedleys feel?

Have they ever had any serious complaints before?

Do you think the Smedleys want to use Fly With Us Airlines again?

PURSUE AN IDEA

1. Create a scrapbook of sales letters and their envelopes. Analyze them for the sales pitch. What kind of attention-getters does each letter use? How does each try to convince the reader of the validity of its product or service? Look closely at the motivation to action. How is it worded? Rank the letters from most effective to least effective.

2. Collect some letters with letterheads and notice how each one is placed. Then design your own letterhead. Include a company name, the complete address, and a logo. Decide whether you would like to include anything else in your letterhead. For example, you might wish to include a slogan or the name of the president of your company.

3. Brainstorm in a group to fill in these blanks: I sure could use a _____ to make this job easier! I wish someone would invent a _____ so I wouldn't have to _____. Then invent the product or service. Write a description of it. Now write a sales letter (include envelope) to persuade someone to buy this

product. Be sure to define your audience (your customer) and follow through with an attention-getter (hook), proof of the merits of your item (sell), and motivation to buy.

4. In a group of five or six, make a list of things you do and don't like about your school. Look at your list. Choose the two or four most important complaints and the two or four most important merits. Divide up topics. Let each person in the group choose one of these topics to write a letter of complaint or a letter of appreciation.

5. You have just found a genie in a bottle. This genie will grant you four wishes—as long as the first wish is a genuine wish for someone you know. Write the names of several people you know, and then make a list of things you know those people would like to have or would like to do. Select one item for one person on your list.

   Now write a good news letter announcing to your friend (or relative) that Genie and Company has the item or event available for free. Decide where your friend will need to go to receive the prize. What will this person need to do in order to claim the prize?

   If you choose to, write the letter from Genie and Company to yourself announcing that you have just been given something you really wanted.

6. Think of the last time you were *justifiably* angry (not when you simply lost your temper). Write down a description of how you felt and exactly what happened to make you angry. Turn your anger into something productive by writing a letter of complaint. Be sure to analyze your audience and complain in a tactful way so that you don't alienate your audience.

7. Make a list of nice things people (your parent(s), a teacher, a friend, a political figure) have done for you this year. Choose the one nice thing that made the biggest impression on you. Write a letter of appreciation thanking this person for something he or she did for you. Now that you've gone to the trouble to write the letter, why not actually send it?

8. If you are currently working on a research project in another class, compose a letter of inquiry to ask for some of the information you need. Begin thinking about this assignment by making a list of things you want to know. Ask your teacher or librarian for help in finding the name and address of an appropriate resource.

Tone

Unlike the objective tone in technical reports, letters give writers a chance to show a range of emotions from apathy to warmth and enthusiasm to anger. While some unanswered complaint letters may appropriately display anger, most of your letters should convey a positive, upbeat, reader-centered tone.

Tone refers to the emotional overtones that words emit. Not only do words give you information, but they also convey feelings that make you feel OK or not so OK about something. Since human beings are both rational and emotional creatures, tone can affect the way readers react to words.

Read this passage. Describe the tone. Which words contribute to that tone?

Dear Parents,

Don't be late picking up your child. The bowling class is held from 11:00 to 12:00. Pick up your child promptly at 12:00. If your child is not picked up by 12:10, your child will be taken out of the bowling program.

Here you see that the short, terse style creates a negative tone. The words "If your child is not picked up by 12:10" may spark anger among parents who perceive that they are being treated like children. A better version would have been

Dear Parents,

We enjoy having your child in our bowling classes.

Please try to pick up your child from bowling class by 12:10. Our instructors have to be at the tennis courts at 12:30 and may be late unless you are on time.

Thank you for your cooperation. If you have any questions, please contact...

A positive tone makes people more likely to cooperate. You can create a positive tone in the following ways:

Avoid negative words. A number of words carry such negative messages that it's best to avoid them if possible. Words like *never, not, failed, cannot,* and *regret* can often be replaced by more positive words.

Use tact. Choose your words with care. Be sensitive to their impact. Instead of saying you *don't like a hat,* try saying *it shows personality.*

Accentuate the positive. Be optimistic. Most people would prefer to do what is right and best for all concerned. Remember the old example: The cup is *half full* (accentuating the *positive*) instead of *half empty* (accentuating the *negative*).

Remember your manners. Say *please* and *thank you.*

Note the differences in the following examples. What did the writer do to change a negative tone in the first column to a more positive tone in the second column?

Do not sign the evaluations.	Keep the evaluations anonymous.
If you fail to sign the form, your return will be late.	Please sign the form to avoid unnecessary delays.
We insist that you include a deposit.	Please enclose a deposit.
We received your fax in which you claim we sent you damaged goods.	Your faxed letter of 5 July indicates you received damaged goods.
If you decide to visit our museum…	When you decide to visit our museum…
Your essay is disorganized.	Concentrate on organizing your ideas.

THE INSIDE TRACK: APPLY WHAT YOU HAVE LEARNED

Make the following statements more "user-friendly" by rephrasing to make them more positive.

1. If you will attend the first meeting, I'll buy you lunch on Friday.
2. We told you to be at work by 8:00!
3. You claim to have had a flat tire on your way home?
4. We cannot allow you to make failing grades.
5. You have had more than enough time to pay the small amount shown on the enclosed bill.
6. If you cannot be at the practices on time, you cannot be on the team.
7. Our sweatshirts will not shrink.
8. You will not encounter any problems with our software.

Employment Communication

Write-to-Learn

Place yourself in the future—ten years from now. Write a one-page description of your life. What kind of job do you have? Are you happy with that job? How much money do you make? Where do you live? Do you have a family?

DEFINITIONS

chronological resume a traditional resume that provides a history of employment and education in reverse chronological order

letter of application a letter accompanying the resume; highlights major qualifications for the job

follow-up letter a letter thanking a prospective employer for an interview

functional resume a non-traditional resume organized according to most important function or skill for the job

parallel structure repeating the same grammatical structure of a phrase or sentence

priority order organized from most important to least important

resume a one- or two-page summary of job qualifications; uses elements of page design to highlight the most impressive qualifications

reverse chronological order going backwards through time

Matthew R. Abboud

Temporary
803 Princeton Road
Albuquerque, New Mexico 87103
(505) 555-0173

Permanent
67B Lakeside Apartments
Albuquerque, New Mexico 87103
(505) 555-0172

OBJECTIVE   Position as computer programmer

QUALIFICATIONS   *2 years' experience on Macintosh and IBM systems
*A.A.S. degree in Business Computer Programming
*Experience in C and C++ programming languages

EDUCATION   **Maddox Community College, San Soma, New Mexico**
A.A.S., May 1995
Major: **Business Computer Programming**. G.P.A. 3.9/4.0

Major Courses

C Language	Fox Base Pro	Technical Writing
C++ Language	Systems Programming	Data Structures
Assembly Language	Math Statistics I,II	Multimedia

CO-OP EXPERIENCE   **Wadell Computer Industries**   **August 1994–May 1995**
Columbia, New Mexico
* Designed test specifications for mainframe computer
* Developed inventory database program
* Supervised spreadsheet applications for accounting

Xenox Computer Designs   **July 1993–May 1994**
Vales, New Mexico
* Wrote tutorial for new employees
* Directed seminar on PageMaker

OTHER WORK EXPERIENCE   **Earned half of college expenses working part-time**   **1991–1993**
Auto Express, Vales, New Mexico. Sales Clerk
Better Burgers, Vales, New Mexico. Cook and Sales Clerk

INTERESTS   Programming, sailing, photography

REFERENCES   Available Upon Request

JUANITA MANUEL
Route 5, Box 332
Charles, Ohio 43605
(414) 555-0195

Objective
Part-time work as an administrative assistant in a business environment

Office Skills
- Experience with Word for Windows, Lotus Spreadsheet, and WordPerfect
- Knowledge of office procedures
- Strong interpersonal skills
- Knowledge of accounting ledgers

Administrative Activities
MANUEL'S FLOWERS, July 1996 to Present
Assisted with clerical duties in family-owned business

BETA CLUB TREASURER, October 1996–June 1997
Maintained account ledger, created annual budget, balanced budget,
wrote checks

CO-CHAIRPERSON, JUNIOR MAGAZINE SALES, January 1996–March 1997
Directed sales staff, planned advertising campaign, sold magazines

Education
Wanoca High School, Charles, Ohio. Expected date of graduation June 1997
Course of Study: Office Technology.
Specialized Courses: Accounting, Office Management, and Word Processing

Interests
Writing, skiing, singing, piano

References
Sam Pollock	Hilda Brad	Greg Wilms
Business Teacher	Manager, Shoe Bargain	City Treasurer
342 Baily Road	8890 Yellowstone Street	89 Braxton Place
Charles, Ohio 26785	Farmville, Ohio 26798	Charles, Ohio 26785
(614) 555-0189	(614) 555-0187	(614) 555-0135

After completing this chapter, you will be able to

- Employ persuasive strategies to impress a prospective employer
- Research your audience's expectations
- Assess your own employment strengths
- Use basic resume headings
- Make decisions to add optional headings
- Highlight your strengths in either a chronological resume or a functional resume
- Organize a resume
- Compose employment letters

The job you seek may be the long-awaited dream job, a part-time job to help you through school, or a transitional job. Whatever the job, you will need employment communication that is both attractive and effective to highlight your strengths for the job market.

Employment communication includes a **resume** (a one-page summary of your qualifications), a **letter of application** (letter to accompany resume), and possibly a **follow-up letter** (letter to thank employer for an interview). Resumes and accompanying letters are important because

1. they give employers something to look at *before you fill out their applications,*
2. they make you look *professional* and *ready to work,* and
3. they allow you to *control the presentation of your skills.* Your skills stand out in a resume you designed instead of being hidden in an application form someone else designed.

Audience: Who Reads Employment Communication?

WARM UP 5.1

If you were the owner of a big corporation, what kind of employees would you want to hire?

To understand how to approach employment communication, consider the job hunter's perspective, the employer's perspective, and the employer's expectations.

Job Hunter's Perspective

In any persuasive communication, the better you know your audience, the better you can tailor your communication to its needs. To approach a prospective employer, you must be smart and do your homework. You should find out all you can about this person and the organization to which you are applying. The Prewriting for this chapter tells you what you should find out about your audience before you write your resume and letter of application.

Employer's Perspective

Prospective employers are interested in your skills, your education, and your references. They are also interested in your ability to get along with others, to solve problems, and to communicate. An employer's goal is to hire the best-qualified applicant available, but finding that person is not easy. Employers can't waste time with unqualified applicants, so they skim through a set of resumes, discarding those of applicants who do not meet their needs. The few resumes selected during this initial screening are read very carefully.

Employer's Expectations

Your prospective employer expects your employment communication to conform to standard employment protocol. Employment communication must

1. Contain no errors. Resumes with misspellings, typos, nonstandard dialect, and punctuation errors are routinely cast aside during initial screenings.
2. Look neat and professional. A resume corrected with white-out and strikeovers, for example, or one whose print is too light would make it look as if the writer didn't care. To look professional, resumes should be printed in letter-quality print on bonded paper.
3. Follow an accepted format. A resume that is too long, for example, or one printed on purple paper or written using an eccentric design would look as if the writer didn't know what a resume was supposed to look like.
4. Assert your best qualities (even if it sounds to you as if you are bragging).

REAL-LIFE CRISIS

Frances was being interviewed for a position when she was asked a question she didn't know the answer to. How should she have handled this?

STOP AND THINK 5.1

1. Why do employers discard some resumes initially?
2. Why do employers read selected employment communication carefully?
3. What kind of impression might a resume with errors make on an employer?

Prewriting: Getting Started on Employment Communication

To get started on an employment package, find out about yourself, find out about your employer, and choose your references.

Find Out About Yourself

Good employment communication begins with some self-assessment. To get started on your employment package, think about your skills, your aptitudes, your goals, your education, and your experience.

Answer these questions to assess your strengths as an employee. Take notes. When you finish, highlight or circle the three most important things about your employable self.

- What are your special talents?
- What kind of work do you think you have an aptitude for?
- What special skills do you have?
- Have you received any honors or awards? If so, what?
- Which of your accomplishments in the past two years might impress a prospective employer?
- What school and/or community activities do you participate in? In your activities, have you worked on committees or been responsible for certain projects? If so, what?
- What are your hobbies or interests?
- What is your GPA?
- Have you had special classes to prepare you for a particular job?
- What past jobs have you held? Write the dates for each job. Describe what you did in each job.

Find Out About Your Employer

In addition to assessing your own strengths, you should find out as much as you can about your audience, the place of business, and the job you seek. Ask people who already work there how they were hired. Call the Personnel Office and find out about the company's hiring practices. Information on major American companies can be found in *Hoover's Handbook: Profiles of 500 Major US Companies*. To continue working on your employment package, take some notes by answering as many of the following questions as possible. Then highlight or circle what you think the three most important pieces of information are.

- Who will be responsible for making the decision to hire you—an individual or a committee?
- If an individual, what position does the individual hold? What does he or she expect from an employee?
- If the responsible party is a committee, who is on it? What are their positions? What do they expect from an employee?
- What is a typical interview like? How long does an interview last? Who conducts the interview? Will you be expected to take a test or perform a task as part of the interview?
- What can you find out about the company—its mission statement/philosophy, its current projects, its organization, its openings, or its past record?
- In what area of the company would you like to work? What would you be expected to do in this area?

Choose Your References

Choose at least three people (no more than five) to include as references. Work references, people for whom you have actually worked, make the best references. After all, your employer is interested in knowing how well you perform on the job. Educational references—teachers, advisors, guidance counselors—can also attest to your knowledge and reliability. Personal references, people who have known you long enough to vouch for your character, should be kept to a minimum. If you have only two work references and need a third one, then you may choose a personal reference. However, if you have three good work references, list them. The only exception might be if one of your personal references is an important and well-known person (for example, a community leader or a respected professional). Before you list someone as a reference, always ask.

Formatting Resumes

WARM UP 5.2

Look at the Abboud and Manuel resumes (pages 77 and 78) for 10 seconds and then look away. What do you remember from this 10-second glance? Look back at the resumes. To what three parts of each resume are your eyes drawn?

Designing a resume is like designing an ad for a newspaper. Have you ever noticed how, in a newspaper ad, some words *jump out* at you? They may be set in bold type, for example, or bulleted to draw your attention. A newspaper ad is designed to create an immediate impression in a small space.

Like a newspaper ad, the resume must make its impression in a short amount of space. After all, you are designing an ad—and you're selling *you*, your skills and expertise, to a prospective employer. You want your most impressive qualifications to *jump out* at your employer during his or her first 10-second glance at your resume. For a high school student or newly graduated college student, the resume should be only one page long. For people with several years of impressive work experience, a two-page resume may be acceptable.

Part of the design strategy is to consider how the resume looks on the page. It should look symmetrical and balanced. White space allowing comfortable margins makes the resume look easy to read and uncluttered. Special features such as **boldfacing,** underlining, *italicizing,* CAPITALIZING, • bullets, or * asterisks make important information stand out. Headings should be easy to spot. Use an easy-to-read font (Geneva, Helvetica, or New York, for example) in 10-point or 12-point type. However, be careful: too many special features will make your resume look cluttered and busy. See Chapter 8 on Document Design and Visual Aids to learn more about design elements.

S T O P   A N D   T H I N K

Look back at the items you circled in your notes during the Prewriting exercise to signal something important. How could you use special features to draw attention to this information?

Organizing Resumes

W A R M   U P

Look at Manuel's resume at the beginning of the chapter. Compare the headings with the headings in Abboud's resume. How are the headings different? How is the organization different? Do you have any suggestions as to why the headings are organized differently?

To organize materials for your resume, follow this sequence:

1. Include all the basic headings.

2. Decide which optional headings to include.

3. Highlight your strengths in either a chronological resume or a functional resume.

4. Use priority order (from most important to least important) and reverse chronological order (backwards through time) to write sections of your chronological or functional resume.

Decide Which Headings to Include

Making decisions about which headings to include in a resume is like making decisions about your daily wardrobe. You must put certain clothes on—jeans, shirts, shoes, socks—whatever your basic wardrobe consists of. You do have choices to make, however, about accessories, items such as jewelry, caps, scarves, belts. The accessories help you express your individuality; they are what sets you apart from others. Similarly, a resume must include the basic headings. Optional headings, like accessories, help to highlight your strengths and minimize your weaknesses.

Basic Headings. Basic headings include your identification, education, work experience, and references. Figure 5.1 illustrates what *must be* included under each basic heading and what *may be* included under each basic heading.

Figure 5.1 Basic Headings

	Must Include	May Include
Identification*	● name, complete address, phone	● permanent and temporary address
Education	● name of school, city and state of school; ● dates of attendance, graduation or expected graduation; ● major or course of study	● list of courses, if helpful to employer; ● academic honors, if any; ● GPA, if good ● extracurricular activities
Experience	● name, city, and state of company; ● position/title; ● most recent jobs (up to 3 jobs); ● description of duties, if related to job sought	● promotions, special accomplishments; ● description of duties, even if not related to job sought
References	One of these: **1.** References Available Upon Request *OR* **2.** names, titles, addresses, phone numbers of three references	

*Identification is not used to name this part of the resume; in other words, identification is not a heading. It merely describes the information given at the top of the resume.

Optional Headings. Optional headings give you an opportunity to show off your strengths and minimize your weaknesses. A number of optional headings appear on resumes but some of the most popular headings are job objective, qualifications, skills, interests and/or activities, achievements and/or honors, and military experience. Figure 5.2 suggests when to use these headings and when not to use these headings.

Figure 5.2 Optional Resume Headings

	USE IF . . .	DON'T USE IF . . .
Objective	● You're applying for a specific job ● The company prefers you to include an objective	● You're not applying for a specific job ● The company prefers to decide in which position to place you
Qualifications	● You wish to summarize your strengths ● You have the qualifications listed in the ad for employment	● Qualifications are not specified
Skills	● You wish to summarize your skills ● The ad calls for specific skills that you have ● You have skills not related to your education ● You have impressive technical skills	● You're not sure what skills the employer needs ● You don't have special skills
Interests and/or Activities	● Your employer wants to know more personal information qualifications ● Your interests complement your qualifications ● You want your employer to see you as well rounded and human ● You have space to fill on page	● Your employer wants to know only about your work ● You don't have space
Achievements and/or Honors	● You have honors and/or awards ● You achieved other significant goals	● You don't have any honors or awards
Military Experience	● You have gained skills you want to highlight ● You have impressive experience	● You have included military experience under another heading ● You don't have military or ROTC training

You may choose another name for some of the headings. Make the name of the heading as specifically related to the information you are giving as possible. Here are a few variations:

Objective: Job Objective, Career Objective, Professional Objective

Experience: Work Experience, Related Experience, Co-op Experience

You can divide Experience into two areas: Related Work Experience and Other Work Experience; Co-op Experience and Other Experience; Related Experience and Military Experience

Education: Military School, Licenses, Certificates

Qualifications: Major Qualifications, Summary, Skills

Interests: Interests and Activities, Activities, Hobbies

Honors: Honors and Achievements, Achievements, Awards

STOP AND THINK **5.3a**

1. What is included under each basic heading?
2. What is included under each optional heading?
3. What purpose do optional headings serve?
4. Which optional headings would you include in your resume?

FOCUS ON ETHICS

Tim, age 28, spent two years in the state penitentiary for shoplifting when he was 19 years old. Since that time, he has attended classes and obtained an Associate degree in Accounting and has spent three years in the U.S. Army. He now has a family and is an involved and respected member of his community. Tim is applying for a job with D & J Accounting. The application asks if he has ever been convicted of a crime. Since his shoplifting offense, Tim has been a law-abiding citizen. Should he tell about the shoplifting?

Chronological Resume

The **chronological resume** takes an employer backward in time through your educational and employment record. Widely used, a chronological resume offers an approach that most employers recognize and accept. This resume

- provides a history of employment and education, regardless of the job
- accounts for every year out of high school with no gaps in time
- tends to emphasize dates in resume design
- uses predictable, traditional headings
- places education and work experience early in the resume.

The chronological resume offers several advantages. First, it is familiar and readily accepted. Second, it can be read quickly. Third, it can draw attention to a steady and impressive work history.

Even though the chronological resume is widely used, it is not ideal for everyone. First, a lengthy work history may make the resume too long. Second, the format is so structured that it may limit someone whose qualifications do not fit into its framework. For example, it may not be flexible enough for someone with little or no work experience. Third, it may be so similar to other resumes that it will not stand out. In other words, it may get lost in the "sameness" of other chronological resumes.

The Abboud resume at the beginning of this chapter is an example of a chronological resume. Abboud is applying for a job directly related to his degree. With only two years of related work experience, he figures his degree is his best asset and his related work experience (Co-op) is his next strongest asset. He lists his other work experience last because it is not as impressive as his related work experience. The dates, separated from the main text of the resume, stand out. Notice he does not describe this work experience because it is not as impressive as his Co-op experience. Also, most of his employers will understand what these part-time jobs entailed and will take note of these only because he worked part-time to support himself in school.

Clay tablets prove that Babylonians used arithmetic skills more than 4000 years ago.

Functional Resume

Resumes organized according to function or purpose offer more flexibility than chronological resumes. Truly tailored to suit the requirements of a particular job, a **functional resume**

- provides a summary of most important qualifications *for the job*
- may not account for every year out of high school
- emphasizes skills, accomplishments, job titles—regardless of time frame
- uses less predictable, nontraditional headings *designed for the job*
- may present education and work experience later in the resume.

The functional resume offers several advantages. First, it helps the employer make judgments about what skills and accomplishments are useful for the job. Second, the functional resume can be used in a variety of circumstances. For example, functional resumes are useful if you have plenty of work experience and skills that would take up too much space on a chronological resume. On the other hand, functional resumes are also useful if you are applying for a job for which you have no formal education but for which you have a number of marketable skills. For example, perhaps you have carpentry skills taught to you at home. Even though you do not have a degree, you still possess the skills.

While the functional resume does offer flexibility and a more original format, employers may want to discuss items such as "holes" in resumes (time lapses that are not explained). Be prepared to account for such lapses in a job interview.

The Manuel resume at the beginning of the chapter is an example of a functional resume. Manuel's circumstances are different from Abboud's, and a functional resume meets her needs. Manuel is not applying for her first full-time job upon graduating from college; she is applying for her first part-time job while she is in high school. Because she does not yet have a degree, her job skills are more important than her education. She has no work experience, so she capitalizes upon her club work and community volunteer work to show she is capable of handling office responsibilities.

STOP AND THINK 5.3b

1. What are the characteristics of a chronological resume?
2. What are the characteristics of a functional resume?
3. Compare the advantages and disadvantages of the chronological resume and the functional resume.
4. Which type of resume will best meet your needs? Why?

Organizational Strategies

Two organizational strategies govern the writing of all resumes: **priority order** and **reverse chronological order**.

Priority Order. Major sections (*except for References:* they are always placed last) are presented from most important to least important. Most important, here, should be what is most important *to your audience*, or your prospective employer. If you have impressive work experience, then work experience may be more important to your employer than education. If so, place work experience before education. If you are a recent graduate without much work experience, then education may be listed first as the most important qualification to your employer. A summary of skills that provides an overview of your qualifications should be placed early in the resume. An employer quickly skimming your resume can focus on your major qualifications even if he or she does not read any further. Within each section, lists of skills, duties, awards, or interests are also organized from most important to least important.

Reverse Chronological Order. Some parts of the resume are always presented in reverse chronological order (backwards through time). Actually, reverse chronological order is an extension of the priority order mentioned above. The priority here is time: what is most recent is considered to be the most important. In particular, past jobs and schools attended should be listed in reverse chronological order. For example, when presenting your work experience, list your most recent job first, your second most recent job second, your third most recent third, and so on.

S T O P   A N D   T H I N K   5.3c

1. Why is there so much flexibility built into writing a resume?
2. Explain priority order and reverse chronological order.

Composing the Resume

W A R M   U P   5.4

Look closely at the diction, or wording, of Abboud's resume and Manuel's resume. How would you describe the diction? Do the writers use fragments or clauses? How are the resumes punctuated?

After you have answered some questions about your audience and assessed your strengths as an employee, you are ready to begin composing the parts of your resume. From the questions you answered about your employer and the employment self-assessment, review the six things you circled as being most important. Add to your "important" list one more item: your name. Now that you know what information to highlight, you are ready to begin composing your resume.

Word Choice

When writing a resume, you want to make sure you have **1)** presented information in as few words as possible and **2)** placed information in an easy-to-read format.

The word choice in a resume is unlike that in anything you've written before. A resume has its own grammar rules: Sentences and paragraphs are out. They take up too much space. Instead, resumes are written in lists: lists of **1)** nouns and nouns + modifiers and **2)** verb phrases—always using **parallel structure** (repeating the grammatical structure already in place). See The Inside Track, page 102.

Nouns and Nouns + Modifiers. For naming Interests, Activities, Honors, and/or Achievements, simple noun lists and nouns + modifiers are useful. Here are some examples:

Nouns

Interests: sailing, reading, programming, gardening (gerunds that name)

Activities: aerobics, Girl Scout leader, member Beta Club, choir member

Honors: Chief Marshall, winner Speech Contest, member Honor Society

or

Who's Who, Honor Society, Quill and Scroll

Nouns + Modifiers

Skills:
- Knowledge of both IBM and Macintosh systems
- Ability to program in a variety of languages
- Experience conducting workshops on software applications

The structure of these lists is parallel because the lists start the same way each time. The bullets draw attention to the skills. Can you see there is an understood "I have" before each item in the Skills section? ("I have" knowledge of....)

Verb + What Phrases. Verb + What phrases are quick, effective ways to describe Skills, Qualifications and Work Experience. Use action verbs to stress what you can do for an employer. Performance is more impressive than qualifications. Notice that the phrases have an understood "I" or "I can" before each item ("I can" repair; "I" encode; "I" sold).

Skills:
- Repair both Macintosh and IBM systems
- Program in a variety of languages
- Conduct workshops on software applications

Be sure that the lists are consistent in tense: present tense for jobs you currently hold, past tense for jobs you no longer hold. If you had (or have) a title, include the title followed by a colon before you list your duties.

Present Tense Phrases to Describe You Jobs Currently Hold

encode data	install equipment	wait tables
provide child care	repair VCR's	take orders

Past Tense Verb Phrases for Jobs You No Longer Hold

sold merchandise	analyzed data	assisted customers
stocked groceries	filed reports	evaluated procedures

Title Before Verb Phrase

Cashier: operated register, greeted customers, and stocked shelves

Foreman: supervised workers, enforced safety measures, and handled payroll

Figure 5.3 shows other action verbs you may wish to consider.

Figure 5.3 Action Verbs

accomplished	completed	earned	initiated	reduced
achieved	composed	established	led	revised
administered	contributed	evaluated	maintained	saved
analyzed	coordinated	expanded	operated	sold
applied	created	headed	organized	solved
assisted	designed	identified	performed	streamlined
built	developed	implemented	planned	supervised
communicated	devised	improved	produced	trained
compiled	directed	increased	promoted	wrote

Punctuation

Since there are no complete sentences in resumes, it's hard to apply traditional punctuation rules. Many parts of the resume have no end punctuation at all. If one piece of information ends naturally on a single line, then you may choose not to put any end mark there at all. For other marks of punctuation,

- use periods to break up big blocks of thought or to indicate a real change in information,
- use colons to introduce lists,
- use commas to separate simple lists of three or more items, and
- use semicolons to separate complex lists (lists that already contain commas) of three or more items.

Refer to the models in the chapter to see how these resumes use punctuation.

STOP AND THINK 5.4

1. What will be the hardest part of writing a resume? Why?

2. How does the diction of a traditional essay differ from the diction in a resume?

3. Describe the diction of every part of the Abboud or Manuel resume. Tell where Abboud used noun lists, noun phrases, verb lists, and verb phrases.

Composing Employment Letters

There are two primary types of employment letters: letters of application that accompany the resume highlighting the applicant's strengths and follow-up letters that thank the employer for the interview. The letters give you another forum in which to sell your skills. They also show the employer how well you express yourself.

Letter of Application

If you think about it, a letter of application is really a sales letter. After all, you are selling yourself as a good candidate for employment. Notice the sales elements in Abboud's letter of application in Figure 5.4.

Parts of Letter.

As you recall from Chapter 4, sales letters are made up of three parts: the hook, the sell, and the motivation to action. Similarly, a letter of application is made up of an opening (attention-getter), a summary of qualifications (proof), and a request for an interview (motivation to action).

Opening. The first paragraph should get the reader's attention. It should

1. state your interest in the job,
2. explain how you found out about the job, and
3. quickly summarize your major qualifications for the job.

Summary of Qualifications. The second (and maybe third and fourth) paragraph(s) justifies your claim that you can work for this company by providing proof of your credentials. To provide specific proof that you can perform this job,

1. describe your education,
2. describe appropriate work experience,
3. describe related skills, and
4. explain something important not mentioned in the resume.

Request for Interview. The last paragraph motivates the reader to action by asking for an interview and making contact convenient. Be sure to

1. refer to the enclosed resume,
2. ask for an interview, and
3. tell how and when you can be reached.

Figure 5.4 **Letter of Application**

803 Princeton Road
Albuquerque, New Mexico 87103
15 June 19--

Dell Yamsung, Personnel Director
Sampson Electronic Industries, Inc.
3902 West Broad Street
Charles, Arkansas 72203

Dear Mr. Yamsung:

I would like to apply for the computer programmer position you advertised in the <u>Daily</u>
<u>Register</u> last week. My education and work experience qualify me for this position.

I earned an Associate's degree in Applied Science in Business Computer Programming from
Maddox Community College. At Maddox's Unix-based computing lab, I learned to program in
the Fortran and C++ languages. In addition, I gained valuable experience in multimedia presentation using Toolbook. Using Maddox's up-to-date facility has given me the knowledge and
confidence I need to adapt to any computer environment.

In addition to my education, I have experience meeting the computing needs of business and
industry. At Wadell Computer Industries, I worked with Fox Base Pro and database management. Just before I graduated, I was instrumental in implementing a database inventory program. I also worked on quality teams to keep production efficient. At Xenox Computer
Designs, I wrote a tutorial for training new employees and directed a seminar on PageMaker.
My supervisor at Xenox gave me superior evaluations, ranking me high in problem-solving
skills and ability to work with people.

My resume is enclosed for your consideration. I would be happy to schedule an interview to
discuss my qualifications. You may reach me at (501) 555-0172 after 3:00 p.m.

Sincerely,

Matthew Abboud

Matthew Abboud

Enclosure

Sentence Structure.

When composing your letter of application, use variety in sentence structure.
Although it's easy to begin every sentence with "I" when writing about yourself, try to begin some sentences with words other than "I." To achieve variety, consider beginning sentences with prepositional phrases, introductory
clauses, and transitional words. See Abboud's letter to observe how he
achieved sentence variety.

Follow-up Letter

A follow-up letter, sometimes known as a thank-you letter, is sent soon after a job interview. The follow-up letter should

1. thank the employer for the interview,
2. remind the employer of something said or done during the interview,
3. explain why you are the best candidate for the job, and
4. express continuing interest in the job.

This way the employer knows you're still interested. He or she is also encouraged to remember something specific about you. Figure 5.5 shows the body of a follow-up letter that Abboud wrote Mr. Yamsung after his interview.

Figure 5.5 Body of a Follow-up Letter

Dear Mr. Yamsung:

Thank you for considering me for the position of computer programmer with your company. I enjoyed discussing ways to improve the personnel database. As you may remember, I have had much experience with the relational database program Fox Base Pro. I would welcome the opportunity to put my knowledge to work for your company designing a more efficient personnel database. I am also willing to relocate to any of your subsidiaries.

I look forward to hearing from you soon. If you have additional questions about my qualifications, please call me at (501) 555-0172.

STOP AND THINK **5.5**

1. What information should a letter of application include?
2. What information should a follow-up letter include?
3. Will you send out follow-up letters for every resume and letter of application you send out?

SUMMARY

1. Content and design are important to get your reader's attention. After initial screening, prospective employers read employment communication very carefully, so writers should spend time and effort to research and design effective employment communication.

2. Before you can write a resume and letter of application, you should find out information about your employer, assess your strengths as an employee, and choose your references.

3. A resume is designed. It should look symmetrical, include ample white space, and use an easy-to-read font. Special features such as **boldfacing,** <u>underlining</u>, *italicizing*, CAPITALIZING, • bullets, or * asterisks make important information stand out. Headings should be easy to spot. Use an easy-to-read font (Geneva, Helvetica, or New York, for example) in 10-point or 12-point type.

4. Basic headings that must be on all resumes include Identification (applicant's name, address, telephone), Education, Experience, and References. Other headings are optional headings, the headings you may include to enhance your resume.

5. Resumes generally fall into two types: chronological resumes that provide an employment history and functional resumes that closely match achievements to the job.

6. Resumes use two organizational strategies: reverse chronological order and priority order.

7. Word choice in a resume uses phrases and lists in parallel structure. Sentences and paragraphs are not used.

8. Applicants may write two kinds of employment letters: letter of application and follow-up letter. Letters of application are like sales letters and follow a three-part structure: opening, summary of qualifications, and request for interview. Follow-up letters should thank the employer for the interview, remind the employer of something said or done during the interview, explain why you are the best candidate for the job, and express continuing interest.

Editing and Revision Checklist

Complete Employment Package

✓ Is everything—resume, letter of application, and follow-up letter—free from any grammar, spelling, and punctuation errors? Remember, there should be no errors in employment communciation.

Resume

✓ Have I addressed the qualifications for the job (either the qualifications listed in an employment ad or the qualifications you think the job requires)?

✓ Have I included all the basic headings?

✓ Do my optional headings reveal my best qualities?

✓ Is the resume organized to reflect my strengths? Are sections organized in reverse chronological order?

✓ Have I used boldfacing, underlining, and capitalization to highlight important items? Does my name stand out?

✓ Is the resume neat? Does it make appropriate use of white space?

✓ Is the length of my resume appropriate to my level of experience (probably one page)?

✓ Have I included proper details throughout, such as phone numbers, easy-to-spot dates, and GPA (if appropriate)?

✓ Have I proofread the resume for grammatical and mechanical errors?

Letter of Application

✓ Do I have a three-part structure (introductory beginning, explanatory body, and request conclusion) with at least (but not limited to) three paragraphs?

✓ Do I have a well-structured first sentence?

✓ Have I explained how I have the skills necessary for the job, referring in particular to any skills mentioned in the ad or job description?

✓ Did I consider mentioning something other than what I could cover in the resume?

✓ Did I refer to my resume?

✓ Did I ask for an interview and give enough information so that I could be reached easily?

Follow-up Letter

✓ Have I thanked the interviewer for the interview?

✓ Have I reminded the interviewer of something specific that took place during the interview?

✓ Have I reminded the interviewer of my most impressive qualifications?

✓ Is the tone positive and polite?

APPLY WHAT YOU HAVE LEARNED

1. Something important is left out of each of the following excerpts from resumes. What is left out?

A. Address
Kareem S. Saleeby
589 Mohican Avenue
Saint Thomas, FL

B. Reference
Howard VanStaldinuin
New Dresden, NY
(518) 555-3214

C. Experience
Neuse Sport Shop, Carnival, NM
*Assisted customers on the floor
*Operated cash register
*Stocked shelves

D. Education
Danville Technical and
   Vocational College
Associate in Applied Science
GPA: 3.5/4.0

2. Here is an ad for an Administrative Assistant followed by an excerpt from a letter of application for this position. In small groups, decide whether the excerpt addresses every qualification in the ad. What, if anything, is left out?

ADMINISTRATIVE Assistant.

High energy, detail-oriented, team player for our Greenville office to learn many office responsibilities. Prefer knowledge of WordPerfect and Lotus spreadsheet. Send resume to....

As a graduate of Montclair Technical Institute, I have gained skills in word processing. In particular, I have worked extensively with WordPerfect and Lotus spreadsheet. In addition, I have experience with Word for Windows and Excel.

I am also familiar with the most up-to-date office management systems. A part-time job with Apex Industries gave me the opportunity to work in an office with an extremely efficient office manager. From the office manager, I learned important tips about filing, turning out timely correspondence, and scheduling appointments.

3. Here is an ad for employment followed by three skills lists. In small groups, decide which skills list is best suited to match the qualifications of this ad.

AUTO TECH NEEDED.
ASE Certified. Experienced in front-end alignment, brake work, and transmissions. Must have two years' experience as auto mechanic. Contact Steve....

A. Major Qualifications
*Two years' experience as auto mechanic
*Knowledge of electrical systems
*ASE certified
*Experience on a variety of foreign cars

B. Major Qualifications
*Two years' experience as mechanic on domestic and foreign cars
*ASE certified
*Extensive experience with front-end alignment, brake work, and transmissions

C. Major Qualifications
*Experience on front-end alignment
*Experience with brake repair
*A.A.S., Automotive Technology
*Knowledge of transmissions

4. Here are two work experience descriptions from the same resume. The first job description lists work experience using the verb + what method. The second job description lists job duties using nouns. Make the first job description parallel to the second by using nouns or make the second job description parallel to the first by using the verb + what method.

Da-Nite Restaurant, Bethel, MN

- manage restaurant
- take orders
- prepare food
- handle money

George's Remodeling, Bethel, MN

- roofing
- painting
- carpentry
- tree cutting

5. The following sentences from letters of application are not specific enough by themselves. They do not provide the details that prove the skill or qualification listed. What kind of information should be added?

a. I have educational experience with personal computers and basic programming.

b. I have worked in my family's construction business for the past seven years, so I have extensive knowledge of how a building should be put together. I have worked on every phase of a job.

c. I am a 19-- graduate of Vancouver Community College with an Associate degree in Medical Office Technology. Throughout my college career, I have gained many skills.

6. The following Education and Experience sections appear on Caroline's resume. In small groups, decide how to arrange each section and how to punctuate each.

EDUCATION

Where: Clifton County Community College in Farmville, South Carolina.

When: Attended August 19-- to present. Expected date of graduation November 19--

Major: Graphic Design

Degree: A.A.S.   GPA: 4.0/4.0

Courses: Adobe PageMaker, QuarkXpress, Adobe Illustrator, Adobe Freehand, Photography, Design, and Production

Senior Project: Ad campaign for local theater production of The Secret Garden.

EXPERIENCE

Where: Logan's Printers, Farmville, South Carolina

When: June 19-- to May 19--

Description: worked on printing press, helped customers decide on business card designs, responsible for laying out ads for restaurant placemats

Where: Cattle Barn, Farmville, South Carolina

When: September 1993–March 1994

Description: greeted customers, accepted money and gave out change, wrote down phone orders and take-out orders

7. Beaumont has listed the following seven people as possible references on his worksheet. In small groups, look at the description of each and help Beaumont decide which references to include and which to exclude on a resume for a construction job.

Joe Garriet: Beaumont's high school drafting instructor

Rosalie Maynard: Beaumont's neighbor, high school secretary

Dr. Gary Wiggins: head of local Habitat for Humanity, for which Beaumont has volunteered (Habitat for Humanity helps build and finance houses for people who could not otherwise afford them.)

Rachael Currier: neighbor, architect in local firm, supervised high school construction project that Beaumont worked on

Roy McDougan: manager of building supplies store, has sold supplies to Beaumont

Marilyn Smith: Beaumont's 12th-grade English teacher

Chevron Williams: Beaumont's uncle

8. Reduce these sentences to phrases. Leave out anything that is not absolutely necessary.

   a. I was responsible for filing reports and answering the phone.

   b. For one summer, I babysat for two preschool children. I played with them and tutored them in reading.

   c. Last year I worked in my uncle's department store. He had me stocking shelves, ringing up purchases, and walking around the departments answering questions from customers. I also ordered some merchandise.

CONSIDER THIS CASE

1. After graduation from high school, Yu-lan Wang plans to apply for two part-time summer jobs: camp counselor for 10- to 12-year-old boys at BSA Camp Wacamaaw and carpenter's helper for the local G & W Construction Company. Because the jobs are so different, Yu-lan will have to write two resumes: one for each job.

Divide into small groups. Then use the following description of Yu-lan's high school record, work experience, skills, and possible references to write a functional resume for either or both of these jobs. Make up the dates and addresses for his resumes and add additional information as appropriate. Refer to the Revision and Editing Checklist at the end of the chapter to help you write. This activity is also on the computer applications diskette as **TEXT5A**.

Yu-lan took Drafting I and II, a developmental psychology course, and Spanish. His GPA was 3.1/4.0 (a B average). Actively involved with the SADD chapter in his school, he helped arrange a safe Junior-Senior prom and campaigned for tougher laws against those convicted of DWI charges. He won Most Popular in the Senior Class poll. Other school activities included member of the Spanish Club, member of the scenery crew for Stunt Night, and member of the swim team. Interests outside school include canoeing, music, and attending antique car shows.

He worked as a Little League soccer coach for two years, as a babysitter for the McDouglas' seven-year-old twins, and as an Eagle Scout in charge of two day camps last fall for a group of Webelos. As an older scout, he has helped plan the Pinewood Derby races for the past three springs.

Yu-lan also worked in a few odd construction jobs with his uncle, including tearing off old shingles and reshingling a roof. Working as a carpenter's helper for Biggsley's Construction (going for supplies, holding wood in place, nailing, sawing, and assisting with porch construction), he learned quite a bit about construction just watching the master carpenters.

Possible references include Josh Biggsley, a carpenter for whom he worked; Sarah Brulet, family friend, and director of the Head Start program for preschoolers; Samuel Bekka, a next-door neighbor (whose lawn Yu-lan has mowed since he was 11) and president of the local Savings and Loan; Geoffrey Grangers, his drafting teacher; Carla Wolinski, his psychology teacher; and Dr. Michael Reddengerger, a town councillor with whom Yu-lan has interned.

2. Now write a letter of application for Yu-lan for one or both jobs. Consider adding some of the following information to the letter: Yu-lan likes children and would like to major in elementary education. He also enjoys the outdoors.

PURSUE AN IDEA

1. Pretend it's three to five years from now. You have just completed the degree you have always wanted with an impressive GPA. Make up a resume and a letter of application to help you get your dream job.

2. Write a resume for yourself for a part-time job available in your area. Use Manuel's resume as a model. Write a letter of application to accompany it.

3. Write a resume for yourself for a full-time job available in your area that you could apply for after graduation. Write a letter of application to accompany it.

4. Write a resume for an adult friend or a relative (any adult who has been in the work force for five years or more). Using the two questionnaires in the Prewriting section, take notes for the resume. Decide whether this adult needs a chronological resume or a functional resume. Ask the adult to supply you with a job objective and description of a job he or she would like to have. Write a letter of application to accompany the resume.

Parallelism

In writing, two sets of words are parallel because they repeat the same grammatical structure.

Your ability to recognize parallel structure depends on your ear and your knowledge of grammar. Words, phrases, and clauses joined by coordinating conjunctions and used in lists should be parallel.

Parallel Words, Phrases, and Clauses

Can you hear that these sets of words are *not* parallel?

1. I like running, biking, and to paint.
2. He told us to wash our dishes and that we must sweep the floor.
3. I like to paint portraits, play the piano, and to read science.

Here is the grammatical structure of these sentences to help you see where the break in parallel structure occurs:

    S V   Gerund   Gerund   Infinitive
1. I like running, biking, and to paint.

               Infinitive phrase   **Dependent clause**
2. He told us to wash our dishes and that we must sweep the floor.

    S V   to + verb/object   verb + object   to + verb / object
3. I like to paint portraits, play the piano, and to read science.

In sentence 1, the infinitive breaks the parallelism because the list has been started with "ing" words, gerunds. In sentence 2, the dependent clause breaks the parallelism because the list has been started with an infinitive phrase. In sentence 3, the "to" wasn't repeated in every part of the list, so the parallelism was broken.

Here are improved versions of the above sentences:

1. I like running, biking, and painting. *OR* I like to run, bike, and paint.
2. He told us to wash our dishes and to sweep the floor. He told us to wash our dishes and sweep the floor. He told us that we must wash our dishes and sweep the floor.
3. I like to paint portraits, to play the piano, and to read science. I like to paint portraits, play the piano, and read science.

Parallel Lists

The itemized list below is not parallel. Which parts of the list are more alike than other parts?

At the next Spanish Club meeting, we will discuss these items:

- next year's budget
- which person to nominate for chair
- implementing our attendance policy
- whether to donate money to the senior class project
- elections

The first list is not parallel because some items are nouns preceded by adjectives, two are listed as questions, one starts with an "ing" word, and one is a simple noun. To make the list parallel, start each part of the list the same way. Use all "ing" beginnings, all questions, all nouns, or all nouns preceded by adjectives.

You can make the list parallel by making every part the same. The following list makes the entire list parallel to the first item by repeating the adjective(s) + noun structure:

- next year's budget
- chair nominations
- attendance policy
- senior class project donations
- upcoming elections

Parallel Order

Using the same order of information also makes parts of a resume parallel. For example, if you present the work experience of Job #1 in this order, NAME (of business), CITY/STATE (of business), DATES (of work), and JOB TITLE, then you must present the work experience of Job #2 in the same order. Don't put DATES first, NAME second, ADDRESS third, and so forth.

INSIDE TRACK: APPLY WHAT YOU HAVE LEARNED

1. Make the unparallel example list above (At the next Spanish Club meeting, we will discuss these items) parallel in other ways. Make the whole list parallel to the second item, "Which person to nominate for chair." Then make the list parallel to the third item, "Implementing our attendance policy." Which do you prefer?

2. Make a list of your morning routine. Set up your list with this statement and a colon. Every morning, I follow the same routine:

3. Make the items in this list parallel:

Activities
- Chairperson of Booster Club
- Delivered Meals on Wheels to shut-ins
- United Way: accepted pledges
- Recorder for Debating Team

4. Correct these sentences for faulty parallelism.
   a. The letter directed us to preview the contracts, sign them, and to return them promptly.
   b. The rules were fair but that they could not be enforced.
   c. Paula and Jenna were told to be home at 2:00 and that they had to refill the car with gas.
   d. She had trouble explaining her position and which decision to make.
   e. Johnny can't read, Johnny can't write, and math performance is poor.
   f. The new product line is noted for its durability, its attractiveness, and it is reliable.

5. Make these two job descriptions parallel in structure.

   Baylor Industries, Glenville, Virginia. June 19-- to April 19--. Sales Representative: called on customers and kept accounts.

   Sales Director. January 19-- to August 19--. United Sales Corporation, Oakdale, Virginia. Duties included supervising sales personnel, training new personnel, and calling on customers.

Oral Presentations

Write-to-Learn

Recall several speakers whose performance you have particularly enjoyed. For instance, you may have an instructor who holds your attention from the moment you sit down until the bell signals the end of class. Perhaps you really appreciated a speaker you heard at a club meeting or special event, such as a July Fourth celebration. Once you have clear images of these speakers in your mind, consider what makes them effective communicators. Make a list in your journal of qualities and actions that you think help these speakers effectively reach their audiences. Your list, for example, might include

a good joke to open

language I can understand

walking through the audience

DEFINITIONS

adrenaline a stimulant, something that excites and creates extra energy

auditory relating to the sense of hearing or perceived through the sense of hearing

feedback verbal and nonverbal response to a communication process or product

rhetorical question a question designed to provoke thought, a question for which the speaker expects no answer

stage fright anxiety or fear experienced when a person speaks to or performs for an audience

After completing this chapter, you will be able to

- Analyze an audience and determine how best to meet its needs
- Plan and organize a message appropriate for the audience, the situation, and your goals
- Prepare notecards suitable for making an oral presentation
- Use visuals effectively in an oral report
- Deliver a message with confidence

> *What is written without effort is in general read without pleasure.*
>
> SAMUEL JOHNSON

Your Write-to-Learn list suggests that you already know a great deal about what it takes to be a good public speaker. In this chapter, we will review some of the things you know and perhaps add some new ideas.

Many opportunities in business, industry, and your school exist for you to speak before a group of people. Sometimes your career success will depend upon your public speaking ability. You may have the best new product idea your company will ever see. For your idea to become a reality, however, you must effectively communicate it to the management team and convince them to try the product. Successful employees share their knowledge and talents with others.

Planning

WARM UP 6.1

Think about your public speaking experiences, perhaps giving a report in class or leading a club meeting. If you haven't had many speaking opportunities, imagine what the experience would be like. Make a list that you can share with your class of the things you like and dislike about public speaking.

The planning stage, akin to prewriting for written documents, occurs mostly in your mind. Regardless of whether you plan for a consistent period of time or at random over a period of time, this is the important part of the process —when you begin to work on audience analysis, topic, and **stage fright**.

Audience

Analyzing your audience is as important in an oral report as it is in a written report. Start by referring to your audience analysis questions on page 25 of Chapter 2, Audience.

Of particular importance to you as a public speaker is how you believe your audience already feels about your topic. If you think your audience will like your ideas, you can use a direct approach for your presentation, starting with the main idea. On the other hand, if you believe you will speak to an audience opposed to your ideas, you would not want to start with the most important or main idea. Why?

If you start with an idea with which your audience disagrees, you run the risk of causing listeners to tune you out immediately after hearing your first statements. Thus, you need to know as much as possible about your audience before you make decisions about what to say and how to say it.

Topic and Message

Sometimes speakers are able to choose their own topics. However, when asked to speak at work (and in school), you will often be assigned a topic. Frequently in the work world, managers ask employees to prepare a written document, such as a report on progress, on a solution to a problem, or on an incident. After submitting the written report, the employee may be asked to make an oral presentation of the same information. For instance, Edith Rivers, a machinist at Tarboro Machine Corporation, wrote a report that suggested three new safety measures for all machine operators. The report was submitted to the plant safety officer, the president and vice-president, and all division heads. Rivers' supervisor then asked her to orally present her plan at the next managers' meeting. The supervisor told Rivers that since Rivers was more knowledgeable on the topic than anyone else, she should present the ideas and answer questions about them.

One way to plan an oral presentation is to list all the things you want to say to this audience. You might list words and phrases for every idea you have.

Remember that prewriting is a creative process. Therefore, leave your judgments, your critical side, someplace else for now. Don't cut out any idea as being too impractical or inapplicable. List all your ideas. Later, you can be critical and cut ideas.

Stage Fright

You may think it odd that a textbook tells you to *plan for stage fright* when most people want to avoid it. Yet, stage fright is not something to eliminate; it is an energy to put to use. Many professional speakers will tell you that you can't get rid of nervous reactions when speaking even if you want to. Those reactions, they say, are natural responses to stress. So, instead of trying to suppress stage fright, get it to work for you. To harness this energy, you should

- note the ways your body responds to anxiety
- expect and plan for these reactions to occur
- use excess **adrenaline** and energy to give your introduction and important points extra emphasis.

Dr. Ralph C. Worthington, a professional consultant and noted speaker, likes to greet members of his audience at the room entrance. By meeting individuals before his presentation Dr. Worthington says he feels as if he is talking to them one-on-one during his presentation.

1. Would an audience of your classmates be more interested in how school policy affects taxpayers or students?
2. Should you try to suppress feelings of anxiety when you speak?

Organizing and Composing

WARM UP 6.2

Thinking of messages you've prepared for oral delivery, as in planning to ask someone for a date or a favor, compare oral composing with written composing. Note differences and similarities in a brief journal entry.

Since listeners can't look back when ideas are unclear or confusing, speakers should organize and compose for the listeners' situation and needs.

Using Direct/Indirect Approach

For most presentations, you will probably use the direct approach. With the direct approach, you state the main idea first and then explain and support that idea with details. Stating the main idea first lets your listeners know how you will proceed. They then know what subject you will pursue and what point you will make. Given that main idea, the audience is ready to follow your presentation. For more information on using the direct approach, see The Inside Track following Chapter 3.

If, on the other hand, you realize your audience opposes the point you support, or if you want to be especially persuasive, you should consider an indirect presentation. With indirect strategy, you can build piece of evidence upon piece of evidence, convincing the audience of your point.

Previewing Organization

Regardless of the organizational strategy, make sure your audience knows what organizational plan you are following by giving them a preview. The preview is like a map that shows a driver where to turn and how far to go. Your preview explains the order of your ideas. A typical preview statement is "This recommendation contains four major parts: review, staffing, operational policy, and production," or "The Standard Operating Procedure for student interns involves completing treatment plans, writing instruction memos, and recording patient progress."

Composing the Introduction

Listeners recall the first and last things they hear. Therefore, be sure you plan for a strong introduction and conclusion. If uncertain how to introduce your presentation, think like your audience. What would get your attention? You would want to know

the topic,

the point the speaker intends to support, and

how this issue affects you, the listener.

Thus, your introduction will usually announce your topic and the points you wish to make. In addition, the speaker should try to give the listener something with which he or she can relate, some connection.

If you have trouble getting started, try one of several formula introductions. They are called formula introductions because they are like math formulas, a pattern into which you plug your information. Some formula openings include use of

a direct quotation (usually from a well-known source)

a **rhetorical question**

a startling fact or statistic (that would grab a listener's attention)

a statement you then disprove

an anecdote or humorous story

For example, if you were making a class presentation on the advantages of modern medicine, you might begin this way:

> If you were born in the United States in 1978, at the time of your birth you had a life expectancy of 73.5 years. On the other hand, people born in 1950 were expected to live only 68.2 years. According to these statistics, you will outlive your mother and father by 5.3 years (Famighetti 972).

The startling fact that the audience's generation is expected to live 5.3 years longer than their parents' should grab the listeners' attention, especially since these statistics relate to the audience's own mortality.

Composing the Body

Usually oral presentations are not prepared in writing. These guidelines will help you with composing the body of an oral presentation:

1. **Address people.** Remember that your audience is made up of people much like you. Include the words *you* and *your* early and often.

2. **Use words your audience will know.** Define terms they do not know.

3. **Use simpler sentences than when writing.** A speaker should not have to say so many words that he or she cannot catch his or her breath.

4. Give your audience the information they want or need. Main ideas and examples or details used for support should be relevant. Explain to listeners how your information impacts upon them; make it relevant. Remember, it is as easy to ramble in speaking as it is in freewriting, so avoid that pitfall.

5. Emphasize main points and make transitions from one point to the next. Since listeners actually take in only a small percentage of what they hear, emphasize the essential ideas. Repeat or restate main points. Also announce transitions so the audience will not miss the connection: it is as if you are saying to the listener, "Now we are leaving the discussion of Point A to move on to Point B. Follow me."

6. Consider questions your audience is likely to ask and try to include answers in your presentation.

Composing the Conclusion

Conclusions, important because they are the last thing the audience will hear, require as much planning as introductions. While the formulas for introductions can be used for conclusions, an effective conclusion needs to hold the audience's attention and then do something more. **1)** It should summarize the key points of the presentation. **2)** It should call for action, if action is being requested.

Preparing

Having completed the thinking process, with your presentation generally clear in your mind, you need to do some things that will help you deliver your presentation. You need to prepare notecards, visual aids, and your image.

Notecards

A practiced performance using notecards yields an informal, conversational style. With this type of preparation, you consider what you want to say, and you say it in an interesting way.

Before you get to this point in the process, you must organize your ideas in the most effective manner. If you were writing a report, your next step would be to compose sentences, build paragraphs, and create a document. For an oral presentation, however, you should avoid extended writing.

Start with 3" × 5" notecards. Since you will write only a few words on each card, this size works very well. However, some people who like notes in extra-large letters use 5" × 8" cards.

On the first notecard, write a word or a phrase that will trigger your memory for your opening point. Then go on to each idea, example, and illustration in your speech.

For each idea, prepare a note-card similar to the one in Figure 6.1. This sample card reminds the speaker that this section of the talk is about tsunamis, the giant, destructive waves that sometimes strike Hawaii and Japan.

When preparing notecards, remember two important points:

1. a notecard should contain only one idea, and

2. a notecard should *not* be written in complete sentences or long phrases or clauses. Even experienced speakers would be tempted to read it if the card contained clauses or sentences.

Figure 6.1 Notecard for Oral Presentation

Notecards should spark your memory. Looking at the word(s) on a card, you should be able to look up at your audience and deliver a portion of your speech. Thus, you can truly converse (in a polished way) with your audience.

Number your cards from beginning to end. Put the card number in the upper right corner and circle it, as in the illustration above. If you drop your cards or get them mixed up, having them numbered will help you reorganize them quickly. Also, be certain that your name is on the back of each card.

Visual Aids

According to recent studies, an audience takes in less than 25% of what a speaker says. Therefore, a speaker should try to increase an audience's comprehension in any way possible. (Alessandra 20–21). One way to help your audience is by using visual aids. Visuals let audiences see as well as hear the message. Thus, the audience has two opportunities to take in your ideas.

Guidelines for Choosing What to Illustrate. When you think of adding visuals, how do you know what to illustrate? You can ask these questions:

● What information is most important?

● What data is the most complex or difficult to understand?

● Am I giving any statistics or figures that are particularly important for my audience to comprehend?

Once you've answered these questions, you will have ideas for illustrations.

Visual aids can include photographs, line drawings, charts, tables, objects, or even people. For instance, a presenter discussing environmental hazards might use a flip chart to diagram the amounts of certain chemicals found in groundwater. One presenter, a student speaking to her class about erroneous ideas associated with cerebral palsy, brought in her brother, a police detective with cerebral palsy, as a visual aid.

Guidelines for Creating Visuals. When you develop visuals, keep your audience's needs in mind. These guidelines may help you:

1. Make the visual large enough for everyone—even those sitting in the back of the room—to see easily.

2. Don't crowd numbers or images on a poster board, chalkboard or projection screen.

3. Remember that, although attractive design counts, message is more important. Bright colors can't replace solid ideas.

4. Consider handouts your audience can keep if you want your audience to think about your ideas later.

Personal Appearance

In addition to notecards and visual aids, image has a tremendous impact on the way listeners receive that speaker's message. You probably know how appearance can affect communication in everyday situations, such as the way some salespeople treat you when you are in your worn jeans and an old T-shirt. If you haven't experienced this treatment yourself, you likely have seen others treated differently because of clothes or grooming.

When selecting clothing for a presentation consider **1)** the audience and its expectations, and **2)** the situation in which you will be speaking.

For instance, someone addressing your city council would probably dress as formally (business suit) as its members typically do. On the other hand, if addressing children at the youth center, the speaker might dress more casually.

Whatever you wear, make sure the outfit is one that feels comfortable to you. If you feel good about the way you look, you will speak with confidence.

If you have done *everything* you can to prepare for success, you are ready to move to the rehearsal phase of the process.

STOP AND THINK

1. Could a machine part be a visual aid? Explain.
2. Would running shorts ever be appropriate dress for a presentation? Explain.

Rehearsing

WARM UP

In other skills you've developed—sports, music, art—how much practice is enough? What does this tell you, if anything, about oral presentations? Respond to these questions in a brief journal entry.

Veteran presenters will tell you that practicing is a critical step in giving a successful presentation. Practicing helps you develop a conversational style. In fact, good speeches are a conversation between speaker and audience, only slightly more polished than the conversations we have with friends.

Using your notecards and visual aids, practice your speech. When you first deliver the talk, you will note parts you like and don't like. Delivering the speech the second time, you may change what you don't like. When you are comfortable with your delivery, you have rehearsed enough. You have reached that conversational style.

Speakers practice in different ways. With experience, you will decide which methods of rehearsing work for you. Here are some suggestions:

1. **Use a tape recorder.** After recording your presentation, take a break. After you have "cooled down" or gained some distance and perspective on the speech, listen to the tape for

> rate (how fast you talked),
>
> volume (how loud or how soft),
>
> pronunciation (the distinctness of your words),
>
> inflections (the changes in pitch or tone), and
>
> time (the amount of time you took to present your ideas).

The first automobile was steam-powered, had three wheels, and motored down the road at a blistering three miles per hour.

2. **Use a mirror.** Put yourself in the role of the audience. What do you *see* that will enhance or detract from the message? Check for

   a. appropriate facial expressions.

   b. effective use of your body and hands. Are your hand movements emphasizing major points, or are you distracting your listener from the topic? Don't lean over the speaker's stand or walk around too much.

3. **Use a video camera.** Again, do not review the tape immediately. Wait until you have greater perspective, perhaps in an hour or after a day or two. When you do play back the tape, pretend to be your audience. Look for strengths as well as weaknesses. With this **auditory** and visual **feedback,** check

   a. how you sound,

   b. how you look, and

   c. what message you deliver.

4. **Use a live, stand-in audience.** Ask a friend or family member to listen to you practice your presentation. After delivering the speech, invite comments and suggestions. You might try some of these questions:

   What was the topic of my speech?

   What point did I try to prove?

   Did I make eye contact?

   Did I talk loudly enough?

   Did I tend to use "and uh," "um," or "like"?

   Was my conclusion effective?

   Did I pronounce words correctly?

STOP AND THINK 6.4

While a tape recorder gives useful feedback during rehearsal, what won't it tell you? In small groups, discuss your answers.

Presenting

WARM UP 6.5

Discuss this question with your classmates: Is it possible for oral presenting to be fun?

Having invested a great deal of thought and preparation, you can present with confidence. The next consideration, before delivering your message to your audience, is preparing the environment in which you will make your presentation.

Checking the Room

Arrive early for your presentation if possible. During that time, make sure listeners will be comfortable and can see and hear well. Consider the following:

seating   lighting

temperature   equipment and visual aids

Seating. Check the placement of chairs. Are they arranged to let you communicate effectively? For instance, if you want group discussion, the chairs should be placed so that people can see each other. Also be sure all persons in the room will be able to see you easily.

Lighting. Be certain your audience will have enough light to see. In addition, correct any glaring and overly bright spots. With an appropriately lighted room, your audience can comfortably see and concentrate on your message.

Temperature. Check the temperature controls. People who are shivering from cold or sweltering from heat will not be the best listeners.

Equipment and Visual Aids. Make sure all equipment is in working order and prepare for possible problems. Remember Murphy's Law: If something can go wrong, it will! Make sure that you have an extra bulb for the projector, markers, chalk, and anything else you might need.

Consider visibility and access in placing visual aids. Visuals need to be located

- where everyone in the room can easily see them
- where you can point to the visual as you talk
- where you can get to equipment, such as overhead projectors, to make adjustments and
- where the equipment will have a power supply.

Also determine how you will hang, post, or display your materials before the event.

Delivering the Message

Having prepared for the presentation, you are ready to enjoy talking with your audience. The pointers listed below are to help you be as effective a speaker as possible.

1. **Use appropriate facial expressions.** For example, if you are talking about the positive outlook for jobs, an occasional smile is suitable.

2. **Maintain eye contact.** By acknowledging your listener with eye contact, you show your interest and concern for that person.

3. **Use visuals effectively**. These suggestions will guide your use of graphics:

   a. Explain every visual. Since each person may see or understand something differently, tell people exactly what you want them to learn from the image.

   b. Post or distribute handouts only when you want them used or read. Otherwise, the audience may be flipping noisily through pages and reading what captures their attention rather than listening to you. If you don't want to leave the speaker's stand or take time to distribute your handouts at the appropriate time, ask someone to distribute materials for you.

4. **Consult your notes, but don't read from them.** Consult your notes only enough to follow your outline and to cue yourself to key details for your presentation. If you read directly from your notecards, you will break eye contact with your audience and lose their interest and attention.

5. **Continue with your talk even if something goes wrong.** Recover as best you can, but "go on with the show." Don't call the listeners' attention to a mistake you've made.

6. **Remember that your audience wants you to succeed.**

7. **Always give your audience an opportunity to ask questions, unless the program does not allow time for questions.** If you cannot answer a question, respond in a positive way: "I'm sorry that I don't have the answer to your question, but I will be happy to check my sources and get back to you later this week."

STOP AND THINK 6.5

1. Should you display your poster before you begin to speak?
2. Is eye contact with your audience desirable?

Travis Woods' project manager has sent him a memo asking for a meeting with Travis and Martha Anne Bright, his co-worker, at 9 a.m. tomorrow. The project manager wants an update on the work for Phase One, drafting construction plans for a retirement community. Travis is on schedule with his part of the drafting. However, he is aware that Martha Anne is at least two days behind schedule. How should Travis reply?

SUMMARY

1. Opportunities to speak to groups abound in schools and in the workplace. Your ability to effectively present your ideas orally to others is likely to affect your degree of success in both areas. Although many people dread speaking in public situations, you can do a great deal toward reducing your anxiety and improving your self-confidence.

2. Planning is the part of the process that occurs mostly in the mind. You should plan for your audience, the topic and content of your presentation, and stage fright.

3. Use audience analysis to decide how to organize, and preview the organizational plan to help the listeners follow you. Compose a strong introduction and conclusion, and create a body that is relevant and meets the audience's needs and expectations.

4. Preparing, a more active step in the process, involves creating notecards and visual aids as well as analyzing and making adjustments in your image.

5. After planning and preparing, rehearse to polish your presentation. Try a variety of rehearsal methods, such as using a tape recorder, a mirror, a video camera, and a stand-in audience to get different types of feedback.

6. *Enjoy* presenting after you've planned, prepared, and rehearsed. First, check the seating, lighting, temperature, equipment, and visuals to make the best possible listening environment. Some guidelines you should keep in mind as you speak are to **1)** use appropriate facial expressions, **2)** maintain eye contact, **3)** use visuals effectively, **4)** consult your notes but don't read from them, **5)** continue with your speech if something goes wrong, **6)** remember that your listeners want you to succeed, and **7)** always ask for questions from listeners.

APPLY WHAT YOU HAVE LEARNED

1. Review an oral report you gave recently—in school or elsewhere, formal or informal. Write in list or paragraph form some of the changes you would make now to improve your effectiveness if you were able to give the presentation again.

2. Attend the presentation of a speaker at school, in the community, or at work. If a live presentation is not possible, watch a videotape or live video of a speaker, perhaps a politician, an editorial commentator, or a promoter from an info-mercial. As you watch and listen to the speaker make two lists: one for positive elements, things that make the speech work; a second for negative elements or things that detract from the effectiveness of the presentation.

CONSIDER THIS CASE

1. You have been asked to speak to your nephew's fifth-grade Social Studies class on Mexico since you worked there last summer as a volunteer for Habitat for Humanity. The Social Studies class lasts 50 minutes. If the teacher does not give you a time limit, how long should you plan to talk?

2. Mrs. Nicci, a counselor, has asked you to explain to a group of 35 first-year students how to complete their registration cards. The entire process involves using decisions the students have made previously and entering data on a pre-printed form. Choose a room in your school with which you are familiar and imagine this as the location. What would be the most effective way to arrange chairs for this presentation? Consider the visuals you might use. Take into consideration how much, if at all, you want the students consulting with each other. Another factor could be the size of the room and location of permanent features, such as built-in cabinets.

PURSUE AN IDEA

1. Choose any written report you have already completed or find a model in the textbook. Write an essay about decisions you would have to make and changes that would be needed to present in an oral report the information found in the written document.

2. Research the career you are currently considering. Look for information on employers, salaries, working conditions, educational requirements, and hiring rates. You could go to the library, talk with a counselor, visit someone working in the field, or see an instructor in that curriculum area. When you have as much data as you need, think of making an oral presentation to classmates who might be interested in the same career.

a. Write a brief analysis of your audience. Refer to Chapter 2, Audience.

b. Decide on the focus or main idea for your presentation. Write this focus in one sentence.

c. List at least two ideas for information that could be enhanced with the use of a visual aid.

d. Create at least one of the visual aids listed in **c.**

e. Prepare the notecards you would use for this presentation.

3. Plan a speech that you could deliver to your own graduating class.

WORKS CITED

Alessandra, Anthony J. "How Do You Rate as a Listener?" *Data Management* (25) Feb. 1987. 20–21.

Famighetti, Robert, et al., eds. "Years of Life Expected at Birth." *The World Almanac and Book of Facts 1994*. New York: Funk & Wagnalls, 1993. 972.

CHAPTER

7

News Releases

Write-to-Learn

Recall a news item relating to business or industry you've seen or read in the last week from television, radio, or print media. With that piece of news in mind, write answers to the following questions in your journal: What parts of the story do you remember? What made the story memorable? What elements of the story do you think were provided by the business or industry and what elements were probably a result of reporters' investigation?

DEFINITIONS

embargo to prohibit or to request that a story not be published

exaggerations overstatements or additions beyond the truth

hook in a news story, an opening element whose purpose is to engage the reader, grab attention, and lead into the subject

media a system or means of mass communication, such as radio, television, newspapers, and magazines

PSA public service announcement, news published for the benefit of the public or public agencies

public relations plans or actions taken by an individual or an organization to create a favorable relationship with the public; the staff responsible for creating an advantageous relationship with the public

tag line feature of a press release or a news story that identifies the location of a story

NEWS RELEASE

Atlanta Committee for the Olympic Games
250 Williams Street, Suite 6000
P.O. Box 1996
Atlanta, GA 30301-1996 USA
Telephone 404 555-1996
Facsimile 404 555-1997

Contact: Laurie Olsen
404 555-1235

400 CHILDREN PAINT OLYMPIC STADIUM FENCE OCTOBER 13 & 14

ATLANTA (October 11, 1993) - - Children from nine schools in neighborhoods surrounding the Olympic Stadium construction site are joining forces this week to add a little local color to the site's construction fence.

More that 400 children, grades 1 through 12, will express their artistic talents along the fence lining Capitol Avenue and Little Street. Approximately 4,500 square feet—nearly half of the four-block barricade—will be painted Wednesday, October 13, and Thursday, October 14, between 9:00 a.m. and 3:00 p.m.

Themed to complement The Atlanta Committee for the Olympics Games' (ACOG's) 1993 in-school curriculum program, entitled "The Olympic Spirit: A Worldwide Connection," children from each participating school have been assigned particular counties to represent in their painting. Educators have been working with children in the classroom to help them formulate ideas for the mural in advance of the two-day paintfest.

"This is an excellent way for children to learn the value of teamwork and participation, important elements of the Olympic Movement," said Ann W. Kimbrough, ACOG's director of community relations, who has been spearheading the fence-painting activity. "They are also demonstrating what they have learned about countries in the Olympic Family while creating a visual panorama that expresses who they are and enhances their neighborhood."

Sponsors of the 1996 Olympic Games will work with the children on site to help guide their activity. Employees of worldwide sponsors The Coca-Cola Company, Eastman Kodak Company, VISA, Bausch & Lomb, *Sports Illustrated,* XEROX, and Panasonic; employees of Centennial Olympic Games Partners NationsBank, Champion Products, The Home Depot, IBM; and Sea World and sponsor John Hancock Mutual Life Insurance Company employees are participating.

Thirty-five gallons of paint, 600 paint brushes, 1000 paint stirrers, and 1200 mini paint buckets are being employed in the creation of the montage. ACOG plans to repeat the painting activity as stadium construction continues until the entire perimeter of the site presents a kid's-eye view of the 1996 Olympic Games.

#

After completing this chapter, you will be able to

- Analyze the two audiences of news releases

- Plan a news release for print media, television, or radio

- Properly format a news release

- Organize and compose an effective news release

News releases, also called press releases, are reports of events or facts prepared to send to the **media.** The goal of the release is to be published and thus to inform the public. Some of these news releases are just that—news stories, such as the promotion of an employee or the expansion of a company. However, some press releases are also known as public service announcements or PSA's. As the name suggests, **PSA**'s differ from other news releases in that they present facts considered beneficial to the public. PSA's, for example, announce Red Cross blood drives, city council meetings, fundraisers, and other public events.

News is uncovered by reporters, as Carl Bernstein and Bob Woodward of the *Washington Post* did in uncovering the break-in at Democratic Party national headquarters on 17 June 1972, now known as the Watergate scandal. News releases are sent to the media by people and organizations anxious to share information with the public.

THE PROFESSIONAL SPEAKS

Susan Nobles, a public relations director for a nonprofit organization, suggests that writers get to know the news agency staff. If the news director or the editor recognizes the contact person's name and trusts that person, then he or she is more likely to consider the release for publication. Developing a strong professional relationship, according to Ms. Nobles, gives writers an edge, perhaps the edge that is needed to compete with all the other releases that land on the news desk.

Who writes news releases? In large organizations, **public relations** departments, responsible for communication between the company and the outside world, try to keep the company name and a positive image before the public. Sometimes this job includes damage control as well. For instance, if a company executive is involved in a scandal, the public relations staff may prepare a news release to present the company's view of the situation and to restore public confidence.

In smaller organizations without public relations departments, virtually any employee may need to write a news release. The maintenance director may write a release describing the company's recycling efforts, a retail sales manager might cover the store's planned expansion, and a volunteer group's secretary may outline the organization's upcoming fundraising project.

Audience: Who Reads News Releases?

W A R M   U P   7.1

Read the model news release at the beginning of this chapter. Without looking back, answer the following questions:

What is the topic of the release?

What organization created and distributed the release?

What elements of the story captured your attention?

What part of the story is most interesting or memorable to you?

Two types of readers see news releases. Editors and news directors review them first. Then, if the editors and news directors decide to run them, the public will see or hear the news. It will appear in its final form in a newspaper or magazine, on a television or radio broadcast, or even on a computer bulletin board.

> *The secret of all good writing is sound judgment.*
>
> HORACE

Editors and News Directors

Since the writer sends the news release to select news agencies, the first readers are editors and news directors who look at the release with a critical eye. They decide if the news release will be run. If the information is newsworthy and the release is well-written, so that little editing is required, the likelihood of its being run increases. Other factors that may influence this decision include space and time constraints.

The Public

If the release is run, the second audience is the public. Sometimes this second audience is anyone who reads a newspaper or magazine, watches television, or listens to the radio—the general public. The second audience could also be a select group of people. Specialized media agencies receive news releases that target a particular audience. For instance, you are probably familiar with television stations that aim for a select group of people: MTV targets teen music lovers; TNN attracts country music fans; CNN focuses on persons interested in world, economic, and financial news; and the Disney Channel targets children. In any case, audiences of the various media are all looking for the same thing—information that is timely and interesting.

Since you rely on the media and since you might be in a situation one day when you need to write a news release, the techniques for this kind of composition are worth learning.

> **STOP AND THINK 7.1**
>
> 1. Before a news release is published, what reader(s) must approve it?
> 2. Should a news release be written for a general or a specific audience?

Prewriting: Getting Started on News Releases

When you decide to write a news release or are assigned by an employer to write one, where do you start? Technical writers should always start by analyzing their audience. For a news release, you will need to consider both types of audiences: the editor or news director as well as the public.

Reporter's Questions

The next logical step is to ask the classic five "Reporter's Questions:"

Who?	What?	Why?
Where?	When?	

Answering these questions will provide you with the most important information to include in your news release.

Beyond the Reporter's Questions, ask yourself

● What will interest my audience?

● What will grab their attention?

● What would they ask about if they could?

Record your ideas for inclusion in your rough draft.

Accuracy

Writers of news releases should strive for accuracy. Writers should check their prewriting notes for accuracy in

- facts
- names
- quotations
- numbers and statistics
- locations
- completeness ("the whole truth")

If you plan for correctness in your text, then your releases will have a much greater chance of being published.

Credibility

Similar to inaccuracies, exaggerations can ruin a news release and destroy a writer's credibility. **Exaggerations** are overstatements or additions above the truth. One way to escape exaggeration is to work with information that can be verified. Another way to avoid exaggeration is to avoid superlatives, such as *the best, the fastest, the first,* and *the worst,* unless you can document or provide proof for the statement.

For instance, if you write a release that opens with "RJ Birch, the fastest 10K runner in the state," are you being honest or are you exaggerating? If you can prove that RJ Birch is the fastest runner, if you have recorded race times, then the release is truthful. If, on the other hand, your statement that RJ Birch is the fastest is based only on your opinion, then you may be exaggerating.

Formatting News Releases

W A R M   U P

Imagine that you are editor of your school newspaper and that you have just received an anonymous story suggesting that one of your classmates is running a successful catering business from home. Although you might like to print the story, you realize that you need more information than that provided by the story. What questions would you like to have answered?

News releases are formatted so that information the reader needs stands out and is easy to see, editors can write and make changes easily on the page, and typesetters and news anchors (who might read the text on the air) can easily follow the document. For our purposes, let's divide the formatting into three units: top of the page or introductory information, the body or story, and pagination cues. As you read about how to format a news release properly, refer to Figure 7.1.

Figure 7.1 News Release Format

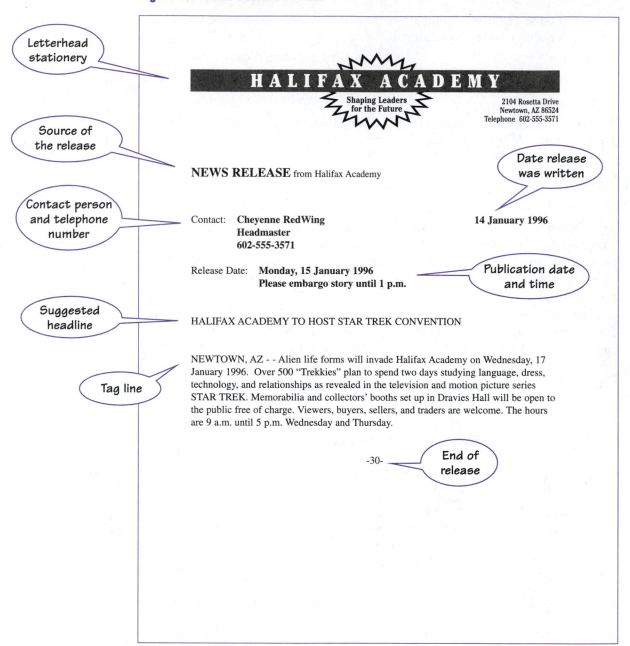

Letterhead stationery

Source of the release

Contact person and telephone number

Date release was written

Publication date and time

Suggested headline

Tag line

End of release

Introductory Information

Many large companies create special letterhead stationery just for news releases. This stationery is printed with such information as the company name, address, telephone number, logo, and the words *NEWS RELEASE*. Writers using this letterhead simply fill in the blanks or add the needed information.

Writers for organizations that don't have special letterhead use plain 8½" × 11" paper. These writers then decide how to organize and present the features at the top of the news release. While the information given is standard, writers have some flexibility in presentation. When you plan your own news release, you may create your unique presentation. The format in Figure 7.1 is typical.

Standard information at the top of news releases answers questions that routinely would be asked. Also, as with memos, formatting makes that essential information very easy to access. Follow these guidelines for top of the page or introductory format:

1. Begin with the words *NEWS RELEASE*, usually in all capital letters. Along with *NEWS RELEASE*, name the source of the document, the name of the agency or organization, in initial caps only.

2. Give the name of a contact person: Type the word *Contact* and a colon. Two spaces after the colon, enter the name of the person who is responsible for the news release or who can answer questions about it. Under the name, enter the job title of the contact person and the phone number where that person can be reached.

3. Record the date the document was written in the upper right corner across from the name of the contact person.

4. Place the words *Release Date* and a colon at the left margin beneath the contact information. Two spaces after the colon, type the date—and the specific time, if necessary—the information in the news release should be made public. Since news should be timely, most releases are slated for immediate publication.

5. As in the model, writers occasionally request a release to be held for a specified period of time before publication. If you want a story to be held, type beneath or beside the release date *Please hold until [desired release time]* or *Please embargo story until [desired release time]*. **Embargo** means to withhold or delay publication.

6. Give the news agency a suggested headline in all capital letters.

Body

These guidelines will help you format releases that are attractive and easy for news agencies to use:

1. Preface the body of your release with a **tag line** that identifies the location of the story. Type the tag line in all capital letters, such as SAN FRANCISCO, CA. In Figure 7.1, NEWTOWN, AZ is where the story is taking place. After the location, **1)** leave a space, **2)** type a hyphen, **3)** leave another space, **4)** type a second hyphen, and then **5)** leave a final space. The body of the release immediately follows this final space.

2. Double-space the body of the press release. Some news directors suggest using double-spaced lines for print media and triple-spaced lines for radio and television.

Pagination Cues

News release writers use a special code to aid readers in following the text and in reading from one page to another. These cues are explained in the formatting suggestions below:

1. Type the word *–more–* centered at the bottom of the page when the release will be continued on the next page.
2. End news releases with *–30–* or *###* after the last line of the body.

STOP AND THINK 7.2

1. What should a contact person be able to do?
2. If a story is embargoed, what happens to it?

Organizing and Composing News Releases

WARM UP 7.3

Pretend that you are the owner of Zone Music Company, a business that has just developed a new compact disc that sounds more true-to-life than anything ever yet produced. What would you want your public relations staff to say in the news release announcing the new product?

Next, imagine that you are the news director of WABC radio station who will receive the press release from Zone Music Company. What information would you most want to find in the release?

American television shows began to broadcast in color in 1954.

As you are composing, be aware that your news release will be competing with others for space or airtime. Since the headline will be the element of your report to be read first, compose it carefully. Include an active verb. The verb will be present tense for current events, past tense for events already concluded, and future tense for scheduled activities. The suggested headline in Figure 7.1, HALIFAX ACADEMY TO HOST STAR TREK CONVENTION, uses an active verb that indicates future time, *to host*, since the event has not yet occurred.

Like the headline, the body of the news release must earn a positive response from an editor or news director as well as from the public. To achieve this goal, the release must do several things: open with a hook, answer the five Reporter's Questions immediately, and be organized with the important ideas placed first.

Beginning the Story

Begin your news release with **1)** a hook, to catch the audience's interest and **2)** answers to the five Reporter's Questions, so the audience immediately gets the essential information.

Provide a Hook. Open your press release with a hook—catchy wording or an idea that attracts attention or entices the audience. Dynamic wording or an intriguing idea is meant to seize the audience's attention and encourage further reading, viewing, or listening. Listed below are several examples of hooks used to open news releases:

- *The nets are still hanging in Memorial Coliseum after last night's City League upset, but only because the Westinghouse-sponsored Knights expect to return for them during the playoffs.*

- *When 600 first-year students show up for orientation at Spilman College on Saturday, they'll get something besides their dorm assignments.*

- *The Marion Michaux Farm owns some birds that will never fly the coop.*

- *The Easter Bunny Brought What?!*

All of these opening sentences use words and ideas designed to gain the reader's or listener's attention. If they are effective, the audience will want to know more.

Answer the Five Reporter's Questions. Answer Who? What? Where? When? Why? immediately. In fact, an effective news release will include the answers to all five questions in the first paragraph. Some will even include all this information in the first sentence. For an illustration of this idea-packed opening, see Figure 7.2.

Figure 7.2 Reporter's Questions In News Release Opening

Who?

Lakeside High's 6'7" senior Rasheed Watson ended a year

of suspense for recruiters from a number of big-name schools

When?   **What?**

Tuesday, March 15, 1996, when he signed a letter of intent

Why?

with his father's alma mater, Notre Dame, here in his

Where?

family's Watauga home.

In March of 1994, the public relations group for a financial planning business owned by three brothers was faced with a great challenge. The youngest brother, Martin Castleberry, was arrested for embezzling from the company. He had been transferring funds from company accounts to his private account for three years and had used the embezzled funds to feed his gambling habit. Should the company have issued a press release? What and how much should have been told? If you worked for this company, what would you have done?

Organize Information

Order ideas from most important information first to least important last. When you place the important ideas first, you achieve several purposes:

- You make editors' work easier and the story's publication more likely.
- You help readers find the most important information quickly and easily.
- If a release must be cut, you make the work easier and you have more control over how it will be cut.

If a news director has only 20 seconds of airtime (time to deliver a news story) and your news release requires 30 seconds, then the news director must either cut 10 seconds from your release or choose not to use it. Likewise, print editors sometimes must cut an inch or inches from press releases in order to fit them into the space available in the publication, as illustrated in Figure 7.3. The triangle shows the part of the release one editor decided to publish. The last two paragraphs, containing the least important information, were cut.

Take a News Writer's Approach

News is what will get editors to publish a release. So, if you are tempted to lavishly promote a product or a service in your release, remind yourself that news is *who* did *what when, where*, and *why,* while advertisements are how great, new, improved, or cost-effective something might be. Editors are unlikely to publish news releases that read like sales literature.

Save your sales pitch, if you include one, for the end of your press release. Statements that praise products or services should appear only at the end of the release and should be concrete and concise.

Figure 7.3 News Release Cut by Editor

CAMELOT
Public Information Office

City of Camelot
Office of the Mayor
1156 West Main Street
Camelot, IL 61808-1908
Phone: (555) 555-0001
Fax: (555) 555-0012

News

For Immediate Release

CAMELOT, IL - - Roller Art has donated $100,000 to Camelot for the development of a park especially designed for rollerblade and roller-skating enthusiasts. The park will feature two oval tracks for straightforward skating as well as another area with five ramps for trick skating.

The 2.45-acre park site is located three blocks west of the city office quad. This undeveloped land was deeded to the city two years ago by Roller Art.

Construction on the property is expected to begin within the month, and Mayor Margie Harker says the park, to be named Roller Royale, will be open by early summer.

Maureen Nowicki, spokesperson for Roller Art, said that her company is happy to be able to give something back to the community that has helped Roller Art to become successful. Roller Art employs 48 people who design and manufacture roller skates.

Roller Art has a history of giving to Camelot. In its nine years of doing business in the community, the company has donated a total of $425,000 to the city and an equal amount to local nonprofit groups.

The local company has the top-selling rollerblades on the market, Rold World. Rold World, developed after years of research, combines speed with the maximum in directional control.

-30-

Although your releases should not make a direct sales appeal as an advertisement would, most releases are good news messages intended to create and maintain goodwill. The message is one to be shared with a large audience and may cover such positive news as the introduction of a new product or service, the expansion of facilities, or the hiring of employees. For instance, when KFC announced its Colonel's Rotisserie Gold roasted chicken, the company certainly could not send a letter to all customers. Instead, press releases announced the new product. Such product introductions are news; however, they also keep the company in the consumer's mind.

Use the writer's notes given here. Place the notes in main-idea-first order as you would before writing a news release.

a) It's St. Patrick's Day.

b) The scene is Harrington Fitness Center.

c) The gymnasium is filled with approximately 150 people, mostly teenagers.

d) At 7:15 p.m., someone yells, "Green rain!"

e) Mist and then small drops of green liquid begin to drop on people.

f) The green rain came from the sprinkler system in the ceiling of the room.

g) Dancing, laughing, and karaoke singing continued for two hours as the participants, covered in green liquid, slipped over the green floor.

h) Harrington Fitness Center's Irish celebration, with the help of enthusiastic party-goers, raised over $1,000 for the new Cultural Center.

SUMMARY

1. News or press releases, prepared by employees, are documents that move news of the organization to agencies that can publish them, such as newspapers, magazines, and radio and television stations.

2. Two audiences benefit from news releases: **1)** the news directors and editors of news agencies and **2)** their readers, viewers, and listeners.

3. Writers of press releases should strive for accuracy and credibility. They should begin by collecting answers to the classic five Reporter's Questions: who, what, where, when, and why. Writers also should consider any other questions editors or the public are likely to have about the topic.

4. The news release has a standard format that editors and news directors expect. At the top of the page, the format features **1)** the words *NEWS RELEASE* along with the source of the release, **2)** the name, job title, and telephone number of a contact person, **3)** the date on which the document was written, **4)** the date on which the release may be published, and **5)** a suggested headline. Formatting for the body begins with a tag line giving the location of the story. The rest of the document should be double- or triple-spaced. Pagination cues centered at the bottom of the page give readers help in following the text: *–more–* indicates the report continues on the next page, and *–30–* or ### indicates the end of the report.

5. The body of the press release must meet the needs of the news director and the public. It should open with a hook, be organized deductively, and use a news writer's approach.

Editing and Revision Checklist

✓ Is my press release appropriate for the audience (general or specialized) for which it is intended?

✓ Does my release answer the five Reporter's Questions (and any others the audience might have) at the opening of the story?

✓ Did I properly format features at the top of the first page, including the words *NEWS RELEASE;* the source of the story; a contact person's name, job title, and telephone number; document date and release date; a suggested headline; and a tag line?

✓ Did I begin the body of the release with a hook to catch the editor's and the reader's attention?

✓ Did I present the essential ideas early in the body of the release? In other words, does the release give details in descending order of importance?

✓ Is my release more news (*who, what, when, where, why*) than advertisement (what product or service is "new and improved" or "a real bargain")?

✓ Did I avoid inaccuracies and exaggerations?

✓ Is my document neat, attractive, and free of errors?

APPLY WHAT YOU HAVE LEARNED

1. Read the paragraph below, which is the opening paragraph of a news release. Then identify which Reporter's Question(s) is (are) not answered.

   NASA: No talk of cutting mission
   CAPE CANAVERAL, Fla. - NASA said Sunday it did not intend to cut short Columbia's 14-day mission despite trouble with a fuel line connected to a crucial auxiliary unit. (From Associated Press Reports, The Daily Reflector, Greenville, North Carolina, Monday, March 7, 1994 PAGE 1)

2. Read the following bodies of news releases to determine what you might do to improve them. Look for a hook to open, main-idea-first organization, and a sales pitch at the end (optional). Include only data you know are accurate, use a news writer's approach, and avoid exaggeration. Activity **b** also appears on the Computer Applications Diskette as **TEXT7A**.

   a.
   DARDEN, KANSAS - - A bad storm left White Farms, a family-owned dairy, devastated. A tornado ripped through the southern part of the county, leveling two barns. However, the owners announced today that they will rebuild the entire operation. This tornado was one of the year's worst disasters for this area. Pamela White and her aunt, Em Llewllyn, the owners of White Farms, say they are determined that no employees will lose their jobs. The tornado did this and other damage in the county yesterday between 3:00 and 3:30 p.m.

b.

CHICAGO, Ill. - - FreshFlowers is a rose producer/wholesale organization. A FreshFlowers spokesperson said the company spent nine years and $12 million creating long-lasting roses. Flowers that are pretty so long people begin to think they're silk, that's what FreshFlower wants to sell you for Valentine's Day. Biotechnology keeps the FreshFlower flowers prettier than any other rose, about 10 days longer than the average rose. The genetic changes enable the grower to cut the flowers at their peak of color and fragrance, ship them to retailers, and still guarantee healthy blooms and foliage for at least two weeks. They look like roses. They smell like roses. But they don't die like roses. FreshFlowers CEO Martha McCarthy says her roses are "perfectly natural and more than safe to people and the environment." The U.S. Department of Agriculture ruled this week the genetically engineered plant poses no risk to the environment.

3. Clip an article of local interest from your newspaper (or photocopy an article from a newspaper in the library). Read the article carefully. Then find answers to the five Reporter's Questions in the article and write them down.

4. In small groups, compare the differences in planning a release for a general news agency, such as a local newspaper, with a specialized media agency, such as an alternative music radio station or an organic gardeners' newsletter. Record your responses to turn in to your instructor or to share with the class.

CONSIDER THIS CASE

For each of the situations described below, write and properly format a news release appropriate to the circumstances. Add details as needed and omit any information not needed.

1. You are the captain of your school's chess team. Your team, having won the regional competition last Saturday, will be participating in the state contest on the first Saturday of next month. The faculty member on campus who sponsors your team has asked you to write a news release announcing your team's success and the upcoming event. The faculty sponsor wants the release sent to the local newspaper and television station.

2. Write a news release announcing your school's First Annual Metalworks Show and Sale and inviting the public to attend. The show will feature wrought iron furniture, candlesticks, cookware holders, and fireplace tools. The public may make purchases during the sale with cash, check, or credit card. The show will be held in Gray Gallery from 6 to 9:30 p.m. on Friday, 28 April and from 9:00 a.m. to 6:00 p.m. on Saturday, 29 April 19--. All items are student work and will be sold to buy new equipment for the metalworks laboratory. This activity is also on the Computer Applications Diskette as **TEXT7B**.

PURSUE AN IDEA

1. If your school or your community has a newspaper or radio or television station, visit the news office. Interview the person in charge of news. Ask the news director to show you a collection of news releases. In addition, ask the news director about the editing he or she usually does with press releases before publication.

2. Look for something newsworthy at your school (events, projects, awards, special programs, sports) or in your community (organizational or club news, neighborhood programs and events, special projects). For instance, you may learn that some of your neighbors are forming a community watch group. Then, analyze the audience—editors and public. Prewrite, compose, edit, and revise a news release that might be sent to a local news agency, such as the area newspaper or television or radio station.

Economy

Good technical writing is economical. As good food is rich in nutrition and low in fat and sugar, good technical documents are rich in meaning and low in unneeded words and phrases. Technical writers who think of their readers try to write clearly and concisely so that documents take less time and are easier to read. The writer also saves production time and costs when economy is the rule. This section provides several tips for cutting out unnecessary words and phrases.

1. **Avoid *There is/There are* openings**. Revise sentences starting with *There is* or *There are* to give the sentence a subject at the beginning where it will get more attention followed by an action verb. *There is* and *There are* sentences are not wrong, but they are weak sentences that waste words. Getting directly to the point of the sentence is better. Look at the examples below:

   WEAK: There are 10 units of Amoxycillin stored in the warehouse.
   IMPROVED: Ten units of Amoxycillin are stored in the warehouse. (Passive Voice)
   The warehouse stores ten units of Amoxycillin. (Active Voice)
   WEAK: There is a direct relationship between speed limits and fatalities.
   IMPROVED: Speed limits and fatalities are directly related. (Passive Voice)
   Fatalities directly relate to speed limits. (Active Voice)

   The technique for revising these sentences is as follows: **1)** Mark out the *There is* or *There are* opening. **2)** Move the real subject of the sentence to the opening position. **3)** Create an action verb, sometimes from a word that followed the subject.

2. **Eliminate *It* sentence openers.** Sentences should not start with *it* unless the *it* refers to a specific person, place, or thing already mentioned. If you see that the *it* in a sentence is incorrectly used, then omit the *it*. Revise the sentence to give a stronger meaning without the unneeded word. Refer to the examples below:

   WEAK: It gives me great pleasure to introduce our new Quality Assurance Officer, Rebecca Bielby.
   IMPROVED: I am pleased to introduce our new Quality Assurance Officer, Rebecca Bielby.
   WEAK: It is the thermostat that received an electrical surge.
   IMPROVED: The thermostat received an electrical surge.

3. **Delete unnecessary modifiers.** In the examples given below, you can see that the modifier placed before each word is unnecessary. These words do not need modification. For instance, can something be very essential? No, something is either essential or not essential. Here are other common examples of unnecessary modifiers:

highly satisfactory	extremely competent
very rare	highly unusual
very precious	slightly expensive
barely visible	perfectly clear

4. **Avoid redundancy.** Redundancy is needless repetition. Thus, redundancy adds words but does not add meaning. The unnecessary repetition should be omitted. You can probably think of other redundant expressions to add to the list below.

refer back	advance warning
blue in color	large in size
personal opinion	mix together
the month of June	the state of Nevada
basic fundamentals	cancel out
3:00 a.m. in the morning	

5. **Reduce needless phrases.** Writers sometimes pad their writing, either intentionally or unintentionally, with unnecessary phrases. Never use an entire phrase when a single word will do. Each phrase listed below would be better replaced by its single-word equivalent on the right:

due to the fact that = because	prior to = before
be aware of the fact that = know	at a rapid rate = rapidly
in this modern day and age = today	in the event that = if
in many cases = often, frequently	at a later date = later

6. **Replace *-ion* nouns with stronger action verbs.** Use of *-ion* nouns often adds words without advancing meaning. These nouns can usually be omitted, making the sentence shorter and stronger. Refer to the examples below. Notice that the *-ion* nouns have been turned into action verbs.

WEAK: The Food and Drug Administration, under public pressure, took into consideration the adoption of several new AIDS drugs.

IMPROVED: The Food and Drug Administration, under public pressure, considered adopting several new AIDS drugs.

WEAK: Hilton came to the conclusion that the report was a summation of court procedure.

IMPROVED: Hilton concluded that the report summarized court procedure.

7. **Avoid cliches and overused expressions.** Most of the overused expressions listed below will sound familiar to you because you have probably read or heard them many times. While these cliches may be easy to write because they jump from our memory stores, they are not exciting to read. Each cliche below is followed by a possible replacement to its right.

every effort will be made—we will try	attached herewith is—attached
as per your request—as you asked	at this point in time—now
during the time that—while	upon receipt of—having received
as a general rule—generally	under separate cover—separately
I will be most grateful if—Please	afford an opportunity—allow
for the reason that—since	based on the fact that—because of

8. **Avoid strings of prepositional phrases.** Some prepositional phrases may be necessary to join ideas, but too many of them can be distracting. Whenever possible, revise sentences to remove excessive prepositional phrases.

WEAK: The drop in deposits by students in their accounts at the bank is of great concern for management.

IMPROVED: Decreasing student bank deposits concerns management.

WEAK: The EPA office in Lawrence plans to send out warnings to residents about possible contamination from lead in the water.

IMPROVED: The Lawrence EPA office will warn residents about possible lead-contaminated water.

THE INSIDE TRACK: APPLY WHAT YOU HAVE LEARNED

These activities are on the Computer Applications Diskette as **TEXT7C**.

1. Revise the following sentences to omit the *There is/There are* and *It* openings.
   a. There are 10 cases of welding rods on order.
   b. It is certain that the SCSI cable to connect the CD-ROM to the computer is missing.
   c. There is a solution that strips the silver from the film to create the photographic contrast.
   d. It is phosphate that encourages growth of algae in the river.
   e. There are several dessert recipes that are low in fat and sugar.

2. Revise the following sentences to eliminate unnecessary modifiers, redundancies, and needless phrases.
   a. The new packaging, which is oval in shape, has proven "quite satisfactory" in tests in the northeast market.
   b. The CAD software is 5% faster than it was prior to the upgrade.
   c. Designers should be aware of the fact that hidden cameras record their production process.

d. In this modern day and age, we expect almost all jobs to involve computer use.

e. My personal opinion is that no advance warning was given.

3. Revise the sentences below to replace the *-ion* nouns with stronger action verbs.

    a. The bulletin provides a description of a closed electrical circuit.

    b. The committee took our amendment into consideration.

    c. The continuation of John's project depends upon the financial support of UpStart.

    d. The Research Division presented a recommendation that all toxic wastes be disposed of through Standard Corporation.

    e. The synthetic fibers make an action like natural filament.

4. Revise the following sentences to omit cliches and unnecessary prepositional phrases.

    a. As per your request, I am sending the antenna to fit your AS302 model.

    b. The combinations of fragrance seem to sell well in areas of large metropolitan population in the United States.

    c. The toner cartridge for the LaserWriter needs to be replaced with care.

    d. With precision and swiftness, the photographer loaded the film into the back of the camera.

    e. I will be most grateful if you can afford me an opportunity to interview for the vacant position in your accounting area.

PART

3

Informative Reports

Document Design and Visual Aids

Write-to-Learn

Using words only, write down directions from school to your house. Then draw a map with arrows to show the route from school to your house. Which is easier to understand? In a short journal entry, explain why.

DEFINITIONS

Charts

chart a drawing with boxes, words, and lines to show a process or an organizational structure

flowchart a drawing with lines and arrows to show a process or series of steps

organizational chart a drawing with boxes, words, and lines to show how an organization is structured

Design Elements

design elements considerations in writing a document that affect page layout: the way a document looks

font the design of individual letters; popular fonts include Geneva and New York

headings the titles of the major divisions of a document; most often in a hierarchy of first-degree headings, second-degree headings, and third-degree headings

highlighters boldfacing, underlining, italicizing, or capitalizing a word or phrase to draw attention to it; also, itemizing a list to draw attention to it

justification how words line up with the right, left, and center margins

point the size of letters; 10 point is smaller than 12 point

sans serif letters *without* tails

serif letters *with* tails

ragged when type does not line up flush or even with the margin

visual aid information presented in a visual form such as a table, graph, or diagram

white space the white, blank areas on the page

Graphs

bar graph graph using a horizontal and vertical axis to compare numerical data, drawn with heights or lengths of rectangular bars

dependent variable the variable whose changes *are affected by* changes in the independent variable; often presented on the vertical axis

double bar graph graph using a horizontal and vertical axis to compare pairs of numbers, drawn with heights or lengths of rectangular bars

double line graph graph using horizontal and vertical axes to compare trends and show relationships between two sets of data

horizontal axis the axis that goes across the bottom of the graph; usually measures the independent variable

independent variable the known variable whose changes are automatic and cause changes in the dependent variable; usually presented on the horizontal axis

key a system that identifies the parts of a visual; similar to the legend on a map

line graph graph using a horizontal and vertical axis to show a trend or relationship between numbers, drawn with lines

multiple bar graph graph using horizontal and vertical axes to compare data, drawn with two or more bars for each measurement

multiple line graph graph using horizontal and vertical axes to compare trends and show relationships between numbers, drawn with different types of lines

pie graph a circular graph showing how parts relate to the whole; the whole equals 100%

tick marks evenly spaced marks on a table or graph that mark off numerical measurement

vertical axis the numerical data presented on the up-and-down axis; usually presents the dependent variable, the variable being measured

Tables

columns information given vertically in a table

footnotes notes given beneath a table to help explain parts of the table

formal table numerical information set up in rows and columns and drawn with rules; used to present figures

informal table a simple table with two or three items, drawn without rules and stubs

rows information across a table

rules the lines in a table or line graph that separate columns and rows

stub the name of a column in a table

verbal table information given in rows and columns; uses words instead of numbers

Diagrams

call outs the names of specific parts of a diagram, connected to the diagram or drawing with lines

diagram a simple line drawing

After completing this chapter, you will be able to

- Design a document using white space, line justification, typeset text, headings, and highlighters

- Select visual aids appropriate to the audience's need and the objectives of the report

- Describe the distinguishing features of each visual aid

- Distinguish the purpose of each visual aid

- Follow basic principles for formatting visual aids

- Construct tables, graphs, charts, and diagrams

Writing entails making many decisions—decisions concerning what to write, how to organize, which words to use, whether the words reflect standard usage. In technical writing, add to this list of decisions, one more: how the document looks on the page. Design your document to make the text easier to follow. Use **visual aids** to convert words into technical "pictures."

Designing the Document

> *Man is still the most extraordinary computer of all.*
>
> JOHN F. KENNEDY,
> MAY 21, 1963

WARM UP 8.1

Remember the last time you went to the library to choose a book for a book report? After thumbing through several books, how did you make your final choice? Did some books look more inviting than others?

Looks play an important role in technical writing. Your audience will feel more comfortable with text that looks a certain way, just as you may feel more comfortable in a room that looks a certain way. A cluttered room with poorly designed lighting may make you feel overwhelmed. In the same way, a cluttered document with poorly designed elements may make your readers feel overwhelmed.

To keep your documents uncluttered and your readers comfortable, use the following **design elements** for your reports:

1. **Create Adequate White Space.** **White space** is just that—space that is white or blank because there is no ink in that particular line or area. The fewer words per page and the wider the margins, the more inviting your text appears.

2. **Use left justification with ragged right edges.** Left justification means that the text is flush with the left margin of the page. **Ragged** right means that words lie unevenly along the right margin. Readers read regular text more quickly if it is left justified with ragged right margins.

3. **Choose a 10–12-point serif font that mixes capitals and lower-case letters.** Two basic differences between **fonts,** the name of a particular letter design, are serif or sans (French for *without*) serif. **Serif** refers to letters with more distinguishing lines or "tails" (like this sentence) that make it easier to see the differences between one letter and another. Sans serif refers to letters with fewer distinguishing lines and no "tails" (like this sentence) and is appropriate for something short—like a short letter, a title, or a heading. Size is described in **points,** with a larger point number (like 12 or 14) representing a larger letter. Letters in 10 or 12 point are large enough to see easily. Never write an entire document in all caps. All caps are harder to read and should be used only for emphasis, a title, or for a major heading.

4. **Use a workable system of headings.** **Headings** are short titles that introduce the main idea of a selected portion of text. They show the bigger divisions of a report and how the subdivisions relate to the bigger headings. Like a formal outline, headings help your reader see the organization of a document in one glance. Most reports use a system of two headings—first-degree headings and second-degree headings—but can use more. Glancing through this textbook and others will show you a variety of systems.

5. **Use highlighters to draw attention to important information.** **Highlighters** are special print styles you use to focus the reader's attention on something in particular—perhaps a word or a series of words. **Boldface,** underline, *italics,* and CAPITALS are popular highlighters, with **boldface** as the most effective and CAPITALS as the least effective. Use highlighters to play up information, but use them sparingly: Overuse clutters the page and distracts the reader, drawing attention *away from* the text instead of *to* the text. Another effective tool for highlighting is to itemize a list. To **itemize a list**, you set up a list separate from the text, indented from the left-hand margin. Bullets (●) often precede each item in the list to draw the reader's eye to the information.

S T O P   A N D   T H I N K   8.1

1. Why do white space, ragged right edges, serif font, and headings make text easier to read?
2. What is the purpose of highlighters?

Audience: Who Reads Visual Aids?

What is being described here?

A circle, 3 inches in diameter, contains three items. At the bottom of the figure, approximately ¾ of an inch from the bottom is a single line, approximately 2 inches long curved in the shape of the bottom half of a small circle. At the top of the 3-inch circle, approximately ½ inch from the top and 1 inch apart are two small circles, ¼ of an inch in diameter. A perfect square encloses the 3-inch circle, the four sides of the square barely touching four points of the circle.

A picture is, indeed, worth a thousand words, isn't it? A visual aid simplifies or clarifies information *instantaneously*. At one glance, your reader can perceive more information than he or she can understand in words.

Technical readers expect to see visual aids in their reading. Most complex technical material can be clarified with some sort of visual—perhaps a table, a schematic drawing, a diagram, or a graph. Where academic writing relies heavily on words to convey meaning, technical writing relies on *words plus visuals* to convey meaning. In fact, technical readers may think it odd if you don't find ways to present your information in visual form.

Technical readers vary in their ability to understand visual aids. As always in technical writing, the decision about which visual aid to use depends on what your audience can understand and what he or she already knows.

Some visual aids are more difficult than others to read. Figure 8.1 on page 148 illustrates the relative difficulty of reading several of the more popular visual aids. Of course, this assessment is general. More data will make an easier visual more difficult to read; less data would make a difficult visual easier to read.

To help decide which visual aid your audience will best understand, ask these questions about your reader:

1. Does my audience know a lot about the subject?
2. Is my audience interested in my subject?
3. Is my audience a technical audience? In other words, does it need or expect technical information or many figures?
4. Is my audience's reading level high (roughly tenth-grade level or higher)?

Count the number of yes and no answers to the preceding questions. Then use this formula as a guide to help you make your decision:

4 no answers, definitely lay reader	4 yes answers, definitely sophisticated reader
3 no answers, probably lay reader	3 yes answers, probably sophisticated reader
2 no answers, probably intermediate reader	2 yes answers, probably intermediate reader
1 no answer, probably sophisticated reader	1 yes answer, probably lay reader

The more no answers, the less sophisticated your audience is and the more help he or she needs from you. The more yes answers, the more sophisticated your audience is and the less help he or she needs from you.

STOP AND THINK 8.2

Consider these topics: scuba diving, popular music, chemistry, sewing, biology. Using the questions and formula presented above, determine whether you are a lay reader, intermediate reader, or sophisticated reader for each of these topics.

Prewriting: Getting Started on Visual Aids

Audience is only one consideration in deciding what kind of visual to use. Other considerations include the purpose of your visual, how much information you have, and what type of information you have. You also choose visuals based on the information you want your reader to pay more attention to.

After you have determined how difficult a visual your audience can handle, ask yourself **1)** what the objectives of your writing are and **2)** how visuals can help you achieve those objectives. Then match your writing objective to the visual aid purpose to the reader level. For example,

Writing Objective	**Visual Aid Purpose**	**Reader Level**
to teach what a cell looks like→	to show what something looks like→	lay

VISUAL AID CHOICE: simple line drawing or diagram

To help you make decisions about which visual to use, look at the purpose column in Figure 8.1. Turn each purpose statement into a question that begins with an understood "Do I want…?" For example, [Do I want] to draw a mechanism or part of a mechanism? If the answer is yes, you may want to consider using a simple line drawing or diagram. Continue through the rest of the table, asking the same question. Jot down which ones you answer "yes" to. Then match writing objective(s) to Visual Aid Purpose(s) to Reader Level. Now you are ready to make a list of possible visual aids to use.

Jupiter is the largest and the brightest of the planets.

Figure 8.1 Visual Aid Purpose and Reader Level

Purpose [Do I Want...?]	Type Of Visual	Reader
to show a mechanism or part of a mechanism	simple line drawing or diagram	lay reader
to show how the whole is divided into parts, to show how the parts relate to the whole	pie graph	lay reader
to present a small amount of data (especially numbers) in an easy-to-read format	informal table	lay reader
to compare several sets of data; to present differences in a dramatic way; sometimes to depict a trend	bar graph	lay reader
to compare several sets of data, sometimes to depict a trend	double bar graph	intermediate reader
to show a trend; to show how data is related	line graph	intermediate reader
to show several trends; to compare trends; to show how data is related	multiple line graph	sophisticated reader
to present information, especially lots of numbers, in an easy-to-read format	formal table	sophisticated reader
to present a process	flowchart	sophisticated reader
to present the structure of an organization	organizational chart	sophisticated reader

*NOTE: Remember that more data will make a simpler visual more difficult to read; less data can make a more complex visual easier to read. The reader levels are meant as a guide only and may not reflect the relative complexity of the visual you design.

Formatting Visual Aids

WARM UP 8.3

Take a close look at the visual aids that are modeled in the following sections of this chapter. What do you notice about each visual? What do they have in common? Notice some of the differences. In what visuals do the differences occur?

Read these principles and observe how the visuals in the following pages use them. When you construct your visuals, be sure to follow these guidelines:

1. **Make sure visual aids are neat.** The quality of a visual is a crucial factor in how carefully it is read. Many computer programs generate graphic material, but you may have to draw your visual aids yourself. If you draw the visual, sketch first in light pencil and go back over your penciled lines with black ink. Make sure the lines and titles are straight and that your lettering is neat. Use a ruler and measure carefully. If you use a pie graph, trace around a circular object. Leave enough white space to make the visual look uncluttered.

2. **Keep the visuals simple.** In general, keep the data you place into a visual centered around one idea, one point. It is better to use two uncluttered, simple visuals to illustrate two concepts than one cluttered visual to illustrate too many concepts. Avoid three-dimensional graphics. They look pretty but are harder to read.

3. **Refer to each visual clearly in the text BEFORE you place it on the page.** Refer to the visual when you think your reader will most likely need to look at it for the first time. Use the word *Figure* to refer to any visuals that are not formal tables. Use the word *Table* to refer to formal tables (tables with rules and titles). Call your reader's attention to figures or tables by **1)** incorporating references into your text, **2)** using parentheses, or **3)** creating stand-alone sentences:

   Table 1/Figure 1 shows the amount of rainfall in Idaho over the past 3 years.

   The rainfall in Idaho over six years varied substantially (see Table 1/ Figure 1).

   The rainfall in Idaho over six years varied substantially (Table 1/Figure 1).

   The rainfall in Idaho over six years varied substantially. See Table 1/Figure 1.

   Choose a method you prefer. Then be consistent and refer to all your figures and tables in the same way. Informal tables need not be referred to as a Table or a Figure. **Verbal tables** are not always referred to as a Table or Figure but are often integrated into the text with an appropriate introduction.

4. **Place each visual—whether a Figure or a Table—in a convenient place for the reader to see.** Always place the visual after you have referred to it. If the visual is small enough ⅛ to ½ page), try to place it on the same page as its reference. If the visual is large (¾ to 1 page), you may have to place it on the next page after the visual is referred to.

5. **For visuals used in conjunction with reports, explain the significance of the visual in the report as you introduce the visual.** Explain, in words, the relationships you want your reader to see. You might point out the parts of a diagram, the trend in a line graph, or the important numbers in a table. You need not discuss every part of the visual, but you should point out what is important for the reader to note. Generally, explanations are presented in the introduction preceding the visual. More complex visuals may be explained before and after placement of the visual.

6. **Provide a title for every visual.** Computer graphics are changing the traditional placement of visual titles. Titles of tables may be centered above the table and titles of figures centered below the figure; however, placement may vary. Whatever placement you use, be consistent throughout your document. Use titles that are specific enough to be readily understood by the reader. For example,

    Salary Distribution for 1955–1956   NOT JUST Salaries

    Regal Powerboat Model OTY-453   NOT JUST Powerboat

    Informal tables do not need titles.

7. **Number Figures consecutively throughout. Number Tables consecutively, but separately from Figures, throughout.** Note how the following example separates the numbering of figures from tables: Figure 1, Table 1, Figure 2, Figure 3, Table 2, Figure 4, etc.

8. **Give credit for the visual if you did not compile it yourself or if you compiled it using borrowed data.** Place the word "Source" below your figure and give the bibliographic reference for the source as you would a footnote or an endnote.

9. **Align decimals when they are presented in columns.** For example,

    8.3

    0.525

    98.6

10. Where possible, spell out words rather than use abbreviations. If you must use abbreviations, use standard ones and provide a key defining them.

S T O P   A N D   T H I N K   8.3

1. Why should visual aids be neat and simple?
2. How do you label diagrams, graphs, charts, and formal tables?
3. When do you refer to figures and tables in your text?
4. What kind of information should you include in your discussion of your visual aid?
5. What should you consider when thinking of a title?

Constructing Tables

W A R M   U P   8.4

Review the definitions for tables at the beginning of the chapter. Preview the sample tables in this section (Figures 8.2 and 8.3), paying close attention to the margin notes. Match the definitions to the samples in the text. Note any questions you have about a particular definition.

To illustrate the variety of choices available to you as a composer of tables and other visual aids, we will show the options available to Theresa. Theresa has embarked on a fitness program. Her goal, to lose 12 pounds of fat and gain 15 pounds of muscle, will require her to change her eating habits and to exercise.

Theresa has been asked to write two articles about her fitness program. One of the articles is for *Fitness,* a magazine for junior high school students or people just beginning to embark on exercise programs. She has also been asked to contribute information to an article for *Mind and Body,* a magazine for college students majoring in Physical Education.

The following tables represent the various ways Theresa can present her fitness program in visuals. Try to understand each decision Theresa makes. Refer to Figure 8.1 on page 148 to help explain her choices.

Informal Table

To present her progress for the first two weeks, Theresa considers using an **informal table**, a visual using **rows** and **columns** drawn *without* **rules** (lines) or **stubs** (column headings). See Figure 8.2 for the informal table and its written introduction.

Figure 8.2 Model of Informal Table with Introduction

Over the next two months, Theresa lost a total of 4.2 pounds. For every pound of fat she lost, she gained approximately $^3/_4$ of a pound of muscle.

Fat lost	14.0 lbs.
Muscle gained	9.8 lbs.
Total pounds lost	4.2 lbs.

An informal table is easy to read because the information blends into the text. The explanation is a brief summary of the information. An informal table is a good choice here because the information is simple—only three items to consider. Theresa plans to use this information early in the article for *Fitness* to motivate beginners.

Formal Table

Theresa wants readers to know at what rate they should be exercising their hearts. To help, she decides to use part of a table from a published book. A **formal table** is a visual that presents numerical information in rows and columns with rules (lines drawn). Figure 8.3 is a portion of the formal table she reproduced from *Exercise and You* along with the brief introduction.

Figure 8.3 Model of Formal Table with Introduction.
Table 1 shows the recommended heart rates during exercise by age. The athlete's training rate is for only the most fit athletes. The average training rate is recommended for a healthy person beginning a fitness program.

Formal table is labeled Table

Stubs

Rules

Superscript letters direct attention to footnotes

Footnotes explain parts of table

Source provides bibliographic data

Table 1. Recommended Heart Rates During Aerobic Exercise

		TRAINING RATES[a]	
Age	**Maximum Heart Rate**	**Athlete, 85%[b]**	**Average, 80%**
20	200	170	160
22	198	168	158
24	196	167	157
26	194	165	155
28	192	163	154

[a]Based on average heart rates of 72 beats per minute for males and 80 beats per minute for females

[b]Percentages represent percents of Maximum Heart Rates in column 2

Source: Alan Grayson and Susanne Brazinski, *Exercise and You*, Clearview, ND: Mountain Press, 1994.

A formal table is appropriate here because of the many different numbers. The many numbers, however, make the table more difficult to read. Notice that the introduction tells what information is included in the Table. Theresa will use this table for the readers of *Mind and Body*, an older and more knowledgeable audience. This audience might better understand the detailed numerical data.

Theresa designs her table carefully. She decides to use only three rules because more rules would clutter the visual. The columns are named with stubs. Notice the "a" and "b" superscripts that direct the reader's attention to the **footnotes** that give additional information about the table. Underneath the visual the word "Source" appears with a footnoted bibliographic entry. Also note that this visual is referred to as a Table, not a Figure.

Verbal Table

A **verbal table** is similar to a formal table with its several rows and columns. The verbal table in Figure 8.4 illustrates how eating habits can affect health.

Figure 8.4 Model of a Verbal Table with Introduction

The following chart shows that some diseases have possible causes in poor eating habits.

Eating Habits	Diseases from Poor Eating Habits
Too much fat	Some cancers, heart disease, strokes
Too much salt	Heart disease, high blood pressure
Too much cholesterol	Heart disease, high blood pressure
Too much sugar	Diabetes, hypoglycemia
Lack of fiber	Some cancers, gallstones
Lack of calcium	Osteoporosis

Source: Marion Newberry, *Nutrition*. New York: Medical Press, 1992, 12.

Theresa is thinking about using the verbal table in Figure 8.4 for both audiences. The verbal table is harder to read quickly than a bar graph, but Theresa thinks both audiences will be interested enough to read all parts of it.

STOP AND THINK 8.4

1. Which table(s) is(are) more appropriate for a lay audience? Why?
2. Which table(s) is(are) more appropriate for a sophisticated audience? Why?
3. Which table needs no table number?
4. What is the difference between a formal table and a verbal table?

Constructing Graphs

WARM UP 8.5

Review the definitions for graphs at the beginning of the chapter. Pay close attention to the margin notes and match the definitions to sample graphs in the chapter. Note any questions you have at this point about a particular definition.

A graph is a visual that *shows* the relationships between numerical data. Three types are bar graphs, line graphs, and pie graphs.

Bar Graph

Theresa decides she wants to show the readers of *Fitness* how much fat she lost per week for the first two months. Figure 8.5 shows the bar graph she designed and its accompanying introduction.

Figure 8.5 Model of Bar Graph with Introduction

Figure 1 shows the progression of fat loss per week for eight weeks. Notice that the greatest amount of fat loss occurred during weeks 1 (3.6 pounds lost) and 2 (2.7 pounds lost). Weeks 3 (1.5 pounds lost) and 4 (1.1 pounds lost) show the least amount of fat loss. Typically, the body will lose more weight at first. Sustained metabolism and significant water loss contribute to this effect. Several weeks into the weight-loss program, the metabolism will slow down the amount of loss in order to protect the body from harm. Notice also that after seven weeks on the program, Theresa's weight loss stabilized at a loss of a little more than a pound a week.

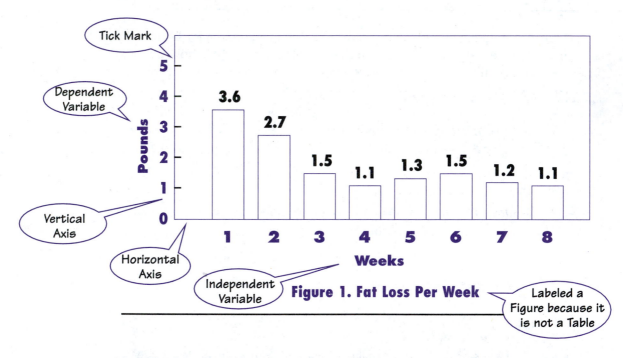

Figure 1. Fat Loss Per Week

The **bar graph** is a visual using a horizontal and vertical axis to compare numerical data presented in rectangular bars. It is relatively easy to read and is therefore appropriate for the *Fitness* audience. The introduction tells Theresa's readers which figures to pay attention to.

In her bar graph, Theresa has used the **horizontal axis** for the **independent variable** and the **vertical axis** for the **dependent variable**. In this case, the independent variable is the number of weeks, and the dependent variable is the amount of pounds lost. The independent variable, the variable that changes automatically, causes or effects changes in the dependent variable. In other words, changes in the dependent variable are affected by changes in the independent variable. Typically, the vertical axis represents the dependent variable and the horizontal axis represents the independent variable. Often the horizontal axis depicts time or distance.

Here, the number of weeks, which pass automatically, has something to do with the amount of weight lost. Put another way, the dependent variable, weight lost, is affected by the independent variable, the passage of time.

Notice that the specific number of pounds has been added atop each bar for easy reference. To do so is not necessary, but is helpful. In fact, Theresa could have left out the numbers next to the **tick marks**, since the actual numbers were placed atop the bars. The decision to add specific numbers depends on your reader and how specific you think he or she wants you to be. Additional tick marks between pounds to mark individual ounces or half pounds were not added because the graph was understandable without them. Additional lines would have cluttered the visual. Notice that the bars are the same width, and the space between the bars is one-half the bar width.

Multiple Bar Graph

To compare how much fat she lost to how much muscle she gained, Theresa uses the **multiple bar graph**, a bar graph with more than one line, in Figure 8.6.

Figure 8.6 Model of a Double Bar Graph with Introduction

Figure 2 compares the amount of fat lost to the number of pounds gained. Notice that the amount of muscle gained is small compared to the amount of fat lost during the first weeks. However, as the fat loss stabilized during weeks 7 and 8, the amount of muscle gain is slightly higher. Muscle is denser than fat. As the body converts more fat to muscle, the net effect is to actually gain poundage while still losing fat.

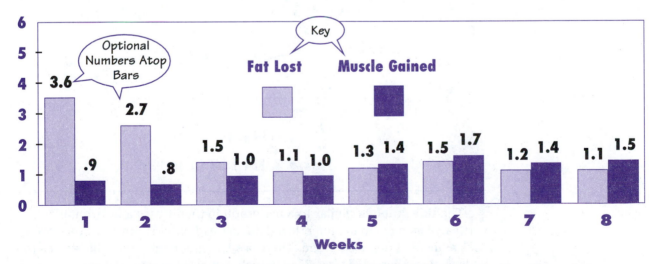

Figure 2. Fat Lost Compared to Muscle Gained, in Pounds (for 8 weeks)

The **double bar graph** uses two sets of bars on a horizontal and vertical axis to compare several sets of numerical data. It is easy enough for both audiences to understand and offers the *Mind and Body* audience more information than a simple bar graph. Also, Theresa wanted to emphasize the difference in fat loss and muscle gain in the first weeks. The bar graph compares data and shows that difference dramatically by forcing the reader to see that one bar is taller than the other. Again, the introduction points out what is most important to the reader. It also gives the reason for the figures.

The bars for fat lost are shaded differently than the bars for muscle gained. A **key** is provided to explain the shading. Also Theresa decided to add the specific poundage atop each bar again as she did in the single bar graph. She could have left out this information but thought her readers might appreciate the specific amount.

Line Graph

Theresa thought about using a line graph to show the same data. To experiment with the change, she tried plotting the same 8-week fat-loss data on a line graph. Figure 8.7 shows the same data in a line graph as Figure 8.5 shows in a bar graph.

Figure 8.7 Model of Line Graph with Introduction

Figure 3 shows how the fat loss peaked in the earlier weeks, dropped remarkably during the middle weeks, and plateaued during the last 4 weeks.

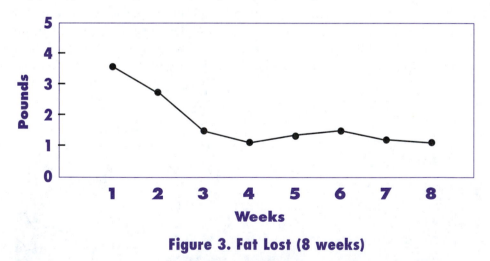

Figure 3. Fat Lost (8 weeks)

The **line graph** is similar to a bar graph in that it uses a horizontal and vertical axis to compare numerical data. Instead of bars, however, this graph uses a line that depicts a trend. Theresa's line graph pictorially illustrates the fat loss over a period of time. Even though it shows the same data as Figure 8.5, it plays up the general trend, not the individual numbers. The introduction focuses on the overall trend: the fat loss "dropped remarkably" and "plateaued." It plays up *relationships* between weeks instead of the stark *differences* between them.

This graph would be appropriate for either audience. Theresa will have to decide for what purpose she wishes to use the graph before she makes her decision.

Multiple Line Graph

See how Theresa's Figure 8.8 puts the same information as the double bar graph in Figure 8.6 into a **multiple line graph**, a graph using more than one line to compare data. Because Theresa's graph compares two sets of data, we will refer to it as a **double line graph**.

Figure 8.8 Model of Multiple Line Graph with Introduction

The relationship between fat loss and muscle gain is more closely matched after the first weeks of the fitness program (see Figure 4). During the first 2 weeks the amount of muscle gain is minimal and fat loss is at its maximum. As the fat loss plateaus, the muscle gain stabilizes, surpassing fat loss by a few ounces.

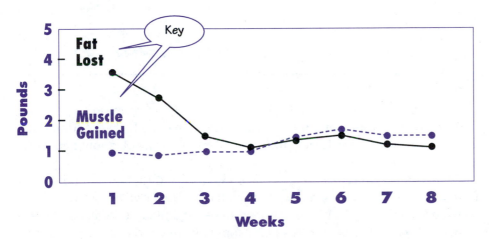

Figure 4. Relationship of Fat Loss to Muscle Gain

Notice how the double line graph illustrates the *relationship* between fat loss and muscle gain rather than the *differences* between fat lost and muscle gained. Again, the introduction emphasizes this relationship. The double line graph is relatively easy to understand and is appropriate for both audiences.

Pie Graph

To represent what percent of her total daily food intake consisted of fat, protein, and carbohydrates, Theresa draws a **pie graph** in Figure 8.9. A pie graph is a circular visual that shows how the parts relate to the whole.

Figure 8.9 Model of a Pie Graph with Introduction

Figure 5 shows how much protein, carbohydrates, and fat a person on a fitness plan needs in one day. Surprisingly, the human body needs more carbohydrates (65%) than protein and much less fat than previously thought.

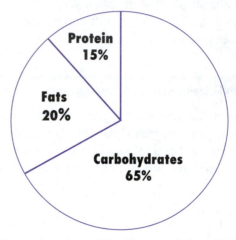

Figure 5. Percentages of Daily Nutrition Required

The whole totals 100% with each piece of the pie representing a percentage of the whole. Notice that the pieces of the pie move clockwise from the 12 o'clock position from the largest to the smallest. A pie graph should contain no more than seven sections.

The introduction repeats the actual percentages in the pie and points out the significance of those numbers. The readers of *Mind and Body* already know these percentages and do not need to be reminded of them, so Theresa decides not to use the pie for this more sophisticated audience. The readers of *Fitness,* who include people just beginning fitness programs, may need this information.

**S T O P   A N D   T H I N K   **

1. Which graph shows a more dramatic change?
2. Which graph shows a more gradual change?
3. Which graph or graphs give the most information?
4. Which graph shows the relationship of parts to a whole?

The availability of spreadsheet programs and drawing programs makes constructing visuals a snap—for those who know how to operate the programs. Programs such as Microsoft Excel and Lotus 1-2-3 create tables, pie graphs, bar graphs, and line graphs. After entering the data onto the spreadsheet, you can click one button to see how the data looks in a pie graph and another to see how the same data looks in a bar graph. Some programs like Microsoft Works and Novell PerfectWorks integrate graphical aids into the word-processing package. This way the writer can type text, create a graph, save, and print in the same document. Computer graphics make it easy to create visual aids.

Constructing Charts and Diagrams

WARM UP 8.6

Review the definitions for charts at the beginning of the chapter. Pay close attention to the margin notes, matching the definitions to the sample visuals in the chapter. Note any questions you have at this point about a particular definition.

A **chart** is a drawing with boxes, words, and lines to show a process or an organizational structure. A diagram or drawing shows what something looks like or how it operates.

Flowchart

Theresa wants a quick way to show the complex process of converting glucose to fat. So she chooses a **flowchart** in Figure 8.10, a drawing with lines and arrows, to show this process.

This flowchart is fairly simple and would be appropriate for a lay audience as well as a sophisticated one. The arrows lead the reader through the process. The introduction summarizes the process.

Figure 8.10 Model of Flowchart with Introduction

Figure 6 shows what happens when sugars and starches are digested to glucose. The glucose that is not used by the brain or the muscles is converted to fat.

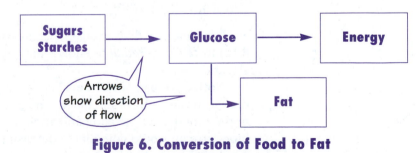

Figure 6. Conversion of Food to Fat

Organizational Chart

Theresa was asked to present her research to the student body during assembly. To make students aware of the school's fitness center, she creates an **organizational chart.** The chart shows the hierarchy of the fitness center employees. Theresa creates her organizational chart using boxes, words, and lines in Figure 8.11.

Figure 8.11 **Model of Organizational Chart with Introduction**

The following chart shows the organization of the school fitness center.

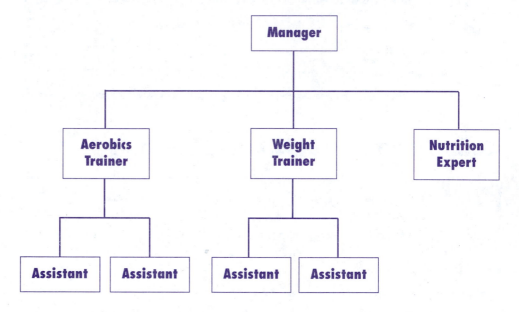

Figure 7. Organization of the School Fitness Center

The blocks contain the job titles. At the top of the chart is the most important position. The lines show who is responsible to whom. The introduction describes information in the chart.

Diagram or Drawing

For her *Mind and Body* article, Theresa uses a **diagram,** or drawing (see Figure 8.12) from *Good Health* to show what triglycerides (fat) look like in the bloodstream.

Notice the use of **call outs**, names of parts of the drawing with lines drawn to the appropriate place. The drawing represents a simplified version of the blood arteriole and capillaries. To add everything else that exists in the bloodstream would complicate the visual. Here, the author drew only what is needed to make the point.

Figure 8.12 Model of a Diagram with Introduction

Figure 8 shows how the blood cells clump together abnormally after a dinner high in triglycerides (fat). Notice when the triglycerides create sludging, blood flow to the capillaries is impeded.

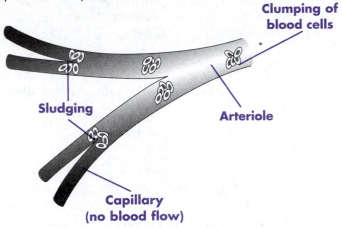

Figure 8. Triglycerides (Fat) in the Blood Stream

Source: Spivey, Sandra. "Fat Affects You." *Good Health* 1996: 212.

S T O P   A N D   T H I N K   8.6

1. Which chart shows a process?
2. Which chart shows an organizational hierarchy?
3. Which chart shows what something looks like?

FOCUS ON ETHICS

Look at the following line graphs. Figure 1 minimizes the trend by spreading the horizontal axis out. Figure 2 exaggerates the trend by shortening the horizontal axis. Figure 3 is more realistic. Is it ethical to make a visual appear to be less or more than what it is?

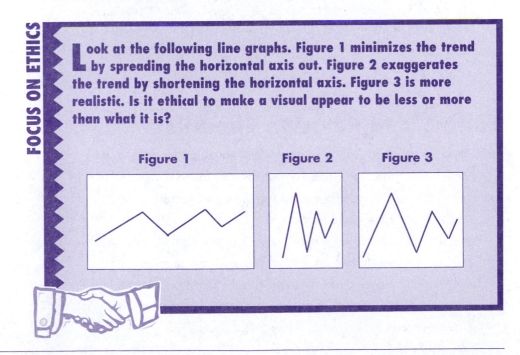

1. Use the following document design for your reports: **1)** Create adequate white space, **2)** Use left justification with ragged right edges, **3)** Use a 10–12-point serif font that mixes capitals and lower-case letters, **4)** Determine a workable system of headings, and **5)** Use highlighters to draw attention to important information.

2. Get started on visuals by trying to match the type of reader to a particular kind of visual aid. Consider the reader's interest, knowledge, and reading ability.

3. Each type of visual has a purpose that can be matched to writing objectives and audience needs.

4. Visual aids should adhere to basic principles. They should be neat, use Figure labels and numbers to refer to anything that is not a table, use Table labels and numbers to refer to formal tables, and be located in a convenient place for the reader (usually right after the referral phrase). They should also use specific titles, give credit when necessary, use words to explain the visual, be kept simple, have aligned decimals, and avoid abbreviations.

5. Tables are useful for comparing numbers or listing verbal information. Informal tables flow into the text; formal tables use rules, columns, and rows; and verbal tables use words in columns and rows.

6. Graphs show numerical data in a variety of formats. Sometimes the same information can be presented in bar graphs and line graphs. Bar graphs, both single and multiple, dramatize differences. Line graphs, both single and multiple, emphasize trends and show relationships.

7. Charts use lines and blocks to convey a process or a structure. Flowcharts show a process, while organizational charts show the structure of an organization. Diagrams are simple drawings to show what something looks like.

Editing and Revision Checklist

✓ Have I determined what kind of reader I have and found a visual to match?

✓ Have I determined my writing objectives and found a visual to match?

✓ Have I followed the guidelines for formatting visual aids?

  ✓ Constructed the visual neatly?

  ✓ Referred to the visual properly as a Table or Figure?

  ✓ Placed the visual in a convenient place for the reader?

  ✓ Provided a specific title for every graph, chart, and formal table?

  ✓ Numbered the visuals consecutively? Table 1,2 etc.? or Figure 1,2 etc.?

  ✓ Given credit for the visual if found in a source?

✓ Explained the significance of the visual?

✓ Kept visuals as simple as possible?

✓ Aligned decimals?

✓ Avoided abbreviations?

✓ Have I attended to these details for various visuals?

   ✓ Drawn pie percentages from largest to smallest clockwise from the 12 o'clock position?

   ✓ Made sure the pie percentages equal 100%?

   ✓ Drawn bars in even widths with spaces one-half the bar width?

   ✓ Placed dependent variables on the vertical axis?

   ✓ Placed independent variables on the horizontal axis?

APPLY WHAT YOU HAVE LEARNED

1. Use the information from this table to generate other visuals.

No. 189. Organ Transplants and Grafts: 1981 to 1991

[As of end of year. Based on reports of procurement programs and transplant centers in the United States]

PROCEDURE	NUMBER OF PROCEDURES							NUMBER OF CENTERS		Number of people waiting	1-year survival rates, 1990
	1981	1985	1987	1988	1989	1990	1991	1981	1991	1991	(percent)
Transplant:											
Heart	62	719	1,512	1,647	1,673	1,998	2,125	8	156	2,267	[1]82
Liver	26	602	1,199	1,680	2,160	2,534	2,954	1	93	1,679	[1]74
Kidney	4,883	7,695	8,967	9,123	8,890	9,433	9,949	157	237	19,416	[1]93
Heart-Lung	5	30	41	74	67	52	51	(NA)	84	155	[1]53
Lung	–	2	11	31	89	187	401	(NA)	79	678	[1]54
Pancreas/Islet cell	(NA)	130	180	243	413	529	532	(NA)	89	602	[1]89
Cornea grafts	15,500	26,300	35,930	36,900	38,464	40,631	41,393	(NA)	[2]108	5,083	[3]95
Bone grafts	(NA)	(NA)	250,000	300,000	(NA)	350,000	375,000	(NA)	34	(NA)	(NA)
Skin grafts	(NA)	(NA)	5,000	5,200	(NA)	5,500	5,200	(NA)	25	(NA)	(NA)

– Represents zero. NA Not available. [1]One year patient survival rates for transplants performed between October 1, 1987, and December 31, 1989. [2]Eye banks. [3]Success rate.

Source: U.S. Department of Health and Human Services, Public Health Service, Division of Organ Transplantation; American Association of Tissue Banks, McLean, VA; and Eye Bank Association of America, Washington; and unpublished data.

Source: U.S. Bureau of the Census, Statistical Abstracts of the United States: 1993 (113th ed), Washington, DC.

- a bar graph to illustrate the number of heart transplants from 1987 to 1991.
- a double bar graph to show the change in the number of centers offering heart, liver, and lung transplants from 1981 to 1991.
- a line graph to illustrate the number of cornea grafts from 1987 to 1991.
- a multiple line graph to illustrate the number of heart, heart-lung, and lung transplants from 1987 to 1991
- a simpler table for any three transplants for 1989, 1990, and 1991.

2. Critique these three visual aids. Look for several mistakes in each one. Make suggestions for improvement.

a.

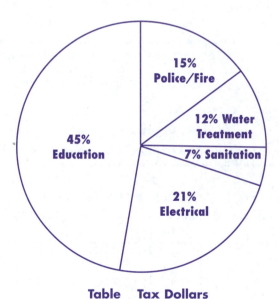

Table   Tax Dollars

b.

Prefix	Symbol		Power of Ten
mega	m	1,000,000	10^6
kilo	k	1,000	10^3
deci	d	0.1	10^{-1}
centi	c	0.01	10^{-2}
milli	m	0.001	10^{-3}

Source: Jay Britain, *The Metric System*.

c.

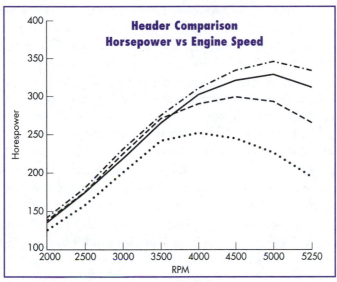

Source: *Summit Catalog,* May June 1994, 10.

---

3. Examine several of your textbooks for design. Describe their design. Which one is better-designed and why?

4. Read your local and national newspapers and magazines. Cut out an example of each type of visual aid presented in this chapter. Identify the parts of the visual. Using your checklist, determine whether the makers of the visual did a good job of presenting data.

5. Look for visuals that are different from the ones presented in this chapter. Note what's different about them. What's been added or changed? Even though they are different, they should fall into one of the categories we have described. Which category do they fall into?

CONSIDER THIS CASE

1. Present the following information in an informal table. In 19-- Champion Industries sold $538,000 in wristwatches, $640,000 in wall clocks, and $717,000 in clock radios.

2. Here are the 1988 pitching averages for 4 major-league pitchers. Decide which data you'd like to work with. (You don't have to use all the numbers.) Present the data in several different visuals: formal table, bar graph for one item, double bar graph for comparison, line graph for one item, multiple line graph for several items. Introduce the visuals by giving the significant information.

   Jack William Armstrong (Reds) pitched 14 games, 65 innings. He gave up 44 runs, walked 38 batters, made 42 errors, and struck out 45 batters. Michael (Mike) Joseph Bielecki (Cubs) pitched 19 games, 48 innings. He gave up 22 runs, walked 16 batters, made 18 errors, and struck out 33 batters. Larry Dean McWilliams (Cardinals) pitched 42 games, 136 innings. He gave up 64 runs, walked 45 batters, made 59 errors, and struck out 70 batters. Michael (Mike) Ausley Maddux (Phillies) pitched 25 games, 89 innings. He gave up 41 runs, walked 34 batters, made 37 errors, and struck out 59 batters.

3. Convert this survey information into a pie chart. You surveyed 400 clients of Iron Works Gym to determine their preferences for new equipment, facilities, or services. Results were as follows: 175 clients want additional weightlifting equipment, 50 clients want child care available while they exercise, 75 clients want a sauna, 50 clients want more trainers, and 80 clients want a juice bar.

   Find the percentages and draw the pie, labeling it as Figure 4. Write an introduction. You can make up some details (for example, comparing some of the percentages to last year's) for the introduction.

4. Here is the organizational structure for Vortex Industries, a small textile company. Place this hierarchy into an organizational chart. Marilyn R. Smythe is the President. Jonathan M. Comas, Executive Vice President, reports to the President. Ursula Boyer, Computer Operations Chief, reports to the Executive Vice President. Rodriguez Malindas, Production Operations Chief, reports to the Executive Vice President. Robert Coleman, Production Supervisor, reports to the Production Operations Chief. Valerie Phatel, Computer Operations Assistant, reports to the Computer Operations Chief. Samuel R. Thomas, Computer Technician, reports to the Computer Operations Chief. Victor B. Garcia, secretary, reports to the Computer Technician. Miranda Felix, secretary, reports to the Computer Operations Assistant. Bryan Shiver, Technical Assistant, reports to the Production Operations Chief. Yolanda Yaseem, Office Manager, reports to Production Supervisor.

5. These are the steps for accessing the mainframe computer. Place them into a flowchart that uses arrows to point to the next step. First, you turn the computer on. Then you key "LOGIN." When the computer asks for your name, enter your name. When the computer asks you for your password, enter your password. Choose the item that you want to access from the main menu.

PURSUE AN IDEA

For each of the Pursue-an-Idea assignments, write an introduction that refers to the visual aid and explains the significance of the visual. Be sure to follow this chapter's guidelines for constructing visuals.

1. Draw the organizational hierarchy of an organization you are familiar with. For example, you could draw an organizational chart for one of the school clubs, the school administration, the town government, or some other business or political organization.

2. Think about some routine or procedure you follow regularly. Perhaps it's a routine you follow at work—closing a store, opening a store, or checking stock. Or perhaps it's a routine you follow at home—doing chores, taking care of a pet, or working on your car. Draw a flowchart of your routine.

3. Each night for a week, take note of the number of hours you spend doing one thing: watching TV, studying, talking on the phone, performing chores, working. Put one or more of these activities onto a bar graph. Then put the same activity on a line graph.

4. Compare your graphs in #3 with someone else's in your class whose numbers on the same activity differ. Put your information into a double bar graph and a double line graph. Be sure to label your figures and title them.

5. Prepare a double bar graph or line graph that compares your hours spent watching TV with hours spent studying.

6. Take notes on the time you spend engaged in five major activities of a typical Saturday. Your activities might include eating, shopping, sleeping, or studying. Put this information into a pie chart.

7. Prepare a table of your expenditures during a month. Consider items like food, gas, clothing, entertainment, and phone. If you're not responsible yet for some of your expenses, ask your parents to help you estimate expenses. Be sure to refer to this visual as a Table, not a Figure.

8. Prepare a verbal table for one of the following situations: a troubleshooting table for emergency first aid, a troubleshooting table for a piece of equipment, a biology chart that explains the classification of the animal kingdom, a computer chart that explains the description and function of a computer, a chart that lists five members of your class and tells the same things about each one (such as hobbies, career goals, and current job status).

9. Draw a diagram of an item you use often. Label the parts and write an introduction that refers to the visual and describes the parts.

10. Draw a diagram of something you are studying in science. Label the parts and write an introduction that refers to the visual and describes the parts.

Using Numbers

The following rules are generally accepted as guidelines to help you decide when to write numbers as figures and when to write numbers as words in technical documents.

1. Generally, use *figures* for numbers 10 and above. Use *words* for numbers one through nine.

> Olsen Community College presented 22 partial scholarships and 15 full scholarships to first-year students.
>
> Two of my cousins and four of my friends accepted part-time employment.

2. Use *figures* if a series contains numbers above and below 10.

> Her fortune included 5,498 acres of land, 173 paintings, 3 mansions, and 5 horses.

3. Use *figures* when several numbers (including fractions) are presented in a single sentence or in several related sentences.

> Fry 2 cups of sliced apples in ¾ cup of honey, ⅛ cup of apple cider vinegar, and 1 tablespoon of cinnamon.

4. Use *figures* for units of measurement. Note that the unit of measurement may be expressed as a word, an abbreviation, or a symbol.

18 meters	5⅓	4.25 liters	55 MPH
5.5 centimeters	66⅔	75 MHZ	35mm film
0.05 margin of error	14.4 K baud	32°	8″ × 10″

> 33% mark up ("%" sign preferred to the word "percent" in technical writing)

5. Use *figures* for fractions and decimals presented with whole numbers.

5⅓	66⅔	72.6	10.25

6. Use *figures* to express exact amounts of money.

$181.95	8¢	$0.95

7. Use *figures* for data presented in tables and illustrations.

Figure 1. Time Spent on Tasks

8. Use *figures* for addresses and dates.

> Route 5 Box 182   103 East Maple Street   January 3, 1865

9. Use *figures* to express age.

> 3 years old   man in his 20s   an 18-year-old woman

10. Use *figures* for identification numbers.

> The correct number is 378-18-3555.
>
> The engine number is JEMH00347WE99678.

11. Use *figures* for one of two numbers written next to each other.

sixteen 2-liter drinks   16 two-liter drinks

12. Use *figures* to indicate time not expressed with o'clock.

8:00 a.m.   12:10 p.m.

13. Use *figures* for statistics and scores.

The odds were 3 to 1 in her favor.

The Grover Bears won the basketball game 76–74.

14. Use *figures* for page and volume numbers.

Turn to page 45 in volume 2 of your manual.

15. Use *figures* and *words* for very large numbers (over 6 digits).

$6 trillion   4 million people   5.3 billion years

16. Use *words* at the beginning of the sentence. Rewrite awkward sentences so that the numbers are written as figures within the sentence.

Nine thousand seven hundred and sixty-six citizens signed the petition.

The petition contained 9,766 signatures.

17. Use *words* for indefinite or approximate numbers.

Over one hundred people attended.

Approximately fifty tickets were sold.

18. Use *words* for fractions not connected to whole numbers.

Approximately three fourths of the children have been vaccinated.

19. Use *words* for ordinals below 10. Use *figures* plus last letters of the ordinal for ordinals over 10.

third base   ninth inning   10th person   21st birthday

THE INSIDE TRACK: APPLY WHAT YOU HAVE LEARNED

Using the guidelines above, rewrite the following passages to present numbers as figures and numbers as words.

1. Penguin is the common name for fifteen species of marine birds. They live on five continents in the Southern Hemisphere. One penguin, the Galapagos, lives within six degrees of the equator. Penguins can swim through the water at speeds of up to twenty-five miles per hour. The largest species, the emperor penguin, ranges from three to four feet tall. The smallest, the Adelie, stands about two feet tall.

2. On the twenty-third of February in the year nineteen hundred and eighty seven, one hundred forty-two mallards were tagged off the coast of Florida. For five years, researchers tracked approximately seventy of the mallards over three hundred and ninety-seven miles. The ducks survived in temperatures down to minus ten degrees Celsius. A report was distributed to twenty-seven agencies in seven states. The research cost six thousand forty five dollars and fifty-six cents. It is estimated that seven and one half million mallards inhabit the southeastern area of the United States. Biologists estimate that ninety percent of the mallards follow predictable patterns of migration.

Instructions

Write-to-Learn

Think of the last time you had to follow a set of instructions. Maybe the instructions were from a teacher, a parent, an employer, or a manual. In a short journal entry, answer these questions: What were the circumstances under which you were asked to follow the instructions? Were the instructions easy to follow? If so, why? Were the instructions difficult to follow? If so, why? If the instructions were poorly written, what problems did they create and how did you handle those problems?

DEFINITIONS

active voice refers to a verb whose subject performs the action of the verb

cautions statements designed to keep a person from harming the mechanism he or she is working on or with

explanation information coming after a step and providing additional data to clarify the step

field test to try out or test your instructions on a small sample of people to see if the instructions are clear before you print final copies

imperative mood the form of a verb that signals a command; uses "you" or understood "you"

passive voice refers to a verb whose subject is "passive," receiving the action of the verb; formed by the verb "to be" plus the past participle

second person writing using "you" or an understood "you" as the subject

set of instructions a step-by-step listing of what actions to perform to complete a task

step one action in performing a set of instructions

warnings statements designed to keep a person from being harmed

First Recording

This page gives the basic steps for recording. You should practice them until you can do them without referring to the manual. To save time, we suggest you record for only two or three minutes.

The following page shows you how to playback the recording you made.

3CH OR 4CH

① Turn on your TV and tune it to the "VCR channel" (channel 3 or 4). The channel switch *(CH3/CH4)* on the back of the VCR and the channel selector on your TV must be set to the same channel to see the picture from the VCR.

② Press the *POWER* button on the VCR. (The indicator above the *POWER* button will light.)

③ Press the *VCR* button to turn on the VCR indicator in the display panel of the VCR. The VCR is now in the "VCR mode".

④ Insert a blank cassette with the safety tab intact. (The cassette-in indicator will light.)

Note: The VCR is automatically turned on when a cassette is inserted. The VCR automatically enters playback mode when a cassette without a safety tab is inserted. Be sure to check this tab before inserting a cassette. If a cassette without a safety tab is inserted, the VCR ejects the cassette when the *RECORD* button is pressed. Details on safety tabs are on page 11.

⑤ Press the *TAPE SPEED* button to select the tape speed. The tape speed indicator (*SP, LP* or *EP*) will appear in the display panel of the VCR. Use *EP* speed for normal recording. It will give you the best picture when using stop action and visible scan.

⑥ Make sure the *LINE/TUNER* switch is set to *TUNER*. The *TUNER* position is used for normal viewing and recording of the picture from the VCR tuner.

⑦ Select the channel that you want to record by pressing either the *CHANNEL* ▼ or ▲ button on the VCR or the number buttons on the remote control. (Remember, you must press two numbers on the remote control to enter a channel. For example, press "0", then "8" for channel 8.)

⑧ Press the *RECORD* button to start recording. The REC indicator will light.

⑨ Press the *STOP* button to stop recording.

Note: Press the *PAUSE* button to temporarily interrupt the recording. Press *RECORD* again to resume recording.

CAUTION: Avoid pausing for more than three or four minutes, because the spinning heads that do the recording are still in contact with the tape and will eventually wear off the active material. This can cause streaks or spots in the picture when you play the worn part of the tape (called dropouts).

After completing this chapter, you will be able to

- Analyze your audience's expectations and knowledge level
- Analyze the steps required for a set of instructions
- Choose an appropriate format for a set of instructions
- Choose appropriate words for writing steps
- Choose appropriate kinds of explanations
- Choose appropriate visual aids
- Write a set of instructions

"Chuck [the ball] like you're gonna throw a paper. When your arm gets here [Bennie shows him], just let go."

Bennie Rodriguez in the movie *Sandlot* uses these words to tell his new ballplayer, Smalls, how to throw a baseball. Smalls knows nothing about how to throw a ball. He is embarrassed, afraid the others are going to laugh at him. Bennie's tone is matter-of-fact and task-oriented—just what Smalls needs. Bennie's instructions are clear and simple, showing a knowledge of the throwing process and an understanding of his audience.

A **set of instructions** tells how to do something. To write clear instructions, writers must break down processes into a sequence of steps.

Audience: Who Reads Instructions?

WARM UP

Do you always read instructions before you attempt a procedure? Why or why not?

People who read instructions need to perform a task or need to understand how someone else performs that task. The waiter or waitress, asked to close the restaurant, needs to know the procedure for closing at night. The surveyor, measuring the road for underground pipes, needs to know how a transit works. You, playing a new Nintendo game, need to know how the controller manipulates your player.

Like Smalls in *Sandlot*, people reading instructions experience a variety of emotions. Most are anxious because they want to understand the procedure. Instructions, with their visual aids and technical language, can be intimidating. Some readers read instructions carefully, paying attention to every word. Some readers use the visuals, not the words. Other readers are impatient and try to go through the steps without reading all of them first.

Even though readers can be inattentive, they expect a lot from a set of instructions. They expect accuracy, precision, and proper sequencing of steps. Readers trust the writers of instructions. Some instructions—electrical installation and medical procedures, for example—can be matters of life or death. In these cases, readers trust writers with their lives and with the lives of others.

Because your reader trusts you, make sure your procedures are accurate and include enough detail. How much detail to include will depend on how knowledgeable your audience is about the process. A beginner, for example, will need more detail than someone with more experience. With good instructions, readers are reassured and motivated to keep reading carefully.

S T O P   A N D   T H I N K **9.1**

What would you have to tell a 4-year-old about making a peanut butter and jelly sandwich that you would not have to tell a person your age?

TECHNOLOGY UPDATE

Many companies are using interactive video to train employees. Instead of employees sitting in classes for 4–6 weeks, reading and studying from books, they sit in front of computer screens, interacting with the computer. The computer will repeat what the employee doesn't understand, and the experience is fun. The employee can learn at his or her own pace and need not spend 4–6 weeks listening to lectures.

Prewriting: Getting Started on Instructions

To get started on instructions, make sure you understand the sequence of events. Use one or more of these suggestions to help you analyze the process and come to a better understanding of it:

Figure 9.1 Sample Flowchart

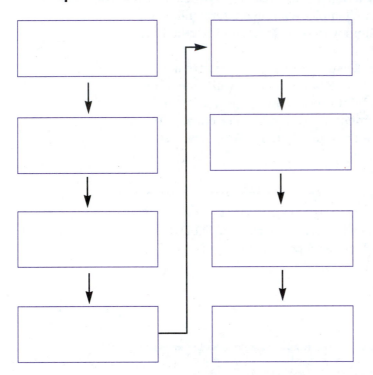

1. Fill in this flowchart with steps to the process. Inside the boxes, write what someone should do first, second, third, and so on. Try not to skip any steps. Add boxes or take away boxes as needed.

2. In your mind, work the process backwards. What is the purpose of the procedure? What is done last, next to the last, third to the last, and so on?

3. Watch a person performing this task for the first time. Take notes. What is the very first step? What is the most difficult step? What steps does the person misunderstand?

Organizing and Formatting Instructions

WARM UP

Look at the VCR instructions that open this chapter. What do you notice about how the instructions are laid out on the page? What special features do the instructions use? What have the writers done to make the instructions easy to follow?

Now that you have analyzed the steps for your set of instructions, you can organize your information into sections for your reader. Then you can place that information into an easy-to-read format.

Organizing Instructions

All instructions include steps of the procedures and appropriate explanations given in chronological order. Instructions often contain other parts as well.

Instructions usually include an introduction, but some do not. Manuals contain an introduction at the beginning but may not contain introductions for every part of the manual. Telling someone how to perform a standard operating procedure may not require a list of materials, but telling someone how to bake cookies would require a list of materials and ingredients. Telling someone how to use an appliance would require only familiarity with the appliance, not a list of materials. Telling someone how to answer questions on a job interview or how to get over the death of a pet would require a different structure from telling someone how to repot plants. Learning how to repot plants, however, might require **cautions** against actions that would harm the plant. Learning how to parachute would require stronger **warnings** to prevent injury.

Understanding your process will help you make decisions about content. Use Figure 9.2 to determine what sections to add to the basic steps.

Figure 9.2 What to Include in a Set of Instructions

PROVIDE	IF
Introduction	Your reader needs any or all of the following information: background information, context for the set of instructions, the purpose of your instructions (what the reader will be able to do when he or she finishes), whom the instructions are for, scope of the instructions (what the instructions cover and what they don't), organization of the instructions, something special about how to read the instructions, what assumptions you are making about reader's knowledge or ability, motivation to read carefully.
Definitions	Your reader must learn new terms to perform the procedure. More than six terms need a separate list or glossary; fewer than six terms need to be defined as you write.
List of Materials, Tools, or Ingredients	Your reader should gather materials, tools, or ingredients before beginning to follow your instructions.
Visuals	A picture, diagram, or flowchart would make the instructions easier to follow; also include visuals if the instructions are new or complicated.
Warnings	Your reader or others could get hurt if a step is overlooked or done incorrectly. Warnings should be written before the reader is likely to do anything dangerous and placed as close to where the reader needs them as possible. Often a symbol or visual aid signifying danger accompanies the warning.
Cautions	Your reader could damage equipment if a step is overlooked or done incorrectly. Cautions should be placed as close to where the reader needs them as possible before the reader is likely to do anything dangerous. Often a symbol or visual aid accompanies the caution.
Notes	Your reader's understanding would be aided by additional information. This information is not an essential step but should be included immediately after the step it is most closely related to.
More Explanation of Each Step	Your reader is performing the process for the first time, the procedure is complicated, or the reader needs to understand more to perform the procedure correctly.
Less Explanation of Each Step	Your reader has performed the process before, or the procedure is simple. You may also provide less explanation for each step of an emergency procedure where reading explanations might prevent the reader from acting quickly enough.

Formatting Instructions

Because readers are unpredictable and often impatient, you need to work hard to make it easy for them to read your set of instructions. Use plenty of white space to make instructions look accessible. Number your steps with Arabic numerals, and align the steps in a list.

Flowcharts and diagrams are practical visual aids for process reports. A flowchart can simplify a process and is especially useful for an intermediate reader, one who has performed this process before and needs only to be reminded about the sequence of steps. Diagrams and drawings are almost always used with a set of instructions. Sometimes different parts of a mechanism are shown at different times during the steps. (See Chapter 8 on Document Design and Visual Aids for help in making decisions about your visuals.) Get into the habit of referring to your visual aids with an explanatory statement such as "See Figure 1 to see the placement of buttons on the VCR." Instructions that include these referral statements remind the reader the visual is there and make the reader consider the visual at the proper time in the reading.

A simple set of instructions may include only a one-sentence introduction and a list of steps. More complex instructions require several sections and visual aids. Figure 9.3 shows options for formatting simple and more complex sets of instructions.

Figure 9.3 Variations in Formatting Instructions

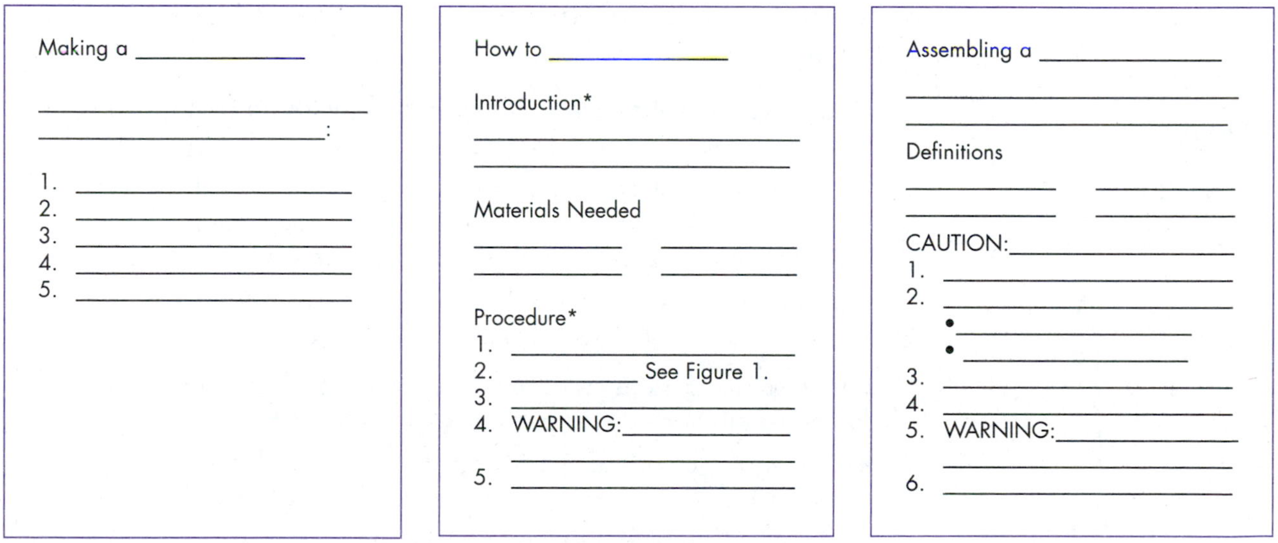

*These sections are not always labeled.

STOP AND THINK **9.2**

1. Why does the organization of a set of instructions change from one set to another?
2. How can page layout help someone read instructions?
3. What visual aids help readers understand instructions?

Composing Instructions

WARM UP **9.3**

Look at the model. Pick out the sentences that actually tell the reader to do something. What do you notice about the wording of these sentences? What do the other sentences do?

Format and visual aids may vary, but all instructions require a chronological sequence of steps. Most, except for instructions written for experienced readers, require explanations to accompany the steps.

Our sun is estimated to be 5 billion years old and has enough hydrogen fuel to supply its needs for 5 billion more years.

Steps

A **step** is the action a reader performs, what he or she actually does. Steps have a consistent and unique structure. Use the following guidelines for writing steps:

1. **Make sure steps proceed forward in time, with no backtracking to pick up a step that was forgotten**.
   - *Incorrect* (Backtracking): 1. Insert the key into the ignition switch. 2. Turn the key forward until you hear the engine hum. 3. Buckle your seat belt before you turn the key.
   - *Correct* (Forward in time): 1. Buckle your seat belt. 2. Insert the key. . . . 3. Turn the key forward. . . .

2. **Begin each step with an *active voice* verb in *imperative mood* (a command: Verb + What) using *second person*.**
   - *Incorrect* (No verb to start): The system needs to be cleaned with a tape cleaner.
   - *Correct* (Action verb to start): Clean the system with a tape cleaner.

   NOTE: Sometimes it's necessary to begin with a modifying word or phrase as in "Thoroughly *clean* the system..." *OR* "If the sound is garbled, *clean* the system..."

3. Use short sentences.

- *Incorrect* (Too long): Slide the brake lever(s) as close as possible towards the grip without limiting the operation of the brake levers or causing the end of the brake lever to extend beyond the end of the handlebar.
- *Correct* (Shorter sentences): Slide the brake lever(s) as close as possible toward the grip. Don't limit the operation of the brake levers. Do not cause the end of the brake lever to extend beyond the end of the handlebar.

4. Write only one instruction for each step.

- *Incorrect* (More than one step): Buckle your seat belt and depress the brake.
- *Correct* (One instruction per step): 1. Buckle your seat belt. 2. Depress the brake.

EXCEPTION: If two steps are so closely tied to each other in time, it may be easier for your reader to read them in the same step: Release the clutch. At the same time, press the accelerator.

5. Make sure each step is truly a step, something to do.

- *Incorrect* (Not a step): The rope will come back to you.
- *Correct* (Step): Grasp the rope when it comes back to you.

6. Unless pressed for space, keep in the natural articles "a," "an," and "the."

- *Incorrect* (Without articles): Send electrician notice to connect power to house.
- *Correct* (With articles): Send the electrician a notice to connect power to the house.

7. Place explanations *after* the step (if you need an explanation).

- *Incorrect* (Explanation before step): Make sure there is an equal distance between each chain stay tube and the wheel. Securely tighten the axle nuts.

NOTE: Even though "Make" is a verb, it is not a step. It *explains how* to securely tighten the axle nuts.

- *Correct* (Step beginning with action): Securely tighten the axle nuts. Make sure there is an equal distance between each chain stay tube and the wheel.

Explanations

An **explanation** is an extension of the step it explains. Explanations use the same number as the step they follow and are always written immediately *after* the step.

1. Step. Then explanation.
2. Step. Then explanation.
3. Step. Then explanation.

The number and type of explanations depend on your reader's prior experience with the set of instructions. Typical explanations include

What not to do and why. Do not place stray pencil marks on the answer sheet. The computerized scanner may read the stray mark as an error.

Significant details to help the reader understand why something is important. Rinse the boiled egg with cold water as soon as you remove it from boiling water. The cold water will cause the egg to contract from the shell, making it easier to peel the shell off the egg.

How to make a decision. Wrap a small section of hair around the wand. If you want curls to flip up, wrap the hair backwards (away from the shoulders). If you want curls to curve under, wrap the hair down (toward the shoulders).

NOTE: This step and explanation could also be written using the following format:

5. Wrap a small section of hair around the wand.

    a. If you want curls to flip up, wrap the hair backwards…

    b. If you want curls to curve under, wrap the hair down…

What will happen when the reader does something. **1)** Press *PROGRAM* on the remote control. The MENU will appear on the TV screen. **2)** To auto-scan for a channel, press *CHANNEL SCAN* on the remote control once. The tuner scans the channels stored in the tuner's memory, stopping on each channel for about two seconds.

More details on how. Tighten the axle nuts. Make sure they are tight. There must not be any space between the inner nut, the wheel slip and the axle nuts. If there is space, tighten more securely.

Quick definitions. Beat the eggs until frothy, or until they look like sea foam. *OR* The antenna is the "signal receiver" that picks up TV broadcasts.

NOTE: If there are a number of definitions, you need a separate section labeled definitions or glossary. If there are only a few, you can define them as you go or place them in the introduction.

Because some readers need more details than others, you must think carefully about how much explanation to add. To determine how much explanation is necessary, consider the answers to these questions:

- What *shouldn't* readers do? Why? (What did you do wrong the first time you performed the process?)
- Would readers be more likely to perform the steps correctly if they knew the significance of the action, the reason for performing the step, or more about the process?

> *Be careful that you write accurately rather than much.*
>
> ERASMUS

- Would it help readers to point out what should happen when they execute a step? (The first time you performed the process, how did you know you had performed a step correctly?)
- Does the reader need help making a decision? Should some steps be subdivided with *If X happens, do this. If Y happens, do that?* (See curling iron example on page 180.)
- Would the reader benefit from a quick definition?
- What questions will a reader have? (What questions did you have the first time you performed this process?)
- What are the most crucial steps, the steps that absolutely must be done correctly?

Precise Details

Make sure you have included enough precise, specific details to show your reader what to do. Details might include distances, sizes, places, or time.

- *Incorrect* (Insufficient): The bike chain should have correct tension. Make sure there is some movement or "give" in the chain.
- *Correct* (Sufficient): The bike chain should have correct tension. Make sure there is ⅜" *of movement* or "give" between the front and rear sprockets.
- *Incorrect* (Insufficient): Connect the short wire from the TV/Game Switch Box to the antenna terminals on your television set.
- *Correct* (Sufficient): Connect the short *twin-lead wire* from the TV/Game Switch Box to the *VHF terminals* on your television set.
- *Incorrect* (Insufficient): Switch the computer on.
- *Correct* (Sufficient): Turn on the power switch. The power switch, *shaped like a light switch*, is located on the *back right side of the CPU*.

Field Test

Always *field test* your instructions by asking several people to try them out before you send out your final copy. Your field testers can provide you with valuable feedback by noting wording that isn't clear, steps out of sequence, or steps left out.

S T O P A N D T H I N K

1. How are steps written?
2. What kind of information do explanations contain?
3. What kind of information makes instructions precise?
4. Why is it important to field test instructions?

1. Readers of instructions can be inattentive readers, so writers must learn to compensate with carefully planned writing. Readers trust writers—to be accurate and to be safety conscious. Readers who have no experience with the process need more detail and more explanation than readers with prior experience.

2. Thoroughly understand the process yourself before you try to write about it.

3. All instructions contain an itemized list of steps. Most instructions contain an introduction and visual aid. Whether or not to include a list of materials, visual aids, warnings, cautions, notes, or definitions will depend on the process you are analyzing.

4. Instructions, always organized chronologically, are written in short sentences using active voice and imperative mood. Each step must show an action. Explanations that follow steps tell what not to do, why a step is performed, what the results of a step are, and how to complete a step. Provide explanation depending on your audience's prior experience. Instructions should provide enough details to enable the reader to perform the step correctly and safely.

Editing and Revision Checklist

✓ Do I thoroughly understand the procedure I am writing about?

✓ Did I consider using a visual aid?

✓ If I did use a visual aid, did I follow the guidelines for using visuals in Chapter 8 on pages 148–150?

✓ Did I field test my set of instructions?

✓ Did I consider using an introduction, list of materials, cautions, warnings, and notes?

✓ Have I written steps that
  ✓ move forward in time?
  ✓ begin with a verb that commands?
  ✓ use short sentences?
  ✓ have only one instruction per step?
  ✓ are truly steps, things to do?
  ✓ keep the articles "a, an," and "the"?
  ✓ place explanations *after* the steps?

✓ Have I written explanations appropriate to my reader's level of experience?

✓ Have I considered including explanations that
  ✓ explain what not to do and why?
  ✓ include significant details to help the reader understand why a step is important?
  ✓ tell the reader how to make a decision?
  ✓ include descriptions of what will happen when the reader does something?
  ✓ give enough details on how something should be done?
✓ Have I included enough precise details—such as distances, sizes, places, or time?

APPLY WHAT YOU HAVE LEARNED

1. What *kind* of information would make these instructions more specific?
   a. Rotate the tool several times around the wire leaving the spring closed.
   b. Draw part of an oval for the head.
   c. If the fitting has a tub spout, make a hole in the wall.
   d. Clean your room before you leave.
   e. Beat the meringue until stiff peaks form.
   f. Place the selvages of the material together.

2. Break up each sentence below into shorter sentences that reflect one step per sentence.
   a. Remove the cover from the mike, press the transmit button on your mike and by using a small screwdriver with a plastic or wooden handle adjust the transmitting frequency.
   b. Take the two upper sections of the handle and using the shortest bolt ($1/4 \times 1 3/4$), with a nut provided, fasten together as shown in the illustration in Figure 1.
   c. Hold the short molding piece up against the edge of the corner shelf and fasten it to the angle brackets using a #6 $\times 7/16$" large-head wood screw through the brackets and into the groove that is in the short molding piece.
   d. Read the passage and locate all the nouns, underlining them with a single line.

3. Rewrite these steps to begin each with verbs in *active voice* and *imperative mood*. The "You" can be understood.
   a. The cook should touch the AUTO DEFROST pad in order to begin the defrosting process.
   b. When you wish to play, you should press the *Start* button.
   c. The aquarium floor requires a layer of gravel that, sloping from the back to the front, is about six to eight centimeters deep at the front wall.
   d. We want you to come to the front of the room and use the podium.

4. How many steps are included in each of these sentences? Rewrite the ones that include more than one step.

  a. Sterilize the infant's bottles, nipples, and caps in a kettle and then fill them directly from the can of formula.

  b. Press the transmit button, talk into the receiver, and turn the radio dial up and down until you find the radio-transmitting frequency in your area.

  c. Enter wages, salaries, and tips for each person, from Form 1040A, line 7.

  d. Take two aspirin and call me in the morning.

  e. To apply decals, cut each out, dip in lukewarm water for 20 seconds, and hold in place until it uncurls.

  f. Press the Command key. At the same time press S for Save.

5. Are these steps, explanations or cautions/warnings?

  a. When paddling, keep the canoe in line with the current.

  b. Make sure that the supply voltage matches the voltage specified on the rating plate.

  c. Separate dark clothes from light clothes to prevent colors from running.

  d. Do not overload your dryer. For efficient drying, clothes need to tumble freely.

  e. Designate a high number of rings (10 or more) for your modem calls.

  f. Install the stem correctly or an accident can occur.

  g. To determine how tight the fasteners need to be, see the Torque Range Chart in the back of this book.

  h. Before you ride the bicycle, check the laws in your area. The reflectors and any lights must operate according to the laws.

6. In groups of two or three, critique this set of instructions and make revisions. What kind of visuals would you recommend? This activity is also available on the computer application disk as **TEXT9A**.

How to Administer Rescue Breathing

Warning: Make sure the victim's tongue does not block the airway.

- Insert the mouth barrier mechanism over the victim's mouth.

- Make sure to turn the victim's face up first and tilt the head back and lift the victim's chin. The mouth should open and create a pathway for air to flow freely over the tongue.

- You are supposed to seal your mouth over the victim's mouth. For a child, seal your mouth over the nose and mouth. If the victim is a child, do not pinch the nostrils.

- An adult victim should have his/her nostrils pinched together.

- Look to see if the victim's chest rises after you blow into the victim's mouth to fill the lungs with air. For a child, blow over the nose **and** mouth simultaneously to force as much air in as possible.

- Remove your mouth, take a deep breath and count to five. During this time, watch to make sure the victim's chest falls as the breath escapes from the lungs.

Warning: Oh, by the way, be sure to use the barrier. It protects you from possible exposure to the victim's bodily fluids.

- Blow into the victim's mouth again.

- After clearing the obstruction, attempt again to breathe in.

  —Straddle the victim with one knee on either side of his/her legs.

  —Place the heel of your hand on the victim's abdomen, midway between the ribcage and belly button.

  —Push upward quickly five times.

- If the victim's chest does not rise when you blow in, check for blockage in the victim's mouth.

- If still unable to get air in, assume obstruction and proceed with abdominal thrusts.

  —Look in the mouth.

  —Use your finger to sweep for anything in the mouth.

  —If you find something, pull it out.

These instructions will show you how to save someone's life if he or she has stopped breathing. Remember, if your first attempts to restore breathing fail, **keep repeating the procedure until a doctor or medical team arrives.**

CONSIDER THIS CASE

Here is a letter Willard sent home describing how he and his tentmates built a fire. What mistakes did the director make in giving them directions? Write a standard set of instructions telling how to build a fire properly. Add appropriate visuals and any details you may already know about building fires.

Dear Mom,

   We built a campfire last night. First, we found lots of wood and a good place to build the fire. The director said it couldn't be too close to the tents or to trees with low branches because we might start a forest fire. Terri and Spencer found a big log. But the director said it wouldn't burn well because it was wet. So Terri and Spencer finally found some big tree branches. The director said they would do but we had to cut them up with the hatchet. We finally chopped up the wood enough, in 1–2 ft lengths like the director said, and placed them alongside one another where we thought the fire should be.

Then we tried striking matches to light the logs, but they wouldn't light. The director said we needed smaller pieces of wood to get the fire started, pieces even as small as sticks in various lengths—from a few inches to 6 or 7 inches long. And then he said we needed something called kindling. Kindling, he said, could be anything from pieces of bark to scraps of paper to dry leaves—as long as it was dry. He said the kindling was supposed to catch fire first because it was so small. He said the sticks would catch fire second and then the smaller logs and then the larger logs.

The director left. We found some small sticks and kindling. We piled them all up on one another. Kareem found a good, dry tree branch and threw it on top. We found some matches in the director's backpack and lit the kindling. The director was right. It did catch fire fast, but it burned out without ever lighting the sticks.

I was beginning to think this fire was never going to be built when the director came over to see how we were doing. He looked a little disappointed and said: "Boys, you have to keep the bigger logs out and feed them into the fire gently after it has gotten started. Now, take some of those real small logs and build a pyramid with them. Stand three or four of the smaller logs on end and make them touch. Then light the kindling—lots of kindling. The fire from the kindling will rise and light those small logs at the top, where they touch. Then when they light, you can feed in some larger logs. The larger logs will burn slowly and you keep the fire going by feeding in the larger logs."

The director left again and we began building the pyramid. After a while, we finally had a fire going! We started whooping and hollering and didn't notice the pinestraw burning close to BJ's tent. Luckily, the director came back in time to rake back the burning pinestraw. And then he told us that we should have cleared a circle around the fire so that there was no wood, no pinestraw, no paper, no sticks, or anything that could catch fire. "You have to watch a fire," he said. "You can't start playing around and ignore it!"

PURSUE AN IDEA

In small groups, write a set of instructions on any of the following processes (or some other process you are familiar with). Be sure to analyze your audience, follow the guidelines for composing instructions, and provide ample explanations.

making a bed	using a calculator
changing oil/tires	setting up a tent
lifting weights	playing a video game/any game
setting up an aquarium	building a model
playing any sport	brushing/flossing teeth
mowing the lawn	constructing any craft
administering first aid	taking pictures
changing a diaper	cleaning a room
creating artwork	

Clarity

Good technical writing is clear. To make your writing clear, follow these suggestions:

1. **Use traditional *S–V–MODIFIERS*, *S–V-OBJECT*, or *S–V–COMPLEMENT* word order.**
   - *Incorrect:* Over the river and two streets down is where we live.
   - *Correct:* We live over the river and two streets down.
   - *Incorrect:* The dishes she washed.
   - *Correct:* She washed the dishes.
   - *Incorrect:* Windy was the day.
   - *Correct:* The day was windy.

2. **Write moderately short sentences (12–24 words).**
   - *Incorrect:* The registration procedure begins with the student making an appointment with his or her advisor at which time the advisor and student will discuss the student's career goals, placement test scores, and transcripts to determine a schedule of classes that the advisor will enter into the computer and that the student will pay for before the registration period ends—that is, unless the computers are down, in which case the student will have to come back another time.
   - *Correct:* The registration procedure begins with the student making an appointment with his or her advisor. At this time, the advisor and student will discuss career goals, placement test scores, and transcripts to determine a schedule of classes. Next the advisor will enter the schedule into the computer. The student will pay for the classes by the end of the registration period. If the computers are down, the student will have to come back.

3. **Place the main idea (the subject or topic) first.**
   - *Incorrect:* Kittens like to chase balls of string around on the floor. They also enjoy chasing their mothers' tails. Kittens like to pretend they are attacking something that's hiding under a table. Kittens like to play.
   - *Correct:* Kittens like to play. They like to chase balls of string around on the floor. They also enjoy chasing their mothers' tails. Kittens like to pretend they are attacking something that's hiding under a table.

4. **Use *active voice*—unless you have a good reason to use *passive voice*.**
   - *Incorrect:* The new computers were purchased by the School Board.
   - *Correct:* The School Board purchased the new computers.

   (See also Chapter 11, pages 223–225, The Inside Track: Active Voice and Passive Voice)

5. Use parallel structure.

- *Incorrect:* Orientation consisted of the following activities:

  meeting our advisor

  tour the campus

  placement tests

  the president of the school greeting us

- *Correct:* Orientation consisted of the following activities:

  meeting our advisor

  touring the campus

  taking placement tests

  meeting the president of the school

  (See also Chapter 5, pages 102–104 The Inside Track: Parallelism)

6. Use *first person* ("I" or "we") whenever possible.

- *Incorrect:* The defective parts were returned to the company.
- *Correct:* We returned the defective parts to the company.

7. Choose precise nouns and verbs.

- *Incorrect:* Last night the local school team won the football game against a nearby rival.
- *Correct:* Wednesday, October 16, 19--, the Midland Junior Varsity Bears defeated the Chocowan Junior Varsity Mountain Lions 26 to 0.

INSIDE TRACK: APPLY WHAT YOU HAVE LEARNED

Using the suggestions presented above, rewrite this paragraph to make the sentences and the message clearer.

First he hoed a small area until the dirt was broken up. Then he raked out the clumps of grass, pulling up those stubborn weeds. The fertilizer was lightly put on and worked into the ground with the hoe. Next, plastic stuff was placed all over the plot of land and stuck to the ground at intervals of three feet to keep the grass from growing and to allow the rain to drain through and bring needed moisture to the roots. Then holes were cut in the plastic stuff, not too far apart. Francois planted some flowers through the plastic stuff into the ground. Then over the plastic stuff and around the plants pebble rocks were placed to help hold down the plastic and so that the area would look neat. Francois made planting a garden look easy.

Other Informative Reports

CHAPTER 10 OBJECTIVES

After completing this chapter, you will be able to

● Write two types of summaries

● Write an abstract

● Write a mechanism description

● Write a trip report

● Write an incident report

Business and industry use many kinds of specialized short reports. Five of the most common are presented in this chapter: summary, abstract, mechanism description, trip report, and incident report.

Summary and Abstract

A **summary** or **abstract** is a condensed version of a longer document. When you write an essay, you are asked to generate details to develop or support a thesis and a number of topic sentences. Summaries call on writers to do just the opposite: to keep the general information and leave out all except the most important of the details. Abstracts are more condensed than summaries, reducing documents to a succinct thesis. Both summaries and abstracts require a writer to separate general information from specific and to make judgements about what information is important enough to keep. The length of the summary or abstract depends on the needs and expectations of the audience.

Many reports begin with an abstract or summary. By condensing the highlights of the report before the audience reads the details, they save your co-workers time and work.

Figure 10.1 contains two summaries and an abstract of "Printers For the Road" below. One summary is longer than the other. Read them both. What has been left out from the original? What information has been left in? How does the abstract differ from the summaries?

PRINTERS FOR THE ROAD

I tested four portable printers and found that portability and capability are on opposite ends of the seesaw. The better the printer, the larger and heavier it is. The smaller the printer, the slower and more limited it is. It's an adventure in compromise, and it's difficult to find a winner.

The two most capable machines are Hewlett-Packard's 4.3-pound DeskWriter 310 and Apple's 4.5-pound Portable StyleWriter. The $379 DeskWriter 310 is an interesting bird. In its most portable configuration, it measures 2.5 inches high by 12 inches wide by 5.75 inches deep. It also holds just one sheet of paper at a time; you must hand-feed the printer for multipage documents. An optional ($99) sheet feeder accepts up to 60 sheets. Another $49 buys a kit that enables the printer to print in color—a nice plus.

Apple's $289 Portable StyleWriter is a bit bulkier than the DeskWriter 310. The StyleWriter also handles just one sheet of paper at a time; a 100-sheet feeder costs $85. The Portable StyleWriter can't print in color—in fact, it can't even print in grayscale. True, most people don't print scanned images in their hotel rooms, but I'd bet many of them print graphs from spreadsheet programs or business graphics from presentation packages. The Portable StyleWriter is not suited to these jobs; think of it as a text-only printer. You could work around the lack of gray-scale output by formatting graphs to use patterns rather than colors or gray shades, but given these compromises you might be better off buying the HP DeskWriter 310 instead.

The $399 Citizen America Notebook Printer II weighs a little more than 2 pounds and is the only portable printer tested that can hold more than one sheet of paper (it holds 5). The Notebook Printer II has a unique emulation mode that lets it imitate an Apple StyleWriter II. With the printer in this mode, you can use the StyleWriter II driver (included with System 7, but not with the Notebook Printer II) to print scanned images using Apple's GrayShare technology; the scheme works reasonably well. The printer can also print in color using Citizen's driver, but don't bother—the quality is poor.

Finally, there's GCC Technologies' $329, 2½-pound WriteMove II. This printer's output isn't bad, but loading paper is guaranteed to frustrate. The Notebook Printer II is a better miniprinter.

I can't enthusiastically recommend any of the four portables tested. If you need occasional hard copy when on the road, consider using your PowerBook's modem to fax a document to the hotel where you're staying. If you need better quality or tighter security, then consider HP's DeskWriter 310. It strikes the best balance on the portability/capability seesaw.

Portable Printers at a Glance

Company	Phone	Product	List Price	Number of Fonts	Paper Capacity? Optional Feeder Capacity (in sheets)	Batteries Included/Pages per Charge	Weight (in pounds)
Apple Computer	408/996-1010, 800/767-2775	Portable StyleWriter	$289*	39	1/100	yes/50	4.5
Citizen America	310/453-0614, 800/477-4683	Notebook Printer II	$399	0	5/NA	no/50	2.1
GCC Technologies	617/275-5800, 800/422-7777	WriteMove II	$329	0	1/NA	yes/16	2.5
Hewlett-Packard	800/752-0900	DeskWriter 310	$379	35	1/60	no/100	4.3

NA = not applicable. *Vendor's estimated street price.

Figure 10.1 Sample Summaries

> The first paragraph introduces the source (the author's name and the title of the article) and the thesis of the article.

> The second paragraph includes the next two main ideas and significant details.

> The third paragraph includes the next two main ideas and significant details.

> The conclusion includes a brief quotation and ends on the same idea as the original.

LONG SUMMARY OF "PRINTERS FOR THE ROAD"

Jim Heid in "Printers for the Road" reviews his top choices for portable printers. Heid claims none of his four choices represent the ideal printer and notes that the heavier printers offer more flexibility and more features.

The Hewlett-Packard DeskWriter ($379, 4.3 pounds) and Apple Portable StyleWriter ($289, 4.5 pounds) are Heid's top two choices. Both printers print one sheet at a time but can print more with the purchase of additional sheet feeders. An additional kit will allow the DeskWriter to print in color, whereas the StyleWriter cannot print in color or in gray-scale.

The Citizen America Notebook Printer II ($399, 2 pounds) and GCC Technologies' WriteMove II ($329, 2.5 pounds) are Heid's third and fourth choices. The Notebook Printer II is lightweight, can hold up to five sheets of paper, and can imitate the StyleWriter to print gray-scale images and color (but color is of poor quality). The WriteMove II is an adequate printer but loading paper is frustrating.

While Heid admits he "can't enthusiastically recommend" any one of these printers," he says the DeskWriter 310 "strikes the best balance on the portability/capability seesaw."

> The first sentence identifies the source. Sentences two and three restate the article's thesis. The body includes only the main ideas. The conclusion ends on the same idea as the original.

SHORT SUMMARY OF "PRINTERS FOR THE ROAD"

Jim Heid in "Printers for the Road" tests four portable printers. He reports that the heavier printers tend to be faster and less limited than the smaller ones. He ranks the following printers from most capable to least capable:

* Hewlett-Packard's 4.3-pound DeskWriter 310: $379
* Apple's 4.5-pound Portable StyleWriter: $289
* Citizen America's 2.0-pound Notebook Printer II: $399
* GCC Technologies' 2.5-pound WriteMove II: $329

Even though the DeskWriter is Heid's first choice, he says that none of the four choices are ideal.

> The abstract includes only the source and the most important information from the article: the ranking of the computers.

ABSTRACT OF "PRINTERS FOR THE ROAD"

Jim Heid in "Printers for the Road" ranks Hewlett-Packard's 4.3-pound DeskWriter 310 ($379) as the best printer. Apple's 4.5-pound Portable StyleWriter ($289) is a close second. The Citizen America's 2.0-pound Notebook Printer II ($399) and GCC Technologies' 2.5-pound WriteMove II ($329) rank as his third and fourth choices.

To write a summary,

1. Include the thesis, or the main point, of the original in your first sentence.

2. Make it clear what you are summarizing early in the summary. When summarizing an article, you can introduce this information by including the name of the author and the title of the article in the first sentence. If you are summarizing a speech or a meeting, you can give credit in the opening sentence.

3. After you have determined the thesis, find the main ideas of the original. Look for the topic sentences that support the thesis.

4. Decide if your audience needs a few details or only the main ideas.

   a. For longer summaries, pick out only those details that are especially important.

   b. For short summaries, leave out all details.

   c. For abstracts, include only the most important general ideas. Be concise. Reduce the original to the thesis in a few sentences.

5. Reproduce the author's ideas in proportion to the original emphasis. If the author spent four paragraphs on one topic and two paragraphs on another, try to make your summary give equal time and emphasis. For example, you would not include more information from the two-paragraph topic than from the four-paragraph topic. You would keep your summary information proportional to the original.

6. Write in present tense.

7. Be sure to paraphrase, not copy word for word.

8. Quote sparingly, if at all, and use quotation marks correctly.

9. End on the same idea as the original.

10. Provide adequate transition to keep the summary from sounding choppy.

DO NOT include too many details.

DO NOT give your opinion about the information contained in the summary, unless asked to do so. A summary should be an objective presentation of what you read or what happened.

TO GET STARTED writing a summary, try one of these:

1. If you are summarizing an oral presentation, take notes during the presentation or as soon after as you can. This way you are less likely to forget.

2. If you are summarizing something written, read the document at least twice. As you read for the third time, cross out everything (all the details) except the main ideas. Paraphrase what is left. For longer summaries, go back and choose a few important details to include. For abstracts, condense the paraphrased material. See Chapter 15 for more information on paraphrasing.

The first coin-operated telephone was patented in 1889 by William Gray.

Mechanism Description

A **mechanism description** describes the main parts of a device or mechanism. It tells the purpose of the mechanism and overall design, what the various parts of the mechanism are, what they look like, and what their function is. In composing mechanism descriptions, writers are called upon to observe details, to understand the purpose of the device, and to separate the mechanism into its relevant parts.

Mechanism descriptions are used in catalogs, in instruction manuals, and in employee training. A description of the mechanism can orient workers to the various parts before they operate it.

Figure 10.2 is a mechanism description of a common household item, a hand-held can opener. What kind of information is included in the introduction to this report?

Figure 10.2 Sample Mechanism Description

> The opening paragraph provides an overall physical description of the mechanism, identifies the purpose of the mechanism, and previews the parts to be discussed.

> Each section includes a detailed physical description and explains the function of each part.

> Notice the attention to precision: the measurements, the color descriptions, and the location of parts.

HAND-HELD CAN OPENER

A hand-held can opener is used to open standard aluminum and tin cans in which food is stored. It will open cans with a ⅛-inch lip around the rim and will not open cans (like soda cans) with a smooth rim. The hand-held can opener (see Figure 1) consists of the following parts: handle, blade and gear, and turning knob.

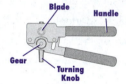

Figure 1. Can Opener

Handle
The handle consists of two 3-inch stainless steel moveable prongs that extend beyond the cutting mechanism. Each prong is encased in a 2¼-inch white plastic sheath to protect it from rust and to make it easier to grip. The prongs of the handle are pressed together by the user's hand to place the blade over the lip on the top of the can and to pierce the top of the can.

Blade
The blade, opposite the gear, is a ⅛-inch diameter circle, approximately the size of a penny and made of gray metal. The outer edge of the circle is sharp, allowing the blade to cut the lid off the can.

Gear
The gear, located directly under the turning knob, is on the back of the can opener. Approximately ½ inch in diameter, or the size of a penny, it is made of stainless steel. Attached to the turning knob, the gear is placed under the lip of the can to grip the can.

Turning Knob
The turning knob is a 2¼-inch-long rectangular lever used to move the blade along the outer edges of the can. Located on the side opposite the blade and gear, it is made of stainless steel. The user turns the knob which, in turn, rotates the blade.

To write a mechanism description,

1. Decide which parts of the description are most important to your audience.

2. Open with **a)** an overall physical description of the mechanism (nothing detailed here), **b)** a statement that identifies the general purpose of the mechanism (i.e., What is it designed to do?), and **c)** a preview of the parts of the mechanism.

3. Divide the mechanism into its parts and discuss each part under a separate heading. Use the proper names of the parts, but if the parts do not have a proper label, make up a label that fits. Place headings in the same order you used in the preview list.

4. Provide a precise physical description of the parts of the mechanism. Include things such things as size, color, location (where parts can be found), and material (what the mechanism is made of).

5. Include the purpose or function of each part. What is this part supposed to do?

6. Provide a drawing of the mechanism.

7. Use active voice, where possible, although passive voice may be your only choice to describe function.

8. Use **spatial** organization through space: left to right, right to left, top to bottom, bottom to top.

DO NOT explain how to operate this mechanism. Instead, describe what it does, what it looks like, what its parts are, what the parts look like, and what each part does.

DO NOT overload sentences with too much information.

TO GET STARTED on a mechanism description, look at the mechanism closely. Pretend that you have to describe this device to someone on the telephone who has never seen it before. Take notes, describing in detail what every part looks like.

Trip Report

Trip reports tell supervisors and co-workers what was gained from a business trip. Often businesses send workers to conferences to learn the latest developments in their field. Sometimes associates visit other places of business to negotiate deals or to learn about their operations. A trip is an investigation, a research mission whose findings must be shared with other members of the organization.

Trip reports have an element of description, but they are more like a condensed **narrative.** Often the report does not include everything about the trip, but includes only those parts that are most critical to your organization—those parts that your supervisors and co-workers will find most helpful. In this way the trip report is similar to the summary because it asks you to pick out what is most important from what is least important.

Figure 10.3 is a trip report from Linda Thompson to her supervisor relating the important findings of an insurance conference. Read the report. Why doesn't Thompson tell her supervisor how to fill out claim forms? Why do you think the report includes only the new policy changes?

Figure 10.3 Sample Trip Report

> The report opens with the dates and purpose of the trip. The last sentence in the introduction previews the rest of the report.

> Each major section summarizes information that will benefit Thompson's audience.

> The Conclusion sums up Thompson's assessment of the trip.

> The Recommendation makes a suggestion about what should be done with the information gained from the trip.

MEMO

TO: Cristina Santana
FROM: Linda Thompson
DATE: 5 November 19--
SUBJECT: Medical Providers HHII conference

The Medical Providers HHII Conference was held in Greensboro, North Carolina, on 28 October 19--. The conference featured speakers from various insurance groups. The seminars focused on new policy changes and the correct way to file a claim. Few changes have been made in filing claims, but Medicaid, Blue Cross Blue Shield of North Carolina, and Workers' Compensation have implemented new policies that are already in effect.

Medicaid of North Carolina
Effective 1 January 19--, Carolina Access requires that a patient be referred by the primary care physician assigned to him or her. The primary care physician's name will appear on the front of the Medicaid card. The referring physician's authorization number must appear on the claim form for payment of benefits.

Blue Cross Blue Shield
Effective 1 November 19--, co-payment to a specialty practice has been changed from $10.00 to $20.00 per visit. Patients are responsible for paying their co-payment on the day services are rendered.

Workers' Compensation
Effective 1 January 19--, treatment for on-the-job injuries will not be covered if treatment was administered by a physician's assistant (P.A.). All claims in which patients were treated by a physician's assistant will be denied.

Conclusion
The seminars were not as informative as they have been in the past, but they gave me an opportunity to meet with other insurance agents, many of whom I have spoken with over the phone. Speaking with them gave me a chance to understand how other physician's offices are run.

Recommendation
I recommend that we circulate the new policy changes among office personnel and mail letters to clients announcing the changes.

To write a trip report,

1. Report on what your audience will find most useful. This means you do not have to include the details of the entire trip, only those things most appropriate to the audience. Use only as much detail as your audience requires.

2. Cover the Reporter's Questions as you write the report: Who? What? When? Where? Why?

3. Set up a list in your introduction that previews the rest of the report.

4. Use bulleted lists for important events or knowledge gained.

5. Decide whether your report needs Conclusions and/or Recommendations. Some trip reports require Conclusions instead of Recommendations, or Conclusions with Recommendations.

   ● Use Conclusions to sum up the benefits of the trip.
   ● Use Recommendations if you have further action to recommend.

6. Choose between chronological order or order of importance for your report.

7. Use "I" or "we" to make the report sound natural.

8. Use active voice to report on what happened during the trip.

DO NOT include all the details of the trip.

TO GET STARTED on a trip report, keep notes during the trip. Collect brochures and/or conference guides, if available. Before the trip, find out from your supervisor what the purpose of the trip is and what you are expected to learn. Make sure you investigate these concerns during your trip.

Incident Report

Incident reports, also called accident reports, report on an unusual incident or occurrence. Often the incident is an accident, but the incident could be something else, a surprise inspection, an angry employee getting out of hand, or a near accident. When police write down the details of your fender bender, they are writing an incident report. When your teacher writes you up for throwing paper airplanes in class, he or she is writing an incident report.

An incident report is a narrative that describes a sequence of events. The report must be carefully written to reflect what really happened, for it can become legal evidence used in court. It must also be written to accommodate a variety of readers. Figure 10.4 recounts an injury at a day-care center. Possible readers include parents, supervisors, and insurance agents—maybe even lawyers or a judge if parents find the day-care provider negligent.

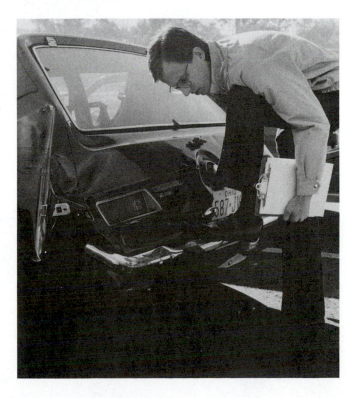

Figure 10.4 Sample Incident Report

> Paragraph one summarizes the incident and tells when it took place.

> The Description provides more details. It answers the major questions: Who? What? Where? When? and Why? It reads like a narrative and covers the incident from the very beginning to the end.

> The Outcome tells what happened as a result of the incident. It may repeat part of what was stated in the Discussion.

> The Conclusion tells what has been learned as a result of this experience and what will help prevent another similar incident.

INCIDENT OF INJURY AT TINY TOT DAY CARE

Summary

On July 13, 1992, David Lechworth was bitten by another child at Tiny Tot Day Care. Miss Holland cleaned the wound, and there was no permanent damage. Mrs. Olsen informed both parents of the incident. The report was filed in the permanent records of both children.

Description

On July 13, 1992, Miss Holland and Mrs. Olsen were supervising a group of 10 children on the playground. At 10:15 a.m., David cried out loudly and ran to Miss Holland. David cried hard enough to give himself hiccups. With tears in his eyes, he showed his arm to Miss Holland. Miss Holland comforted David by picking him up in her arms and holding him. Miss Holland then took David inside to wash the wound caused by the bite.

While inside, David told Miss Holland who had bitten him. Apparently the other child wanted the wagon David was using. The other child grabbed David and then bit him on the upper right arm. There was no blood, but the skin was slightly broken. The area was cleaned with soap and water and then dried.

David returned to the playground but stayed away from the child who had bitten him. Mrs. Olsen and Miss Holland talked to the other child about how much it hurts to be bitten and what he is allowed to bite.

Outcome

No permanent damage was done to David's arm. Incident reports were filed in the permanent records of both children. Parents of both children were informed of the incident.

Conclusion

In the future, both children will be watched more closely. Since biting is a common problem with this age group, it is important to know 1) which children are under stress and therefore more likely to bite and 2) indirect guidance techniques to help eliminate such aggressive behavior.

To write an incident report,

1. Begin your report with a quick summary of what happened.

2. Add a Background heading if you think background information (events leading up to the incident) would be helpful for your reader.

NOTE: Some incident reports fuse the summary and background together and do not use a separate heading for this part, if it is short.

3. Under Description, tell exactly what happened—in chronological order. Include sufficient details for multiple audiences: supervisors, customers, insurance companies, judges, lawyers, parents, victims. Be sure to cover the Reporter's Questions: Who? What? When? Where? Why? Also answer the question: How?

4. Be completely honest and objective in your recording of data. (See Chapter 11 p. 213 for a discussion of objectivity).

5. Use the Outcome to tell the observable results of the incident.

6. Use the Conclusion to tell what was learned from the incident, what to think about next time, or what can be done to prevent a repeat incident.

7. Keep an objective tone throughout.

DO NOT include information that you cannot verify.

TO GET STARTED on an incident report, take careful notes about evidence you see. Interview people who have some knowledge of the incident.

PURSUE AN IDEA

For each assignment, review the model in this chapter and the guidelines for writing each report.

1. Write a long summary, a short summary and an abstract of an article on one of the following: an article from a magazine in a field that interests you, a chapter of a textbook, this chapter (Chapter 10), a sporting event, a meeting, a TV show, a movie, a classroom lecture, a speech.

2. Make a list of 5–10 mechanisms you know well. These mechanisms could be something you use at work, at home, or at school. Consider using household appliances such as VCR's, telephones, or curling irons. Other suggestions include stereo equipment, car equipment, telescopes, farm equipment, computers, exercise machines, cash register, or special tools. After you have made your list, choose one of the items about which to write a mechanism description. Include a diagram of the mechanism in your report.

3. Take a trip to gather information about something that interests you. Before you go, prepare a list of questions you'd like answered during the trip. You could visit a college, a business, another school's lab facilities or sporting event, a museum, a play, or a natural or historical site. Write a trip report to your teacher, your parent, or a real or made-up supervisor that answers some of the questions you posed. Use a memo format.

4. Think of the last time something went wrong. It might have been a problem at school or work. Perhaps you observed someone else's difficulty. Write an incident report describing the incident and what you learned from it.

5. Watch a regular news show or docu-drama on TV. Write up one of the show's unusual occurrences as an incident report.

6. Write an incident report from this account of an armed robbery that occurred on October 17, 19-- at approximately 8:10 p.m. when Tierny Cox was working at the concession stand at Tryon Cinema, 513 Mainland Pike. Use the headings suggested in this chapter for an incident report. Include the final action as the Outcome. Determine your own Conclusion based on the description. Remember to keep your tone objective. This activity also appears in computer application **TEXT10A**.

> At 8:45, a 911 call was made to Tryon City Police: A woman in a shaky voice said, "We've been robbed! Help! The man told me to lie down on the floor. There was over $1,000 in the safe. He said he'd kill me if I screamed."
>
> At 8:58, two police officers arrived, Sergeant O'Roark and Officer Gilliam. They found an open safe, a frightened 19-year-old woman, and a cinema full of people watching the movie, unaware of the robbery. Here is what Cox told the police:
>
> A man wearing a blue ski mask, black jeans, and a black jacket and gloves barged past the concession stand into the office where we keep the safes. He was tall—probably over six feet—and thin—under 200 pounds, I'm sure. He pointed a gun in my face and told me if I screamed he would shoot me. He said to open the two safes. I opened the top safe with a key, but the bottom safe could be opened only with the proper combination. He took money out of the top safe and ordered me to use the combination to open the bottom safe. I told him I didn't think I could remember it, but he said I had to. I hardly ever open that safe and wasn't sure I could remember the combination. I started turning the lock. My first attempt failed. I tried again, trying to make it look like I knew what I was doing. My hands shook and I felt dizzy. Then the man said if I didn't open that safe, he was going to shoot anyone who came into the lobby.

Suddenly, I thought of the right combination and the door opened. He grabbed the rest of the money and told me to lie down on the floor and not to call the police. He said if I moved, he'd shoot the first person he saw. Then he left. I could hear a loud motor start and then a vehicle screech away. I waited awhile before I called you. I was too scared to move.

PART

4

Analytical and Persuasive Reports

Science Lab Reports

Write-to-Learn

How do your science classes differ from your other classes (such as English, history, business, vocational, physical education)? Make a list of those differences. Write a short paragraph explaining why you think those differences exist.

DEFINITIONS

active voice when the subject of the sentence performs the action of the verb; preferred in most technical writing

conclusions the logical, inductive leap made after considering all the details of an experiment; what is learned from an experiment

deductive reasoning reasoning from the general to the particular

experiment the controlled observations of natural phenomena

hypothesis the explanation of a pattern to help organize knowledge and predict other events

inductive reasoning reasoning from the particular to the general

objectivity an attitude signifying that no personal bias or opinion has distorted or slanted a researcher's thinking

precision accuracy; communicating something in such a detailed way that no one will misunderstand; often numbers make writing precise

passive voice the verb "to be" plus the past participle of the main verb; used in scientific writing to focus on the process instead of the performer of the process

results observable effects of an experiment

scientific method using inductive and deductive reasoning and a system of controls to objectively explore natural phenomena

---

ECOLOGY LAB: HOW LOCATION AFFECTS MICROCLIMATES

To show how just a small change in location can make a difference in microclimate range, a simple experiment was set up at River Park in Walston, South Carolina.

Materials and Method
Min-max thermometers were set up in groups of three locations in the park for a 21-hour period. The thermometers were placed at a pond with minimal shading at heights of 1 meter and 10 cm above the surface, and at 10 cm below the surface. Two more thermometers were set up on a flood plain under a canopy of dense foliage at 1 meter and 10 cm above the ground. Two thermometers were placed at the river's edge under moderately dense foliage at 1 meter and 10 cm above the river's edge. The relative humidity was also taken at each location using a sling psychrometer.

Results and Discussion
Table 1 shows the variations in temperature and humidity of the three sites.

Table 1. Temperatures and Humidity of Microclimates at River Park in Walston, SC, 26 August 19--.

TEMPERATURE AND HUMIDITY	POND			FLOOD PLAIN		RIVER	
	1 m above	10 m above	10 cm below	1 m above	10 cm above	1 m above	10 cm above
Maximum	32[a]	27	26	26	27	28	31
Minimum	23	24	24	2	21	22	22
Current	25	27	25	2	23	29	24
Range	9	3	2	5	6	6	9
Humidity	96%			91%		100%	

[a] Temperatures in degrees Celsius

The data lead to these observations:
1. The range of temperatures within each location is greater with increased distance from the surface. The wide range is probably due to the insulating effects of the ground and water or perhaps reduced air flow. In fact, the submerged thermometer had the least variation, testifying to the water's insulating qualities.
2. The pond location generally had higher temperatures and a greater range of temperatures perhaps due to the lack of cover and the insulating effects of the water. The water's resistance to temperature fluctuations may have kept the higher thermometers warm.

Conclusions
A microclimate can extend to a range as small as a few centimeters. In all, a microclimate must be considered species specific. An organism will thrive only when the climate surrounding it is within that species' tolerances.

After completing this chapter, you will be able to

- Distinguish between workplace audiences and educational audiences

- Devise a system for keeping lab notes

- Answer basic questions in a lab report

- Describe the scientific method

- Explain objectivity

- Write a science lab report

Henry David Thoreau used his creative mind to write *Walden*, a literary and philosophical masterpiece. However, he also used his creative mind to explore Walden Pond using scientific calculations.

> . . . I surveyed it carefully, before the ice broke up, early in [1846] with compass, chain, and sounding line . . . .
>
> I fathomed it easily with a cod-line and a stone weighing about a pound and a half, and could tell accurately when the stone left bottom, by having to pull so much harder before the water got underneath to help me. The greatest depth was exactly one hundred and two feet . . . . (191)

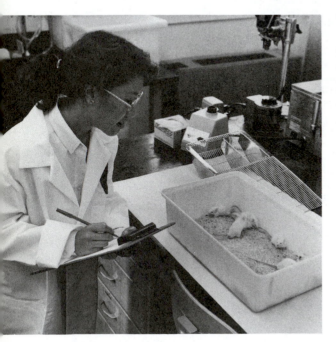

Creative genius—the inspiration for the writing of *Walden*—is also the inspiration for the design of the incandescent light bulb, the theory of relativity, and the binary language of computer programming. In fact, creativity, coupled with curiosity and a sense of adventure, is the driving force behind scientific exploration.

However, scientific exploration adds little to the community of knowledge unless the scientist writes down what was done and what happened. Hence, the science report, unique in its insistence on the scientific method, is a necessary vehicle for sharing knowledge.

In your biology or chemistry lab, you may already be performing experiments or testing hypotheses. If so, the lab report may not be new to you. In physics and psychology classes, you have no doubt read about famous experiments that advanced scientific knowledge.

Audience: Who Reads Lab Reports?

WARM UP **11.1**

Think about the science classes you've had in school or some of the science magazines you like to read. What branch of science (or technology) do you like to read about and why?

Lab reports are read by two audiences: **1)** workplace scientists and **2)** educators. Both audiences will expect a professional and ethical presentation of data. Both are captive audiences who read lab reports with great interest and a critical eye. They are experts in their fields, apt to note any inconsistencies in the research. Work audiences and school audiences, however, read for different purposes.

In the workplace, lab reports are read by research scientists with a professional and/or financial interest in the subject. The research represents new knowledge, and audiences are eager to find out the **results.** Often these lab reports become the basis of more involved science reports submitted to major magazines such as *Analytical Chemistry* and *Journal of Medicine*.

In school, lab reports are read by teachers of lab classes. The procedures and experiments do not represent new research (except in upper-level classes) but are replicated in the school lab to teach students scientific concepts. In the classroom, the lab report is a test to see if students have performed an experiment correctly and understood what happened. Here, teachers are interested in more detailed explanations than workplace audiences, which are more interested in results (Blicq 95).

Whoever the audience, all readers of lab reports respect, understand, and follow the **scientific method,** the reasoning on which scientific experimentation is based. The scientific method calls for **precision,** accuracy, **objectivity,** and carefully drawn **conclusions** based on sufficient data. Data must be presented clearly, much of it in visuals such as tables and graphs.

THE PROFESSIONAL SPEAKS

Ashley Respess, a chemist, says that lab reports must be clear. He says it's important to consider what the reader does not know and to explain that information carefully.

STOP AND THINK **11.1**

How do workplace audiences differ from educational audiences?

Prewriting: Getting Started on Lab Reports

Once you begin your lab, you should take careful, meticulous notes. Those notes become the prewriting from which you will write your report.

Recording Data

Workplace labs and school labs may require you to keep data logged in a workbook, in a lab notebook, or on some type of electronic medium. If you record data in a workbook provided to you by the class or company, then all you have to do is make sure the information you are recording is accurate and precise.

If you record data in your own notebook, be sure to include all the information you need to complete your report. Try placing your notes into this format:

- materials used
- method followed
- results seen
- conclusions drawn

Such a system will organize notes for your lab report later. Be precise: formulas, properties—even mistakes—should be written down. If you have a lab partner, one of you can perform the steps and the other can take notes on what happens.

Technology provides other ways of taking notes. Audio and video recordings, computer databases, photos—all are helpful to record notes for different kinds of experimentation. Whichever method of notetaking you choose, make sure the data you record is accurate, organized, and clear enough for you to read later when you can no longer depend on your memory.

Sir John Harrington, a godson of Queen Elizabeth, developed the first toilet in 1596.

WRITERS ON THE JOB

Beth Irlandi, marine biologist, spends much of her time scuba diving off the eastern coast of North Carolina and trudging through the wetlands. About 50% of her time, however, is spent writing. To fund her projects, Irlandi must write grant proposals. In fact, each year she must write the grant that pays for her position! Irlandi also writes lab reports describing the work she is doing. Some of those lab reports are written for publication in professional journals.

System of Consistency

When you keep your own notes, arrange a system for consistency. Record the same type of data every time you record something. For example, if you are to record how tall a plant has grown under different light sources, be sure to record the height at the same time of day using the same system of measurement. Devising a chart like Figure 11.1 would keep your entries consistent. Also, data aligned in a table might help you see any patterns that develop.

The raw data (your handwritten notes) can be redrawn into a more professional-looking table for the final report.

Some scientific research may require a survey of current research. Notecards are useful for recording library research. Include the information, the source of the information, the subject matter of the information, and whether the information is a direct quote or not. See Chapter 15 for more tips on how to take notes.

Figure 11.1 Sample Chart.

Growth Record for Plant #1

TIME	Artificial Light Direct	Artificial Light Indirect	Sunlight Direct	Sunlight Indirect
8 AM				
1 PM				
6 PM				

Formatting and Organizing Lab Reports

WARM UP 11.2

Look at the sample report at the beginning of the chapter. What kind of information goes under each heading?

The structure of a lab report varies little. Sometimes the names of the headings change or something is added, but lab reports always answer these questions: What was the purpose of the lab? What materials were used? What was the procedure? What were the results? What are the conclusions?

A typical lab report includes the following four parts:

1. **Introduction**
   - ALWAYS tells objectives/purpose of the lab, what the lab is expected to prove
   - SOMETIMES gives the background of the problem under research
   - SOMETIMES tells under whose authority the lab was conducted
   - SOMETIMES is given a separate heading if the lab report is long

2. **Materials and Method** (also called *Experimental Section, Methodology, Procedures*)
   - ALWAYS describes and/or lists materials or instruments used
   - ALWAYS describes the procedure used, including relevant calculations
   - ALWAYS uses chronological order (through time)

3. **Results and Discussion** (also called *Results* or *Discussion*)
   - ALWAYS presents test results with relevant calculations; usually includes accompanying visuals—tables, graphs, etc.
   - ALWAYS discusses the results, explains why things happened, tells what is significant
   - USUALLY uses chronological order for results seen and cause-to-effect order for discussion of results

4. **Conclusions**
   - ALWAYS includes a brief summary that tells how the test results, findings, and analysis meet the objectives established at the beginning of the report.
   - SOMETIMES uses chronological order; SOMETIMES uses priority order

Depending on the type of lab and the length of the report, other sections are added: a *Theory* section explaining the scientific theory behind the lab, an *Instrumentation* section if the lab tests equipment, a *Calculations* section if the lab uses involved mathematical computations, a *Recommendation* section (comes after *Conclusions*) if necessary for the assignment. Longer reports may also use an *Appendix,* a separate section at the end of the report, that contains tables and graphs whose complexity and length disrupt the flow of the report itself.

Just as English teachers vary formats of the papers they assign you, science teachers may also vary the format of their lab reports to meet their own preferences or to meet the requirements of the lab. Very short reports may use fewer headings. The sketches in Figure 11.2 show two variations.

Figure 11.2 Variations of Lab Reports

Lab Report #1

Introduction

Methodology

___ See Fig. 1.

1._____
2._____
3._____

Results

_____ See Table 1.

Conclusions

Lab Report #2

Introduction

Experimental Section

Discussion

_____ See Table 1.

Conclusions

Composing Lab Reports

W A R M   U P   11.3

Suppose your best friend, someone you don't know, and someone you don't like were running for class president. Could you decide on the best person for the job without letting your personal feelings influence your decision? Explain.

Scientific exploration explores physical phenomena according to basic inductive and deductive reasoning called the scientific method. The scientific method is responsible for the structure of a lab report.

Inductive and Deductive Reasoning

Inductive reasoning can best be explained with an example. Suppose your mother receives roses for Mother's Day, and you start sneezing. The next day you send your boyfriend roses. While you're at his house, you start sneezing. Later, you walk by the neighbor's roses growing on a trellis and sneeze. What are you to infer from all of this? It seems obvious: roses make you sneeze. Reasoning from the particular (I sneeze every time I am around a rose) to the general (the conclusion: Roses make me sneeze) is called inductive reasoning.

If this experience makes you give your mother a box of candy, not roses, next Mother's Day, then you are using **deductive reasoning:** reasoning from the general (conclusion: I think roses make me sneeze) to the particular (If I send my mother roses, they will make me sneeze; so I will give her candy).

The details of inductive reasoning become the evidence on which a conclusion is based. The details are pieces of a puzzle that scientists put together to make a complete picture. Once the picture is complete, the puzzle is examined to ensure it really is the picture the puzzle pieces were intended to create. In the same way, once scientists draw a tentative conclusion, they use deductive reasoning to test that conclusion to make sure it is valid. The tentative conclusion becomes the hypothesis tested in other experiments. Figure 11.3 illustrates this process.

Figure 11.3 Inductive and Deductive Reasoning

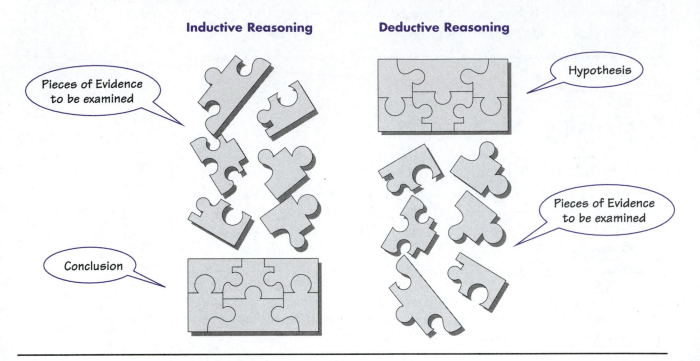

Testing a Hypothesis

Experiments are the controlled observations of natural phenomena. After a series of experiments, an experimenter may see a pattern emerging. Scientists try to explain the pattern with a **hypothesis,** a tentative explanation that helps organize knowledge and predict other events.

To illustrate how a hypothesis is tested, let's go back to the sneezing. Suppose you've reached a tentative conclusion that roses make you sneeze, but you want to make sure. Turn this conclusion into a hypothesis: Roses make you sneeze. Now test that hypothesis:

1. Place different varieties of roses under your nose and breathe deeply. Note whether you sneeze or not. Let's say you don't. Conclusion: Roses don't make you sneeze! Question: What did make you sneeze?

2. Try another hypothesis. The cologne, which you haven't worn since Mother's Day, made you sneeze. Place the cologne under your nose. You still don't sneeze. Conclusion: The cologne doesn't make you sneeze.

3. Try another hypothesis. Maybe all the roses had the same kind of pesticide on them. Find out what pesticide the florist uses. Find out the pesticide your neighbors use. Place it under your nose. Bingo! It makes you sneeze.

How did you find out what really made you sneeze? You set up an experiment that used the same nose but different substances each time you conducted the experiment. You systematically tested each hypothesis, changing the hypothesis each time you gathered new data.

Results vs. Conclusions

Experiments require writers to observe results and to draw conclusions from those observations. Observable **results,** however, are different from the **conclusions** drawn. When Paul Broca measured women's brains in the mid-1800s, he observed that they weighed an average of 181 grams less than a man's brain. His observation, the result of his measurements, was correct. The brains did weigh less. However, he wrongly concluded that smaller brains meant women were less intelligent than men (qtd. in Gould 409). Less weight doesn't lead to the conclusion that women are not as smart.[1]

So you see, a result is not the same thing as a conclusion. A result is simply what happened; a conclusion goes *beyond* what happened. A conclusion requires a scientist to draw an inference, to make a point *about* the results.

Objectivity

Objectivity is an important concept in scientific thinking. Objectivity means that the conclusion reached is based on facts and not a whim or bias. When Broca weighed women's brains in the mid-1800s, his bias that women were intellectually inferior kept him from analyzing his data objectively. Objectivity also means that another experimenter can follow the *same* procedure and come out with the *same* results.

Objective knowledge is different from subjective knowledge. Subjective knowledge, based on personal opinion, is difficult to measure and can vary from one person to another. To say that your hair makes you look sophisticated is subjective, a personal interpretation of sophistication. Not everyone, however, would agree that your hair makes you look sophisticated. To say that your hair is black, cut in a block style with strands approximately 11 inches long is an objective description. Everyone can see this description and agree on it because it's measurable.

Active Voice vs. Passive Voice

Because objectivity is important, lab reports often make use of **passive voice.** Passive voice uses a form of the verb "to be" plus the past participle of the verb. Use of passive voice keeps the reader focused on the *process,* instead of on the *scientist* performing that process. Science strives to be objective, and some people think that the naming of the person makes the lab report sound too subjective and personal.

- ACTIVE FOCUSES ON THE PERSON: *Dr. Cuomo* used the Winkler method to test the oxygen saturation in all three locations. *OR We* used the Winkler method to test the oxygen saturation in all three locations.
- PASSIVE FOCUSES ON THE PROCESS: *Oxygen saturation* was tested in all three locations using the Winkler method.

What is now proved was once only imagined.

WILLIAM BLAKE

---

[1] What would Broca have concluded if he had known that Einstein's brain weighed nearly ½ pound less than the average man's brain?

Most advice in this text encourages writers to avoid passive and to write in **active voice.** While active voice sounds more natural in most contexts, the lab report is unique: Lab reports typically rely heavily on passive voice sentences. Note the following examples:

- Tiny shifts in blood flow to parts of the brain *were detected* with functional magnetic resonance imaging.
- A 50ml solution *was prepared* using distilled water in volumetric flasks.

If your lab instructor tells you to use passive voice when describing the method and the results, then follow your instructor's advice. See The Inside Track at the end of this chapter for a more complete discussion of active and passive voice.

Precision

Your grandmother cooked with a pinch of this and a pinch of that—which was a workable system of measurement as long as *she* was doing the pinching. The real problem came when someone else tried to duplicate the recipe. How could someone else duplicate the precise size of Grandmother's pinch?

Precision is extremely important in a lab report. Usually it takes a number to make something precise enough to be understood in the same way by other people. If Grandmother's pinch of salt is also ¼ teaspoon of salt, then others can now duplicate the pinch with a measuring spoon.

Lab reports use numbers in several ways. Make sure you are using the numbers with precision and in the way your scientific field requires. Some examples are

- **Chemical formulas** Al_2O_3 (aluminum oxide), NaCl (sodium chloride)
- **Mathematical Formula** $y = ax^2 + bx + c$
- **Metric Measurements** centimeter, millimeter, microsecond
- **Percentages and Decimals** $19.56cm^3$ $12.12cm^3$ 35.41%
- **Scientific Notation** $A \times 10^n$ 3.00×10^8
- **Significant Figures** 3.15 cm, 0.315 cm, 0.00315 cm, 3.00 cm
- **Tables**

Table 1. Data on Voltage Measurements

Resistance	Voltage (measured)	Voltage (theoretical)	Voltage (AC)
6.80	3.25	4.08	6.00
2.20	1.03	1.32	5.20
1.00	0.45	0.60	4.00

Word Choice

The language of the science lab report is straightforward. The purpose is to include as much data in as clear and concise a manner as possible. Here are some examples of typical sentences from different sections of various reports:

To Verb + What Phrases

- *To determine* what differences there may be between several aquatic ecosystems, samples were taken in early November from three sites in eastern South Carolina.
- This lab is designed *to identify* fatty acids in internal standard, known and unknown mixtures.

Lists

- The system consists of a z-80A microprocessor, 16-bit DAC, 12-bit ADC, 24 K RAM, 60 K ROM, potentiostatic circuit (current follower/filter), plotter, dot-matrix printer, monitor, keyboard, and an auto cell stand.
- The survey was sent to 25 students, 25 teachers, and 10 administrators.

Description of Processes

- For this experiment, *25 males and females were selected at random* from the graduating class.
- The *blood was drawn* from the patient's finger and placed onto the slide. Then the *sample was examined* under a microscope.

Cause-to-Effect Reasoning

- The data from the above table *suggests that* the resolution is highest with the pH 7/45% MeOH buffer solution (alpha=3.35).
- The warmer temperatures *indicate that* the air is capable of holding more moisture.

Visual Aids

Think about data that could be presented visually. If that data would help your reader understand your lab report, then use the visual aid. For lab reports, consider using

TABLES	if your results use a lot of numbers
SCHEMATIC	if your method or results require an understanding of the circuitry (inside workings) of a mechanism
DIAGRAM	if your method or results involve an understanding of special instruments or mechanisms

MAPS	if you are working with an outdoor lab where places are important
GRAPHS	if you wish to compare numerical data
PHOTOGRAPHS	if the actual picture would help your reader understand your data

Review the guidelines for using visual aids in Chapter 8.

Review the guidelines for using visual aids in Chapter 8.

S T O P   A N D   T H I N K   11.3

1. Describe the scientific method.
2. What does objectivity mean?
3. Why are numbers important in a lab report?
4. Describe the language of the lab report.

SUMMARY

1. Workplace audiences are more interested in the results of a lab test. Educators are more interested in an explanation and that the procedure has been done properly. Both audiences expect the writer to follow the scientific method, presenting data precisely and accurately and using visuals where appropriate.

2. Devising a consistent system for taking notes is important for a lab report. Notes can be taken in a workbook or a lab notebook. Electronic media such as audio- and videotapes can also be used for taking notes.

3. Lab reports always answer these questions: What was the purpose of the lab? What materials were used? What was the procedure? What were the results? What are the conclusions? Some lab reports answer other questions, depending on the type of report and audience.

4. The scientific method determines the structure of the lab report. The scientific method uses inductive and deductive reasoning, maintains objectivity and records precise data. Lab reports often employ passive voice, focusing on the process rather than the person performing the process. Lab reports also use visual aids such as diagrams, graphs, and tables to present data.

Editing and Revision Checklist

✓ Have I answered the basic questions of the lab report: What was the purpose of the lab? What materials were used? What was the procedure? What were the results? What are the conclusions?

✓ Is my data precise and accurate?

✓ Have I placed that data in appropriate visuals?

✓ Have I included appropriate headings?

✓ Have I included appropriate visual aids?

✓ Have I written the methods and results using chronological order?

✓ Have I discussed and explained the results and not simply stated them?

✓ Does my conclusion section provide a true conclusion and not simply restate the results?

✓ Have I employed passive voice where necessary and asked about the appropriateness of active voice?

✓ Did I maintain objectivity?

APPLY WHAT YOU HAVE LEARNED

1. Are these statements subjective or objective? Why do you think so?

   a. This is the best English class I have ever had.

   b. This class covers the basic style and formatting of technical writing.

   c. The patient seemed angry, probably because of something that happened on the way to the office.

   d. The patient was depressed and disoriented.

   e. It's a good day for surfing.

   f. The temperature is in the mid-80s with little chance of rain.

2. What type of visual do you think these statements call for? Consider calculations, figures (What kind?), and tables.

   a. The experiments in this lab were designed to demonstrate the unique properties of inverse functions. We experimented with several types of functions, including transcendental functions and polynomial expressions.

   b. The area of the platinum disk was found by using simple algebra.

   c. An energy flow diagram (see Figure 1) was developed illustrating the energy flow and the student's position on the food web.

   d. The circuit in Figure 1 uses an op-amp as a multiplier.

   e. Table 5 shows the subtraction of input voltages as predicted by theory.

   f. The caliper consisted of the following parts.

   g. The five male students' caloric intake for one day exceeded the average intake for a male in his late teens.

3. Which part of the following statements could be made more precise?

   a. The brown bear drank from the water hole several times in the early afternoon.

   b. The decibels were tested at levels too low for human ears.

   c. The robin sat on a few eggs in the nest for a couple of weeks.

   d. The CPU costs around $500, the monitor costs about $350, and the printer costs $398.99 plus shipping and handling.

   e. The diver dove to approximately 15–20 meters below the surface of the water.

   f. A stock solution of standard copper was prepared by dissolving a little more than a gram in a small flask of nitric acid.

   g. The new Mustang engine is pretty big.

4. Read these sentences. Where do you think they belong in a lab report—under Introduction, Materials and Method, Results, Discussion, or Conclusions?

   a. For this activity, 4 potatoes, 4 pieces of wood, 4 cans and a flame were used to determine evidence of carbon.

   b. The larger the food supply, the larger the guppy population.

   c. The data for absorbencies in Table 1 show excellent correlation and show a strong linear relationship (R=1.00) for Plot 1.

   d. It is obvious from the results (Table 3) that the deciduous forest outnumbers the coniferous in species type by 13:8 and number 83:33.

   e. Exactly 0.00, 1.00, 2.00, 3.00, 4.00 and 5.00 ml of standard solution (100 ppm) was added to the 100ml volumetric flasks containing the unknown sample.

   f. The results of Table 1 suggest that the circuit performed as expected with minimal error.

   g. The purpose of this lab is to trace land use changes through time in a section of Washington, Nevada.

   h. A sheet of white paper was attached to the bottom of an aluminum pan. The paper and pan were then placed outside an apartment building on 43rd Street in New York.

   i. The results indicate that the sound bends around corners.

5. Here is a lab report that should have the following headings: Materials and Method, Results and Discussion, and Conclusions. Place the paragraphs under the proper headings. Then decide where the figure and table should go.

Electricity creates an electromagnetic field that is conducted to the bolt. The batteries' electromagnetic field creates a magnet out of the bolt. The batteries with more amps, the larger D- and C-cell batteries, create the most powerful magnets.

A paper clip count was taken to give a relative reading of the strength of each bolt. Table 1 shows the results of the count for each of the batteries. All bolts attracted and held at least one paper clip. Some bolts held more paper clips than others. Notice that the D-cell batteries enabled the bolt to hold the most paper clips.

The batteries created electromagnetic fields that attracted the metal of the paper clips. The bigger the battery, the more paper clips the bolt would hold. Therefore, the bigger batteries created a stronger electromagnetic field.

Table 1. Paper Clip Count for Select Batteries

BATTERY TYPE	Number of Paper Clips[a]			
	Battery #1	Battery #2	Battery #3[b]	Average
D-Cell	3	2	3	2.66
C-Cell	2	2	1	1.66
AA	1	2	1	1.33
AAA	1	1	1	1

[a]Standard paper clips
[b]Three batteries of each type were used

Twelve ³⁄₁₆" × 3" carriage bolts were wrapped with 20 AGW noninsulated wire, leaving 2 inches of extra wire at either end of the bolt. The bolts were then taped to the following sizes of new 1.5 volt batteries: D-cell, C-cell, AA cell, and AAA cell. Three of each kind of battery were used to ensure more reliable results.

Electrical tape was used to secure one end of the surplus 2-inch wire to the negative end of the battery and the other end of the 2-inch surplus to the positive end of the battery. The wire was left on the batteries for one minute. Figure 1 shows how each battery and bolt was wrapped.

Figure 1. Wire-Wrapped Bolt Taped to Battery

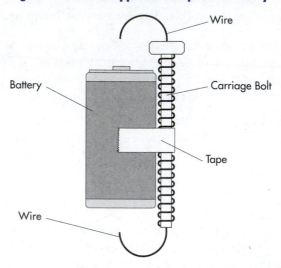

The purpose of this experiment is to determine the relationship between electricity and magnetism.

The bolt and battery were held upright. Paper clips were then touched to each bolt to see how many paper clips the bolts would hold in a string. Figure 2 shows how each battery was tested with the paper clips. A count was made of how many paper clips the bolt would hold before all the paper clips fell.

Figure 2. Paper Clips Attracted to Bolt

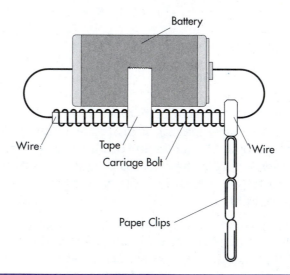

CONSIDER THIS CASE

Here is a narrative telling what Frankie did to grow crystals. Pull from the narrative what is important and leave out extraneous details. First, take systematic notes on the experiment as if you were taking the notes in a lab notebook. Then place the information under the proper headings of a lab report. Reword the narrative to reflect the language of a lab report. Create appropriate visuals and incorporate them into your report. Draw conclusions and include them under a Conclusions heading about the effect of a humid environment on the crystals. Add a title. This activity also appears on the computer applications diskettes as **TEXT11A**.

First, Frankie found three 6-ounce paper cups. Then he took out a saucepan, filled it with three fourths of a cup of water and brought it to a boil. Then he measured 2 cups of sugar and stirred the sugar until it dissolved into the water. He wanted to see if he could grow crystals and if humidity made them grow faster or slower. Granulated sugar is actually crystals of sugar ground up for convenience. After he finished heating the mixture, he turned off the stove. Then he waited 20 minutes for the mixture to cool a little bit. He didn't want to burn himself when he continued with the rest of the experiment.

Next he poured one third of the cooled mixture into each cup. Then he put each cup in a different place. He was curious to see if crystals would grow differently in different places. He put one cup in the bathroom, where the humidity was likely to be high; one cup in the living room where there was a dehumidifier creating low humidity; and one in the kitchen where the heat from cooking created moderately humid conditions. Then he left the cups alone and did not disturb them. For six weeks, he measured the crystals in each cup once a week. Here is a rough table he kept in his notebook.

Location	WK 1 Amt	WK 1 Size	WK 2 Amt	WK 2 Size	WK 3 Amt	WK 3 Size	WK 4 Amt	WK 4 Size	WK 5 Amt	WK 5 Size	WK 6 Amt	WK 6 Size
Kitchen	0	—	0		1/8	pin	1/3	pin	2/3	pin/pea	1	pin/pea
Bathroom	0	—	0		0	—	1/4	pin	1/4	pin	3/8	pin
Liv. Room	0	—	1/8	pin	1/4	pin/pea	1/2	pin/pea	1	pin/pea	1	pin/pea

pin = crystals approx. the size of a pinhead.
pea = crystals approx. the size of a green pea.
fractions = approx. how much of the solution has crystallized.

PURSUE AN IDEA

1. Ask your science teacher to help you perform a lab in science class. Write about that lab for English class.

2. Look through a series of science experiments for children. Scout handbooks, Mr. Wizard's science program, and the Discovery Channel are good sources of simple experiments for children. Try an experiment, keep notes in a notebook, and write a lab report for English class.

3. Think about something you'd like to know more about. Maybe you'd like to know under what conditions your car gets better gas mileage; whether some additive makes your car run better; whether one brand of polish, lipstick or sunscreen works better than another. Maybe you'd like to test several brands of film, several stain removers, several writing pens, or different foods for your dog or cat. Ask your science teacher to help you design an experiment to give you the knowledge you seek. Perform the experiment and write up the results.

4. If your school has science fairs, write up one of your science projects into a lab report; or collaborate with someone who has created a science project to write a lab report.

WORKS CITED

Blicq, Ron S. *Technically-Write! Communicating in a Technological Era.* 4th ed. Englewood Cliffs, NJ: Prentice Hall, 1993.

Gould, Stephen Jay. "Women's Brains." *The Blair Reader.* Ed. Laurie G. Kirszner and Stephen R. Mandell. Englewood Cliffs, NJ: Prentice Hall, 1992. 407–413.

Thoreau, Henry David. *Walden.* New York: New American Library of World Literature, Inc., 1964.

Active and Passive Voice

Which of these sentences do you like better and why?

ACTIVE VOICE: Maria hit the ball during Saturday's game.
PASSIVE VOICE: The ball was hit during Saturday's game by Maria.

Most people prefer the first sentence because it is direct, shorter, and more interesting. As a result, it is easier to read.

Look at the verbs in each sentence. The active voice sentence uses only one verb. The passive voice sentence uses two verbs: the verb "to be" + the past participle of another verb. (The verb "to be" includes *is, am, are, was, were, to be, been, being.*) The past participle is simply the past tense form of the verb that uses a helping verb.

Look at the subjects in each sentence. In the active voice sentence, the subject is the *doer* of the action. In other words, *Maria* performs the action: She hits the ball. In the passive voice sentence, the subject is being acted upon. In other words, the ball was acted upon (was hit) by Maria.

Use active voice when you want to emphasize an action. Because active voice sentences are more direct, we encourage you to write in active voice unless you have a very good reason for writing in passive voice. Sometimes there are good reasons to use passive voice.

1. If you do not know the doer of the action, passive voice gives you the opportunity to leave out the doer.

   P: The money was taken.

   A: ? took the money.

2. Maybe you know who the doer is, but don't want to say. Sometimes passive voice can help you be diplomatic or polite.

   P: Your blueprints have been delayed.

   A: We lost the blueprints.

   P: The vase was broken.

   A: You broke the vase.

3. Scientific writing calls for an objective tone, which is hampered when the doer of the action is included in the sentence. Scientific writing tries to focus on the process, not the person.

   P: Dr. Wems increased the fluid volume by 20% by adding sodium.

   A: The fluid volume was increased by 20% with the addition of sodium.

4. Sometimes the receiver of the action is more important than the doer. You might want to emphasize the receiver by using passive voice. Ads, in particular, like to stress "you" as the receiver of services companies can offer.

P: Richard Nixon was elected president for two terms.

A: The people of the United States elected Richard Nixon president for two terms.

P: You are kept up-to-date with *Newsweek*.

A: *Newsweek* keeps you up-to-date.

Changing Voice

Passive to Active. Look for two-word passive voice verbs, the verb "to be" plus the past participle. If you see that a report contains too many passive voice sentences, convert the passive verbs to one-word active verbs by **1)** placing the doer as the subject of the sentence, **2)** adding a doer that is not included in the sentence, or **3)** turning the simple subject of the verb into a direct object.

P: The car was repaired by the mechanic.
A: The mechanic repaired the car.
P: The window was replaced last month.
A: Andrew replaced the window last month.

Active to Passive. If your science report calls for more passive voice constructions, decide what process, material, or mechanism you want to emphasize and place that item in the subject position. Make sure your verb includes "to be" + the past participle.

Try changing the direct object of the verb into the simple subject of the passive voice verb.

A: The scientist added a cooling agent to the compound.
P: A cooling agent was added to the compound.

THE INSIDE TRACK: APPLY WHAT YOU HAVE LEARNED

1. Find the passive voice verbs in the following sentences. Then change these passive voice sentences to active voice:
  a. The accident report is submitted by the manufacturing engineer.
  b. My homework was lost on the computer.
  c. The key to my house has been lost.
  d. The Area VI Tennis Classic is being sponsored by the Alpha Deltas in May.
  e. The blueberry bushes were ordered by my sister who is landscaping the backyard.
  f. According to our parents, my brother and I are needed to run errands for the family business this Saturday.

2. Locate the active voice verbs. Then change these active voice sentences into passive voice.
   a. John Hinkley shot President Reagan.
   b. The chemist introduced sulfuric acid to the mixture.
   c. Sally Martin, your teacher's aide, sent three difficult students to the office last week.
   d. An unknown person robbed Mr. Miller's convenient mart.
   e. Onyx Computer provides you with complete support.
   f. You waste fuel when you idle your car at stop signs.

Progress and Periodic Reports

Write-to-Learn

Think about where you stand today on the path of your long-term educational goals. Your plan may require a high school diploma or GED. You may want to earn a two-year Associate degree. Perhaps your career will require you to pursue a four-year Bachelor's degree, or beyond that a Master's or a Doctorate degree. Write several paragraphs answering the following questions: What have you achieved thus far toward reaching your long-term educational goals? What do you still need to do to reach those goals? When do you think you will reach your goal? What problems might get in your way?

Your audience could be your parents or guardians, a scholarship committee, or other people who have supported you in your educational career.

DEFINITIONS

fiscal the operating or business year, a calendar that may run from July to June, rather than January to December

progress report a report that tells the audience what work has been completed and what remains to be done on one particular project during the reporting period

periodic report a report, issued at timed intervals, informing the audience of the progress made on all the projects of an organization during the reporting period

reporting period the time span covered by the report

Pitt County Communities In Schools

MEMORANDUM

TO: Board of Directors

FROM: Ann S. Burden, Executive Director *A.S.B.*

DATE: May 15,19--

RE: Progress Report: Planning for a Community Outreach Program at
         D.H. Conley High School

Since our meeting in January when you asked me and my staff to begin planning for a
community outreach program at D.H. Conley High School next year, I have been amazed by
the interest and cooperation this project has generated. This report will acquaint you with the
work completed, the work scheduled, and the problems encountered.

WORK COMPLETED (January 15–May 15, 19--)
Cooperation and hard work by many people have made these accomplishments possible.

Public Relations
A brochure defining the community outreach program and its goals was developed and in
March 1,000 copies were distributed. The brochure helped with one of our first and most
critical activities, which was to educate faculty, staff, students, and parents about the program.

Faculty Recruitment
Duffy Lincoln has been selected as Site Coordinator. In addition, the three faculty members
needed for the program have been named: Mack Jones, Lillian Outterbridge, and Joan Manning.
All personnel volunteered for the coming academic year with full knowledge of the demands
that developing a new program will place on them.

Program Planning
The faculty has adopted a plan for integrating academic and real-life skills in the curriculum
to make learning more meaningful. The program will begin with a group of 60 ninth graders.
Teachers have begun developing lesson plans which integrate English, biology, and social
studies with emphasis on the practical applications to life.

Ann S. Burden, Executive Director
209 East Third Street, Greenville, NC 27858
Office (919) 555-0191 • FAX (919) 555-0194

Board of Directors
Page 2
May 15, 19--

WORK SCHEDULED
As you can see, a number of tasks are on the upcoming schedule, but the workload does not seem impossible. The faculty and I are determined to see this program effectively serving students and the community.

Program Evaluation
The faculty will spend the next three months determining ways to assess the program as well as the students' progress.

Program Planning
A number of tasks need to be completed in the next reporting period:
1. Six field trips to regional business sites for the students will be scheduled before August.
2. The Adopt-a-Grandparent Program will be coordinated by faculty over the summer.
3. A list of guest speakers and mentors for students will be developed.

Student Selection
By June 30, the faculty will select 60 students to participate, and by July 15 all students who are selected will be notified by mail.

PROBLEMS/PROJECTIONS
The only problems we have encountered thus far are the good kind: We have experienced overwhelming interest in the program and had twice as many faculty members apply as we expected. Student interest has also been greater than we expected.

If work continues as it has up to now, we will be ready to begin the program on schedule. We look forward to a productive summer. I will continue to report progress to you.

After completing this chapter, you will be able to

- Identify the writers and the audiences of progress and periodic reports

- Format progress and periodic reports

- Compose a progress report, using the standard organizational plan, that includes all the information the reader will need

- Compose a periodic activity report, using the standard organizational plan that includes all the data the reader will need

- Edit progress and periodic reports for organization, completeness, accuracy, and headings

Progress reports—the name tells us the purpose. These documents report on progress for a period of time; they tell what has been done. Likewise, periodic reports, reports given periodically, also tell about progress. Yet, an important difference separates the two report types.

The **progress report** describes what has been done during a specified time on *one particular project*, such as work completed on the construction of a building. A progress report covers in detail *all* the achievements toward one project. Anyone in an organization, from the president to a security guard, might need to report the progress he or she has made on a project.

On the other hand, the **periodic report** usually explains accomplishments for *all of the projects* of a unit or of the whole organization over a specified time period. For instance, if you have ever listened to your governor make a State of the State address or the President make a State of the Union address, then you have heard a periodic report. These speeches explore the many ongoing projects of the state or the nation for the year. Periodic reports may cover different periods of time: a week (weekly), a month (monthly), three months (quarterly), or six months (semi-annually). Anyone responsible for a unit or organization is likely to prepare periodic reports of activities for a superior or others who need the information.

Audience: Who Reads Progress and Periodic Reports?

W A R M   U P   12.1

1. Read the model progress report at the beginning of this chapter and then try to determine the relationship between the writer and the audience.

2. What is the writer's purpose in presenting this report?

Decision-makers and managers within organizations, as well as stockholders of companies, use the information related in progress and periodic reports to evaluate projects and the way they are being handled. Managers also use these reports to determine how to deal with other projects under way or to decide if continuing certain projects is worthwhile. Consider the way the progress report described below is used.

> Students in your school decided to collect books, maps, magazines and other supplies for the library of a school in California badly damaged by a recent earthquake. The task was divided: several clubs were collecting books, the Ecology Club was gathering magazines, the Beta Club was asking for money to buy items not donated, and the Volunteer Club was responsible for arranging shipment. The Volunteer Club's first progress report outlined the cost estimates for packaging and shipping the materials. Because books are heavy, the shipping costs were estimated to be more than $300, almost equal to the value of the books and materials to be shipped.

This progress report could have changed the thrust of the entire project. The students at your school could have decided that the students in California would benefit just as much if they were sent money to buy books locally. That way no shipping charges would be involved. Another option someone might have suggested is that the Volunteer Club look for a corporation to deliver the materials along with one of their shipments to the California area.

What is important to remember about readers of progress and periodic reports is that they are busy people looking for specific data. They expect to find in a specific place the information they're looking for and don't want to hunt for it. Also, since they are basing decisions on this information, they expect it to be complete and accurate.

WRITERS ON THE JOB

Ron Howard, Corporate Photographer for SAS Institute, a leading software developer in the United States, reports spending a great deal of his work time communicating with people at all levels of the organization. One challenging aspect of the job, says Howard, is to be certain he understands exactly what the user wants. Since almost anyone in the company who needs pictures—from programmers who want to include photographic images as icons in computer applications to public relations staffers who need shots of visiting dignitaries—is a "customer," Howard notes the value of effective communication skills.

STOP AND THINK 12.1

1. What is the purpose of progress and periodic reports? In other words, what do these documents report?
2. What is the difference between progress and periodic reports?

Prewriting: Getting Started on Progress and Periodic Reports

In the planning stage, think of your audience and the information these readers most need. Think also of your plan and what tasks you need to report.

Consider Audience

Whether you are preparing a progress report or a periodic report, the first thing to consider is your audience. Try to put yourself in the position of the reader. Ask yourself what this reader needs to know. Anticipate not only the reader's questions, but his or her concerns as well. Also in the planning stage, be sure to check your facts and figures for accuracy.

Consider the Project Schedule or Plan

Begin by noting the time period of your report. Are you sharing information about the last two weeks, the past month, or the fiscal year? (A **fiscal** year is the operating year, such as the academic year, which often runs from August to July.)

With a time frame clearly in mind, review any plan or schedule you had for the project or the organization. Many projects, such as the construction of a building, have detailed plans for when work will begin, who will do each phase of the work, when each phase should begin and end, and on what date the project will be completed. Likewise, most organizations develop plans, such as short-term and long-range goals and objectives. From these goals, the companies describe the actions they plan to take and the time frame suggested for achieving these goals. By examining the plan or schedule, you can compare what was actually achieved with what had been planned for this particular time span.

Consider Organization of Tasks

You might even make a chart by listing what was scheduled to be done in this time period in one column and what was actually done in another column. Another list would cover what needs to be done next. These lists can then be used in composing your report.

Once the lists are complete, you may see that some things belong together in a category. The groupings or categories become subheadings under a major heading. For instance, if you were to report on your gardening, then fertilizing, weeding, and making rows could all be discussed under the heading of Soil Preparation. In turn, Soil Preparation could be a subheading under Work Completed and Work Scheduled or under only one of them. Soil Preparation would be listed under both headings if you had completed some soil preparation tasks but still needed to do others. If you had completed all soil preparation work, then the subheading would appear only under Work Completed.

Formatting Progress and Periodic Reports

WARM UP 12.2

1. Think of a form you completed recently, such as a class schedule, a job application, or a magazine subscription card. Would you prefer to fill in a form with data or compose paragraphs for presenting the data? Why?

2. Do you think forms are easier to read than paragraphs? If so, why?

WRITERS ON THE JOB

Yvonne M. Jones, a teacher of preschool students with developmental disabilities, stresses the importance of accuracy and precise observation in progress reports. Miss Von, as she is known to her students, says teachers are aware that parents and guardians want their children to succeed academically, physically, and socially. Sometimes teachers are tempted to overstate a child's progress to make the family feel better. However, greater disappointment is certain to follow when family members witness the child's true abilities if they are less than what the family had been led to expect.

Progress and periodic reports are often, though not always, internal documents. If the report is written for an internal reader, it would probably be formatted as a memo. If the report is written for an external reader, then it would probably be formatted as a letter. For a more formal tone, manuscript format may be used for either an internal or external audience. A formal tone may be called for if the audience is distant from the writer in the organization or if the readers are numerous or varied.

Composing Progress Reports

Since the information contained in progress reports is meant to keep managers informed of work being done on a particular project, the reports are organized to answer the readers' most important questions first. For instance, most managers will *first* want to know what has been done. Then the writer should answer other questions the manager will use to make decisions, such as what needs to be done to complete the project and whether any problems have delayed completion.

Ellen Hardee-Laking and co-worker Andre Carver, soil scientists with CIC Inc., have been working on a 36-acre tract of land to determine if the land is appropriate for building homes. Until a year ago this tract was the site of a junkyard stacked high with all kinds of vehicles leaking oil, gas, antifreeze, and other chemicals into the soil. Hardee-Laking and Carver were assigned to the project by their supervisor when the new landowner contracted with CIC to determine if she could safely go forward with her plans to develop a luxury community. The landowner and the CIC supervisor are pushing for a rapid decision from the scientists. Feeling the pressure, Hardee-Laking prepares a progress report that indicates test results for twice as many tests as she had actually run. She tells Carver that she used the actual results of tests completed to anticipate the results for tests not yet run. She claims that the report shows what they would find if they had time to run all the tests.

Should Carver sign the report and go along with Hardee-Laking's suggestion that "this is what we would find anyway"? Or should he report her to the supervisor? Should he tell the client? What should Carver do?

Organizing

The outline given below is typical of the plan frequently used for progress reports. Most progress reports include the following sections:

Heading in Report	What That Section Covers
Introduction	Report topic, purpose, and **reporting period**
Work Completed	What has been done
Work Scheduled	What needs to be done
Problems/Projections	What has gone wrong, if anything, and when the work will be finished

Under each of these section headings, the writer may add subheadings if a number of ideas are to be covered in that section of the report. For a more detailed look at what to include in a progress report, refer to Figure 12.1.

Figure 12.1 Model of an Internal Progress Report

Indicates that this is the third progress report on this project; notes the report topic

INTRODUCTION: Describes the project being reported upon; gives the reporting period; states the purpose of the report. May give more background in a first progress report

Memorandum

To: Senior Class Members
From: Senior Trip Committee
Date: February 1, 19--
Subject: Progress Report 3: Planning for trip to Disney World

Since our Senior Trip to Disney World is less than two months away, we are working hard to make an enjoyable adventure possible. This report outlines the accomplishments, the work remaining, and one problem encountered during January.

Covers what has been done on the project

WORK COMPLETED (January 1–February 1, 19--)

We are marking a few things off the to-do list. If we can maintain the current level of enthusiasm, we will get there.

WORK COMPLETED may include subheads if the work accomplished falls under two or more categories

Finances
The class sponsored two doughnut sales during the month to add $350 to the travel fund.

Reservations
Three buses from the White Goose Line have been reserved at a cost of $800 each. In addition, reservations have been made for three nights at the Disney Dunes Hotel, and a deposit of $500 has been paid to the hotel.

Chaperones
School policy requires 11 adults to accompany groups the size of our class on overnight trips. To satisfy that requirement, 4 teachers, their spouses, and 3 parents have agreed to serve as chaperones.

Covers work yet to be done

WORK SCHEDULED

The primary responsibilities remaining are earning the rest of the money required for the trip and making additional reservations.

Finances
The fund balance now contains $9,675 of the $11,000 we need to earn for the trip. Five other fund-raising projects have been scheduled before the trip. However, if the future projects are as successful as the last two, we may raise the remaining $1,325 after only three projects have been completed.

Omits the subhead Chaperones under WORK SCHEDULED because nothing else concerning chaperones needs to be done

Reservations
We will order two-day passes for Disney World and one-day tickets for Sea World next week. Also, Mr. Marshall will make reservations for the Senior Banquet at Seaside Restaurant. The Banquet Committee will request a seafood buffet for Saturday evening.

Senior Class Members
Page 2
February 1, 19--

PROBLEMS/PROJECTIONS
The School Board has agreed to consider our request to be excused from school early on the day we leave. Otherwise, we cannot reach Orlando before 3:00 in the morning. If we arrive in the middle of the night, we will probably waste half the day planned for Disney World catching up on sleep. We might think of changing the schedule if the School Board denies our request.

Other plans are proceeding as expected, and we should have all work for the trip completed by March 16, two weeks before departure.

> Explains any difficulties that may affect the project; gives a revised completion date if problems have caused delay

Drafting the Introduction

In the opening or introductory section of the report:

1. Name the project.
2. Note the time period you cover in this report.
3. State the purpose of the report (to tell readers of the status of the project).

Be direct and remember that using *I* or *we* is acceptable and even encouraged. By using first person, you are taking responsibility for your actions and opinions.

Drafting the Work Completed Section

In the Work Completed section,

1. Note again (optional; usually beside the heading or in the opening sentence of the section) the time period you cover in the report.
2. Use past tense verbs.
3. Improve readability by using subheadings (to separate kinds of jobs) or bulleted lists.
4. Provide enough details and explanations about each job completed to meet the needs of the reader.

Since your reader is probably most concerned about what you have done on the project, be certain that this section is clear and accurate. Use your most important ideas first. After all, this is the good news section; it is your opportunity to tell others what you've achieved.

Drafting the Work Scheduled Section

In the Work Scheduled section, tell your audience what work needs to be done in the next reporting period or what remains to be done to complete the project. Use future tense verbs in this section. As with the Work Completed section, you may need to separate and emphasize each major task or job with subheadings.

Drafting the Problems/Projections Section

In the Problems/Projections section of the progress report,

1. Describe any obstacles to the completion of the job. You may choose to list and number these problems, or to describe them in paragraph form. Be honest and direct. Unless you need to assign responsibility, report just the facts.

2. Give a completion date for the project. If problems have stalled the project so that the original completion date cannot be met, then you will need to give your audience a new date.

STOP AND THINK 12.3

1. What are the standard headings used for almost all progress reports?

2. If you were reporting your progress in training for a marathon to your corporate sponsor, under what section/heading in the monthly progress report would you note the sprained ankle you suffered this week?

Composing Periodic Reports

WARM UP 12.4

Suppose that your best friend must miss an entire semester of school and has asked you to keep him or her informed of classwork and assignments each week. If you were to write a letter or note to this friend about what happened at school during the first week, what topics would you cover and how would you organize your ideas? What might you write the first week that you might not write in the weeks following? Write a list of what you would include in a weekly report to your friend; then organize the list in the order you think it should be presented.

Organizing

Remember that a periodic report reviews what an entire organization or unit of an organization has done in a specified period of time. The report keeps decision-makers informed. It should be organized so that the reader can find important information easily. The structure usually consists of

1. An *overview* that briefly presents the highlights of the entire report.
2. A *section for each category of activity or work undertaken* during the reporting period, with section headings and sometimes subheadings, organized from most important activity or work to least important.
3. A *conclusion* that refers to the next report.

STOP AND THINK 12.4

To see how easily a reader can pick important ideas from a periodic report, read Figure 12.2 on pages 239 and 240 and answer these questions.

1. What time period does this report cover?
2. For how many areas or types of work is Ove Jensen reporting progress?
3. What is the most important task or topic mentioned in Jensen's report?

Drafting the Introduction

The introduction needs to be brief and to the point. When you compose the periodic report's introductory section, keep in mind that the reader may be very busy and will expect a summary of important points first. The summary should mention each idea included in a major heading. Also note the reporting period, the time for which the document describes progress. Use your best economical style, but include transitions to connect ideas. (For more information on transitional techniques, refer to The Inside Track following Chapter 16, pages 330–332.)

Drafting the Work Progress Sections

After the introduction, the rest of the report body is determined by the types of work done. The report will have a heading and discussion for each area or type of work undertaken during that reporting period. For instance, the monthly activity report of a United States Navy recruiter might include the following areas of work (and thus headings for): Job Fairs, School-Based Meetings, Office Conferences, and Public Speaking Events. Under each heading in the body of the report, the recruiter describes what he or she has accomplished during the reporting period. Organized by priority, these sections explain what work has been done in each area of the organization.

While detailing work accomplished, the writer may note any problems encountered as well. The writer should report problems factually, omitting personal opinions and attitudes and allowing the reader to draw his or her own conclusions.

Figure 12.2 Periodic Activity Report

Memorandum

To: Miss Helen Wooten, Advisor

From: Ove Jensen, Student Intern

Date: March 5, 19--

Subject: Activity Report for February 19--

    February has been a productive period in my second month of job-shadowing Ms. Antoinette Clavelle, Radiologic Technologist at Grove Park Hospital. The month was filled with action and variety. I observed work in the Neonatal Intensive Care Unit, the MRI (Magnetic Resonance Imaging) section, and the Radiology Lab. In addition, I have completed one of the three research papers required for earning academic credit.

Neonatal Intensive Care Unit

    During my first session with Ms. Clavelle last month, which took place in the Neonatal Intensive Care Unit, I watched radiologists work with medically fragile premature and newborn babies. Ms. Clavelle used an ultra-sound machine to obtain images of the brains of two patients. I further observed her use a portable X-ray device to take film of the chest and abdomen of another young patient. Some of the infants in this unit weigh as little as one pound and are connected to many pieces of support equipment, such as respirators and heart monitors. These patients present unique challenges to radiologic technologists.

MRI Section

    Since Ms. Clavelle is a Rotation Supervisor, I was able to observe the oper-ation of the MRI machine while she worked in that area. This room-sized piece of imaging equipment serves a variety of purposes in diagnosing patients' problems. During the four hours I shadowed Ms. Clavelle in the MRI section, she worked with the following patients:

    1) an 82-year-old stroke patient,
    2) a 14-year-old auto crash victim with head trauma,
    3) a quarterback for the university football team with a knee injury, and
    4) a 36-year-old woman suffering back pain.

Everything about this machine is computer-driven, so I became a little restless in the control room while the patients were undergoing treatment. The problem was that I did not understand the computer jargon used by the technologists, nor did I understand what I was seeing when I looked at the images on the computer screen.

Radiology Lab

    Observing Ms. Clavelle in the Radiology Lab gave me an opportunity to witness a wide range of the uses of radiologic technology as well as to see the necessity for accurate reporting. A patient's well-being may depend on the technologist's communication skills.

Gives highlights of entire report

Organizes from most important information to least

Provides as many specifics as possible

Notes and explains problem area

Miss Helen Wooten
Page 2
March 5, 19--

Researched Reports

As my goal is to earn academic credit toward graduation, I am submitting one researched report, <u>Using Ultrasound in Diagnosing Brain Hemorrhage</u>, along with this monthly report. I am researching now for the second report and plan to finish it by the end of March. The final paper should be completed by the end of April or the first week in May.

Conclusion

My experiences with Ms. Clavelle in February were worthwhile and exciting. In fact, after observing technologists use several types of equipment, my interest is greatest in ultrasound, and I am considering work in that area as a career goal. When we meet next, I would like to discuss the educational requirements for such a career and the possibility, during my last semester of high school, of shadowing someone who works only with ultrasound.

Looks forward to the next report and meeting

One key to effective writing in each section is to be specific and accurate.

Rather than   *I had meetings with several employees this month.*

Try   *I held performance evaluation conferences with six of my ten employees during March.*

Another tip that might help with the writing and the reading of these sections is to use lists, numbered or set in columns, when possible. Divide long discussions into shorter paragraphs to reflect groups of ideas and to make the document easier to read.

Drafting the Conclusion

The concluding section of the report looks to the future, to the next periodic report the writer will compose.

STOP AND THINK 12.5

1. How many major headings will a periodic report have?
2. In what section of the report does the overview or the summary of progress go? Why?

1. The progress report describes the status of work on one particular project for a specified period of time.

2. The periodic report describes the progress of all the projects ongoing in an organization or in a division of an organization during a specified period of time.

3. Prewriting for both of these reports involves considering the audience's interests and the project's or the organization's schedule.

4. Report writers choose memo, letter, or manuscript format based on audience.

5. The progress report, most often written by a project manager to his or her supervisor(s), covers work that has been done, work that is scheduled to be done in the next reporting period, problems hindering work (if there are any), and the completion date of the project.

6. The periodic report begins with an overview or highlights of work done during the reporting period and is followed by a detailed description of work completed in each area. Subheadings help the reader easily identify areas in which work has been done.

Editing and Revision Checklist

✓ Have I designed, organized, and written the report with the audience in mind?

✓ Have I taken into account the project schedule or company plan and told the readers what they need to know?

✓ Is my format—memo, letter, or manuscript—appropriate for the audience and the situation?

For Progress Reports

✓ Does my report include these headings and discussion: Introduction, Work Completed, Work Scheduled, and Problems/Projections?

✓ Is this the first progress report and, if so, how much background does your audience need to understand the project?

✓ Are the data under each heading organized deductively?

✓ Did I use past tense verbs in the Work Completed section and future tense verbs in the Work Scheduled section?

✓ Do the reporting period dates appear in the Subject line (if I am using letter or memo format) or as part of the Work Completed heading?

✓ Is the information complete and accurate?

✓ Have I used lists where appropriate for easier reading?

For Periodic Reports

✓ Does the opening section of the report, which could be given the heading *Introduction*, summarize or give the important points from the body of the report?

✓ Does the body of my report discuss all the types or areas of work undertaken by the unit or organization during the reporting period?

✓ Is my discussion of progress made easier to read by the use of descriptive headings, and do the headings follow parallel structure?

✓ Is my discussion organized deductively, with an overview or main idea first?

✓ Do I present accurate, specific details to explain progress and problems?

✓ Do I mention any problems encountered under the appropriate heading in the body of the report?

✓ Have I presented problems as facts, not accusations?

✓ Does my report end with a Conclusion section that looks forward and refers to the next periodic report to be filed with the reader?

APPLY WHAT YOU HAVE LEARNED

1. The statements listed in **a** through **j** will go into a progress report. The writer needs to know in which section of the report to place them. Help the writer by identifying each statement as Work Completed, Work Scheduled, or Problems/Projections. This exercise is also available on the computer applications diskette as **TEXT12A**.

   a. A site license has been purchased from NetBright for our network.

   b. The CD-ROM, which was delivered last Friday, was damaged in shipping so that it is inoperable.

   c. We installed screen savers on all computers.

   d. If all work scheduled is completed as we expect, the network will be ready for the team orientation on September 23.

   e. This week the System Director will order the serial cable we need.

   f. The hardware security system we requested was $300 over our budget.

   g. Each computer will be named so that it can be easily identified by users.

   h. A system administrator will have to be trained before we can become fully operational.

   i. The laser printer has been connected to the network and tested.

   j. We forgot to order a surge protector for the computer attached to the LCD projection panel, so we cannot use this equipment until the order comes next week.

2. Some of the sentences below are vague and some include personal opinions of the writer. Revise each sentence to make it specific and factual. Invent details as needed.

   a. The calibrator is several minutes off schedule.

   b. The phenomenal response to our new computer safety education program shows that employees will benefit from this new program.

   c. To get to the warehouse, go down the hall a bit and turn left.

   d. The line was down for quite awhile last Friday because of one of those lectures on safety.

   e. The original air purifier can be assembled in 45 minutes, but the fancy case of the new model causes a much longer assembly time.

CONSIDER THIS CASE

1. Write a progress report based on the information given here. This activity is also available on the computer applications diskette as **TEXT12B**.

Your school has agreed to a new approach to graduation this year—a ceremony organized and carried out by students. You have been elected the chair of the student committee developing the graduation plans. Part of your responsibility is to send monthly progress reports to the School Administration Team.

It is April 1 and your group is well on its way toward completing graduation plans. The committee wanted music that reflects the graduates' preferences rather than the traditional, formal band or orchestra music often used. The Free Band has agreed to perform, and their contract will be ready for signing in two weeks. The results of the committee survey given to students concerning graduation speakers revealed that 62% wanted a brief speech (no more than 10 minutes) given by a graduate who has found success in the community. Lyle Anasaza, a young entrepreneur who owns three indoor basketball entertainment centers called Slam Dunk, has accepted an invitation to speak. The following donations have been pledged: 173 red roses, one for each graduate, by Kate's Flower Kart; 16 pots of yellow mums for the stage by South Hills Farm; 20 gallons of fruit punch by Central Dairy; a carton of prepared carrot sticks and two quarts of vegetable dip by Country Corner Kitchen; and 15 dozen chicken salad sandwiches by Norfolk Bakery. Programs and invitations have been designed by the Graphics Arts class. Invitations will be printed by Quik Print and distributed to seniors within the month. The auditorium will be decorated and chairs set up by Mr. Hall's Theatre class.

2. Write a periodic report using the case study given below.

As chair of the Drafting Club, you receive funds for your organization from the SGA. Therefore, you present reports to the SGA twice each semester to keep them aware of what the club is doing. Your next report is due January 6, 19--. In this report you want to discuss work in the following areas: Professional Pursuits, Service, and Membership. You believe the club is a more active and useful member of the campus community than it ever has been. Over the holidays, five members attended the national American Institute of Building Design (AIBD) meeting in Las Vegas, Nevada. They brought a great deal of information back to share with the other club members. The club began the school year with 21 members, and two students who moved into the district joined during the second semester. The club's service project for this school year has been to draw the plans for the city's first Habitat for Humanity house. Club members have completed the exterior drawings and submitted them for approval. They will need to finish the interior drawings before school ends. All 23 members of the club have participated in this service project.

3. Write the progress report Marcus Lytle would send to Gulf Coast Catfish using the following situation and information.

A farmer, diversifying his corn and soybean operation, contracts with Gulf Coast Catfish to operate two 5-acre ponds for raising catfish on Hathaway Farms. Gulf Coast Catfish hires Sheldon Excavations to dig the two ponds. Marcus Lytle, the job supervisor for Sheldon, brings in equipment and a crew and begins to dig. When the first day of digging ends, the pond holds 3 feet of water. The next morning the water level is at 1 foot. After the second day, the water is at 4.5 feet and the next morning it is at 1.75 feet. At the end of the third day the water is at 5 feet and overnight drops to 3 feet. After three days, the first pond is nearing completion, but Lytle is dissatisfied with the soil he has uncovered and the pond's loss of water. Certain soil types, such as those with high levels of clay, hold water in ponds; sandy soil, however, allows water to percolate through until it reaches the water table below the soil. In a first progress report to Gulf Coast Catfish, Lytle explains the situation as of the current date.

PURSUE AN IDEA

1. Consider any project you are working on at home, school, or work as a topic for a progress report. Your audience will be a person or group of people who have an interest in the project or who make decisions regarding the project. Use the format and organization appropriate for the topic and audience to prepare your progress report.

2. Evaluate the progress you are making on a hobby or collection. For instance, if you are building a sound system in your room, you would explain the pieces of equipment such as speakers and receivers you have acquired and describe the equipment you hope to add to the system. If you are collecting baseball cards or comic books, your progress report would note the cards or books you have in your possession now as well as the items you wish to trade for or buy in the future.

3. If you are seeking a summer or part-time job or if you are applying for admission to a school or camp, then write a progress report to your advisor or family concerning what you've done toward accomplishing your goals.

4. To compose a periodic report, think first of the organizations of which you are a part: a family, a club, a neighborhood, a school. With one of these organizations and a particular time period in mind, plan and write a periodic report for a particular audience. Describe the progress and the ongoing activities for your entire group or your unit of the larger organization.

Unbiased Language

Technical writers should be sensitive to diversity in the workplace. One way to begin is to use unbiased language.

1. Avoid sexist language by choosing words that include both genders.

USE	RATHER THAN
representative	Congressman
firefighter	fireman
police officer	policeman
mail carrier	mailman or postman
chair/presiding officer	chairman
supervisor/manager	foreman
synthetic	manmade
polite	ladylike
doctor	woman doctor
nurse	male nurse
people/humanity/human beings	mankind

2. Avoid sexist language by using pronoun references that include both genders.

The sentence below implies that all scientists are men:
Each scientist files his laboratory's OSHA report after completing his quarterly review.

Two ways to solve this problem are **1)** to reword the sentence to omit any reference to gender and **2)** to include both genders:

  a) Each scientist files the laboratory OSHA report after completing the quarterly review.

  b) All scientists file their laboratories' OSHA reports after completing their quarterly review.

  c) Each scientist files his or her laboratory's OSHA report after completing the quarterly review.

Using *his* or *her* can be awkward if repeated in a number of sentences.

3. Avoid sexist language by referring to men and women in the same way when using courtesy titles and in similar situations. The preferred title for women (unless you know the woman's preference) is *Ms.*

USE THIS	NOT THIS
David Tyson and Erica Stokes	David Tyson and Erica
Mr. Jordan and Ms. Carlisle	Peter Jordan and Ms. Carlisle
John and Cara Peterson	Mr. and Mrs. John Peterson
Carol and Anthony Russo	Carol Russo and her husband

4. Avoid sexist language in letter salutations by including both genders.

Of course, you should use the receiver's name if at all possible. If you cannot determine the receiver's name, then these options may be used:

  a) Use a job title.
  Dear Personnel Officer:
  b) Omit the salutation and complimentary close (simplified letter style).
  c) As a last choice, use either of the following:
  Dear Sir or Madam:
  Dear Madam or Sir: (alphabetical)

THE INSIDE TRACK: APPLY WHAT YOU HAVE LEARNED

Revise the sentences below to eliminate biased language.

1. Each of the paratroopers was trained to his maximum ability.
2. Miss Maxine Faulkner, Ralph Huston, and Karl Heinz are listed as having senior security clearance.
3. Jake should address his employment cover letter to "Dear Sir."
4. Any businessman needs to be aware of his educational options.
5. The nurse must record her observations in the patients' charts.
6. All mankind is responsible for making the earth a cleaner, safer place to live.
7. Mrs. Hillary Rodham Clinton, Attorney General Janet Reno, and Al Gore appeared in the photograph.
8. The foremen will file their reports with the CPD Director each Friday.
9. The woman doctor should begin her letter to the Swiss hospital administrator with "Dear Sir" since she does not know the administrator.
10. Did you ever want to be a fireman or a policeman when you were young?

Recommendation Reports

Write-to-Learn

Think of the last time you had to make a choice between two things. Maybe you had to decide between two classes, two cars, two outfits, or two restaurants. In a one-page journal entry, describe the process you went through to make your decision.

DEFINITIONS

criteria the plural form of criterion; the factors on which a decision is made; things to consider when making a decision. *The criteria are cost and safety.*

criterion singular; a factor on which a decision is made; something to consider when making a decision. *The criterion is safety.*

point-by-point organization a comparison/contrast structure that covers two or three items under one criterion

rank the relative importance of one criterion to another; usually ranked from most important to least important

recommendation report a report that helps decision-makers make choices; after comparing and contrasting two or three items to a common set of criteria, it recommends (strongly suggests) one item over the other(s)

standard the limits to a criterion; further defines each criterion

subcriteria a smaller category of criteria that fall under a criterion, the larger category; helps to define the criterion

MEMO

TO: Roberta Boles

FROM: Lisa Smith and Richard Riley

DATE: July 15, 19--

SUBJECT: Purchase Recommendation for New Swing Set

INTRODUCTION

The purpose of this report is to recommend which new swing set Tender Care Center should purchase. The old swing set is rusted through and poses a safety hazard to the children. We have narrowed our choices to two sets: Play Time Gym Set and Kiddie Swing Set. To determine which set should be recommended, we developed the following criteria:

1. Safety
2. Special Features
3. Cost

RECOMMENDATION

We recommend that Tender Care Center purchase the Play Time Gym Set. First, its plastic slide and rounded edges make the set safer for the children. Second, this swing set offers more of the special features we want. Third, the cost of the Play Time Gym Set is within the allocated budget.

SCOPE

The Center's directors have suggested that we rank safety as the first criterion. Concern for the children and compliance with federal guidelines require us to be safety conscious.

Special features is our second criterion. The teachers have said that the children play less on the old swing set because there is no special equipment to interest them. We'd like the new swing set to have special features that provide some variety for the children.

To make sure we stay within budget, we have ranked our third criterion as cost. The director has allocated $300 to spend on the new swing set.

The remainder of this report will compare both swing sets to the three criteria.

DISCUSSION

Safety

A new swing set must include

a. smooth edges with no rough places that can cause cuts and scrapes
b. few cap covers to wear thin and reveal rough edges that may cut
c. a slide under 10 ft. long so children can climb safely
d. a slide that will not absorb heat and thus burn the children's skin

Play Time Gym Set. We visited Samson Sales to see the Play Time Gym Set. The Play Time Gym Set has plastic seats with rounded edges. Fewer caps are needed because of the rounded edges. The slide is 6 ft. in length. In addition, the slide is plastic and will not absorb heat from the sun.

Roberta Boles
Page 2
July 15, 19--

Kiddie Swing Set. According to the Fun and Exercise catalog, the Kiddie Swing Set has galvanized steel frames with rounded edges and would require more caps to cover the sharp edges. The slide is under 10 ft. in length, but heat from the sun will make the metal slide hot.

Conclusion. The Play Time Gym meets the subcriteria, while the Kiddie Swing Set has rough edges, more caps, and a metal slide that will absorb heat.

Swing Set Special Features
The swing set must include enough variety to please different children. The preschool teachers suggest the following features:
   a. Glide ride
   b. Swings
   c. Two-passenger swing
   d. Slide
Table 1 compares these subcriteria to both swing sets.

Table 1. Comparison of Swing Set Features

FEATURES	PLAY TIME GYM SET	KIDDIE SWING SET
Glide Ride	Yes	Yes
Swings	Yes	Yes
Two-Passenger Swing	Yes	No
Slide	Yes	Yes

Play Time Gym Set. The Play Time Gym Set has the features that the preschool wants. Other features such as the pony ride and the adult swing are not necessary.

Kiddie Swing Set. Although the Kiddie Swing Set meets most of the subcriteria, it does not have a two-passenger swing. Like the Play Time Gym Set, the Kiddie Swing Set includes a pony ride and adult swing that are not needed.

Conclusion. The Play Time Gym Set meets and exceeds our subcriteria for special features. The Kiddie Swing Set lacks a two-passenger swing.

Cost
The cost of the swing set must not exceed $300.

Roberta Boles
Page 3
July 15, 19--

Play Time Gym Set. According to Carlton Muroulis, sales representative for Samson Sales, the total cost of the Play Time Gym Set is $282.99. Here is a cost breakdown:

Play Time Gym Set		$249.99
Tax		15.00
Delivery and Setup		18.00
	Total	$282.99

Kiddie Swing Set. The total cost of the Kiddie Swing Set is $226.39. Suzanne Dickenson, sales manager for Fun and Exercise, gave us the following cost breakdown:

Kiddie Swing Set		$189.99
Tax		11.40
Delivery and Setup		25.00
	Total	$226.39

Conclusion. At $282.99, the Play Time Swing Set meets the third criterion. The Kiddie Swing Set, at $226.39, also meets the third criterion—the budget allowance for the swing set.

After completing this chapter, you will be able to

- Adjust the structure of a recommendation report to accommodate the reader's attitude

- Devise criteria for evaluation

- Organize a recommendation report using major headings

- Organize the discussion using point-by-point comparison/contrast structure

- Evaluate criteria and draw conclusions using a systematic, point-by-point analysis

- Conduct research appropriate for the topic

- Write a recommendation report

> *The direction in which education starts a man will determine his future life.*
>
> PLATO

The **recommendation report** is a problem/solution report, a written answer to a need that arises in the workplace. Most problems, however, have more than one solution. The recommendation report recommends the *best* solution to a problem or need. In other words, it helps readers make a choice.

Sometimes the recommendation is the purchase of equipment. In the model at the beginning of the chapter, Lisa Smith and Richard Riley examined two swing sets and recommended the Play Time Swing Set for Tender Care Center. Throughout the chapter, we'll look more closely at some of the decisions Smith and Riley made while writing their report.

Sometimes the report recommends a course of action. For example, Myers Logging has decided to expand and has narrowed the location of its new plant to three towns in West Virginia. A recommendation report will compare and contrast the three sites against the **criteria** the company thinks are important. Finally, the report will recommend a location. Later in this chapter, we will see how the writer of this report gathers data and plans the report.

The last time you bought school supplies, you went through the process of choosing from among several alternatives. Knowing that you needed a three-ring binder, you probably sought out several different three-ring notebooks. The choice you made depended on a number of factors including cost, special features like clipboards or zipper pencil pouches, durability, and color. In the work world, major companies go through this same thinking process when they make choices.

Audience: Who Reads Recommendation Reports?

WARM UP 13.1

Look at the model recommendation report that introduces this chapter. Where is the actual recommendation made? Is this a good place for the recommendation? Why do you think so?

Decision-makers who have the power to implement your recommendations read recommendation reports. Sometimes one person reads the report; often, a committee or board votes on recommendations. The report is usually written to a supervisor, but sometimes recommendations are made to co-workers.

The report can be solicited (asked for) or unsolicited (not asked for). In solicited reports, your reader *asks* you to analyze several alternatives. This reader understands the need and will be more receptive to your suggestions.

In an unsolicited report, your audience is not expecting your recommendations. You may have difficulty gauging this reader's reaction. Your reader may be receptive and may appreciate your initiative in helping to make decisions. On the other hand, your audience may be unwilling to accept your recommendations for a variety of reasons.

Analysis of your audience's attitude may affect how you organize your report. A receptive audience will be ready to read the recommendation itself up front, early in the report (as is presented in the model at the beginning of this chapter). An unreceptive audience will require more careful research up front, with the recommendation itself coming last. Carefully lead this reader to your recommendation. Figure 13.1 shows the strategies for accommodating a receptive and unreceptive audience.

Figure 13.1 Strategy for Receptive and Unreceptive Audiences

RECEPTIVE	UNRECEPTIVE
Introduction	Introduction
Recommendation	Scope
Scope	Discussion—with more details
Discussion—with fewer details	*Recommendation*

Recommendation reports are persuasive. Persuasive writing always requires you to analyze audiences carefully, for your job is to convince your reader to act on your recommendation. Researched facts, opinions of authorities, and logical thinking are the tools you need to be convincing. Find out what information your reader expects in the final report and how detailed the research should be. Review Audience Identification in Chapter 2, page 25 to help you analyze your audience.

. . . .

STOP AND THINK **13.1**

1. If the reader of the swing set recommendation had been unreceptive, where would you have placed the Recommendation section?
2. Why must writers of persuasive reports analyze audiences carefully?
3. Name several possible readers for the swing set recommendation report.

Prewriting: Getting Started on Recommendation Reports

Before you can begin writing, you must define your problem, brainstorm solutions, and devise criteria.

Define Your Problem

In a solicited report, the problem is usually self-evident, but put it into words anyway. In our model, Riley and Smith stated the problem in one sentence: "The old swing set is rusted through and poses a safety hazard to the children."

In an unsolicited report, the problem may need more explanation. If the problem needs more explanation than one or two sentences, consider placing the explanation in a separate paragraph in the Introduction.

Brainstorm Solutions

Now brainstorm solutions. You may need others to help you generate possible solutions. Remember to brainstorm freely and record all the ideas you and your colleagues generate. Next, narrow your choices to two or three. Again, you may use the advice of others to help you narrow your choices.

When Riley and Smith brainstormed solutions to the rusted swing set problem, they generated a list of six kinds of equipment they would like to have on the playground. Their list included things like a Jungle Gym, an eight-swing gym set, and a swing set and slide combination. They narrowed the list of six to two when they decided that a swing set with special equipment would give them more variety for the price.

Devise Criteria

Now that you have narrowed down your choices, decide what criteria to use. Interview people in your organization to help you decide what is important to consider when making the choice. Ask all concerned: administration, workers, people who may have used one of your solutions before. Every area of an organization brings its own unique perspective.

Elaina West was asked to write the report for Myers Logging to recommend the West Virginia town for the new plant. After several management meetings, three sites in West Virginia were selected as possible locations.

After the sites were chosen, West consulted with others to help her devise criteria. Figure 13.2 shows some of the preliminary information she gained after consulting the administration at Myers Logging, the workers who will relocate, and a local furniture manufacturer who purchases wood from Myers Logging.

Figure 13.2 Preliminary Notes for New Plant Location

FROM	TOWN SHOULD HAVE
Administration	• 10-acre plot of land
	• available workforce
	• adequate power supply
Workers who will relocate	• good schools
	• affordable housing
Local furniture manufacturer	• good roads
	• good water supply

From this preliminary list, West was able to classify like items under larger categories. The categories—resources, utilities, and living conditions—became her criteria for her first draft. The smaller units under each category became the **subcriteria**:

Resources	Utilities	Living Conditions
land	power	schools
workforce	water	housing
roads		

Next, she worked to further define each of the subcriteria. Again, she went back to her colleagues and asked these and other questions: What is a fair price for the land? How many people are needed in the workforce? What kind of labor is needed—skilled or unskilled?

If your list of criteria is longer than four or five, reevaluate their importance and see if you can limit your list to no more than five.

Formatting and Organizing Recommendation Reports

WARM UP 13.2

Look closely at the headings in the model report. What kind of information goes under each heading?

The recommendation report is a highly structured report, using a consistent outline and a comparison/contrast discussion.

Outline

The recommendation report consists of introductory material, a recommendation (summary of discussion), scope (what the report covers and why), and discussion (analysis of criteria—the factors used in making the decision). Here is a typical outline.

Introduction
- Gives the purpose of the report
- Briefly explains the problem
- Narrows the choice to two or three items
- Gives a list of criteria
- Provides a preview of the rest of the report
- <u>May</u> include the method of investigation

Recommendation
- Makes the recommendation
- Uses criteria to summarize reasons for the recommendation

Scope
- Lists criteria, in descending order, that were given in the Introduction
- Explains why the criteria were chosen and why they are ranked as they are

Discussion
- Analyzes each of the criteria thoroughly
- Draws conclusions about which item is better for each of the criteria

Remember, receptive readers are interested primarily in the recommendation, so it appears early in the report as a summary/recommendation. Unreceptive readers, however, would need the recommendation placed last, after the Discussion.

Comparison/Contrast Discussion

The discussion follows a comparison/contrast structure. There are several ways to organize a comparison/contrast document. One effective way, the way presented in our model, is to organize **point by point**.

Point by point zigzags from one item to the other, comparing some aspect of one item to the same aspect of another item. Under the Safety heading in the swing-set model, the writers compare the *safety features* of the Play Time Gym Set to the *safety features* of the Kiddie Swing Set. Both swing sets are collected under one point or **criterion,** in this case, Safety. Figure 13.3 shows the zigzag from one item to another.

Figure 13.3 Point-by-Point Organization

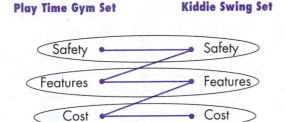

Point by point is the preferred method for the recommendation report. Figure 13.4 links a general outline for this section of the report to the headings found under Discussion in the swing-set model.

Figure 13.4 Point-by-Point Organization in Swing-Set Model

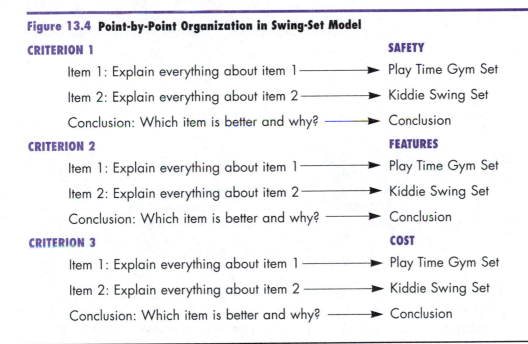

CRITERION 1		SAFETY
Item 1: Explain everything about item 1	→	Play Time Gym Set
Item 2: Explain everything about item 2	→	Kiddie Swing Set
Conclusion: Which item is better and why?	→	Conclusion
CRITERION 2		**FEATURES**
Item 1: Explain everything about item 1	→	Play Time Gym Set
Item 2: Explain everything about item 2	→	Kiddie Swing Set
Conclusion: Which item is better and why?	→	Conclusion
CRITERION 3		**COST**
Item 1: Explain everything about item 1	→	Play Time Gym Set
Item 2: Explain everything about item 2	→	Kiddie Swing Set
Conclusion: Which item is better and why?	→	Conclusion

S T O P   A N D   T H I N K   13.2

1. What heading of a recommendation report contains the most diverse information?
2. What does it mean to "provide a preview of the rest of the report"?
3. How many times does *criteria* appear in the typical outline on page 256?
4. Which part of the report will be the most difficult for you to write? Why?

Sarah Williams is an accountant for Gildstein's Business Managers. She has the tough job of recommending to her supervisor which construction company should build a small office building: Wilmore Construction Company, Inc., or Grayson Builders. Wilmore is a larger company and has a better reputation for finishing tasks on schedule. Bids from both companies fall within Gildstein's budget, but it is imperative that the office building be up in time for holiday sales. Grayson Builders is owned by Williams' brother-in-law, Jeff Grayson. The Graysons have a child with a serious medical condition and really need the money Grayson would earn from this contract. Williams' husband wants her to recommend his brother's company for the job. He claims families should look out for one another. What should Williams do?

Composing Recommendation Reports

W A R M   U P   13.3

John likes contact sports (football, soccer, boxing), Italian food, country music, and horror films. In small groups, design a perfect Saturday for John. Why did you choose the activities you chose? Design a perfect Saturday for your group. Why did you choose these activities?

The Introduction of a recommendation report provides information basic to many technical reports—the purpose and focus of the report, an explanation of the problem, the focus and a preview. The method of investigation could be described in the Introduction or throughout the report as the research is introduced. Basic information, however, is secondary to setting criteria, evaluating criteria, and researching criteria.

Setting Criteria

Criteria, the factors on which you base a decision, play an important role in the recommendation report. Figure 13.5 tells where and how criteria are used in this report.

Figure 13.5 Criteria

CRITERIA ARE		
INTRODUCED	in the	**INTRODUCTION**
SUMMARIZED	in the	**RECOMMENDATION**
EXPLAINED & RANKED (Why chosen & ranked?)	in the	**SCOPE**
EVALUATED (one-by-one)	in the	**DISCUSSION**

The criteria you choose will depend on what you, your audience, and your colleagues think is important. After you select criteria, you must present it in a logical, consistent way. All criteria must be presented with a name, a rank, and a standard (Holcombe and Stein).

Choose a simple name, usually a noun, that is in parallel structure to the other criteria. Some reports turn criteria into questions.

Give each criterion a **rank** to show its relative importance to the other criteria. Which is the most important criterion? second most? third most? List them in descending order, from most important to least important. If necessary, ask others to help you with this decision.

The rank of criteria may change depending on the circumstances. For example, younger workers with families moving with the Myers Logging operations to West Virginia might rank the criteria for an acceptable town as **Schools (1st), Family Entertainment (2nd),** and **Medical Facilities (3rd).** Older workers might rank the criteria as **Medical Facilities (1st), Family Entertainment (2nd),** and **Schools (3rd).**

Finally, determine the **standard** of (or limit to) the criteria. For example, if Tender Care Center will not pay more than $300 for a swing set, then $300 sets the standard for cost.

You may need help refining your criteria. In the swing-set model, the playground equipment had to meet several subcriteria under Safety and Special Features. In your report, list subcriteria when you get to the appropriate criterion section of your report. Like criteria, subcriteria should be listed in descending order of importance. Figure 13.6 summarizes how to develop the criteria in your report.

Figure 13.6 How to Develop Criteria

NAME	noun, noun phrase, or question
RANK	criteria listed from most important to least important
STANDARD	a limit that clarifies each criterion (cost, size, quantity, etc.)
SUBCRITERIA	a list of more detailed criteria that fall under one criterion heading

Evaluating Criteria

Evaluating criteria is a logical, step-by-step process. The structure of a recommendation report invites careful analysis. Look back at the three subheadings—Play Time Gym Set, Kiddie Swing Set, and Conclusion—under Safety in our model. Under Play Time Gym Set, the writers discuss the safety subcriteria for one set of swings. Under Kiddie Swing Set, the writers discuss the *same* safety subcriteria for another set of swings. Figure 13.7 shows how the discussion checks off each of the subcriteria, one-by-one.

Figure 13.7 Checklist to Evaluate Swing-Set Safety

The Play Time Gym Set meets these subcriteria easily:

Smooth edges	✓	It has plastic seats with rounded edges.
Secure cap covers	✓	Fewer caps are needed because of the rounded edges.
Slide under 10 ft.	✓	Slide is 6 ft. in length.
Slide not to absorb heat	✓	Slide is plastic and will not absorb heat from the sun.

The Kiddie Swing Set does not meet all the subcriteria:

Smooth edges	X	It has galvanized steel frames with few rounded edges.
Secure cap covers	X	More cap covers are needed.
Slide under 10 ft.	✓	Slide is 6 ft. in length.
Slide not to absorb heat	X	Slide is metal and will absorb heat from the sun.

The checklist shows at a glance that the Play Time Gym Set meets the preschool's needs for safety more completely. The Play Time Gym Set meets four out of four needs; the Kiddie Swing Set meets one out of four needs. A simple count shows that the Play Time Gym Set wins in the category of safety. After the comparison is made, it's easy to summarize the results in the Conclusion, which follows the discussion of each item.

Suppose that the Kiddie Swing Set had met only the Special Features and Cost criteria and the Play Time Gym Set had met only the Safety criteria? Then you would have a judgment call to make. Safety is ranked as the first concern, more important than special features and cost. You would therefore recommend the Play Time Gym Set.

Suppose, however, that the comparison yields a draw—where both items meet the criteria? Then look for some deciding factor. Maybe the cost of one is lower. Maybe the delivery is quicker, the guarantee better. In those rare cases, where there is truly no difference between the two items, then you are free to recommend either one, or you may wish to set other criteria.

Researching Criteria

Research data for a recommendation report can come from a variety of places. Much of the research you conduct for a recommendation report will be field research—research using surveys, interviews, and visits. Manuals and catalogs can provide product information. Print media in the library can be useful, too. *Consumer Reports*, government publications, business indexes, and professional journals can all provide data you need. Refer to Chapter 15, Data Collection, for more advice on researching a topic.

Elaina West, in her recommendation report to Myers Logging, used all of these sources in her report. She interviewed her co-workers and workers of another logging operation. She surveyed the employees who would move to the new site. West visited the three towns in West Virginia and interviewed town officials. She reviewed government documents on the tax base.

Because the writing task was not as involved, the writers of our swing-set model did not need to conduct as much research as West. Preschool personnel, sales brochures, a visit to a store, and sales representatives provided all the information they needed.

Be alert to opportunities to present research data in visual aids. The swing-set model uses tables of costs and features. Other possibilities for visuals include pictures or diagrams of equipment, pie graphs of survey results, or bar graphs to compare items.

S T O P   A N D   T H I N K   13.3

1. Tom's doctor has told him to eat a nutritious diet low in fat, cholesterol, and salt and high in complex carbohydrates. Help him evaluate the butter substitutes listed on the next page. What conclusion can you draw from your evaluation?

Subcriteria	1 tbsp. margarine	1 tbsp. table spread
#1 Low in fat	17% fat	11% fat
#2 Low in cholesterol	0% cholesterol	0% cholesterol
#3 Low in salt	4% salt	5% salt
#4 High in complex carbohydrates	0% complex carbohydrates	0% complex carbohydrates

2. What sources might you use to research the following recommendation report topics?

   a. bass fishing boats   **b.** novels   **c.** uniforms for nurses

S U M M A R Y

1. Decision-makers (sometimes several people) read recommendation reports. Reports can be solicited (asked for) or unsolicited (not asked for). For receptive audiences, place the Recommendation section early in the report. For unreceptive audiences, place the Recommendation section later in the report.

2. Get started on a recommendation report by defining the problem, generating possible solutions, and devising criteria. Interview colleagues to help you with the prewriting process.

3. The recommendation report follows a tight structure, using a consistent outline and a comparison/contrast discussion. The major sections include an Introduction, the Recommendation, the Scope, and a thorough Discussion. The comparison/contrast organization follows a point-by-point pattern that discusses all solutions (usually two) under one heading or criterion.

4. The Introduction contains basic information. The remainder of the report examines criteria. Criteria are *introduced* in the INTRODUCTION, *summarized* in the RECOMMENDATION, *explained* in the SCOPE, and thoroughly *discussed* in the DISCUSSION.

Editing And Revision Checklist

✓ Have I devised a reasonable set of criteria by which to judge the items under analysis?

✓ Have I further defined the criteria by setting standards and including appropriate subcriteria?

✓ Does my Introduction give the purpose of the report, define the problem, narrow the choices, and introduce the criteria in their proper rank?

✓ Have I considered whether my audience is receptive or unreceptive? If the audience is unreceptive, did I adjust the placement of the Recommendation and the number of researched details to accommodate an unreceptive audience?

✓ Does the Scope explain why the criteria were chosen and why they were ranked as they were?

✓ Is the organization of the Discussion clear? Does it follow a point-by-point organizational pattern?

✓ Have I used visual aids appropriately and designed the document to be attractive?

APPLY WHAT YOU HAVE LEARNED

1. Here are excerpts from recommendation reports that are mislabeled. What should the proper heading be?

Example A   **RECOMMENDATION**

The purpose of this report is to recommend the best drawing program for Interform Art Department. The drawing program we are currently using is slow and unable to access the computer's full capabilities. Following your suggestion, we have narrowed the choice to three: Draw Plus, Draw III, and Creative Freehander. I have evaluated them using the following criteria, in ranked order:

1. Capabilities
2. Ease of Use
3. Cost
4. Compatibility

Example B   **INTRODUCTION**

A survey of customers' preferences clearly shows that our golfers' number one concern is a club with good weight balance. Upon their suggestion, I ranked weight balance as the first criterion.

A second concern revealed by the survey is that golfers are not getting enough distance out of their clubs. For this reason, I ranked distance as the second criterion.

The third criterion is cost. Most of our customers have indicated that they would not pay more than $500 for a set of clubs.

The remainder of this report will compare both sets of clubs to these three criteria.

Example C   **DISCUSSION**

I recommend the purchase of the Barts UVC. First, the cost is within the average student's budget. Second, the durability/warranty far exceeds those of the other brands. Third, Barts regularly carries its UVC in stock, whereas the other brands have to be ordered quarterly from retailers. Fourth, our school has an ongoing contract with Barts that would allow discounts for students.

2. What has been left out of the following sections? Edit the passages to add missing information. Make up circumstances, if necessary. This activity is also available on the computer applications diskette as **TEXT13A**.

Example A   DISCUSSION

Gas Mileage
The car should average over 30 miles to the gallon.

Athena ESL. The Athena ESL averages approximately 50 miles per gallon on the road. In town, the gas mileage drops to approximately 46 miles per gallon.

Omni Sedan. The Omni Sedan averages approximately 33 miles to the gallon. In town, the gas mileage drops to approximately 29 miles per gallon.

Example B   INTRODUCTION

We have narrowed our choice of computer desks to three: Archway Desk and Hutch, Tilliton Computer Desk #WS-1, and Sawyer Office Desk #IOT-68. After consulting with the support staff, we chose the following criteria, in ranked order:
1. Flexibility
2. Storage capacity
3. Size
4. Cost

3. In small groups, use one of the following scenarios to answer questions **1–5**. You do not have to use the same scenario for all five questions.

a. You are on the Entertainment Committee to decide which band to hire for the Junior/Senior Prom. According to the survey you sent out, students are evenly divided among a choice for three groups: Newton Jazz Ensemble, Midnight City Rock Band, or Down and Dusty Country Band.

b. You are on the Hampton Scholarship Committee. Hampton Company gives a $1000 scholarship to a deserving high school senior every year. The North High guidance counselor has chosen Wilhelm Nagorski and Annetta Jackson as the top two contenders for the scholarship. You, and the committee, must select one of these students.

c. You are on the Ammsco Chemical's Quality Circle that must decide what goes into the new employee lounge. You've narrowed your choice of microwaves to two: the Trintron Model 1400 and the Even Cook Model 550. You, along with the members of your Quality Circle team, must choose the new microwave.

1. Write an introduction to a recommendation report for **a, b,** or **c** on preceding page. Add details if necessary. Look at the model and at the outline under Formatting and Organizing Recommendation Reports in the chapter. You may begin your introduction with "The purpose of this report is to . . . ."

2. For any two of the preceding scenarios, brainstorm a list of criteria. Narrow your list to the top three or four. Rank them in order from most important to least important.

3. Choose one of the lists of criteria from question **2.** Apply a standard, or limit, to each of the criteria. Devise subcriteria for one of the criteria.

4. In an oral or written scope section, tell your classmates why you chose the criteria you chose and why you ranked them the way you did.

5. Generate an outline for two of the scenarios. Follow this format. For now, make your best guess for the conclusion under each criterion.

CRITERION 1 _____
    ITEM 1   _____
    ITEM 2   _____
    CONCLUSION   _____
CRITERION 2 _____
    ITEM 1   _____
    ITEM 2   _____
    CONCLUSION   _____
CRITERION 3 _____
    ITEM 1   _____
    ITEM 2   _____
    CONCLUSION   _____

CONSIDER THIS CASE

Draw information from the following narrative to write your own recommendation report:

Ursula Potter is trying to decide whether to attend Tyndall Community College, located in her home town, or Nash State University, a four-year college located 30 miles away. After talking to her family, you realize that they do not have a lot of money (total yearly income less than $50,000), but they are committed to finding a way to send Potter to college.

Potter wants to be a high school biology teacher. Tyndall offers a state-accredited Pre-Education AAS that includes general college courses and some courses required for a teaching certificate. After completing this two-year program, Potter could transfer to a four-year school and declare her major. Nash State offers a state-accredited BS in secondary Biology education.

Tuition at Tyndall is $356 per semester. Tuition at Nash State is $788 per semester. Books at both schools average

$135 per semester. If Potter attended Tyndall, she could live at home and ride the bus to classes ($1 per day fare—estimated total $140). If she attended Nash State, she would have to either move there and live in a dorm ($560 per semester) or commute ($2,000 to buy a used car and $1,060 for gas and maintenance for two semesters).

Admission at Tyndall is open door. Potter would not need to use her SAT scores or grades from high school for admission. Nash State would look at her SAT scores and grades. Potter's SAT score was 810, slightly below average and only 10 points higher than the university's requirement. Her high school grade point average, 2.8, meets the school's requirement but is not high enough to offset the marginal SAT score.

PURSUE AN IDEA

1. Write a purchase recommendation to the audience indicated for one of the following situations. Enlist the aid of others to help you narrow choices and devise criteria and possibly subcriteria. Decide what problem your purchase will solve. Research your products using the library and/or other resources.

   a. Think about organizations you belong to—clubs at school, for example. Is there something that one of these organizations is considering purchasing? If so, write a report to the group recommending which item to purchase.

   b. Make a list of things you would like to purchase in the next two years, or think about a piece of equipment that would make life in your household more convenient—maybe another TV, a VCR, a telephone, or a CD player. Write a report with yourself or your parents as the audience recommending which item you should buy.

   c. Look around your school. Make a list of things the school needs. Write a report to your principal recommending the purchase of your item.

2. Write a report recommending a course of action to the audience indicated for one of the following situations. Enlist the aid of others to help you narrow choices and devise criteria and possibly subcriteria. Decide what problem your recommendation will solve. Research your courses of action using the library and/or other resources.

   a. Make a list of problems in your school or community. Focus, for a moment, on one you care about. Are there two or three courses of action that might solve this problem? Write a report to your principal or city official recommending a course of action.

   b. Think of two places you would like to go. Maybe you're considering two schools, two vacation sites, or two apartment locations. Then write a report with yourself as the audience recommending the best place.

   c. Help some club or committee at school make a decision by writing a recommendation report to the members of that group. Help the drama club choose a play, the choral group choose a musical, the Spanish club choose c project, or the prom committee choose a theme.

"You" Attitude

With the exception of the science lab report, most technical writing should be reader-centered rather than writer-centered. A reader-centered approach, or "you" attitude, attempts to look at things from the reader's perspective instead of the writer's perspective. The "you" attitude points out advantages to the reader and makes him or her more likely to accept what you say.

Notice the difference between the "I" or "we" attitude and the "you" attitude in the following examples. The "you" attitude sounds friendlier, more positive.

PARENT:

"I" or "we" attitude: I don't want to see that basketball left outside again. The wind will blow it down the street and it will be gone!

"You" attitude: Remember to put away your basketball. If you leave it outside, the wind might blow it down the street and you might not be able to find it.

MANUFACTURED-HOME DEALER:

"I" or "we" attitude: Do we, at Mountain View Homes, have deals! Our 14 × 70 single-wides have been marked down 20%. And our 14 × 80s can be purchased with a rebate of $1000!

"You" attitude: You can find a real deal at Mountain View Homes. You can purchase our 14 × 70 single-wides at 20% off the regular price. And you can receive a rebate of $1000 on a brand new 14 × 80.

In the first example, the "you" attitude points out the advantages to a son or daughter of putting away a basketball. In the second example, the "you" attitude stresses how a customer can benefit from buying a home from Mountain View Homes. Not only is the "you" approach psychologically smart as a motivator, but it also makes a good sales pitch.

To use the "you" attitude, simply consider the situation from your reader's standpoint. What is the advantage to him or her? Then, where appropriate, add more you's and your's to your message and take out some of the I's, we's, or company names. Point out the benefit of your message to your reader.

INSIDE TRACK: APPLY WHAT YOU HAVE LEARNED

Rewrite these sentences to reflect a stronger "you" attitude. Remember, you can't eliminate uses of *I, we,* and company names, but you can slant the writing to be more reader-centered. Add any information that may help the reader see the advantages to him or her.

1. We will ship the rest of your order next week.
2. Powell Insurance Company is reliable. We have been in business for over 50 years at the same location.
3. I want you to take the conversational Spanish classes for several reasons.
4. Your overdue account must be paid within 30 days or we will give you a poor credit rating and stop taking your orders.
5. We do not have your order in stock. We will notify you when we do.
6. I expect you to be home by 12:00 for several reasons.
7. I don't think you should choose clothes that are difficult and time-consuming to take care of.
8. We want all students to stay on the school grounds during lunch so they won't be late for class.
9. We have marked down all furniture for our moving sale. We'd rather sell the furniture than move it. Everything must go!
10. The university requires you to take 30 semester hours of general college courses.

WORKS CITED

Holcombe, Marya W., and Judith K. Stein. *Writing for Decision Makers: Memos and Reports with a Competitive Edge.* Belmont, CA: Lifelong, 1981.

PART

5

Researched Reports

Problem-Solving

Write-to-Learn

Read the following exchange between Tyson and Constance. Then identify the problem or problems. Which problem(s) needs to be solved?

Constance: Tyson, what are you doing?

Tyson: I'm cleaning up some problems with this design going to Carter tomorrow. Some stray marks on the brick wall you drew for the north boundary need to be erased.

Constance: Wait a minute! That's my design. I spent hours developing those stray marks; they're a new pattern for the brickwork.

D E F I N I T I O N S

factor a subpart or division of the problem
limitations what you will not be able to do in your search to solve a problem
scope what you will examine in your efforts to solve a particular problem

---

CHAPTER 14 OBJECTIVES

After completing this chapter, you will be able to

- Determine if a problem exists
- Define the problem and your purpose
- Conduct preliminary research
- Set scope and limitations for the study
- Identify factors of the problem
- Use a problem-solving process to identify solutions
- Collect data to support possible solutions
- Determine the most effective solution for a particular problem

Problems. Problems. Problems. Undoubtedly, you face problems every day. The problems may be small ones, such as losing a button from your favorite shirt, or the problems may be more significant, such as not having enough money to go to the school you choose. How do you solve those problems?

The best solutions seem to be those reached through a systematic approach. Workable solutions don't often fall out of the sky; they usually don't appear effortlessly; they typically require a system of creative and critical thinking that uses as many available data resources as possible. Using a problem-solving process, or methodical development of solutions, is an effective strategy to help you keep your focus and discover good ideas.

You have probably developed a system for dealing with the everyday problems, the little aggravations, that often crop up in life. If you have a successful system, then you can adapt what you understand about solving problems from that system to help you solve problems in the workplace. However, you may solve problems every day without ever thinking about how you do it or without being aware of the system you use for problem-solving.

Understanding the problem-solving process will help you improve your problem-solving skills. Moreover, since virtually every report begins with a problem or a need, good problem-solvers are also good report writers. A problem-solving strategy, such as the one listed below, can make your work as a student, as a writer, and as an employee easier:

1. Find out if you have a problem.
2. If you do, define the problem and your purpose.
3. Conduct preliminary research.
4. Determine the scope and limitations of your study.
5. Identify the factors or subparts of the problem.
6. Formulate possible solutions.
7. Gather data to support the possible solutions.
8. Test and evaluate possible solutions.

Find Out if You Have a Problem

W A R M   U P   14.1

Joan Lohr works from her home as a medical transcriptionist, someone who types medical reports from audiotapes doctors or researchers have dictated. She contracts with two physicians' offices and one medical laboratory. Recently the workload has become difficult for Lohr to handle. One of the physicians' offices has hired two additional doctors, and they expect Lohr to accept the additional work. If she doesn't, Lohr believes the office will look for another transcriptionist. Yet, Lohr would have to work at least 10 hours a day, six days a week in order to keep up with the work. This is more time than Lohr wants to devote to her job. Does Lohr have a problem? If you think Lohr does have a problem, how might she look at the situation as an opportunity, rather than as a problem?

The first step in the problem-solving process is to decide if a problem even exists. Sometimes situations that at first seem to be problems may, in fact, be opportunities. For example, a man who spent $600 on a painting believed he had a serious problem when he noticed bubbles and other imperfections in the paint surface. Later, he discovered the paint concealed an extremely valuable 17th century masterpiece.

In other circumstances, such as with Joan Lohr in Warm Up 14.1, a problem exists, but it may have an obvious, simple, or ready solution. Lohr does have more work than she can handle, but the situation also gives her an opportunity to expand her business by hiring an employee. If a satisfactory resolution is available, then the problem-solver does not have to work to find a solution.

STOP AND THINK 14.1

How do you define the word *problem*? Compare your definition with those of other members of your group.

Define the Problem and Your Purpose

WARM UP 14.2

Consider Joan Lohr, the medical transcriptionist mentioned in Warm Up 14.1. What is Lohr's problem? Describe the problem fully. Have you ever had a problem similar to Lohr's? Explore your thoughts in a journal entry.

Defining the problem and understanding your purpose are the next things you need to do. This is the step in the process where you determine exactly what the problem is. In the examples mentioned above, you learned of problems that had ready solutions. On the other hand, some problems are harder to identify. When such a situation arises, it is your job as the problem-solver to determine what the problem actually is. To define the problem, it may help to compose a written problem statement or question.

To show how the problem statement and question, as well as the subsequent steps in the problem-solving process, are developed, let's follow Joan Lohr as she attempts to solve her problem. Lohr has found four partners who want to establish Oakmont Medical Transcription Service with her, a company that will type medical reports from tapes doctors or research scientists have dictated. The partners have asked Lohr to investigate whether to hire 8 full-time employees, 16 part-time employees, or 8 to 10 independent contractors who will work at home on their own schedules. Lohr's study will affect whether the new business signs a lease on prime office space now available. The space, if leased, will accommodate 8 transcriptionists and a secretary. To begin her investigation, Lohr writes a clear statement of the problem:

Problem Statement: *Oakmont Medical Transcription Service must decide what type of employees to hire to open the business. Prime office space for full-time employees is available now.*

Lohr then makes the problem statement even more specific in this question:

Question: *Should Oakmont Medical Transcription Service hire full-time, part-time, or independent contract transcriptionists?*

Now that the problem is clear, Lohr needs to be clear about her purpose as well. First, she must know what her partners expect. Do they want Lohr to present data so that the group can make a decision? Do they want her to make her recommendation and support it with evidence? Do they want Lohr to analyze potential clients and suggest the type of employee to best match client needs? Do they want to know how feasible a particular choice is? After talking with her partners, Lohr writes this statement of purpose:

Purpose: *I will recommend a plan for staffing Oakmont Medical Transcription Service.*

The purpose statement is the problem-solver's goal. In this case, it will keep the investigation on track, give Lohr a focus.

S T O P   A N D   T H I N K   14.2

1. How does a problem statement help the person working with the problem?
2. What does a purpose statement include that a problem statement does not?

THE PROFESSIONAL SPEAKS

Roland H. Smythe, owner of a pork processing plant, says problem-solving skills are essential in today's workplace. According to Smythe, employees who succeed are those who take the initiative to seek solutions without having to be told step-by-step what to do. Most managers, he notes, spend too much of their workday solving little problems and putting out fires for others when they could be planning for greater productivity.

Conduct Preliminary Research

W A R M   U P   14.3

Think about Joan Lohr's problem. What would you want to know before you make a decision?

Once you have defined your problem, you need to explore it and understand it completely. If you already are familiar with the problem, then preliminary research could be minimal. If you don't know what the problem entails, then preliminary research can help you with a basic understanding of the issue as well as conditions and events that surround it.

Preliminary research may begin with a search through company reports to discover the history (what has been done and said) of this topic inside the organization. Some businesses and industries even have their own libraries within the company. This research might also involve talking with other employees or experts in the field. You could begin in the library with background reading to explore what is already known in a particular area. (Library research is discussed in greater detail in the next chapter, Data Collection.)

Occasionally this preliminary research will show that the problem has already been solved by someone else. If the same situation came up previously, you can profit from the knowledge and experience of employees who dealt with the problem at that time.

Continuing with the example of the problem for staffing the new transcription business, Joan Lohr is aware that her new business has no history to depend upon, so she chooses to explore other sources of information. She heads to the library to learn more about the advantages and disadvantages of hiring part-time employees, full-time employees, and independent contractors. She also checks materials that discuss business administration and employee management.

S T O P   A N D   T H I N K   14.3

Why is preliminary research important? What could happen if a problem-solver skips this step?

Determine Scope and Limitations

W A R M   U P   14.4

Review the definitions for *scope* and *limitations* at the beginning of this chapter.

Preliminary research should also aid you in determining the scope and limitations of the study to solve your problem. Since scope is a positive statement about how far-reaching and comprehensive your investigation will be, it explains what elements or issues of the problem will be studied. To determine the scope of your work, you may need to brainstorm for the important elements of the problem that you already know.

Having determined how far your study will go by looking at scope, use these six questions to set some boundaries or limitations for the study:

- Who is involved? Who is going to be studied and by whom?
- What do I want to do? What is involved in the research?
- Where is the physical area I will include in this study?
- When is it to be done? When is the most effective time to do it?
- Why am I doing it?
- How should I do it?

As with academic research projects, a writer cannot effectively cover a topic that is overly broad. For instance, if Joan Lohr were to recommend a copy machine for her new business to buy, would she investigate all the copy machines manufactured around the world or would she check those sold and serviced in her region? Checking into every copy machine manufactured anywhere in the world could be an overwhelming task. Most researchers try to limit the search.

Likewise, if Lohr and her partners had only $3,000 to spend on a copy machine, then a search to find the best copy machine for her office should not include machines that cost more than $3,000. Thus, the study has been limited by cost. Many problems must be resolved within a specified period of time; thus, the solution is limited by time. A solution may be limited by time, cost, space, personnel, and other elements.

Joan Lohr has defined the scope of her problem with the three types of employees she will research. In addition, she has a limitation of time to consider: Her partners expect her report in two weeks because the potential office space is only available through the end of the month.

> *In the middle of difficulty lies opportunity.*
>
> ANONYMOUS

STOP AND THINK **14.4**

Using the situation below, describe the scope and limitations of Martin's problem-solving.

Martin, who has a babysitting business to raise money for an electric guitar, has discovered a scheduling problem today, Thursday. He agreed last week to sit for the Robinsons on Friday from 5:30–11:30 p.m. However, he forgot to write the appointment in his calendar, so today his mother accepted another sitting job for him for Friday night from 8:00–10:30 p.m. with the Garcias. The Garcias have a four-month-old baby, and Martin is the only sitter they will hire. How can Martin solve this problem without ruining his business reputation?

You are the city planner for a town of about 40,000 people. The city's landfill has become overextended, and you have been assigned to acquire a new site for the city. After studying a dozen potential sites, you narrow your choices to three:

- A small property in a rural area. The land would be inexpensive, but the city would need to expend a considerable sum on drainage and roadways, and local residents are vehemently opposed to a landfill.
- A condemned factory belonging to a local developer. The developer is willing to sell to the city, but the price is much higher than those of the other sites.
- A large, inexpensive property near the river. Environmental regulations would require the construction of expensive facilities to safeguard the water.

Which would you choose, and why? What other information might you need to acquire before making your decision? What problems might you need to solve in implementing the decision?

Identify Factors or Subparts

W A R M   U P   14.5

Read the following situation and explain in a paragraph or two why Mary Helen's approach is more likely to get positive results than Fernando's.

Fernando thinks he could be an Olympic contender in ice skating, but the training he really needs now is very expensive and 800 miles away from home. Fernando decides the money and distance are impossible obstacles and defers his Olympic aspirations for another year.

Mary Helen, who wants to be an Olympic ice skater like Fernando, faces the same challenges he does. She determines the amount of money needed for coaching and equipment as well as ways she can acquire the money. She also examines the idea of moving 800 miles away from home and alternatives to moving.

Some problems may be too complex and overwhelming to deal with in their entirety but may be quite manageable one part or element at a time. For instance, consider the stranded motorist on the freeway who knows almost nothing about automobile mechanics. The motorist sees only a disabled car. A knowledgeable technician would look at the car as a collection of parts, any one of which might be the single nonfunctioning element preventing the car from working properly. The technician would search for the solution by examining the car's parts.

Most problems can best be solved by identifying factors or subparts. **Factors** or smaller parts of the problem are issues you will investigate, which may lead to solutions for the problem. To find the factors of the problem, be specific about the problem's elements. Search beneath the surface of the problem. Think about causes of the problem as well. What are its component parts? You may use the Reporter's Questions—who, what, when, where, why, —to help you break the problem down.

In the case mentioned above, the car may not run because a belt broke. Therefore, the entire car is not the problem; the broken belt is the problem. Accordingly, the solution lies in this factor or smaller part. When the broken belt is replaced, the car will run and the problem is solved. As you can see, factors can give a framework or outline for your research. Sometimes factors are possible solutions to the problem. Each possible solution becomes one more factor or element to be studied.

For Joan Lohr, three obvious parts of the problem are the types of potential help: full-time employees, part-time employees, and independent contractors. As Lohr looks beneath the surface of the problem, she will add other factors, such as space, salary and benefits, licenses, and insurance. Information she uncovers could lead her to add or delete factors. For instance, she could discover a new employee arrangement, one she had never heard of before; this factor would be added to the search.

S T O P   A N D   T H I N K   14.5

Have you ever made a snap decision to resolve a problem? Are these quick decisions generally effective or ineffective? What kind of problem calls for a snap decision? Write a brief journal entry responding to these questions.

Formulate Possible Solutions

W A R M   U P   14.6

Do you think of problem-solving as boring or exciting? Is it something to avoid whenever possible, an opportunity, or a challenge? In your group, share your views with others. Compare your answers and attitudes about how successful you are at problem-solving.

With a full understanding of the problem and its subparts, you, the problem-solver, are ready to formulate possible solutions for the problem. This is one of the most creative phases of the process. In this phase, you should be as free-thinking and noncritical as you can.

Be sure to consider the factors of the problems and brainstorm for solutions for each part. Each factor may suggest a number of possible solutions. Some factors may share the same potential solution. For instance, Joan Lohr brainstormed for each factor of her problem: full-time, part-time, and independent contract transcriptionists. Considering hiring full-time employees, she decided that she would need a minimum of 1,500 square feet of office space. She also realized that she and her partners would know many well-qualified transcriptionists and be able to select the best job applicants. Brainstorming in this way, she created many possible solutions for her problem. One solution Joan listed was to hire two full-time and as many additional part-time employees as the workload required.

Some problem-solvers think out loud; in other words, they speak the ideas as ideas occur. Others like to create lists. Often, as in other types of brainstorming, one idea will lead to others.

Another approach to creating possible solutions is to start with the most obvious solutions and work your way to those that might be considered far-fetched or even ridiculous. Sometimes the least likely solutions turn out to be winners.

STOP AND THINK **14.6**

Why is it important not to be judgmental or critical when you are formulating possible solutions?

Gather Data

WARM UP **14.7**

Libraries are not the only places where research can be done. Write a journal entry or a list of other information sources that may be used to help solve problems.

Since a solution is only as good as the data on which the solution is based, one of the most important parts of the problem-solving process is research or data collection. It is wise to allow adequate time to locate sources of information, to evaluate those sources, and to collect the data you need.

Although you have already completed the preliminary research and have discovered the necessary background information, this phase of collecting data is more specific and analytical. You may want to prepare a research plan. A research plan is like an outline of your project. It forces you to develop a logical plan, a strategy for collecting and evaluating data. It is a statement of what you're doing and where you're going. A research plan includes

- a statement of the problem and what you already know
- your purpose—including scope and limitations
- a list of sources and methods you will use to collect data
- a list of questions you want to answer about the problem and its factors
- a schedule of tasks

One of the first computers. the ENIAC (Electronic Numerical Integrator and Calculator), was a 30-ton, 2-story-high machine that covered 15,000 square feet.

Figure 14.1 below is the research plan Joan Lohr developed. She used the plan to guide her search to solve the problem she and her partners had concerning staff for the new business. Using the research plan, Lohr was able to focus her study and use her time efficiently.

Figure 14.1 Research Plan Model

Problem

Oakmont Medical Transcription Service needs to hire a staff of trained transcriptionists to open the business. We want to hire the most economical and productive staff possible. Prime office space suitable for the number of people in a full-time staff is available now through the end of the month but may not be available to us after that.

Purpose

The purpose of this study is to determine whether to hire full-time, part-time, or independent contract transcriptionists. The study will compare types of employees hired and the level of satisfaction of their managers at other transcription firms in our area. It will compare costs for each type of staff, including office space and benefits such as insurance. I will survey potential clients, limited to 50 organizations within a 100-mile area, to measure their preference for working with the same or different transcriptionists. The study will be restricted to state-licensed transcriptionists.

> Explains purpose, scope, and limitations

Sources and Methods of Data Collection

Magazine and newspaper articles relating to office management, transcription services, and customer service for the past year will be examined. Managers and employees of transcription services in the area will be interviewed. In addition, I will mail a survey to 50 potential clients asking about their needs and preferences. I also will speak with real estate agents regarding the cost and availability of office space for the business.

> Tells where the information will be found

Questions

What are the advantages and disadvantages of full-time employees?
  What will the costs of office space and payroll (including benefits) be?
  Do clients prefer to work with the same person each time?
  Is management/administration easier? Less costly?

What are the advantages and disadvantages of part-time employees?
  Are part-time workers more productive because they are fresher?
  Does the cost of benefits go down with part-time staff?
  Is continuity of work lost with the constant change in employees each
    day?
  How much office space is required for a part-time staff?

What are the advantages and disadvantages of independent contract employees?
  Must we carry liability insurance for independent workers?
  How can we control quality with this type of staff?
  Are there savings in the amount of office space or equipment needed?

> Offers questions to be answered and uses factors to break the problem into workable units

2

Would a combination of the three types of employees be beneficial?

Schedule

Read newspaper and magazine articles	March 24–30
Interview managers and employees	April 1–10
Survey potential clients	April 1–20
Interview real estate agents	April 11–15
Evaluate and analyze data	April 21–27

> Schedules time for each research task

Since collecting information is one of the most important steps in solving a problem, the subject is covered thoroughly in the next chapter, Data Collection. Chapter 15 will explain how you effectively gather information from printed materials as well as electronic, video, and other sources. In addition, the chapter discusses the acquisition of firsthand information through interviews and surveys, observation, and experimentation.

STOP AND THINK 14.7

Review Figure 14.1, the Research Plan Model, to answer the questions below.

1. Using Lohr's questions as a guide, determine the factors Joan has identified.

2. List the four methods Lohr will use to gather information and the resources from which she will obtain it.

Test and Evaluate Possible Solutions

WARM UP 14.8

You have an interview tomorrow morning for a job you really want, but your parents have had to go out of town on business for two days and you are responsible for your six-year-old sister. Here are some possible solutions:

● Call the interviewer, explain the situation, and try to reschedule the interview.

● Hire a sitter and go to the interview.

● Take your sister with you to the interview.

Which do you think is the best choice?

While generating ideas for possible solutions is a creative activity, the last phase of the problem-solving process requires your critical and analytical skills. With the data you've collected, you test and evaluate possible solutions. You eliminate solutions that prove impossible or unreasonable. In working with Warm Up 14.8, you probably realized, for example, that taking your sister with you would be an unreasonable solution because you could not take care of her while you were being interviewed, and to bring her would be unprofessional. Of the solutions remaining, you determine, based on information you found, the most desirable of the choices.

These questions might be valuable as you test and evaluate solutions:

- Do you have the means (money, equipment, time, space, and others) to carry out the solution?
- How easy or difficult will the solution be to implement?
- How will people feel about the solution? How will they react?
- What is likely to be the result of the solution?
- Will it solve the entire problem or only part of the problem?
- Will it create any new problems?

Sometimes solutions that are generated too quickly or without much thought create additional problems. Consider the "home fix-it fiend" who decides to fix the leak under the sink without calling the plumber. The result of the repair is that there is no longer a leak but the faucet above the sink sprays water everywhere. As in this case, a quick and easy solution may be no solution at all.

Joan Lohr discovered through her research these facts about part-time (PT) employees:

- large numbers of applicants seek PT positions
- administrative costs are 1.5 times those for full-time (FT) employees for an equal number of work hours
- compensation packages cost two thirds of the amount expended for FT employees
- twice as much office space is required for PT as for FT employees

Thus, in evaluating PT employees as a possible solution to the problem, Joan determines that having a large number of applicants and needing only two thirds as much money for salary and benefits would be nice. However, she decides the extra costs for administration and office space outweigh any benefits that seem likely. Therefore, she eliminates hiring part-time employees as a solution.

STOP AND THINK 14.8

If Joan Lohr, after eliminating impossible and unreasonable solutions, is left with two possible solutions for staffing the new transcription business, what could she do?

SUMMARY

1. Since problems challenge us every day, developing effective problem-solving skills can make all facets of our lives better. First, we must understand that problem-solving is a process. Then we must learn to apply the steps of the process to our problems.

2. The problem-solving strategy begins with finding out if there is a problem.

3. Next you must define the problem and your purpose.

4. With a clear view of your problem and purpose, you may begin conducting preliminary research.

5. Next, determine the scope and limitations of your study.

6. The problem can be handled best if you break it down into its parts or identify its factors.

7. For each factor, formulate possible solutions. Be creative rather than critical during this phase.

8. With the possible solutions in mind, gather data relating to each solution.

9. The last step in problem-solving is testing and evaluating possible solutions.

BUILD ON WHAT YOU KNOW

1. Compare the way you solved problems before studying this chapter with the methods recommended here.
   a. What similarities, if any, do you find?
   b. Which problem-solving method will take more time?
   c. Which will have the best outcome?

2. Write an outline of the steps you took to solve a problem successfully.
   a. Using the outline of what you did, identify any of the eight steps of the problem-solving process discussed in this chapter.
   b. Make a list of any of the eight steps you omitted when you solved the outlined problem.
   c. Brainstorm for things you could have done to complete each of the eight steps.
   d. Write a brief composition describing whether or not you think completing the omitted steps would have resulted in a *more successful* outcome.

CONDUCT YOUR OWN RESEARCH

1. Make an appointment to call or visit with a professional in the career field of your interest. Prepare questions in advance. Try to learn about problem-solving and the types of problems this person handles on the job. Prepare a report of your findings to share with your class or to publish in a class or school periodical.

2. Interview any employee concerning a particular problem and the solution for which that employee was responsible. Write a description of the problem, the methods the employee used to solve it, the effectiveness of the solution, and the satisfaction of the employee with his or her work.

3. Use library research or interviews to learn more about a great problem-solver or innovator, such as Thomas Edison, Albert Einstein, Franklin Roosevelt, or Jonas Salk. Try to find out as much as you can about the methods the person used in seeking solutions. Make an oral presentation of your findings to your class.

APPLY WHAT YOU HAVE LEARNED

1. Using a problem mentioned in this chapter or one of your own discovery, prepare a research plan that could be used if you were to follow the process through to its conclusion.

2. Chronicle (keep a journal or diary) the strategies you use and their results as you attempt to resolve a problem.

3. In an essay, explain how and why using a problem-solving *process* might benefit you in your career.

CHAPTER 15

Data Collection

Write-to-Learn

Do you currently do research? If so, what does it involve? Respond to this question in a brief composition. Be prepared to share your answer in class or group discussion.

DEFINITIONS

archives a collection or repository of documents

citations written indications of the source for borrowed materials

close-ended questions questions that restrict the number of possible answers

direct quotation the use of borrowed ideas, words, phrases, and sometimes sentences exactly as they appear in the original source

documentation a system of giving credit for borrowed ideas and words

on-line transmission of information by electronic means

open-ended questions questions that encourage the respondent to provide any answer he or she likes; the question gives no suggested answers

paraphrase presenting someone else's ideas in your own words, phrases, and sentence structure

periodicals materials published at specified intervals of time, such as magazines, journals, newsletters, and newspapers

plagiarism the use of another person's words and/or ideas without properly documenting or giving credit

population the group from whom you want to gather data

primary sources direct or firsthand reports of facts or observations

reliable data results that can be duplicated under similar circumstances

respondents people chosen to respond to or answer questions

sample a subgroup with the same characteristics as the entire population

secondary sources indirect or secondhand reports of information

summarizing condensing longer material, keeping essential or main ideas and omitting unnecessary parts, such as examples and illustrations

valid data accurate measurement of what you intend to measure

After completing this chapter, you will be able to

- Identify and locate secondary data

- Evaluate sources

- Document secondary sources

- Take notes from a source

- Collect primary data using surveys, interviews, observation, and experimentation

Employees rely on information they collect to solve problems, make decisions, answer questions, and carry out many other work functions. Unlike writing for school, report writing on the job provides information to help the business operate effectively, not to show the writer's knowledge of the topic.

Researchers can get some data easily but must search for other information. Employees and other data collectors have two basic sources of information: secondary sources and primary sources. **Secondary sources** are reports of what someone else saw or heard or thinks. **Primary sources,** on the other hand, are direct or firsthand reports of facts or observations. The writer or speaker is the one who witnessed the event or developed the idea. For example, a diary is a firsthand account of the writer's experiences and is, therefore, a primary source. However, if you use ideas from another person's diary in a report on healthy lifestyles, the borrowed ideas become secondary data in your report because they are not something you experienced or observed.

Researchers generally start with secondary sources. Several characteristics of secondary materials make them a good place to begin. They often give general overviews and offer good background knowledge. Although some secondary sources are likely to be older, they usually are easier and less expensive to consult than sources of primary data. The overviews of the topic and background explanations help researchers understand the topic, the factors involved, and what is already known about the topic. A problem-solver may even learn that someone has already discovered a solution for the problem.

Finding Secondary Data

W A R M   U P

As a new sales representative, you are going to Japan to meet with your first prospective customer. If you know little about Japanese people and customs, where do you go to find out whether you should take the customer a gift, and if so, what gift would be a good choice? List several things you'll need to know and where you think you'll find the information.

To solve most problems, your first step will be to explore the available secondary data. After all, you don't want to "reinvent the wheel." If the answer already exists, you won't need to spend time, effort, and money to rediscover it.

Secondary data, usually in paper and electronic format, may come from several places. For work-related research, you will probably use one or more of the following sources of secondary data: your organization's correspondence and report archives, a library catalog, periodicals, general reference materials, and electronic resources.

Correspondence and Report Archives

A logical place to begin to look for an answer to a problem is in the organization where the problem occurs. Most organizations keep **archives** of all correspondence and reports. Employees may use these documents to learn about the history of the problem or topic. They may find letters, memos, or reports explaining when this or a similar problem was first noted; what kind of investigation was conducted; and whether the solution was successful. Some small businesses file paper copies of documents while most organizations maintain files on computer disks or tapes.

Library Catalog

After the archives, the researcher's next stop is either the company's library or a public library. Some large businesses have an in-house library. Often these libraries contain specialized materials relating to the nature of the business they serve. Today many materials businesses use are available **on-line,** so these internal libraries may contain more electronic than paper resources. If no in-house library is available to the problem-solver, then he or she would need to go to a school, municipal, or regional library.

Whether in an internal or a public library, employees looking for secondary data find materials as you do—through the library catalog. The library catalog will help you find books, pamphlets, periodicals, and audiovisual materials. While some libraries still use 3" × 5" paper cards filed by subject or author, most libraries have computerized catalogs. After the user types the author's name, a title, or subject into the computer terminal, the on-line catalog will display a list of sources and their locations. Most systems also can send the information to a printer for printing entries the user needs.

Many libraries have integrated systems so the on-line catalog can tell where a book is and whether it is checked out. The on-line catalogs are generally user-friendly, but you should never hesitate to ask a librarian for help.

Librarians can explain how to use the equipment, what the standard subject headings are, and how to make a search more successful by limiting the topic. Remember that the catalog, on-line or otherwise, will lead you to sources for background and in-depth information. For more recent data, you will need to use periodicals.

Periodicals

Magazines, journals, newsletters, and newspapers are called **periodicals** because they are published at specified intervals of time. (Journals are magazines that have a scholarly or academic intent.) When you need the most current information, periodicals are usually the sources you should seek. All periodicals will be more current than books, but newspapers, especially daily papers, provide the most current information.

The next question is how to find the articles you need in the periodicals. Most library catalogs will tell you what periodicals the library holds in different subject areas, but to find specific articles you need to use an index. In the past, indexes were printed on paper and bound as books or magazines. Today, most periodical indexes are electronic: some are CD-ROM-based, such as the magazine indexes *ProQuest* and *InfoTrac* and the newspaper index *NewsBank*. Some are available through on-line connections, such as Dialog, Dow Jones News/Retrieval, or *FirstSearch*. *FirstSearch,* for instance, is an index provider with databases giving users access to holdings of 17,000 libraries worldwide (Meet Your New). Other indexes may be accessed through a service provider such as OCLC (Online Computer Library Center, Inc.).

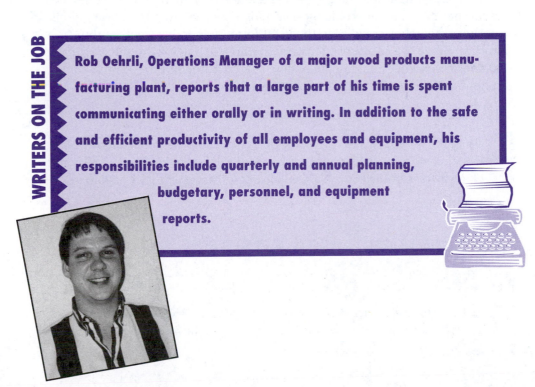

WRITERS ON THE JOB

Rob Oehrli, Operations Manager of a major wood products manufacturing plant, reports that a large part of his time is spent communicating either orally or in writing. In addition to the safe and efficient productivity of all employees and equipment, his responsibilities include quarterly and annual planning, budgetary, personnel, and equipment reports.

General Reference Materials

Ready reference sources such as encyclopedias, dictionaries, handbooks, almanacs, and factbooks are quick ways to get information. These reference materials come in general interest versions, such as *World Book Encyclopedia*, *Encyclopedia Britannica* and *Webster's Dictionary*, as well as special interest versions, such as *Automation Encyclopedia: A to Z in Advanced Manufacturing* (1988), *Taber's Cyclopedic Medical Dictionary* (1985), and Rosenberg's *Dictionary of Business and Management* (1993).

Electronic Resources

In addition to periodical indexes, computer connections make available a wealth of information on countless topics. Users reach databases by CD-ROM, an on-line provider such as *FirstSearch*, a commercial on-line service such as Prodigy or America On-line, or the Internet. The Internet is a worldwide collection of computer networks, an information highway connecting government, military, educational, and commercial organizations and private citizens to a range of services and resources. One database, Knowledge Index, accessed through CompuServe for slightly over $20 an hour, contains approximately 100 databases ranging from language and legal information to chemistry and corporate news (Bjorner 3, 19). Note that on-line searches, whether done through your library or your home computer, can be costly. Along with databases, researchers use on-line books, encyclopedias, bulletin boards, e-mail, consumer information.

Remember that you can get the same data in many different ways. One researcher may find an article by skimming a journal from the library shelf. Another researcher could scan the print form of an index, such as the *Readers' Guide to Periodical Literature,* to find a listing for the same article. Another researcher could do an on-line search in the library or on a home computer. Explore the many resources available to you for research.

> **STOP AND THINK 15.1**
>
> Using the list you drafted in Warm Up 15.1, underline the information that would come from secondary sources. For those underlined items, add any other sources or methods you can think of for accessing information.

Documenting Secondary Sources

> **WARM UP 15.2**
>
> Has someone else, intentionally or accidentally, received credit for your ideas or work? If so, how did you feel? If not, imagine how you might feel.

Documentation is a way of giving credit to another person (writer or speaker) for his or her work; it is using a citation system to note whose ideas or words you are using and where you found them. Responsible writers document ideas and materials they borrow.

You may ask, "What exactly do I document?" The answer is anything you borrow. You should give proper credit for borrowed ideas, phrases, and sentences. Therefore, you will document

- summaries,
- paraphrases, and
- direct quotations

in your writing since these are borrowed phrases, sentences, or ideas. For instance, if reporting on the environmental impact of a new soy ink for your company's publications division, you would document researched facts and statistics, contradictory statements, and unique ideas or opinions.

On the other hand, common knowledge or information typically known by your audience requires no documentation. It is the kind of information usually found in an encyclopedia entry. Yet, common knowledge may differ for each audience, particularly expert audiences. For instance, that Bill Gates is Chief Executive Officer of Microsoft Corporation is common knowledge for an audience of computer engineers while Gates' management philosophy might be common knowledge for business school graduates.

The format for documentation is determined by the field in which the writer works. For example, Modern Language Association (MLA) format, most likely taught in your English class, is the system of documentation used in the humanities. Other documentation systems include the American Psychological Association (APA) system for social sciences and the Council of Biology Editors (CBE) system for biological sciences. Most fields have a style manual. *The Chicago Manual of Style,* the stylebook of the University of Chicago Press, is the preferred style manual for many technical fields.

While all systems explain how to identify facts for each source, the emphasis, order, and punctuation may be different. The APA and CBE, for instance, emphasize publication dates in citations because dates are critical in the sciences. The MLA emphasizes the author and location in the text. This book uses the MLA system. Having learned one form of documentation, you can understand the others easily.

Documentation comes in two parts: **1)** the Works Cited (or Bibliography) or listing of sources at the end of the document and **2)** the internal or in-text citations. The process of documentation begins with a working bibliography.

Men trust their ears less than their eyes.

HERODOTUS

Bibliography and Works Cited

A working bibliography is a collection of information identifying each source you used. While collecting data, researchers develop a working bibliography, which later becomes a final bibliography at the end of a report or paper. A bibliography accomplishes three purposes: **1)** it establishes credibility by showing readers what sources you consulted, **2)** it allows others to find your information path so that they may continue or evaluate the study, and **3)** it acknowledges indebtedness.

As you look at secondary sources, enter data for each source on a 3" × 5" card. Cards allow you to arrange entries easily for preparing the final list of sources. If you use a computer or word processor, you may maintain bibliographic data on disk. Since each documentation system has a particular format, consult your teacher (or employer) for the appropriate style manual. All the systems, however, require similar bibliographic entries. For each source you consult, write the following information required by MLA:

1. author's full name (last name first)
2. title and subtitle of book *OR*
   title of article and title of journal
3. publication information
   BOOKS—place of publication, name of publisher, and date of publication
   JOURNALS—volume number, publication date, and inclusive page numbers

Many variations exist for different publications, such as newspapers or edited or translated books. For these variations, refer to the style manual. Figure 15.1 below shows one card for a book and one for a journal article.

Figure 15.1 Model Bibliography Cards

Book

> Land, James. <u>Audio Testing:</u>
> <u>Saving the System</u>. Boston:
> Bartlett, 1991.

Journal Article

> Sturdivant, Cindi. "The Effect
> of Alcohol Consumption on Anemia."
> <u>American Medicine</u> Sept. 1995:
> 29-42.

After the research is complete and the report drafted, cards for sources not used in the report are pulled out. Cards for sources you did use are put in order. For MLA, use alphabetical order by the author's last name or whatever word appears first in the entry. For some other systems, the order could be that in which sources are used in the report. You will use the appropriately arranged cards to compose the Works Cited page, as seen in Figure 15.2. This page goes at the end of the report so readers can refer to it while reading the report.

Figure 15.2 Model Works Cited

Works Cited

Antonio, Walter. "In-house Arrest: Is It Working?" <u>Corrections Today</u>
    26.2 (1990): 55–63.

Garibaldi, Marcia, and Cecelia B. Moore. <u>The History of the U.S. Prison</u>
    <u>System</u>. New York: Morrow, 1993.

National Corrections Institute. "Prison Caps: Early Release is the Easy
    Way Out." Washington, D.C. 1992.

Walkman, Rivers. "The Prison Dilemma." Editorial. <u>Townesville News</u>
    26 Jan. 1994: C11.

Internal Citations

As people read your report, they will assume the ideas are yours unless they see a citation in the text. **Citations** are written indications of the source of borrowed materials. Most style manuals, like MLA style, now recommend internal or in-text documentation rather than footnotes (citations at the bottom of the page) or endnotes (citations collected at the end of the report before the bibliography). Enter internal documentation immediately after summaries, paraphrases, and direct quotations to tell your reader where you found the information. In MLA format, internal citations consist of the author's last name, or the title of the source if no author is named, and the inclusive page numbers. If the author's name is mentioned in the introductory sentence, only the page numbers appear in the citation. Readers then use the author's name or the title to find the full bibliographic entry in the alphabetical listings of Works Cited. At the end of the sentence (or group of sentences) containing the source material in your report, place the citation. Enclose the citation in parentheses and place the period on the outside, as in Figure 15.3.

Figure 15.3 Internal Citation and Works Cited

Text with Internal Citations

Endangered sea turtles visit this strip of southern beach every year to lay their eggs (Walker A1). The females, sometimes weighing up to 1000 pounds, clamber from the water up the beach while the male turtles wait about five miles out in the ocean. Females in season come every two weeks from mid-May to mid-August (Jackson-Dews 5); however, a female has a fertile season only once every two years (Miller 44–45). On each trip to land, according to Jackson-Dews, a local expert, a female turtle will lay between 100 and 200 eggs the size of a ping-pong ball (5–6).

Corresponding Works Cited

Jackson-Dews, Alicia. "Turtle Watch." <u>Coastal Living</u> June 1994: 4–8+.

Miller, Arthur W. <u>Endangered Species: Can They Be Saved?</u> Boston: Conservation Press, 1995.

Walker, Erich. "Here Come the Turtles!" <u>Swansboro Gazette</u> 20 May 1994: A1.

STOP AND THINK 15.2

What are the costs of poor or unethical documentation practices? In other words, what happens when writers incorrectly or incompletely cite sources?

Evaluating Sources

WARM UP 15.3

Have you ever repeated something someone else said only to have others say it is untrue? If so, how did you feel about the person who told you the story in the first place? Did you continue to share information he or she told you? How do you decide whose information to repeat and whose not to repeat? Have you reached any conclusions concerning sources you trust versus those you don't trust?

As you have no doubt discovered, not everything that appears in print (or on the airways) is true. In fact, many mistakes, untruths, and half-truths are published that you will not want to repeat. A financial planner who uses an unreliable source's information to make investments for clients probably will not get new clients. Therefore, choose your data sources with care.

These guidelines for evaluating sources will help you get started:

● **Check the publication date.** If you want to know the most recent discoveries and happenings in a particular area, you need up-to-date information. Data in a book may be even older than the copyright date indicates since some books take two or more years to be published.

● **Check the author's credentials.** Often the preface or introduction at the beginning of a book outlines the education and experience of the writer(s) or editor(s). Likewise, magazine and journal articles sometimes include brief biographies. If the publication gives no information about the author or editor, consider factors such as the reputation of the journal or the publisher. You also might check an author's reputation in such reference sources as *Who's Who in America, Contemporary Authors, Who's Who in Science,* or *Who's Who in Small Business and Entrepreneurship Worldwide*. Based on what you learn about the author's credentials, determine whether he or she qualifies as an expert in the field. If you have two sources on the same topic, you might find one author more credible than the other.

● **Check the author's methods and resources.** Usually in the introduction of a book or in the opening paragraphs of an article, the author or editor will explain the methods used in reaching the conclusions. If you believe those methods are flawed, then the book or article loses credibility as a potential source. Likewise, you may evaluate a potential source by the resources its author uses. Resources may be mentioned in the text as well as listed in a Works Cited section or Bibliography.

S T O P   A N D   T H I N K   15.3

Read the case below and consider possible outcomes of the situation:

John received time and money to study the effects of a particular veterinary medicine on humans. His report requesting permission for this project was based primarily on one study published in an animal science journal. Over the last year, this study has been largely discredited in animal and human medical journals.

Taking Notes from Sources

Examine the notes you take during class lectures or discussions. Approximately what percentage of the notes are written exactly in the teacher's or speaker's words? Approximately what percentage are written in your own words, your interpretation of the teacher's or speaker's comments? How many notes are *your* ideas or perhaps conclusions you came to as a result of something someone else said? Write a brief journal entry describing what you found in your notes and your answers to these questions.

Employees doing research make notes of information they collect, just as you do when working on a paper in school. When you discover data you believe will be helpful, write complete and careful notes. Most researchers prefer to use 4" × 6" notecards because they are easy to arrange and carry. At the same time, the availability of easy-to-carry computer notebooks encourages some researchers to make notes directly on the computer. The computer user can then transfer the notes into the first draft of the report without having to retype them.

Before making notes, read the source material carefully. An important part of being a successful researcher is to understand your sources thoroughly.

Read the excerpt below from an article describing current theories on the function of the left and right hemispheres of the brain. We will use this passage to discuss notetaking.

The left hemisphere, which controls the right half of the body, is responsible for language and logic; the right hemisphere, which controls the left half of the body, handles such intuitive, nonverbal processes as emotions and spatial relationships. Uncovering this dichotomy earned a 1981 Nobel Prize for Roger Sperry, the Caltech psychobiologist who has experimented with people whose hemispheres have stopped speaking to each other. Ordinarily, the two halves of the brain are connected by a bundle of millions of nerve fibers, the corpus callosum, that allows signals to pass between the hemispheres and enables us to function as an integrated unit. By observing epileptics whose corpora callosa had been severed to prevent the spread of seizures, Sperry learned how the hemispheres divvy up the chores. In one classic experiment, he showed a different picture to each hemisphere simultaneously. (What the right eye sees is processed in the left hemisphere, and vice versa.) The left, verbal hemisphere was shown a picture of a spoon. Asked to name what he saw (to use language, a left hemisphere skill), the subject said knife. Asked to feel with his left hand (a spatial skill, controlled by the right hemisphere) and pick up what was in the picture, the subject chose a spoon from a group of objects. The right brain didn't know what the left brain was doing.

On each card, include three pieces of information: **1)** the information you want to use—only one idea per card, **2)** the topic, and **3)** the source and page number(s) from which the data were taken. The card in Figure 15.4 illustrates the way some researchers handle notecards.

Figure 15.4 Model Notecard

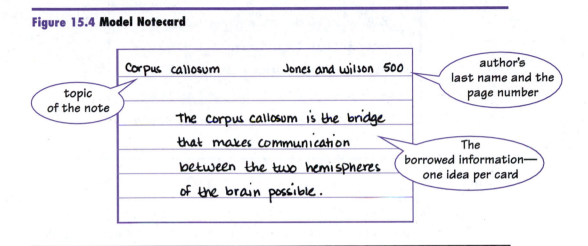

Since the notes you take may be your own ideas, ideas borrowed from other sources, or a combination of the two, distinguish your own ideas by writing them in a different color, highlighting them, or putting them in brackets.

Beginning writers sometimes copy material directly from source after source onto their cards. Copying this way means the writer, at some point, must still reword or condense most ideas for use in the paper. After all, borrowed material cannot be consistently quoted without turning the paper into a cut-and-paste patchwork of style. The notes should be ready to incorporate into the document. You can use this information in these three ways: **1)** summary, **2)** paraphrase, and **3)** direct quotation.

Summary

To **summarize** is to condense longer material, keeping the essential or main ideas and omitting nonessentials such as the examples and illustrations. Remember to be consistent with the source's idea but to use *your* words. (For more information on summarizing, refer to the Chapter 10 section on Abstracts, pages 190–193.) You may have summarized in book reports in school. When doing job-related research, perhaps to solve a problem and to write a report, you might summarize a journal article or chapter of a book whose main idea is helpful. You would summarize the article or chapter in a few sentences or less to use as supporting evidence in your report. You also might summarize in a sentence or two a portion of an article or chapter, maybe a paragraph, for use in your report. The note in Figure 15.5 summarizes the original material on functions of right and left brain hemispheres you read in the article on page 294.

Figure 15.5 **Summary Notecard**

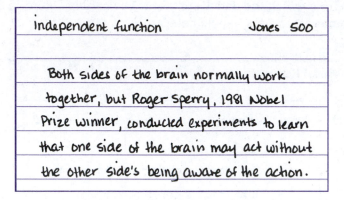

> independent function   Jones 500
>
> Both sides of the brain normally work together, but Roger Sperry, 1981 Nobel Prize winner, conducted experiments to learn that one side of the brain may act without the other side's being aware of the action.

Paraphrase

To **paraphrase** is to borrow someone else's idea and to present it in your own words, phrases, and sentence structure. While a summary should be shorter than the original material, a paraphrase generally is about the same length or even a bit longer than the original. A writer paraphrases when the material supports a point but is not unique or dramatic enough to need to be quoted. Most of the materials writers use from other sources will be paraphrased. Paraphrasing allows writers to include the thinking of many others while putting the borrowed ideas into the writer's own words and sentences to keep the report in one consistent style. As you practice paraphrasing, you may find it helpful to try this process:

1) Read the original carefully,

2) put it aside,

3) write the idea in your own way,

4) compare your version with the original, and then

5) be certain you have used your own words and sentence structure and have accurately conveyed the author's idea.

Figure 15.6 **Paraphrase Notecard**

> function of each hemisphere   Jones 500
>
> As Jones and Wilson explain, the left side or hemisphere of the brain controls speech and thought processes as well as the right side of the body. The right side of the brain, controlling the left side of the body, manages such unspoken innate functions as emotions or gauging distances.

Figure 15.6 contains a paraphrase of the first sentence from the excerpt on functions of the left and right hemispheres of the brain.

Notice that the wording and sentence structure is significantly different. Changing or moving a word or two is not effective paraphrasing. Avoid **plagiarism** by stating the borrowed idea in your own way, choosing words and sentence structure you would normally use, and properly crediting the author of the source.

Direct Quotation

Direct quotation is the third way writers incorporate borrowed material into their reports. It uses ideas, words, phrases, and sometimes sentences exactly as they appear in the original. Copy phrases and sentences directly only when you cannot present the idea as well in your own words. For instance, if the original writer or speaker chose unusual words or composed unique sentences, you may want your reader to get the flavor of the original by quoting directly. Another reason for using direct quotation is to enhance your credibility. But be careful not to overuse quotations; avoid that cut-and-paste patchwork style by making less than 20% of your report direct quotations. Figure 15.7 is a model of a notecard using direct quotation.

Figure 15.7 Direct Quotation Notecard

independent function	Jones 500

Roger Sperry, a Caltech psychobiologist, "has experimented with people whose hemispheres have stopped speaking to each other" to discover that the two halves of the human brain control different functions.

Introduce quotations. Writers introduce quotations to make the writing smooth. Never let quoted sentences stand alone. You can integrate quotations into your text with words, such as "according to one expert" and "Greg Markham claims," or with complete sentences, such as

Benjamin Franklin gave this advice in Poor Richard's Almanac: "Early to bed, early to rise, makes a man healthy, wealthy, and wise."

Indicate added or omitted material. When you need to add to or edit a direct quotation for clarity or conciseness, use brackets to set your changes apart from the quoted words, as in the sentences below.

ORIGINAL: "After the board meeting in which a 2% fine was approved, she signed her resignation letter."

ADDITION FOR CLARITY: "After the board meeting in which a 2% fine was approved, [Margaret Fletcher] signed her resignation letter."

You may need to quote only part of a sentence. In this case, use an ellipsis, three spaced dots, to show where you have omitted words from the original. If the reason for Fletcher's resignation is not important to your work, you might quote the source this way:

OMISSION: "After the board meeting . . . , [Margaret Fletcher] signed her resignation letter."

The ellipsis shows that the clause "in which a 2% fine was approved" was left out of the quotation.

STOP AND THINK 15.4

1. When should a writer use direct quotation?
2. Would you use an ellipsis or brackets to indicate you have left out part of a quoted sentence?

FOCUS ON ETHICS

Recently given more responsibility and a promotion, Sam has been overwhelmed by the additional duties while trying to learn the new job and has not done some of the work assigned him. One job left undone was to plan a product recall. The company had learned of a potentially dangerous problem with a power drill it makes. When the supervisor asked Sam how many of the machines need to be called back, Sam made up a number. What might the consequences be?

Collecting Primary Data

WARM UP 15.5

What could you do in the following situation? Make a list.

You have a stain caused by a chemical from the chemistry lab on your new wool sweater. You don't know the name of the chemical, but you remember the experiment and probably would recognize the bottle containing the chemical.

Many job-related problems are too unique or too current for secondary sources to answer. The commercial fisher may learn more about a new net's effectiveness by asking other users and by experimenting than by reading the literature on nets. To solve work-related problems, primary data may be of more help. Primary data are gathered through field research: surveys, interviews, observation, and experimentation.

Surveys

Surveys gather facts, beliefs, attitudes, and opinions from people. Many businesses rely on surveys to collect information for decision-making. One example is the questionnaire accompanying the registration form for small appliances such as hair dryers. The manufacturer uses the data to determine who is buying the product, how the buyer learned of the product (what advertising method worked), and how satisfied the buyer is.

A survey will work only if you know what you want to learn before you begin. Once you decide, you should do these things: **1)** carefully select your audience or respondents, **2)** decide how you will administer your questionnaire, and **3)** carefully plan your questions.

In choosing an audience, you need to select a sample broad enough to be representative. **Population** is the target group from which you want to gather data. A garden center owner who wants to know whether customers would use a repotting service would have a population of all customers of the business. If the owner cannot question all customers due to expense, time, or distance, then he or she may choose a *sample* to provide representative answers. A **sample** is a subgroup that represents (has the same characteristics as) the entire group. Keep in mind that the sample must be small enough for you to be able to tabulate and analyze the results but large enough to provide meaningful results. For very large or important questionnaires, companies hire trained people to design and conduct surveys.

Once you know your audience, the next step is to decide how to administer the survey. You can administer questionnaires in person, by mail, or by telephone. This decision is often based on the kind of data you are seeking, how much time you have, and your budget. Telephone and in-person surveys offer faster responses than mail surveys. However, if you are asking personal or controversial questions, use a confidential mailed survey to ensure a higher return rate. Also, remember that all three methods of surveying can be costly.

Consider these suggestions as you prepare surveys:

Explain why you need the information and how it will be used. Since you are asking **respondents** to share data, they have the right to know what you plan to do with the information. In a cover letter or opening paragraph, explain what prompted the survey. Then describe the benefits. Estimate the time required to complete the survey. Many surveys also offer to send respondents results of the study.

Convince your audience to participate. After all, you are asking for their time and thoughts. They may wonder what you are giving them in return. You might consider offering an incentive such as coupons, free merchandise or services, improved services—even money.

Start with easy-to-answer questions. If respondents have difficulty with the first questions, they are not likely to continue. The initial questions should ask for information that is easy to supply and not too personal.

The first balloon flight was made by the Montgolfier brothers in a hot-air balloon in Paris in 1783.

Ask only necessary questions. If you don't need the answer, don't ask the question. For example, don't ask about income if income isn't relevant. People will not respond if they believe you are wasting their time.

Logically order questions. Arrange questions in logical groupings to aid memory. Move from easy to difficult questions.

Write clear and non-leading questions. In order for responses to be useful, questions must be clear and precise. Compare the following two questions:

- Do you shop by mail often?
- Do you shop by mail once a month?

With the first question, the respondent will answer based on his or her definition of *often*. Such an answer may not be useful. Likewise, questions should not lead respondents to particular answers. Consider the following questions as an illustration: "Don't you believe that the cost of class rings is outrageous?" "Why don't you buy your lunch in the school cafeteria?" The wording suggests a particular answer.

Make the question's purpose clear. If the survey is to learn about consumers' reaction to your newspaper's new type style, don't ask such general questions as "Why did you purchase this newspaper?" Answers to this general question may vary tremendously, from "It was the cheapest one on the newsstand" to "This is the one my father reads." Such responses will not help you find out what you wanted to know—whether people like the new type style.

TECHNOLOGY UPDATE

Many word processors and computer software programs contain features helpful to researchers and writers. One such feature operates like a stack of notecards. Because word processing allows writers to make changes in text easily, these notecards may be manipulated by the writer, placed in any order desired, and copied directly into a draft of the report.

Prefer facts over opinions. When designing questions, seek facts whenever possible. Facts provide stronger, more credible evidence. For example, ask "Do you purchase from a mail-order catalog once a month or more?" rather than "Do you like mail-order shopping?"

Stick to one topic per question. While it may be tempting to include several issues in one question, the answers will be useless if you don't know to which topic the answer is responding. Suppose respondents say yes to the question, "Are you ever concerned for your safety as you walk through the parking deck and up the stairs into the Whitley Building at night?" You don't know what concerns them—the deck, the stairs, the building, or the darkness of the evening.

Plan for tabulation. Remember that once responses come in, you will need to evaluate and interpret them. Your job will be easier if you design questions whose answers may be stated as numbers. When you already know the range of possible answers, **close-ended questions,** such as these two, allow for a limited number of responses and are easy to tabulate:

Do you live within five miles of one of our stores?

Yes _____   No _____

Please indicate your level of satisfaction with your purchase.

Extremely Satisfied	Satisfied	Somewhat Satisfied
1. < >	2. < >	3. < >
Somewhat Dissatisfied	Dissatisfied	Extremely Dissatisfied
4. < >	5. < >	6. < >

Although more difficult to tabulate, **open-ended questions** are sometimes necessary to discover respondents' thoughts and feelings; unexpected attitudes or information may be uncovered this way. Open-ended questions ask respondents to supply words, sentences, or short essays:

How do you think RFG's Board should respond to the new regulations?
What could Apgard Limited do to improve service to you and your organization?

Be certain to leave adequate space for answers when asking open-ended questions. On the next page, Figure 15.8 gives examples of different types of questions.

Be sure to review your questionnaire for appearance, length, and clarity. As with resumes, design questionnaires to be attractive and inviting. If you do not use white space and organization to make the survey appear easy to read and answer, people may not complete it. Likewise, design the survey so that it will be short—two pages or less. Also, field-test your survey to be sure questions that seem perfectly clear to you are as clear to others. You may ask colleagues to test your survey and point out any concerns. If the questionnaire is quite important and will go to a large sample, you might field-test it on potential respondents.

Figure 15.8 A Mailed Survey

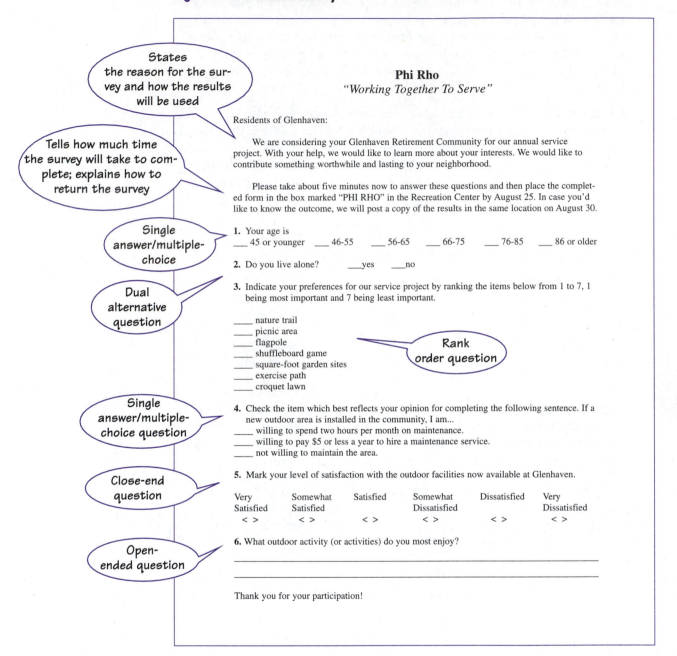

States the reason for the survey and how the results will be used

Tells how much time the survey will take to complete; explains how to return the survey

Single answer/multiple-choice

Dual alternative question

Rank order question

Single answer/multiple-choice question

Close-end question

Open-ended question

Phi Rho
"Working Together To Serve"

Residents of Glenhaven:

We are considering your Glenhaven Retirement Community for our annual service project. With your help, we would like to learn more about your interests. We would like to contribute something worthwhile and lasting to your neighborhood.

Please take about five minutes now to answer these questions and then place the completed form in the box marked "PHI RHO" in the Recreation Center by August 25. In case you'd like to know the outcome, we will post a copy of the results in the same location on August 30.

1. Your age is
___ 45 or younger ___ 46-55 ___ 56-65 ___ 66-75 ___ 76-85 ___ 86 or older

2. Do you live alone?   ___ yes ___ no

3. Indicate your preferences for our service project by ranking the items below from 1 to 7, 1 being most important and 7 being least important.

____ nature trail
____ picnic area
____ flagpole
____ shuffleboard game
____ square-foot garden sites
____ exercise path
____ croquet lawn

4. Check the item which best reflects your opinion for completing the following sentence. If a new outdoor area is installed in the community, I am...
____ willing to spend two hours per month on maintenance.
____ willing to pay $5 or less a year to hire a maintenance service.
____ not willing to maintain the area.

5. Mark your level of satisfaction with the outdoor facilities now available at Glenhaven.

Very Satisfied	Somewhat Satisfied	Satisfied	Somewhat Dissatisfied	Dissatisfied	Very Dissatisfied
< >	< >	< >	< >	< >	< >

6. What outdoor activity (or activities) do you most enjoy?
_____
_____

Thank you for your participation!

Interviews

Interviews, like surveys, are an excellent source of primary data. Interviews can give you access to experts' facts, opinions, and attitudes that you might not find in any other way. However, interviewing can be time-consuming and costly. To make the process as successful as possible, use the following guidelines.

Define your purpose. Know exactly what information you want from each interviewee. Write down the purpose and review it before talking to the interviewee.

Make an appointment. Telephone or write the respondent to describe the topic and request an interview. Whether you are interviewing someone in person or by telephone, ask the respondent in advance for a convenient time. If the interview will be in person, offer to visit the respondent or arrange a suitable place to meet for a personal interview. Be certain that the respondent understands the topic and that you have allowed reasonable preparation time.

Do your homework. Don't expect the respondent to make all the effort. Know as much as possible about the topic before you conduct the interview.

Plan and write out your questions. Prepare questions to bring out specific, detailed information. Avoid vague questions such as "How do you feel about responding to emergency calls involving hazardous materials?" in favor of clear, specific ones, such as "What training experiences have you had to prepare you for emergency situations involving toxic gases?" Also avoid questions which ask for a "yes" or "no" response as they don't encourage the speaker to elaborate. In addition, avoid questions that reflect an opinion or bias such as "Isn't it true that management overemphasizes shop safety?" Instead, ask for the respondent's views: "In regard to shop safety, does management underemphasize, overemphasize, or adequately emphasize?" Some interviewers write questions on one sheet of paper and record answers on another. Others prefer to write each question along with its answer on a notecard. A tape recorder may be helpful, but first ask permission to record the interview. Choose the system that works best for you.

Conduct the interview in a competent and courteous manner.
Remember, you are in control and the success of the session depends on you, not the respondent. Try these suggestions:

- Be on time.
- Introduce yourself.
- Explain the purpose of the interview.
- Keep on track; stick to the topic.
- Take notes, but not excessively.
- Listen attentively.
- Ask for clarification or more details, if needed.
- Dress appropriately.
- Speak in a clear, distinct voice.
- Be assertive, but not arrogant.
- Avoid small talk.
- Thank the respondent for his or her time.
- Offer a handshake as you leave.
- Add to your notes with a more complete summary as soon as you leave.

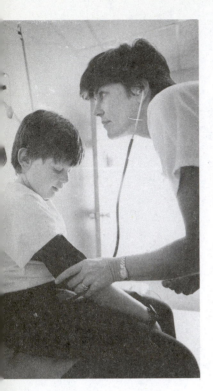

Observation

In addition to surveying and interviewing, observation is another method of collecting primary data. Professionals frequently rely on observation to solve problems in their jobs. Medical professionals observe patients to diagnose illnesses. Crop scientists observe the numbers and types of weeds and insects in a field to decide if the crop should be sprayed. Highway departments count vehicles to decide where to place traffic signals. However, be careful when gathering data by observation; observers may be biased, or subjects may act differently than normal if they know they are being studied. To ensure the credibility of data you collect by observation, use these guidelines:

Train observers in what to look for, what to record, and how to record. If you want to know about traffic at a certain intersection, you could train people to count vehicles. You would need to tell the observers the rules. For example, how would they count mopeds? If one observer counts mopeds with passenger vehicles, another with commercial vehicles, and the third doesn't count them at all, the data will be flawed. Also be sure all observers are using terms the same way.

Be systematic in your observations. For instance, if the observers counting vehicles work only from 7–9 a.m. and 4–6 p.m., will you get an accurate picture? Since people are commuting to work and school during these times, you are likely to get inflated numbers.

Observe only external actions. You cannot project internal actions or reasoning. For example, you may observe that 24% more people displayed flags this Independence Day than last, but you cannot say that more people are flying flags because they feel more patriotic. Report only actions you can see.

Quantify findings whenever possible. Being able to assign statistics adds to credibility, showing that an action or event was consistent.

Support your observations. If you cannot quantify, support generalizations with details, examples, and illustrations. You might even make drawings or take photographs.

While observation can be a valuable source of primary data, consider the time, equipment, and cost. For instance, hiring and training people to count vehicles can be time-consuming and expensive. Even if you decide to place a mechanical device across the highway to count vehicles, it must be paid for, and it will not describe the vehicles.

Experimentation

Experimentation is causing an event so that an observer can test an assumption or hypothesis (a statement of what you believe will happen). Experiments test whether a change in one factor will cause a change in another factor. For example, if the owner of a car cleaning business wants to know whether his current car wax or a new product gives the longest-lasting shine, the owner might polish one-half a car with the current wax and the other with the new wax. He would then check the car periodically for shine.

Workplace experiments are frequently used. Manufacturers often test new products in limited markets to gauge their likelihood for success. Managers may compare a current operating plan in one plant with a new one in another plant. Some experiments involve researchers gathering samples of air, water, soil, food, medicines, body tissues, or even building materials for testing.

As with observation, experimenters must be careful to avoid problems. Sometimes other factors or variables can affect the results of an experiment. For instance, using different cleaners on the two halves of the car would affect the results of the wax study. Therefore, when you design an experiment, try to eliminate as many outside factors as you can.

Surveys, interviews, observation, and experimentation all serve as useful tools for getting information, and many researchers use a combination of these methods. Remember the stain on the wool sweater in Warm Up 15.5? Even this everyday problem may call for interviewing, observation, and experimentation in seeking a solution.

Validity and Reliability

To maintain credibility, primary researchers look for valid and reliable data. You have **valid data** when you have accurately measured what you intended to measure. For example, a clothing store owner wanted to know if his business would attract as many customers if it were open on Sunday as it did on weekdays. He devised a test to collect data. The Sunday that he chose was during a weekend two important football games were being played in town, and visitors filled all the area hotels. Comparing the number of customers on that Sunday with the number of weekday customers would not generate valid data. The large number of visitors in town on that particular Sunday would influence the results.

Reliable data means that, under similar circumstances, the results can be duplicated. If you explain that mixing two liquid chemicals will create a solid, then others could try the same test. If they follow your procedures, the mixed liquids should solidify. Being able to repeat the test with the same results represents reliable data.

The first flight of a mechanically-propelled airship was made by Henri Giffard of France in 1852

STOP AND THINK 15.5

1. Name at least three methods of collecting primary data.
2. Why should observations be planned?

SUMMARY

1. Secondary data, reports of information from someone other than the witness or the person directly involved, are usually found in a business, school, or public library through print or electronic means.

2. When a writer uses a secondary source in a report, the writer must give credit for the borrowed material by documenting the source. Documentation includes in-text citations and a Works Cited or Bibliography at the end of the report.

3. Writers should evaluate sources by checking publication dates, the author's credentials, and the author's methods and resources.

4. As researchers find useful material, they take notes in one or a combination of three methods—summary, paraphrase, and direct quotation—on notecards or a computer disk.

5. Primary data, information direct from the witness or the person involved, may be collected by surveys, interviews, observation, and experimentation. Such data are often necessary to solve problems in business and industry.

BUILD ON WHAT YOU KNOW

1. Think of a subject or hobby you know a lot about. In a brief essay, describe how you acquired your knowledge.

2. Watch a televised or videotaped interview. Note the strategies the interviewer uses to make the interview effective.

CONDUCT YOUR OWN RESEARCH

1. Prepare questions and interview someone in your field of interest. From that person, collect information about a particular research project he or she undertook. Ask about methods, difficulties, and the outcome of the research. Record your findings on the sheet of prepared questions.

2. In a small group, identify an issue at your school.

   a. Develop a survey to collect facts and opinions about the issue.

   b. Administer the survey in person.

   c. Tabulate the results of your survey.

3. Identify a problem at school, in your community, or at work.

   a. Decide what information you need to solve the problem.

   b. Determine how and where to find the information.

   c. Conduct the necessary research.

   d. Submit your bibliography and notecards.

4. Choose a topic relating to the career field of your interest. Search for secondary information to provide basic background information. Write an essay summarizing your findings and prepare a bibliography of your sources.

APPLY WHAT YOU HAVE LEARNED

1. Compose a notecard for each item below.

   a. On page 14 of *Farm Review*, Edwin F. Roberson's and Julius Schwartz' article, "Hog Farmers and Homeowners: Zoning Solutions," notes that municipal and regional governments are "legislating distance" between the farms' waste lagoons and residential areas. The article appears in the November 1994 issue of the magazine.

   b. In her 1991 book *Swine Herd Disease Management,* Dr. April P. Nuñez writes, "Careful recordkeeping and close observation are the key to disease management." The book is 463 pages long, and this statement appears on page 259. The book was published by Delmar, a publisher located in New York.

2. Paraphrase each of the items below.

   a. The Center for Marine Conservation reported that volunteers scouring ocean beaches and inland shorelines cleaned up more than 7 million pieces of trash including cigarette butts, bottles, cans, lightbulbs, syringes, and plastic bags.

   b. The Highway Department yesterday reported approval of a plan to open an 8.5-mile corridor between Henderson and Mount Clemmons. However, the new road may be a little bumpy because two sections of experimental asphalt, one designed to combat hydroplaning and the other made of crumbled tire rubber, are being used.

3. Visit your library to write at least five bibliography cards for reference sources relating to your career field of interest. Your librarian can offer help with finding sources.

WORKS CITED

Bjorner, Susanne. "The KI Companion: A Search Strategist Explores Knowledge Index." *Link Up* July–Aug. 1994: 3, 19.

Meet Your New Research Assistant: First Search. OCLC.

CHAPTER

16

Informal Proposals

Write-to-Learn

Think of a problem you solved by talking with someone. How did you do it? Did you have a plan for your talk? Compare the methods you used to solve the problem by talking with the methods you would use if you had to write instead of speak. Think of planning time, words used, length of message, needs of audience, and effect of message.

DEFINITIONS

proposals persuasive documents that offer a solution to an identified problem or need

RFP Request for Proposal; an advertisement seeking proposals to solve a problem or fill a need and often listing criteria for the solution

solicited proposal a proposal that is written in response to an RFP or upon the request of a supervisor or manager

unsolicited proposal a discovery proposal, one that is written because the writer discovered a problem or need and has a solution to offer

---

PHILLIPS'
CONVENIENT MART STORES

Donovan Phillips, President
3301 Heritage Plaza/ Columbus, Ohio 43209/ 614•555•9854

MEMO TO:	Donovan Phillips, Owner	*csc*
FROM:	Carl S. Cordova, Management Intern	
	Convenient Mart #27, Newsome, Ohio	
DATE:	10 March 1996	
SUBJECT:	Proposal for Improving Traffic Flow	

SUMMARY

Customer complaints, accidents, congestion, and delays in service point out the need for improvements in traffic patterns through our parking and gas service areas. The addition of guide rails and painted traffic lanes throughout the lot would add order and increase the speed with which we can serve customers. Dimpoulos Paving Company, with reasonable prices and reputable work, offers the best solution to our problem. The project should take less than two weeks from the date of approval, and customers are certain to appreciate the convenience and safety added to the good value they already receive every time they shop at Convenient Mart #27.

STATEMENT OF PROBLEM

Convenient Mart #27 has wide entrances (30' and 50') from two streets, and the entire back property line is open to the Tunbridge Shopping Center parking lot. Therefore, traffic may enter our lot from all directions except the west, the Burger Barn property line. Customers walking to the store after pumping gas are in danger of being hit by a moving vehicle, and customers attempting to wedge in between two other vehicles to get gas have bumped into our pumps. Having drivers enter from any direction they choose and park anywhere they choose creates serious safety and efficiency problems.

SOLUTION

Dimpoulos Paving Company can remedy our problem by installing six guide rails and painting traffic lanes and parking spaces on our lot. Guide rails (metal tubes filled with concrete) at the end of each pumping station will keep vehicles in the proper lanes. Likewise, standard-size painted traffic lanes with yellow directional arrows will improve the traffic flow as well as our ability to offer speedy service. In addition, parking spaces will give in-store customers easy access to the store without impeding gas customers.

BACKGROUND

Our current situation will not improve unless we take action. Congestion and accidents will continue. Three collisions, minor yet causing costly damage—more than $750 for each incident—to the cars involved, have occured in the last two months. Slow service is another result. Gas customers can't get to the pumps, and other customers can't get to the store. In addition, these problem situations harm our reputation.

Donovan Phillips
Page 2
10 March 1996

METHODS
Dimpoulos will install six guide rails, one at the end of each pumping station. Workers will fill these round metal tubes with concrete to make them stable and paint them yellow to make them visible. Dimpoulos' engineer said that we have room for five parking spaces around the store, so four will be painted white and one for handicapped access will be painted blue. The company also will paint yellow traffic lanes with directional arrows on both sides of each pumping station to create six lanes. As you can see in Figure 1 below, three lanes will enter from the north, of which one will exit to the east on Myrtle Street and two to the south into Tunbridge Shopping Center. One lane enters from Myrtle and exits to the north onto Highway 102. The other two lanes will feed from the south, vehicles entering from the Tunbridge lot, and exit onto Highway 102.

Figure 1. Proposed Traffic Lanes, Guide Rails, and Parking Spaces

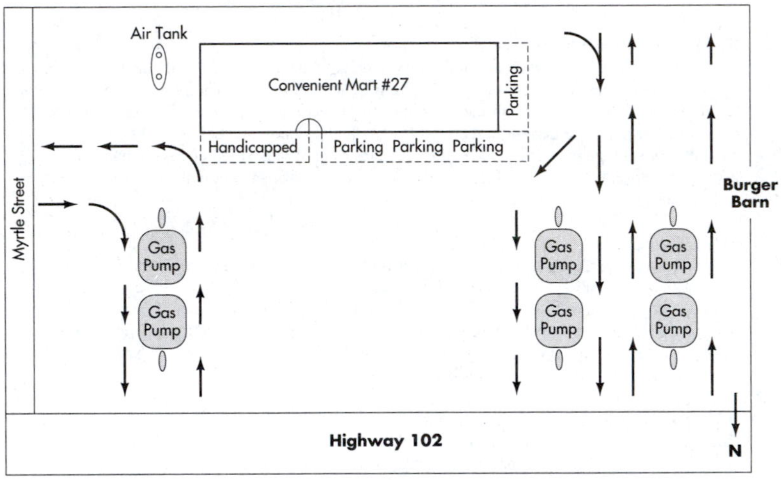

Tunbridge Shopping Center Parking Lot

Donovan Phillips
Page 2
10 March 1996

SCHEDULING
The construction schedule will run as follows:

April 20	April 27	May 2
installing guide rails	painting lanes, arrows, and parking spaces	job completed

Dimpoulos' site supervisor has assured me that all work can be done at night or during our least demanding hours.

BUDGET
The following is a budget for the improvements I suggest:

six guide rails	$1,049.00
paint -2 gallons of white	32.86
3 gallons of yellow	48.24
1 gallon of blue	18.98
labor	2,499.00
engineering costs	945.00
	$4,593.08

CONCLUSION
Congestion, accidents, delays in service, and customer response all require that Convenient Mart #27 do something to improve traffic flow. I recommend that you authorize the placement of six guide rails and the painting of traffic lanes and parking spaces to enhance order and efficiency in the way we do business. I believe that the improvements will more than repay the $4,593.08 cost in customer satisfaction and goodwill.

After completing this chapter, you will be able to

● Define and explain the function of a proposal

● Identify the various types of proposals used in business, industry, and the academic world as they relate to the audience

● Plan a proposal using a prewriting chart to demonstrate how the solution fulfills the needs of the problem

● Effectively format and organize a proposal using data collected

● Compose a convincing proposal that addresses the audience's needs, concerns, and questions

The Greek geographer Pytheas was the first scholar to say that the tides are caused by the influence of the moon.

What would you do if you disliked your school's new policy requiring all students to spend their lunch hour inside the cafeteria?

● You could organize a strike.

● You could start a food fight.

● You could sit around grumbling.

● You could collect signatures on a petition disagreeing with the new policy.

● *OR* you could write a proposal to the school administration identifying the problem as you see it *and* offering a solution.

What is a Proposal?

WARM UP 16.1

Read the model document at the beginning of this chapter and review the definition of *proposals* on page 308. How does this document fulfill the definition of a proposal?

Persuasive documents that offer a solution to an identified problem or need are **proposals.** Sometimes proposals attempt to sell an idea, sometimes a product or a service, and sometimes a new concept or plan. Proposals may be brief or long. The one-page request for a room assignment change you write to your club advisor and the 2,000-page, multivolume document selling a new type of amphibious tank to the Department of Defense are both proposals.

The term "proposal" hints at the use of this type of document. "Propose" is the base word from which "proposal" comes. What does "propose" mean?

Have you "proposed" a party idea to your friends recently? You might think of one person who has proposed marriage to another. If you are thinking of "to suggest" or "to make an offer," then you are beginning to understand the proposal's purpose. More precisely, a proposal is a request, either oral or written, for support. Frequently the support requested is in the form of money. For instance, the local Boys and Girls Club may direct a proposal to the United Way for money to resurface the club's tennis court. Another proposal might offer a customer or client goods or services. If your band or other school organization carries out a fund-raising drive by selling candy or wrapping paper, the project probably began with a proposal from the candy or paper supplier.

Some proposals don't involve money at all. They simply seek permission or approval. If you wrote a proposal to your school administration asking for open lunch privileges for seniors, no funds would be needed, only permission. The successful proposal, whether it seeks money, permission, or both, is one that persuades your audience to accept your offered solution and to invest in your idea, product, plan, or service.

A proposal is a type of report that can be very empowering. Like the students unhappy with the new lunch policy, employees can use proposals to respond to problems rather than sit around complaining. The proposal provides them with a professional means of presenting their ideas for change within the system.

STOP AND THINK 16.1

As you think about each area of your life—school, home, work, community, and organizations—make a list in your journal of problems or needs for which you might like to seek solutions.

WRITERS ON THE JOB

Troye Hackworth, a technical writer for Burroughs Wellcome, realizes the importance of specific, accurate, audience-centered writing. Since her company produces drugs, federal agencies continuously check company records to monitor safe manufacturing procedures. If employees do not write clear and accurate documents, drugs could be made incorrectly or manufacturing could be halted by these federal inspectors. Thus, not only employees' jobs but also public health are endangered by poor writing.

Audience: Who Reads Informal Proposals?

W A R M   U P **16.2**

In small groups, discuss the impact of audience on the methods you use to be convincing. Do you, for example, use the same techniques to persuade your parents or guardian to allow you to go to some event that you use to persuade your teacher to give you more time on an assignment? Consider elements such as length, personality, expectations, and types of evidence or appeal.

Decision-makers in many different positions in business and industry read proposals. Yet, most of these proposal readers will read only a portion of the document. They read the section or sections of the proposal that deal with their area of interest and expertise. Thus, each reader evaluates the proposal and votes to accept or reject the suggestion based on the data presented in the section he or she reviews.

As Figure 16.1 illustrates, proposals may be divided into several different types or categories relating to these readers: **1)** internal or external, **2)** informal or formal, **3)** solicited or unsolicited, and **4)** sales, research, grant, or planning. Understanding these types of proposals will help you to see the role of the proposal in the worlds of science, technology, education, and business.

Figure 16.1 Types of Proposals

Category	Definition of Category
A. internal	within the organization
external	outside the organization
B. formal	contains parts used in formal reports
informal	omits elements of formal reports; often briefer
C. solicited	written in response to a request
unsolicited	written independently, without a request
D. sales	attempts to sell a product or service
research	seeks approval for a research study
grant	asks for funding for a project
planning	attempts to persuade audience to take a certain action

Internal and External

Readers of some proposals will be internal, that is, inside the writer's own organization. Other readers will be external or outside the writer's organization. Internal proposals usually attempt to sell an idea or a plan, such as how providing on-site day care can reduce the absentee rate at work, how merit-raise funds should be distributed, or how eliminating classes on the day before achievement tests could ease stress and improve scores. External proposals frequently try to sell goods or services as well as ideas.

Informal and Formal

A proposal is called informal or formal based on the degree to which conventions of formal report writing are followed, how "dressed up" the document looks. Formal reports contain more parts than informal proposals. Writers decide how formal a document should be based primarily on the audience and its needs.

Because they frequently address an internal audience who understands why the document was written, informal proposals are often brief, generally from one to eight pages. An informed audience eliminates the need for background information or an explanation of the problem. In addition, the report has a flexible organizational plan, is less formal in language usage, and frequently is presented as a letter or memo. Occasionally, however, a brief informal proposal may be written to an external audience if the subject matter and offered solution are simple and require little explanation.

A proposal going to someone close (in the ranks of the organization) to the writer is usually informal. Likewise, a problem and solution that can be explained in a simple manner are presented in an informal report. The proposal writer would not invest the often lengthy preparation time involved in a formal proposal to suggest something as simple as perhaps changing lunch schedules to allow for a pep rally.

Formal proposals, on the other hand, usually address an external and often unfamiliar audience. They are more "dressed up" and are organized according to standard elements of formal, researched reports: cover page, letter of transmittal, title page, table of contents, list of illustrations, executive summary, body discussion divided by headings and subheadings, appendices, glossary, and bibliography. (These terms will be defined and illustrated in Chapter 17, Formal Proposals.)

> *All our words from loose using have lost their edge.*
>
> ERNEST HEMINGWAY,
> *DEATH IN THE AFTERNOON*, vii

Solicited and Unsolicited

A proposal is labeled solicited or unsolicited depending upon the audience's role in its initiation. A **solicited proposal** is one the reader asked the writer to create. Sometimes the request will come from a manager at work who sees a problem. The manager then asks for a solution to be presented in a proposal. The request also might appear in a classified ad called an **RFP** or Request for Proposals. The RFP will state exactly what the customer seeks; the proposal writer then prepares his or her document to address the needs stated in the RFP. On the other hand, the **unsolicited proposal** or discovery proposal is begun when the writer "discovers" a problem, such as an inefficient production line or a lack of water fountains for wheelchair-bound employees. The writer independently identifies a problem, explains it, and offers solutions.

Sales, Research, Grant, and Planning Proposals

Based on function or what the writer wants the audience to agree to do, proposals fall into one of four categories: sales, research, grant, and planning.

The sales proposal tries to sell a product or service. The research proposal asks for approval to begin a study or investigation. A marine biologist at a university, for instance, might request approval, and perhaps funds, for a study of the effect of acid rain on a particular species of fish. The grant proposal seeks money for a specified project, such as beginning a horseback riding program for children with cerebral palsy. The planning proposal attempts to persuade an audience to take a particular action, as in a plan to improve the efficiency of food service at a pizza restaurant's drive-through window.

A single proposal may combine several categories mentioned here. As you read proposals, you may discover that as many as four categories apply to one document. For instance, the proposal presented on pages 309–311 at the beginning of this chapter is brief and familiar, identifies a problem, speaks to an internal audience, and attempts to persuade readers to take an action. Thus, the report is an informal, unsolicited, internal planning proposal.

STOP AND THINK 16.2

Using the information given in Figure 16.1 on page 314, decide what proposal categories apply in the following situation:

Ai-ling Shen, hoping to train a group of retired Chinese-American men and women in her community as literacy volunteers, developed a proposal asking for money with which to buy handbooks and audiotapes. She submitted a three-page proposal to her employer through the company's Community Partners Division.

FOCUS ON ETHICS

Sean Williams is an administrative assistant at Pathmark House, a nonprofit agency that serves children from low-income families. The director, Nicole Thomas, has recently expanded Sean's responsibilities to include writing grant proposals. Sean enjoys the work and is good at it; already, three of the proposals he has written have been approved, bringing in a total of $65,000. Last week, the Board of Directors, whose members Sean is getting to know, called him into a meeting to thank him for the good work.

Nicole wants to hire an assistant to help with the office work, but there isn't enough money in this year's budget. Nicole tells Sean that they will pay the assistant's salary with the $15,000 Tyler Foundation grant, a grant that Sean wrote. The Tyler Foundation gave the grant monies specifically to purchase computer equipment and to pay for classes for Pathmark House clients.

What should Sean do?

Prewriting: Getting Started on Informal Proposals

Now that you have seen the different types of proposals, you are ready to plan for writing such a document. As with any report, the proposal begins with a problem or a need. The problem may be one you have discovered yourself or one someone pointed out to you, as in an RFP or in a memo or letter from another professional.

Once the problem is identified, you should develop a plan for solving the problem (Refer to Chapter 14, Problem-Solving). Developing a research plan and carrying it out can help you to use your time efficiently. Planning for solutions to a problem usually requires research to collect information. Research can mean a long, involved project with hours spent in a library or laboratory. On the other hand, research can be the observing, questioning, and experimenting that you do on an everyday basis, as in comparing composition books to decide which one to buy. The informal proposal explained and illustrated here requires a minimum of research. (Formal proposals, which are longer and usually require more in-depth investigation, will be presented in Chapter 17, Formal Proposals.)

Generating solutions should be a creative process, so suspend your critical nature as you brainstorm for as many solutions as you can. Remember that the most obvious solution may or may not be the best solution. Sometimes the improbable ideas work best. For instance, many devices we use every day, such as televisions and microwave ovens, were once only science fiction; they were improbable solutions that worked.

With a long list of possible solutions in hand, reopen that critical part of your brain. Consider which of the solutions will best solve the problem or meet the need. A methodical listing of positive and negative aspects for each solution may help you to narrow the list. Try thinking of each solution separately and noting in the "good" column the positive outcomes as well as its feasibility or "do-ability." In the "bad" column list any negative results that are likely along with any problems related to implementing the solution. The solution, or the top two solutions, with the greatest number of positives and the lowest number of negatives go into the proposal.

Another prewriting technique may help you strongly appeal to your audience. Create a chart using a sheet of paper with a line drawn down the middle. On the left half of the page write everything you think the reader needs or wants in the solution. For instance, if you have an RFP, then the criteria, as with a job advertisement, are probably noted there. If you have no RFP, make the list based on your research and insight into the problem and audience.

On the right half of the page, list what your solution offers that the reader wants or needs. In other words, for every want or need in the left column, explain how your plan will fulfill that want or need. Thus, you will have the tools of persuasion ready for composing your proposal.

Formatting and Organizing Informal Proposals

W A R M   U P   16.3

Explain why long proposals, perhaps 10 pages or more, should *not* be formatted as memos or letters.

Proposals may be developed in letter format for an external audience, memo format for an internal audience, or manuscript format for any audience that is distant or that contains multiple readers. Manuscript format also is used for very long documents.

If manuscript format is chosen, then the proposal begins with a *title page*. The title page contains the title of the report; the name of the person or group who will receive the report; the author's name, job title, and company; and the date. Whether a proposal begins with a title or cover page (along with other formatting decisions) may be dictated by guidelines in a company style manual. If no manual or guidelines are available, then analyze your audience and communication situation and make decisions based on the needs you identify.

Following the title page is a condensed version of the proposal known as an Executive Summary or Abstract. Place this summary, usually one to six paragraphs, on a page alone with the heading *Executive Summary* or *Abstract* at the top of the page. The heading often is typed in all caps.

Headings and subheadings should be used within the proposal to enhance readability and comprehension. Although many writers use all capital letters for headings, proposal writers may choose from many techniques for highlighting, such as underlining or boldfacing. *Remember to be consistent once you have made your choice.*

The organizational strategy of the informal proposal, like that of many technical reports, is designed with the busy decision-maker in mind. The proposal usually opens with what the reader most needs to know. In other words, the organization follows priority order. Proposal writers follow priority order by giving information about the problem and solution at the beginning of the report. The organizational plan for the rest of the proposal is flexible to fit the many different situations a writer is likely to encounter within his or her working environment.

As with most effective writing, informal proposals contain an *introduction, body,* and *conclusion* (although those particular headings usually are not used). The introduction presents the problem, the solution, and whatever background the reader needs. The body of the proposal is the main section; it covers the facts, the specific evidence to convince the reader that the plan is worthy. The conclusion, then, wraps up the report and tries to spur the reader into action.

The specific information contained, and thus the headings used, within each section—introduction, body, and conclusion—may vary from situation to situation. Depending on the needs of the problem and solution being proposed, the writer decides which subsections to include and which to omit. Possible headings that may be used in each section follow.

SECTION	POSSIBLE HEADINGS
INTRODUCTION	Problem Addressed and Solution
	Objectives of Proposed Plan
	Background
	Data Sources
	Scope and Limitations
BODY	Methods
	Scheduling
	Capabilities, Qualifications of Personnel
	Materials and Equipment
	Expected Results
	Plan for Evaluating Results
	Feasibility
	Budget (usually in tabular form)
	Justification of Budget Items, where necessary
CONCLUSION	Summary of Key Points
	Request for Action

STOP AND THINK

1. In what three ways may an informal proposal be formatted?
2. In which section of the proposal—the introduction, body, or conclusion—does the writer describe the problem and solution?

Composing Informal Proposals

WARM UP 16.4

Recall several convincing people: when they talk, you listen and believe. What gives these people the persuasive edge, credibility? List any traits, characteristics, or actions that you think lend credibility to persuade people. Be prepared to share your list with the class.

Whether long or short, the proposal must be carefully composed to convince the reader to accept the proposer's request. As you plan your own short, informal proposal, remember your audience throughout the writing process. Ask yourself if you are answering all of the reader's questions and doubts.

Drafting the Summary

The *summary* or abstract is designed with the busy decision-maker in mind. In an informal, short proposal, this section may appear on the title page or, typically, as the first paragraph(s) in the report. It provides a brief—often only one paragraph—overview of the essential ideas presented in the proposal. The summary should include a statement of the problem, the objectives of the proposed work, the impact of the project, and the plan of work. Cost is not usually discussed in the summary. Since this is a very important element of the proposal and since it must accurately give the important ideas in the report, you should complete the proposal before you attempt to write the summary.

Drafting the Introduction

The introduction of the informal proposal answers the "Why" in the reader's mind; it explains why the proposal was written. First, you must identify the problem being addressed. Another very important element of the Introduction is your proposed solution to the problem. This statement should be clear, but brief. Later, in the body or technical discussion section, you will provide further details and justify your proposal.

The introduction further explains your objectives or what you hope to accomplish and makes clear the value of the work—why it is worth the investment you seek. This section may also require a brief historical background of the problem. For example, a proposal recommending a change in the way student newspapers are distributed might be viewed more seriously if the writer can prove that the current distribution system encourages littering: Because the papers are placed in stands near doorways only one hour before students leave campus, students have papers in hand as they walk outside and away from recycling bins and waste receptacles. Such an explanation of the background will prove to your reader that you have a grasp of the problem.

In addition, the introduction may explain the need for a solution to the problem. Some readers may ask, "Why can't we simply leave things as they are?" You should note the effects of ignoring the problem. Another element of the introduction is to discuss how you or other personnel are qualified to solve this problem. In addition, you might describe where you will seek information to help solve the problem. Those sources of data could be printed materials (such as from books, reports, or brochures), interviews, observations, or experiments. The introduction also might define the limitations, such as restrictions on time, space, money, or staff, and the scope or the outer boundaries of the project.

Drafting the Body

After the problem and solution have been described in the introduction, the *body* of the informal proposal becomes more specific about your plan of work. The specific details—the facts, figures, statistics, dates, locations, costs—are the ammunition you use to persuade your audience. For this technical section of the proposal, you might address the following topics.

METHODS
- Explain your methodology, what your approach to the problem will be, what criteria (perhaps from the RFP) you will meet, and what outcome or product you will deliver at the date you specify. Justify your plan of work and any exceptions to the RFP as needed.

SCHEDULING
- Present a calendar of the work planned and expected completion dates to assure your audience that you anticipate efficiency. Effectively illustrate scheduling, as appropriate. Flowcharts or time lines are excellent for visual presentation of timetables.
- List personnel, numbers and perhaps qualifications, scheduled for this project.
- Describe facilities, both available and needed, to be used.

CAPABILITIES
- Assure your audience that you can deliver the work that you propose by **1)** noting the abilities of people involved and **2)** describing the successful track record of your organization.

MATERIALS AND EQUIPMENT
- Review materials and equipment to be used. This section is particularly important in scientific projects. Even on a proposal dealing with construction of a building or another product, the type of fabrication material is likely to be critical to the audience.

EXPECTED RESULTS
- Explain what you think the result of your work will be.

PLAN FOR EVALUATING RESULTS
- Outline your plan for determining the degree of success reached by the project.

FEASIBILITY
- State whether you find the conclusion reasonable to implement.

BUDGET
- Present, typically in a chart, the costs for the work, including salaries, equipment, materials, travel, communication costs, services, and other expenses.

JUSTIFICATION
- Clearly (and persuasively) explain the reason for any expenses your audience may question.

Drafting the Conclusion

The *Conclusion* should be straightforward and brief. It might include a summary of key points, such as those to be noted in the summary section, and it should call for the audience to take action.

Exploring the Composing Strategies with a Model

Let's use a sample problem to carry through the composing process: The problem Sharon Reaves, a senior at Martinique High School, has noted is that the local newspaper, *The Martinique Times*, contains very little information from her school. Occasionally *The Times* carries a report of a football, soccer, or basketball game, but she would like to see the newspaper cover other areas of school news as well. Now let's follow Reaves through the process of writing a short, informal proposal in which she suggests a solution to the editor of her hometown newspaper, Gary Owens.

Reaves decides to write a summary and to place it on the title page, but she will wait to write it until later. After the proposal is written, she will pull major ideas from it for her summary.

In order to help *The Martinique Times'* editor understand the problem she has identified, Reaves considers the "Why" question. She writes a clear statement of the problem. Beneath that statement, she lists her goals:

- to include club news
- to note the dates of special events
- to report on students who deserve attention for academics or other achievements
- to highlight teachers and their contributions
- to give students a forum
- to encourage more students to read the local paper

These goals are the things she would like to have happen as a result of her proposal.

Reaves then brainstorms about how these objectives could be met. She thinks of several alternative solutions: **1)** developing a student-owned and -operated paper, **2)** requesting that students be given space for contributions, **3)** asking the newspaper to cover the school's news in a more comprehensive manner, or **4)** suggesting that the school administration submit articles occasionally. She also thinks about the need for the action she proposes: Is there any other way to accomplish these goals? Is anyone else concerned?

The next step Reaves takes is to move from brainstorming to analysis, to become more critical in her thinking. For each of the alternate solutions she developed, Reaves lists "positives" and "negatives," as explained in Prewriting on page 317. For example, under Solution Number 1, developing a student-owned newspaper, she lists the following:

Positive	Negative
Students have complete control.	A great deal of money is needed.
Students would learn by doing.	Would students have the time to do a good job?
Students would read and support their own paper.	Would work and quality be maintained with student turnover?

Reaves realizes her proposal is directed to a business leader interested in the effects of her proposed action on his work—profits, personnel, schedule, public image. She knows that a solid plan with accurate facts and figures is necessary to convince her reader. Having chosen the plan with the most "positives" and the fewest and least serious "negatives," she again brainstorms for ideas to be included in the Body or the technical section of her proposal.

Reaves decides the best solution to the problem is to have a student-written column placed weekly in *The Martinique Times*. She then must assure the editor of a sound plan for implementing this idea: She notes who will be involved and their qualifications, who will be responsible, and how the work will be done. Using the outline for the body of the proposal given on page 321, Reaves explores the types of information she will need to convince her audience. To make the work schedule clear, Reaves develops a chart that shows each step in the development of the student-written column. The chart also is labeled to identify the person responsible for each phase. She uses this chart to check for anything she might have overlooked or anything that could go wrong in getting the column into the paper.

Reaves prepares to write her Conclusion by reviewing her strongest selling points. In addition to a summary of key points, Reaves knows that her closing should include a clear statement of exactly what she wants the editor to do: Does she want him to announce the beginning of the new column in the paper, call her principal with an invitation, write to the school journalism teacher, or speak with students or a student group?

If you would like to see the result of Reaves' brainstorming, researching, analyzing, critical thinking, drafting, revising, and editing, read her final draft in Figure 16.2.

STOP AND THINK 16.4

In a large organization, different people are likely to read only the sections of a proposal relating to their area of expertise. What section(s) would these employees most likely read?

1. CEO (chief executive officer)
2. technical expert
3. comptroller (financial officer)

Figure 16.2 Informal Proposal for an External Audience

Route 1, Box 704
Martinique, MI 12002
23 October 19--

Mr. Gary Owens, Editor
THE MARTINIQUE TIMES
113 South Main Street
Martinique, MI 12002

Dear Mr. Owens:

As a senior at Martinique High School interested in pursuing a career in
commercial art, I read your newspaper regularly. I have always been impressed
with the innovative designs and attractive page layout of your publication.
However, I also have noticed one element of the TIMES that could be improved.

Problem

The problem is in the area of news from Martinique High. Your reporters cover
basketball and football games very well, yet many other events and activities
supported by the student body go unmentioned. I believe that students and your
other readers are interested in seeing information on Martinique High's special
events, academic and other achievements, teachers and their contributions, and
club activities as well as sports.

Solution

News from all areas of interest at Martinique High could be covered and at no
expense to the TIMES. If you include a weekly column devoted to Martinique
High news, students can serve as reporters, gathering and writing the stories.
Other students can take photographs to accompany the articles. To assure you of
high-quality work, the column can be managed through the Journalism Club and
supervised by Mr. Jan Justesen, an English teacher as well as advisor to the
club.

Objectives

Including the news students want to read could have several effects. One result
of a change in coverage probably will be that more students buy and read the
paper. Thus, the students will benefit by being better informed and by improving
their time spent reading. Further, the paper will benefit by Mr. Gary Owens'
developing readers (customers) early in their lives. In addition, the community,
by being made more aware of high school events, may become more supportive
of education and become avid readers of the school column. Moreover, being
given a forum certainly will encourage some students to become better writers
and readers, better athletes, better at whatever they do. After all, most of us
enjoy seeing our names in the paper for having done something well!

Mr. Gary Owens
Page 2
23 October 19--

Methods and Scheduling
If you accept this proposal and invite students to submit a weekly column, informing the student body and organizing participants should take no more than one month. During that time, we will choose a name for the column and assign specific duties. Mr. Justesen also will develop a chain of command and guidelines for everyone to follow. We already have some experienced writers in the Journalism Club, some who have contributed to your paper before. These people will help the new writers and photographers to polish their work.

Our flow of work, as you see illustrated below, is designed so that all work will be done well and on time. Once organized, we will have an editorial board whose job will be to review story ideas, select the best, assign writers and photographers, help with editing, and submit work to Mr. Justesen. Mr. Justesen will supervise the entire process and will approve all work before sending it to you.

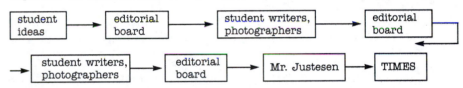

Maintaining the Column
During the summer break and school holidays, the column could be suspended. On the other hand, it would be nice to hold on to readers by continuing the column, perhaps with a student intern reporting on holiday activities in which Martinique High students are involved. For example, a student intern could cover the marching band's performance in state semi-finals over the Christmas break.

Conclusion

A student-generated column in the TIMES will be beneficial in many ways. It will sell papers by creating new readers. It will keep readers informed of all areas of Martinique High. It will not cost the paper anything in time or wages. It will encourage students to be their best. It will instill pride in students and the community. It will bring us all closer together. Please help us to make these things happen by making space for a student column in your paper. Please call Mr. Justesen at 555-1234 with an invitation now.

Sincerely,

Sharon Reaves

Sharon Reaves

SUMMARY

1. The informal proposal is a persuasive document that suggests to the audience a solution to a problem or a change. An informal proposal may range in length from one to several pages.

2. Proposals are defined and categorized according to the audience and its needs:

internal	informal	solicited	sales
external	formal	unsolicited	research
			planning
			grant

3. In prewriting, consider how your solution meets the needs of the audience.

4. Proposals may be presented in memo, letter, or manuscript format, the choice being determined by the audience and complexity of the proposal. Headings and subheadings within the proposal delineate sections of the introduction, body, and conclusion. Information in the proposal is usually put in priority order.

5. The writing strategy for an informal proposal includes a summary (optional), as well as other sections that fall into an outline of introduction, body, and conclusion.

6. The introduction identifies the problem and offers a solution, along with any background information the audience might find helpful.

7. The body of the informal proposal uses facts, figures, statistics, visual aids, and other evidence to *convince* the reader(s) to accept the solution or change.

8. The conclusion of the informal proposal restates key points and calls on the audience to take action.

Editing And Revision Checklist

✓ Have I identified the problem I wish to see resolved?

✓ Have I carefully analyzed my audience and then listed the audience's needs?

   Is my audience internal or external?

   Is my audience aware of the problem already?

   Is my audience at the same level, above, or below me in the organization?

   Will my audience understand the terms and concepts without definitions or explanations?

✓ Have I brainstormed for alternate solutions? Have I listed positives and negatives for each solution on my list?

✓ Which format have I chosen to write my proposal and why?

   Letter format?

   Memo format?

   Manuscript format?

✓ Have I thought about and listed my goals for this proposal?

✓ If my reader(s) is unaware of the problem, have I explained the problem clearly in the introduction?

✓ Does the body of the proposal give my reader enough information to make a decision? If I put myself in the reader's place, what would my reader ask? What will he or she need to know?

✓ Have I provided enough evidence—facts, figures, testimony?

✓ Does my conclusion contain the most important ideas from the proposal? Does it also call for action from the reader(s)?

✓ Have I made information easier for my reader to use by including headings and subheadings?

✓ Have I checked for spelling errors, typographical errors, and grammatical problems?

APPLY WHAT YOU HAVE LEARNED

1. Choose two problems for which you would consider proposing a solution. Write a paragraph or two describing the problem and the decision-maker (audience) for each.

2. Brainstorm a list of possible solutions to a problem or need you have identified.

3. Using a problem whose solution has already been implemented, recreate the thinking proposal writers might have done by

   a. developing a list of positive and negative aspects of the solution.

   b. creating a list showing how the solution meets the needs of the audience or problem.

4. Imagine that you have asked your parents for a car. They have said, "Yes, but—." Your responsibility will be to pay for insurance, gas, and maintenance if they purchase this car for you. In an informal proposal

   a. Explain the type of car you want and why.

   b. Describe how you will pay for the car's expenses if you do not have money and your parents do not want you to work regular hours, such as would be required at a restaurant, grocery store, or department store. Identify your problem and consider alternate solutions. Be creative! Try to think of ways to earn money other than applying for a job. List as many options as you can.

   c. Write out the solution you would propose to your parents.

CONSIDER THIS CASE

1. This activity is also available on the computer applications diskette as **TEXT16A**. As a stocker (a person who places stock on the shelves) at Food King, a grocery store near your home, you, Deborah Culver, have noticed that many senior citizens have trouble reading the signs hung from the ceiling over the aisles. Since they cannot read the signs labeling products located on each aisle, they often stop stockers, clerks, or other employees to ask about the location of a particular item. You do not mind helping these customers, but you don't get as much work done with frequent interruptions. Also, because you have a visually impaired brother, you realize how frustrating it is not to be able to find things independently. A solution to the problem, you think, might be to post, at eye level, signs in print and in Braille on the end of each aisle of shelving. Pronto Printers can create 2' × 4' plastic signs with print and Braille lettering for $36 each. The store would need 12 signs, 2 for each of the 6 aisles.

   Write an informal proposal to Merle Mareaux, Store Manager, suggesting the installation of these signs. Convince him that the cost is justified. Create and add any other details or visual aids you need to produce an effective informal proposal.

2. Write an informal sales proposal to Karen Gorham, owner of Mason Office Center. You own an indoor plant service, Green Thumb Planting, and you are asking Gorham to become a new client. Having visited the office complex, you have determined that the building could use 31 large and 14 medium-sized low-light plants. Your service will provide plants and pots, weekly maintenance, and monthly replacement of imperfect plants. If Gorham accepts your proposal, you are ready to install the plantings within one week. For your service, Gorham will pay a $350.00 installation fee and $35.00 per month thereafter. Your proposal should persuade Gorham to sign a service contract. Create and use any additional details or visual aids you need to prepare an effective document.

PURSUE AN IDEA

1. Search regional or state newspapers or professional journals in your school, public, or home library for Requests for Proposals or Requests for Bids.

   a. Make copies of the RFP's and RFB's so that you can bring them to class for discussion.

   b. From a careful reading of one RFP or RFB, identify the problem that needs to be solved.

   c. Identify the audience the proposal writer would need to address.

   d. Create a brainstorming list of ideas to include in the proposal introduction.

2. Write a proposal convincing your parents to take you (or to allow you to go with friends) on the perfect vacation. Identify the problem, explain the solution, convince them of the reasonableness of your plan, and justify the cost by preparing a budget.

3. Write a proposal to your principal suggesting a change in a school policy or procedure or to your supervisor suggesting a change in benefits, schedules, work routine, or use of equipment.

Effective Transitions

Like any good writing, technical documents need logical connections between ideas. These connections make writing smooth and improve comprehension. Four techniques help a writer to achieve these logical relationships between ideas and between sentences and paragraphs:

repeated key words	parallel structures
pronouns	transitional terms

Repeated Key Words

Repeated key words often refer to the topic or the important information in a document. They remind readers of what is significant in the discussion or what the document is trying to achieve. For example, if you were writing about lumber cut for housing construction, you might begin with the word *lumber* and later repeat that word or use synonyms, such as *boards, logs, planks,* or *timber.*

Pronouns

While repeating key words can improve coherence, using the same word over and over can become boring. Thus, writers also use pronouns to tie ideas together. Read the partial instructions given below to see how the use of pronouns connects ideas and improves coherence:

> When you're planning to paddle down a river, get an accurate, large-scale map and mark the rapids on it. Study it and keep it handy. Rapids are caused by a drop in the riverbed, so remember that you might not see them when you approach.

The pronoun *it* refers to *map,* and the pronoun *them* refers to *rapids.* The difference in the singular *it* (*map* is singular) and the plural *them* (*rapids* is plural) keeps readers from becoming confused.

Parallel Structures

Writers also use parallel structures to link content within and between sentences. Like parallel lines in math, parallel structures in writing mean grammatically similar words, phrases, and sentences, as in these examples.

> My favorite winter sports are <u>ice fishing</u>, <u>skiing</u>, <u>snowboarding</u>, and <u>skating</u>.
>
> NOT
>
> My favorite winter sports are ice fishing, skiing, snowboarding, and <u>to skate</u>.

As a parent, I care about the safety of my children. As a police officer, I care about the rights of individuals. And as a citizen, I care about getting criminals off the streets.

NOT

As a parent, I care about the safety of my children. The rights of individuals is important to me in my role as a police officer. Because I am a concerned citizen, I want to get criminals off the streets.

The repeated grammatical structure helps to connect ideas.

Transitional Terms

Transitional terms or transitions, the fourth technique for improving coherence, are words and phrases that highlight the relationships between ideas.

Below is a list of some transitional terms you might use. The note on the left indicates the relationship the term implies in its connection.

Meaning	Transitional Terms
Addition	also, in addition, moreover, furthermore, and, as well as, besides
Contrast	but, however, yet, nevertheless, on the contrary, on the other hand
Time	before, after, currently, afterwards, during, later, now, recently, then, meanwhile, while, at the same time
Emphasis	in fact, of course, indeed, truly
Example	for instance, for example, to illustrate
Sequence	first, second, third, ..., next, finally, last
Cause and Effect	therefore, consequently, thus
Similarity	likewise, similarly, also, in the same way

THE INSIDE TRACK: APPLY WHAT YOU HAVE LEARNED

This activity is also available on the computer applications diskette as **TEXT16B**.

1. Identify transitional elements in the following passages.
   a. A thunderstorm is a process. It begins with warm air rising. The storm then feeds on moisture and heat. As the rising air becomes cooler, water drops form from the condensing vapor. A picture of the air currents inside a thunderhead could look like a nest of writhing snakes.
   b. In 1940, Comity's hired its first female employee. In 1948, Comity's made that employee the company president.
   c. The PTO shaft was slightly bent in the crash. Consequently, I cannot operate the conveyor belt.

2. Revise the following sentences to create parallel structure.

   a. With Najik, enjoy scanning that is faster, works more precisely, and which can be more economical than ever before available.

   b. First is the group who reacts to the trend by selling every energy stock in the portfolio. As a result of the trend, the second group responds with a threat to sell every energy stock in the portfolio.

   c. First, select a single or double mat for the print, and then the picture will need a frame, and finally you must choose whether to use non-glare or plain glass.

   d. Security officers will be stationed in the following locations:
   - in the entrance foyer
   - the computing center
   - the president's office will be heavily guarded
   - Two officers will be on top of the chemical manufacturing building.

   e. According to some users, the Turbo 040 is the best upgrade available; others say the best upgrade is the ChipStar.

3. Combine each of the following groups of short, choppy sentences into a single sentence by using transition strategies.

   a. The veterinarian prescribed an anesthetic. The anesthetic was for the dog. The pharmacy could not fill the prescription.

   b. Sound waves that hit a plain wall bounce back to distort the sound. Sonex-covered walls absorb the sound waves that hit the walls. Absorbing these waves enhances the sound.

   c. The problem with the collating machine is worn gears. The mirrors on the collating machine are scratched and are part of the problem. The collating machine's levers, which are bent, are a problem.

   d. To apply for the position, job candidates must fill out an application form. They must fill out the form completely. The candidates must submit a resume. They must supply a list of three references.

Formal Proposals

CHAPTER 17

Write-to-Learn

In your journal, write a narrative of a successful sales experience, a situation in which you persuaded someone or a group of people to purchase a product or service or perhaps to agree to an idea.

DEFINITIONS

appendix usually the last element or special part of a formal report; a place to include documents, data, or visuals not necessary to the discussion in the report but perhaps helpful or interesting to the audience

glossary an alphabetical listing of terms accompanied by their definitions

letter of transmittal a letter formally or officially conveying a formal report from the writer(s) to its external audience

memo of transmittal a memorandum formally or officially conveying a formal report from the writer(s) to its internal audience

prefatory material parts or elements of a report that come before the main text (introduction, body, and conclusion)

pagination the assignment of sequential page numbers within a document

---

MEMORANDUM

TO: Barkley Wolfe, Manager
            Eastbrook Shopping Center

FROM: Delores O'Malley, Chief of Operations

DATE: November 23, 19--

SUBJECT: Proposal for Improving Exterior Lighting at Eastbrook

I am submitting for your review my department's proposal to upgrade the exterior lighting system at Eastbrook Shopping Center. This document responds to our October 15, 19--, tenants' meeting and subsequent discussions with you regarding safety on the property.

Of special note are the following sections addressing questions you or our tenants brought up:

Thank you for reviewing our data and suggestions. We look forward to your response. If you decide to accept our proposal, we are eager to implement the needed changes.

**PROPOSAL FOR IMPROVED EXTERIOR LIGHTING
AT EASTBROOK SHOPPING CENTER**

Prepared for
Barkley Wolfe, Manager
Eastbrook Shopping Center

Prepared by
Delores O'Malley, Chief of Operations

November 23, 19--

TABLE OF CONTENTS

List of Illustrations

EXECUTIVE SUMMARY

Evidence from our security office, police records, and customer attitude survey proves that Eastbrook Shopping Center does have a problem with inadequate lighting outside our building at night.

To improve the lighting so that it meets recommendations of the Illuminating Engineering Society and other experts, we will need to exchange our current 150-watt bulbs for 400-watt bulbs and install five new pole lights and six new wall-mount lamps.

The recommended changes will cost less than $1,700 and will improve our security level, liability rating, and public image along with decreasing our energy costs.

INTRODUCTION

Problem

Inadequate illumination in Eastbrook Shopping Center's parking areas is a serious concern. As good corporate citizens, we have a responsibility to the community to maintain a safe environment. As merchants, we recognize that shoppers and employees expect and have a right to a safe environment. We will lose customers if Eastbrook loses its secure, peaceful image. We must also watch expenses. However, it is evident from our research that, as a result of poor lighting, safety on our grounds at night is not assured.

Solution

Problems with lighting can be eliminated if we upgrade our exterior lighting system to meet recommendations of local law enforcement and utilities personnel and Illuminating Engineering Society (IES)* guidelines. (Terms designated by an asterisk are defined in the glossary on page 6.) To increase illumination sufficiently in all areas outside the building, we must exchange our 150-watt mercury vapor* bulbs for 400-watt HPS* bulbs as well as add six wall-mount lights and five new poles in the parking areas.

Objectives

The purpose of this proposal is to improve the quality of exterior lighting at Eastbrook Shopping Center so that customers, employees, and staff feel safe moving to and from the building and their vehicles and so that our parking area will not become the site of illegal activities.

Background

Our records for the last six months prove that we do, indeed, have a problem:

8 incidents of shoplifting (unresolved)	3 purse snatchings
1 assault and battery	1 kidnapping

In addition, the survey our marketing agency conducted last month showed that more than 50% of the 400 respondents feel some concern for their safety in entering or exiting our building after dark. Refer to Figure 1 for the breakdown of the responses:

Figure 1. Attitudes Regarding Eastbrook's Exterior Environment at Night
(by percentage)

Respondents By Age	Extremely Comfortable	Slightly Comfortable	Comfortable	Slightly Uncomfortable	Uncomfortable
18–20	5	31	15	42	7
21–35	15	19	39	15	12
36–50	5	14	22	23	36
over 50	1	9	13	28	49
TOTAL	26	73	89	108	104
PERCENTAGE	7	18	22	27	26

If this unsafe image continues in the public mind, we will begin to lose valuable customers and eventually business occupants of our shopping center. Businesses will move to a location where they and their customers can feel safe. Moreover, we risk a lawsuit if incidents occur that we could have prevented.

Data Sources

The data used to create this proposal came from interviews with experts at Edison Electric and public safety directors at other shopping centers, a customer survey we commissioned, data and recommendations from law enforcement and the Illuminating Engineering Society*, and an experiment conducted by our staff.

Scope and Limitations

In seeking solutions, we wanted to increase safety without creating the image of an armed fortress. The solution must appeal to the public and our business occupants. In addition, any changes we make should be visually attractive and not unpleasant for our commercial and residential neighbors. We have also considered cost and energy consumption.

DISCUSSION

Methods

To determine the amount of light currently being produced, we used a footcandle meter* at the base of each pole. An Edison Electric representative recommended an average of one footcandle* per square foot (Smith). Research revealed that IES Lighting Handbook supports

3

this recommendation, suggesting 0.9 or more footcandles (Kaufman 20–26). Our results indicated that Eastbrook's lights are generally lower than the suggested illumination. The readings ranged from a high of 1.8 to a low of 0.4, as you can see in Figure 2 below.

Figure 2. Exterior Light Intensity and Proposed Fixture Additions

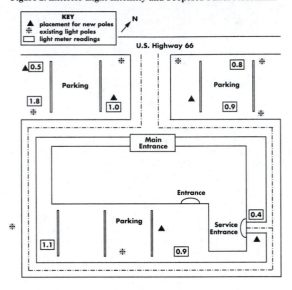

Additionally, a videotaped experiment revealed that in landscaped sections of our parking lots, a person could stand beside a tree or large shrub undetected until the observer was as close as 2 feet. Our research shows almost all parking and pedestrian walkway areas need increased lighting.

Given the videotaped experiment and the footcandle meter readings we collected, an engineer at Edison Electric recommended placement of five new poles outside our building, as indicated on the map in Figure 2 above. Along with the new pole lights, the engineer said that six wall-mount lights installed on the building should bring illumination up to the standard recommended levels. The six lights will be mounted as follows: one on each side of the main entrance and one on each side of the back entrance with the remaining two going on the northeast and the southwest walls (Smith).

Scheduling

We would like to make the suggested improvements as soon as possible. Once equipment has been ordered and received, the project should take less than two weeks, as you can see in Figure 3.

Figure 3. Schedule for Improving Eastbrook's Exterior Lighting

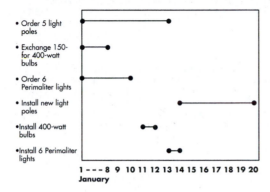

The installation of the five new poles according to IES guidelines will require an outside contractor. Edison Electric has the special equipment needed and can install them in one week. The utilities company also will need to replace our 150-watt bulbs with the new 400-watt bulbs since we do not have the cherry picker required to do this job. This task should take approximately one day. Three members of our own maintenance staff can install the six wall-mount lights in less than one day. The entire project should be complete and lighting improved within a month.

Materials and Equipment

We can purchase the 400-watt bulbs from our current supplier, Witherspoon Inc., for only $10 per unit more than we are paying now for the 150-watt bulbs. Moreover, they will exchange our current stock of 150-watt bulbs for 400-watt bulbs.

Edison Electric will order the materials and erect the five new poles we need. We should contract with Edison to service the pole lights since we do not own the equipment to do so ourselves.

5

Cost

The adjustments necessary to upgrade exterior lighting and implement IES guidelines will cost $1,688.75. The following budget details the expenses for this project:

Five 40-foot metal poles	5 @ $211.95	$1,059.75
Six Perimaliter lights	6 @ $70.00	420.00
Shipping charges for exchanging bulbs		34.00
Edison Electric service fee		175.00
		$1,688.75

In addition to the one-time installation costs, service costs will affect our budget. Operating costs will decrease if this proposal is implemented. Two reasons for the decrease are the longer life and the lower energy consumption of HPS lamps. Mercury vapor lamps have an average rated life of 18,000 to 24,000 hours (Kaufman 8-102) while HPS lamps are likely to be good for 24,000 hours or more (Sorcar 57). In addition, Edison Electric experts suggest we will see an 8–10% reduction in energy use with the HPS lamps, even taking into account the increased wattage (Smith).

CONCLUSION

If Eastbrook's exterior lighting is not improved, future problems are likely to occur. We might face a decrease in the number of customers willing to shop with us in the evening hours and an increase in our insurance rates as a result of liability suits. This proposal is a corrective as well as a preventive measure that increases the safety level for everyone on the property at night. Eastbrook will benefit from a stable environment, night and day.

We recommend that $1,688.75 be allocated in this quarter's operating budget for the installation of 5 new 40-foot metal light poles and 6 new wall-mount fixtures along with the replacement of all 150-watt mercury vapor bulbs with 400-watt HPS lamps. These changes will enhance our security and our image at a reasonable cost.

6

GLOSSARY

bulb. A synthetic light source operated with electricity.

footcandle. A unit of illuminance.

footcandle meter. A meter that indicates the amount of light one candle will produce in one foot of space.

HPS. High-Pressure Sodium. A bulb whose light is derived mainly from sodium vapor.

IES. Illuminating Engineering Society of North America, a professional organization founded in 1906 and dedicated to the theory and practice of illuminating engineering.

lamp. A synthetic light source operated with electricity.

mercury vapor lamp. A bulb whose "light is mainly produced by radiation from mercury vapor" (Sorcar 333).

7

WORKS CITED

Abbott, Marvin, Chief of Security, Golden Crossing Mall. Personal Interview. 5 November 19--.

Kaufman, John E., ed. <u>IES Lighting Handbook: A Reference</u>. New York: Waverly Press, 1984.

------. <u>IES Lighting Handbook: The Standard Lighting Guide</u>. 5th ed. New York: The
    Illuminating Engineering Society, 1972.

Smith, Jason, Chief Engineer, Edison Electric. Personal Interview. 1 November 19--.

Sorcar, Prafulla C. <u>Energy Saving Lighting Systems</u>. New York: Van Nostrand Reinhold,
    1982.

8

APPENDIX A. Police Security Ranking for Shopping Centers and Malls

Metropolitan Police Quarterly Report
June 19-- Security Ranking—Shopping Centers and Malls

1 = Most Secure Environment   5 = Least Secure Environment

Rankings are based on a formula including reported incidents, severity of crime, victims, and cost.

Monrovian Heights	1	Wrightly Way Mall	3
Riggan's Place	1	Anandana Plaza	3
Crossroads Mall	2	Caruso's Crossing	4
South Dunbury Center	2	Eastbrook Shopping Center	4
Newtown Shopping Center	2	Benton Shopping Center	5
Village Mall	2	Bargain Hunter's Way	5

After completing this chapter, you will be able to

- Analyze the needs of typical readers of formal reports

- Use prewriting techniques to collect and organize data for a formal proposal

- Choose appropriate parts of the formal proposal outline to use

- Correctly format each of the special parts of the formal proposal

- Appropriately organize each section of the proposal to convince reader(s)

- Compose each section of the proposal with consideration for the needs of the reader(s) and the importance of the outcome

In Chapter 16, you read about informal proposals. Informal and formal proposals are virtually the same:

- *in function;* they are persuasive documents that offer the writers' answers to the readers' problems or needs.

- *in organization;* writers choose from the same optional subsections in the same order under Introduction, Body, and Conclusion.

On the other hand, formal proposals may differ from informal proposals in several ways:

- tone

- additional report parts

- complexity of the outcome, such as the construction of a new building or the $2 billion purchase of jet airliners

Although not used as frequently as informal reports, formal proposals are called for in many circumstances. The following examples are typical:

- A marine biologist, disturbed by the fish kills in a local estuarine system, wants to study the effect of municipal waste-water dumping on the fish. The biologist seeks funds from the State Department of Fish and Wildlife for a five-year project.

- Having received an RFP (Request for Proposals), a major defense contractor proposes its plan for a new amphibious tank. The potential customer is the United States government, and the price tag is just over $3 billion.

- A mechanic in a ball bearing plant is inspired to improve the precision of a robotic welding machine after studying similar machines at another facility. Having decided on the adjustments needed and the cost in work hours and materials, the mechanic requests approval from the new plant manager.

Bear Marucci, Nuclear Medicine Technologist, says that as a Radiologic Technology student he could not understand why he was required to take technical communication courses. Now effective communication skills are more important to his career than he ever imagined. Writing patient records, protocols, articles detailing research findings, and position papers is essential to Marucci's work and to his success as a medical professional.

Audience: Who Reads Formal Proposals?

W A R M   U P   17.1

When your school needs a new building or needs to remodel an old one, who decides which contractor will be offered the job? Is the decision-maker one person or a group of people? What characteristics would you expect the decision-maker(s) to have? Record possible answers to this question.

Understanding some characteristics of your potential audience will be helpful as you plan to write a formal proposal.

Single, Multiple, and Distant Readers

The audience of a formal proposal may be one person. When one executive makes the decisions for an area addressed by the proposal, then that person is the audience. The proposal developed by the mechanic in the ball bearing plant mentioned previously would be reviewed by one person, the new plant manager. However, formal proposals more often go to multiple readers. When decision-makers collaboratively decide to accept or reject an idea, as would probably be the case with remodeling at your school, then proposal writers should remember to identify and analyze the different audiences. Each reader must have his or her questions answered and be satisfied in order for the writer to be successful.

Readers may be higher on the organizational ladder than the writer(s). In the style of participative management frequently used today, employees from all levels of a business or industry provide ideas for decision-making. Likewise, proposals may travel great distances on the map—from one state to another or even from one country to another. A formal presentation of ideas is often appropriate for readers of higher rank and for readers whom writers don't know.

Audience Analysis Tips

One technique some proposal writers use in analyzing audience is to try to imagine how the reader thinks and feels. Imagining the reader's questions and concerns may help you to understand the reader's point of view and to anticipate his or her needs.

Another technique you might try is to gather audience information relating to the proposal issues, as in the following examples:

Problem

Is the reader aware of the problem?

How much does the reader know about the problem?

What factors of the problem are of the greatest concern to the reader?

Solution

What do the criteria (perhaps in an RFP) established by the audience tell me about the audience?

Prioritize the decision-maker's concerns: personnel, money, time, production, public image, ethics.

How open-minded or how critical will your audience be?

Add other questions to this audience analysis list as you consider the problem, solution, and benefits of the solution.

S T O P   A N D   T H I N K   17.1

If you are writing a proposal to sell a new line of CD's to a music store, how much do you need to know about the company? If, for instance, you know the president/owner of the business and several things about that person, do you know enough?

Prewriting: Getting Started on Formal Proposals

Prewriting techniques should help you plan. During the prewriting phase of preparing a formal proposal, you collect and organize data and determine your objectives. Since a formal proposal is often longer and more involved than other technical reports, prewriting is especially important.

Planning for Problem-Solving

To begin, refer to Chapter 14, Problem-Solving, to review techniques: defining the problem, identifying factors, generating solutions, and selecting the most desirable solution. Remember that you may have to convince your audience that a problem really exists. What evidence do you have to prove that there is a problem and that the problem is important?

If you have an RFP, you might try a two-column listing. In the left column note the reader's criteria (listed in the RFP) and any other questions/concerns, and in the right column, your responses to those questions or concerns. The following example relates to a sales proposal for football helmets.

Criteria	Response
protects players	one inch of solid tempered plastic covered with fiber-glass for resistance
	¾-inch foam padding from ear to ear
	adjustable liner for greater protection
economical	$29.90 per unit, 10% less than the average
	10-year warranty/automatic replacement

After you have a list of the data you need, brainstorm for how or where to gather the data. Ask yourself:

- What information do I need?
- Is it inside/outside my organization?
- Where will I find the data?
- Who can help me get the data?

REAL-LIFE CRISIS

A team of employees at Blue Vale Packing had worked for two months on a sales proposal to a major national mail order company. The proposal offered to supply all foam packaging materials for the mail order business. Since this proposal could represent a major portion of Blue Vale's business, the team had worked diligently to develop and present the best plan possible. However, a serious problem the team had not anticipated arose.

Most sales proposals, as well as many other external proposals, must be approved and signed by a person or people at the head of the organization. The team had scheduled time for research, pre-writing, composing, and editing before the submission deadline. What they had not anticipated was that Blue Vale's CEO left 10 days before the due date for a four-week business trip. Therefore, the CEO would not be available to approve or sign the proposal in time to meet the submission deadline. What could the team do? Could they salvage the situation and meet the submission deadline? How?

Planning for Research

After clearly defining the problem and its factors, you will probably need to conduct research to find and prioritize possible solutions. Refer to Chapter 15, Data Collection, to review research techniques. Outline specific tasks, note dates, determine the personnel to be involved, and figure costs. Writing or mapping your ideas in this way will help you to see more clearly the strengths and weaknesses in your proposal. Be systematic and careful in recording information on bibliography cards and notecards if you use outside sources. This information will be essential in documenting materials within the report and in preparing a Works Cited or bibliography page.

Review the subsections within the formal proposal outline to ensure that you have all the information your audience needs and to determine which subsections you will use in your formal proposal. Possible subsections are listed in the chart below:

Figure 17.1 Formal Proposal Subsection Choices

INCLUDE THIS SUBSECTION	IF YOUR AUDIENCE NEEDS TO KNOW...
INTRODUCTION	
Problem Addressed and Solution	● (AUDIENCE ALWAYS NEEDS)
Objectives of Proposed Plan	● Goal for the project
Background	● History and explanation of the problem
Data Sources	● Where you found the information you used
Scope and Limitations	● How far your study will go for the solution and what you will **not** consider to solve the problem
BODY, DISCUSSION, or TECHNICAL SECTION	
Methods	● How you want to carry out the plan
Scheduling	● Dates on which each phase will begin and end or length of time each phase will take
Capabilities and Qualifications of Personnel	● Who will be responsible for the job and what credentials they have
Materials and Equipment	● Precise descriptions of materials and equipment to be used in the project
Expected Results	● What is likely to happen if the proposal is implemented
Plan for Evaluating Results	● Tools you will use to judge the effectiveness of the work and of the project
Feasibility	● Whether the proposed plan is workable
Budget (in a table)	● The monetary costs of the project
Budget Justification	● Explanations for certain costs

Figure 17.1 Formal Proposal Subsection Choices (continued)

INCLUDE THIS SUBSECTION	IF YOUR AUDIENCE NEEDS TO KNOW...
	CONCLUSION
Summary of Key Points	● (AUDIENCE ALWAYS NEEDS)
Request for Action	● (AUDIENCE ALWAYS NEEDS)

Once you have decided what information (and therefore which subsections) your audience needs, you will know what data you have and whether you need to do more research. Having all the information in front of you will allow you to organize your proposal in the most convincing manner possible.

Planning for Persuasion

Formal proposal readers need to be convinced, as a salesperson convinces a potential customer. If you are to be a successful proposal writer, you must address your audience effectively and erase any skepticism.

Here are some prewriting guidelines for convincing your audience:

1. Collect as many facts as you can to support your proposed plan. You may also use opinions or testimonials, but facts are more persuasive.

2. Be accurate. Plan to check your data. If your reader discovers a discrepancy, exaggeration, or mistake, you lose your credibility.

3. Study your audience and the situation so that you can understand the reader's point of view. Planning with an understanding of the reader will allow you to write a more convincing proposal.

4. Be realistic in your planning. Don't propose to do a job in two weeks in order to make the sale if you honestly believe the work will take a month. You may have to suffer the consequences later since your proposal will become a legal document if it is accepted.

Planning for Integration

Another goal of prewriting the formal proposal is to plan for integration. The entire document must come together as a logical whole. The description of the problem, for example, will affect how the reader views the effectiveness of the solution. When different writers are composing different sections, a primary writer or editor must consider the entire report, not just one section, as he or she plans and edits.

Planning for Visuals, Definitions, and Supplemental Materials

As you gather data, consider whether a visual format could help your audience understand the information. Then decide what type of graphic aid will most clearly depict the idea. (Refer to Chapter 8, Document Design and Visual Aids, on pages 142–169 for more help with planning graphics.)

Plan for terms you will use and whether your readers will need definitions for them. If the proposal does need definitions, decide whether you better serve your audience by placing the definitions within the report or in a glossary at the end. If you need to give only a few definitions, then it may be easier for you and your reader to have definitions within the text. However, proposals that need numerous definitions should probably include a glossary.

In addition to visuals and definitions, think about materials you might like your readers to have access to but do not want to include in the body of the proposal. Consider placing relevant, but not necessary, materials in an appendix. For example, if you have used the results of a survey in your proposal, then you may wish to show interested readers exactly how you gathered data by including the survey instrument as an appendix.

Formatting Formal Proposals

WARM UP

Compare the formatting of the model proposal at the beginning of this chapter, pages 334–345, with formatting in one of your textbooks. What are the similarities?

The format of formal proposals is designed to aid the reader(s). Each formal proposal follows the same basic plan so that readers and writers know what to expect and where to find information they seek. Remember, many expert readers review only one or two sections of a formal proposal.

Parts of Formal Proposals

The parts listed below make up the formal proposal. (Those parts followed by an asterisk are used in informal proposals as well.)

Letter/Memo of Transmittal	Body (or Discussion)*
Title Page	Conclusion (or Summary)*
Table of Contents	Glossary
List of Illustrations	Appendices
Executive Summary (or Abstract)*	Works Cited
Introduction*	

The writing of each of these special elements will be discussed in more detail later in this chapter, under Composing Formal Proposals. Formatting options for the special parts are explained here.

Letter/Memo of Transmittal. The **letter** or **memo of transmittal** is similar to the cover letter mailed with a resume: It is an official greeting and introduction of the document to the reader. Write a letter to accompany a proposal addressing an external audience and a memo when addressing an internal audience. Use any accepted or standard letter or memo format.

Title Page. The title page of a formal proposal, like the cover of a book, gives the reader important information about the document. In designing the title page, make use of white space to spread the words over the full page and to make the page attractive. Notice the placement and type style on the title page of the model formal proposal on page 335.

Table of Contents. The table of contents should be designed so that it is attractive, easy to read, and clear. Refer to the Table of Contents for the model on page 336. The table of contents may appear on a page alone or it may be combined with the list of illustrations on a page. The words *Table of Contents,* in all capital letters or only initial capitals, should be centered at the top of the page. Beneath these words, the listing of contents should, by indentation, visually demonstrate relationships between ideas. For example, section headings may be at the left margin while less important ideas are indented toward the right; the farther right, the less important the idea is.

You may choose to double-space a short listing for a table of contents, but a longer listing should be single-spaced to make reading easier and to save space. Enter headings and subheadings on the left side of the page, **pagination** on the right, and dots (periods) between the heading and its page number.

List of Illustrations. Begin with the words *List of Illustrations* (in all capital letters or only initial capitals) centered at the top of the page or two to four lines beneath the last table of contents entry, as in the model on page 336. Two to four lines beneath the title, provide the label, number, and title of the visual aid on the left and the page location on the right side.

Executive Summary (or Abstract). At the top of the page, centered (in all capital letters or only initial capitals), key the words *Executive Summary* or *Abstract.* The Executive Summary is usually written in paragraph form, generally two to four paragraphs, on a page by itself. It may be single- or double-spaced.

Introduction, Body or Discussion, and Conclusion. In long reports (perhaps 20 pages or more), each of these major section headings may begin a new, separate part of the formal proposal. Each starts on a new page with the heading name, such as *Introduction,* in all capital letters or with only initial capitals centered at the top of the page. In shorter reports, the entire body may flow from one section to another without page breaks.

X-rays were given the name x-ray because the German physicist Wilhelm Roentgen who discovered them in 1895 didn't know what they were. X stood for the unknown.

Glossary. If you choose to include a **glossary**, focus its design on the reader's ease of use. In the text of the proposal, designate words appearing in the glossary by using asterisks, italics, or some other highlighting technique. Include a footnote or a parenthetical note beside the first entry telling the reader he or she can find definitions in the glossary.

At the top of the glossary page, center the title, *Glossary.* Use all capital letters or just an initial capital *G.* Make the entry word, the word being defined, stand out by using boldface or columns. When using columns, place the entry words on the left and definitions on the right. Alphabetize all words, acronyms, and symbols, as dictionaries do. Choose to single-space or double-space entries, depending on how many entries you have and, of course, on what will be most helpful to the reader(s).

Appendices. Appendices are materials that you want your reader to have access to but that are not a primary part of the proposal. Each **appendix** must be labeled with the word *Appendix* (can be in all capitals) and given a number (or a letter of the alphabet) and a descriptive title, similar to the system for identifying visual aids. Make every document an individual appendix.

Works Cited. Prepare Works Cited or documentation pages according to the guidelines of the style manual you are using. For example, this text uses MLA format, which calls for the words *Works Cited* (can be in all capitals) centered at the top of the page and double-spacing within and between all entries. Consult the style manual your organization or the RFP requires and follow it precisely.

Generally writers include most, if not all, of the formal proposal elements listed above. However, the format, length, and even organization of formal proposals may be dictated in the RFP. Federal funding agencies, for instance, often have very strict criteria and will reject proposals that do not follow the guidelines.

Page Numbers

Assigning page numbers for formal proposals works the same as pagination in books. **Prefatory material**, as in preface or before the report begins, is numbered with lowercase Roman numerals. Prefatory material includes

letter/memo of transmittal   table of contents

title page   list of illustrations

Since the letter or memo of transmittal is the first page of the document, it needs no page number. In addition, a title page is never numbered. Therefore, the table of contents, the third page, would be numbered *iii.*

Use Arabic numerals for the remainder of the proposal, except for the first page of the report itself, which usually begins with the Introduction. This first page carries no page number. Place an Arabic *2* on the next page. Number all other pages of the body of the proposal, the glossary, appendices, and Works Cited with Arabic numerals in sequence.

Place page numbers centered at the bottom or in the upper right corner of the page. Use the pagination in the proposal at the beginning of this chapter as a guide.

Placement of Text

Format the lengthy text of your formal proposal so that readers, particularly those who will read only one or two sections, can gain easy access to the information they seek. Use headings and subheadings to show relationships between ideas and to emphasize the important ideas. Itemize, boldface, italicize, and underline to call attention to essential information. Use visual aids to clarify complex points and to break up long blocks of text. When text is placed carefully, even a long proposal can look inviting and be easy to understand.

STOP AND THINK 17.2

How does the table of contents for the opening model on page 336 make clear the difference between important ideas and less important points?

Organizing and Composing Formal Proposals

WARM UP 17.3

Review the proposal outline included in Prewriting on page 351. Notice that the Budget subsection, where the reader is told how much the proposed idea will cost, is placed near the end of the document. Why do you think writers delay budget information in this way? Explain the strategy in a journal entry.

As you organize and compose your formal proposal, keep these tips in mind:

- Give yourself a reasonable amount of time to write the proposal. RFP's usually state a deadline that is not negotiable.

- Prepare your proposal carefully. Follow guidelines and due dates strictly. Your proposal may compete with other proposals, either directly for a sales contract or indirectly for a portion of your company's budget or work load.

- Use a tone appropriate for the audience. Writers usually address distant or unfamiliar audiences with a more formal tone (for example, spelling out contractions such as *can't* or *I'll*).

- Demonstrate your understanding of the subject and the specifications (found in the RFP, if there is one) with specific details.

The owner of a small waste disposal business competes with other small operators for commercial and government accounts in the region. One county government is accepting proposals for the coming year's business. Normally the owner submits a proposal to each of the seven county governments in the area. While she is preparing this proposal, a neighbor who was recently employed by this particular county, without being asked for it, gives the business owner some inside information that could help win the contract if the business owner uses it.

What should the business owner do? Should she use the information and say nothing? Should she report the neighbor? If the owner desperately needs the business, should the level of need affect the decision? If no one is hurt, is it OK to do something you aren't sure is right?

Organizing Sections within Formal Proposals

The sections from which you choose, as explained in Formatting Formal Proposals, will be the same for most formal proposals. However, the organization of sections within the proposal will vary. For example, your Executive Summary should follow a problem/solution/justification plan to tell the busy executive what he or she most needs to know. The Introduction should use a cause/effect plan with the explanation of the problem being the cause and the objectives being the effect. Then sections within the body of the proposal might use different organizational strategies. If you outline schedules, you organize chronologically. If you describe a product, you organize spatially. For each formal proposal section, choose and stick to an appropriate organizational plan.

Organizing the Document as a Whole

What is the most effective and persuasive organization for the entire formal proposal? It is the organization given in the standard outline. Follow the outline and choose subsections to provide the data your audience needs. Check for proposal sections that always need to be included, such as Executive Summary and Problem and Proposed Solution. Present sections and optional subsections in the order in which they appear in the outline.

The outline and organization have been designed and tested to convince readers. Each part meets a particular need, sometimes for only one type of reader, as the Executive Summary helps the busy executive by condensing the report. At the same time, the parts work together to create a powerful and influential effect. For example, the Introduction gives the reader the main ideas behind the proposal; it explains what is wrong or what is lacking as well as how the problem should be fixed. If the reader is skeptical, the Body or Discussion section provides the facts and details to convince him or her. Only then, after the reader is persuaded that the proposed plan is the right idea, does the writer mention cost. Thus, even if the cost is more than anticipated, the case has been made that the plan is worth the price. When proposals are created by a group within an organization, each writer, and particularly the editor or chief writer, must carefully attend to organizing persuasively.

Composing Sections within Formal Proposals

By the time you get to the composing part of the process, you have already done a great deal of work toward creating the formal proposal. During composing, use all your planning and preparatory work to create a draft of the full proposal. The writing process will be easier if you work with one section at a time, keeping in mind that the entire document must work as a logical whole. The suggestions below will help you with composing the special parts of a formal proposal.

Letter/Memo of Transmittal. As with a cover letter for a resume, the letter/memo of transmittal officially passes the formal proposal from the writer to the reader. Since the message is usually good news for the audience, this letter or memo uses the direct strategy:

1. Begin with your purpose, the fact that you are submitting a proposal. Name the topic of the proposal and explain whether you are responding to an RFP, responding to a request, or initiating the proposal on your own.

2. Note any areas of special interest to the reader.

3. Thank the audience for reviewing the proposal. You may offer to provide more information if it should be needed or to answer questions.

The letter/memo of transmittal is usually written last, after the rest of the proposal is complete.

Title Page. Be clear, accurate, complete, and precise in composing the title page. Provide

- a descriptive title of the proposal
- the company or companies involved
- the name(s) of the writer(s)
- the date the proposal is being submitted

Some writers of internal proposals include, as a part of the title page, a routing list of readers who will review the document.

Note that a precise title, such as

PROPOSAL TO DEVELOP A POLICY GOVERNING SUBSTITUTE STAFFING FOR ABSENTEE TECHNICIANS IN THE FIBER TWIST AREA

or

PROPOSAL TO PURCHASE AND INSTALL THE EVERMORR SECURE 3120 SECURITY SYSTEM IN GLYNNDALE CONDOMINIUMS is useful because it gives the reader more information than a vague title, such as PROPOSAL TO DEAL WITH ABSENT WORKERS or PROPOSAL TO IMPROVE SECURITY IN GLYNNDALE CONDOMINIUMS.

Executive Summary (or Abstract). Write the Executive Summary after you have finished the rest of the report. Keep the reader in mind as you compose. Busy executives want the story quickly and only the essential information—the problem, the solution, and the benefits of the solution.

Introduction. The introduction is the framework to prepare readers for the body of your proposal. The introduction answers the questions "what" and "why." No matter which subparts of the introduction you choose to include in your document, clearly state for your reader(s) the problem and a solution or alternate solutions. If you determine that the reader needs background information, summarize the situation and the proposer's qualifications. Include information about your company and personnel, such as the number of years in business, staff and equipment resources, previous clients, and success with similar projects, that will enhance the credibility of your proposal. Since any proposal reviewer might read the introductory material, remember to communicate so that administrators, managers, technical experts, and financial managers all can understand.

Body or Discussion. If the introduction sets the framework of ideas, the body of a formal proposal is the crux of the argument, the specifics of persuasion. The body is the section in which the technical data prove that your idea (solution) will work. Describe methods for carrying out the project, specific tasks, time schedules, personnel, facilities, and equipment. Include an organizational chart of people working on the project so the reader will know who is responsible for particular areas. In addition to outlining what you will do, these specific details convince the reader that your approach is the best one for the situation. The project's budget should clearly show specific costs and perhaps justify the costs. Remember that the visual aids you have planned should enhance the text of your proposal, not take the place of the text.

Conclusion. Be concise and direct when you write the conclusion for your formal proposal. You have already provided all the information to sway your audience to your point of view. This is not the time to add to your sales pitch. Instead, summarize your most convincing points regarding the importance of the project and the benefits of the solution. Then suggest a course of action.

Glossary. Choose words to define and determine the extent of your definitions based on what you know your audience will need. Don't define words the audience already understands. At the same time, if your proposal is to have several reviewers, define a term even if only one of the readers will need the definition. Write definitions using language the reader understands.

1. What section of the formal proposal do writers compose last? Why?
2. Which section of the document—Introduction, Discussion, or Conclusion—contains the specific facts and figures to explain the writer's plan and to convince the audience?

SUMMARY

1. A formal proposal, like an informal proposal, tries to get an audience to approve or accept the writer's plan, product, service, or idea. In contrast to an informal proposal, a formal document uses a more formal tone, includes additional report parts, and often seeks a complex potential outcome.

2. Formal proposal readers, like wary customers, may need to be convinced that whatever is being sold is worth the cost. The audience may be one person or many and may be distant from the writer, either in actual location or on the organizational ladder. Knowing the audience is extremely important in planning a successful proposal.

3. Prewriting techniques will help the writer(s) identify and analyze the problem as well as gather data for solving the problem. During prewriting, the writer(s) should consider which sections and subsections of the formal proposal outline are needed for presenting the collected data. Prewriting also includes realistic plans of what the proposer can accomplish. Particularly if several writers are involved, prewriting should include plans for integrating the various parts of the report into a smooth, logical whole.

4. Formal proposals include many special parts that have unique formatting guidelines. These parts may include a letter/memo of transmittal, a title page, a table of contents, a list of illustrations, an executive summary (or abstract), an introduction, a body (or discussion), a conclusion (or summary), a glossary, appendices, and a Works Cited or bibliography.

5. The various sections within the formal proposal should each be organized according to the data they present and their function, such as the Executive Summary—problem/solution/justification.

6. Writers should **a)** allow a reasonable amount of time for preparing the proposal, **b)** follow guidelines and due dates carefully, and **c)** demonstrate a thorough understanding of the problem and the criteria for the solution by providing a complete, detailed plan. While writers may compose one section at a time or different writers may each compose a section, everyone should work together to create a logical and unified proposal.

Editing And Revision Checklist

Have I reviewed each part of my proposal for the following:

✓ *Letter/Memo of Transmittal.* Does it use a direct organizational strategy? Is it neat and attractive? Is the page number omitted?

✓ *Title Page.* Does it include a descriptive title, the name of the preparer(s), the audience, and the date? Is it visually appealing? Is the page number omitted?

✓ *Table of Contents.* Does it show what is covered in the report and where it is located? Are major sections and subsections obvious? Does it include a lowercase Roman numeral page number?

✓ *List of Illustrations.* Are labels, numbers, descriptive titles, and page numbers included? If on a page alone, does it include a lowercase Roman numeral page number?

✓ *Executive Summary.* Should it be on a page by itself? Is it clear and concise? Does it follow a problem/solution/justification strategy? Does it include a lowercase Roman numeral page number?

✓ *Introduction.* Should it begin on a separate page? Does it clearly describe the problem and the proposed solution, using a cause/effect organizational plan? Are appropriate headings and subheadings used and are they clear and consistent? Is the page number omitted on the first page? Do all subsequent pages use an Arabic numeral?

✓ *Body or Discussion Section.* Should it begin on a separate page? Does this section demonstrate a carefully thought-out plan with specific details to support it? Is organization appropriate for the function of each subsection? Are facts and figures complete and accurate? Are visual aids included where they can enhance the reader's comprehension? Are headings, subheadings, itemization, and other special features used effectively to promote understanding and to enhance eye appeal? Are pages assigned Arabic numerals?

✓ *Conclusion.* Should it begin on a separate page? Does it use headings and subheadings effectively? Does it concisely summarize the key points and call for the audience to take action?

✓ *Glossary.* Are entry words boldfaced or in some way highlighted? Are terms arranged in alphabetical order?

✓ *Appendices.* Is each appendix labeled with sequential numbers or letters?

✓ *Works Cited.* Are ideas or words borrowed from other sources properly documented? Are outside sources listed alphabetically by author's last name or by the first word in each entry? Is the information accurate and correctly formatted according to your organization's style manual or the RFP requirements?

✓ Is the proposal free of grammatical and mechanical errors?

APPLY WHAT YOU HAVE LEARNED

1. Use the following information to create an effective title page for an internal formal proposal.

   Sandra Thomas-Liu, Development Officer, and Dean R. Willoughby, Public Relations Officer, both work for Topeka Memorial Hospital. Together they wrote a formal proposal. It was submitted by the writers on June 11, 19--, to be reviewed by their supervisor, Dr. Linwood Z. Ulio, Director, Public Affairs and Institutional Development Department. The title of the formal proposal is <u>Proposed Restructuring and Division of the Public Affairs and Institutional Development Department</u>. In addition to going to Marjorie O'Malley, Executive Vice-President, for final approval, the proposal will go to Peter N. Riggins, Vice-President of Finances, and Dr. Leah South, Vice-President of Operations.

2. Revise the following table of contents and list of illustrations to make them more useful. *HINT:* Think about relationships between ideas in the Table of Contents.

   Table of Contents

Executive Summary	iv
Introduction	1
Problem	1
Profit Loss	1
Loss of Work Space	2
Figure 1. Useless Manufacturing Space	2
Figure 2. Wasted Space in the Warehouse	3
Lack of Employee Satisfaction	4
Solution	5
Discussion	6
Methods	6
Scheduling	7
Budget	8
Conclusion	10
Works Cited	11

3. Read the following Executive Summary from a sales proposal. Change the order of the paragraphs to follow the problem/solution/justification strategy.

   Built according to current government specifications, Eagle products are guaranteed to be effective. With the addition of these state-of-the-art safety products and a trained response team, insurance rates will decrease by 5–10%. Therefore, the equipment investment can be recouped in three years or less.

Tragic accidents may threaten the health of employees and the life of a company. Now OSHA standards, along with requirements posed by insurance companies, have become increasingly strict for manufacturing facilities. Public confidence also wavers without a safe working environment and a trained response team.

Pilot Mountain Motors can meet or exceed government and insurance guidelines and maintain public confidence with the use of Eagle fire extinguishers and carbon monoxide detectors. With the installation of Eagle safety equipment, a unit of five experts will spend two days on-site training a response team.

CONSIDER THIS CASE

1. This exercise is also available on the computer applications diskette as **TEXT17A**. Using the information given below, write an introductory section for a formal proposal.

At Rockport Child Care Center, the two-year-old group and the four-year-old group are both on the playground during the same time period. Center policy requires that all children be given at least 30 minutes each day on the playground. Andrew Young, a caregiver for the two-year-olds, realizes that a great difference in level of maturity and appropriate play activities exists between these two age groups. Young is responsible for 18 children. Marguerite Gordo has 11 children in the two-year-old group. During the past six months, five accidents and four conflicts involving a child from each age group have occurred, and incident reports were filed. Also, the children compete, usually with the larger children winning, for certain pieces of equipment, such as the swings. The director, Marsha O'Shea, is responsible for scheduling. She has told Young that she has no extra money for a fence to divide the area into two sides or for additional caregivers.

2. As a salesperson for Sound Advice, you are preparing a sales proposal for Green Bay Electronics, a retail store that sells televisions, audio and video equipment, and satellite systems. Installing Sonex wall tiles, you suggest, would improve the quality of sound in the retail store's listening salons and, thus, would increase sales. Green Bay Electronics has four luxurious listening rooms in which employees set up audio and video equipment for demonstration purposes. The Sonex should be applied on one wall (behind the speakers) in each listening room. All four rooms are 10' × 10'; one wall will require 35 blocks of Sonex tile. The blocks cost $9.25 each. Sonex must be installed using an adhesive bond. Each wall will take three tubes; the tubes are $3.50 each. Labor charges for installing the Sonex will be $150. The sealer, sprayed on to preserve the material from the effects of sun and chemicals in the air, is $20.85 per tank. One tank should cover all four walls. Workers will need a sprayer for one hour, and rental fees are $12.95 per hour. Present this information as a budget to include in the formal proposal.

PURSUE AN IDEA

1. Interview a proposal writer to find out how his or her company uses formal proposals, who else (within this writer's organization) writes them, and how successful the proposals have been. Ask what this writer feels is essential in preparing an effective formal proposal.

2. With a group of classmates who share your interests, write a formal proposal to solve a specific problem. Identify a problem at school, at work, or in the community that must be dealt with by decision-makers distant from you on the organizational ladder—for example, a superintendent, president, or member of the board of trustees. Your proposal should require some research. Here are examples of problems to solve:

SCHOOL

equipment—new, replaced, or improved

time/access for the computer lab

snack bar

new club, sport

needed programs, classes

new policy or procedure

WORK

equipment or work space

salary or department budget

training or education

improved working conditions

sponsorship of sports team

insurance/benefits

uniforms

grievance procedure

COMMUNITY

sidewalks/bike paths

zoning or use of land

street/traffic signs

access for handicapped to neighborhood stores

street/park lighting

stray animals

civic group fundraiser

3. Critique a proposal from business or industry. Analyze how the writer(s) met (or did not meet) the needs of the audience. Review formatting features. Determine organizational patterns. Share the results of your critique orally or in an essay.

Technical Reading

CHAPTER

18

Guidelines to Technical Reading

Write-to-Learn

How does your science (or computer or shop) textbook differ from your literature textbook? Do you read scientific or technical material differently from the way you read literature? If so, how? Which do you prefer to read and why?

DEFINITIONS

literary reading reading literature such as short stories, poetry, and novels

margin notes notes made in the margins of text

preview to look over a reading assignment before reading it; to determine subject matter and questions you may have about the material before reading it

technical reading reading science, business, or technology publications

Exercise

Exercise is a popular technique used today by many people to help cope with stress, improve cardiovascular and metabolic capacity, and experience an elevation in mood. The exercise needs to be strenuous for a long enough period of time to put an overload demand on the body. Such endurance or aerobic conditioning exercises include hiking, jogging, brisk walking, running, swimming, bicycling, calisthenics, and active sports.

Stress and Illness. One way exercise seems to have an effect on behavior is by reducing the levels of epinephrine and norepinephrine in the bloodstream generally. Exercise accomplishes this by training the adrenal glands to respond to stress more efficiently. Recent research with previously nonrunning students indicates that pushing the heart and lungs to their maximum capacity by doing aerobic exercise for a semester causes the adrenal glands to respond with higher levels of epinephrine and norepinephrine in a stressful situation (Dienstbier, 1982). This response enables the person to deal with the stress without depleting the body's immune system as much. People who exercise on a regular basis are less likely to develop heart disease or diabetes and have fewer heart attacks and less severe heart attacks than people who are not active . . . . Some studies are even indicating a link between cancer and how a person responds to stress. Thus, there is some evidence that a person who exercises a lot will be ill less often.

Brain Function. Endorphins have been shown to rise in the nervous system during a long-distance race (Colt, Wardlow, and Frantz, 1981), and it appears that regular, vigorous exercise increases endorphin levels even more. Because endorphins are the body's own pain killers working like morphine, people who exercise on a regular basis usually report that they feel better generally, experience more freedom from pain, have the ability to withstand more pain, and experience more peak experiences of exhilaration than when they do not exercise regularly. It has also been speculated that the "runner's high" may be caused by a temporary shift from left hemisphere dominance to right hemisphere dominance (Sachs, 1984).

SOURCE: A. Christine Parham. *Psychology: Studying the Behavior of People*. 2nd ed. Cincinnati: South-Western Publishing Co., 1988. 63.

TECHNICAL READING
Model

Exer— can cope w/ stress, improve heart/lungs & metabolism.

Must be strenuous — aerobic

Exer lowers epinephrine? and norepinephrine?

Exer makes adrenal glands more efficient.

Exer —→ less disease

Stress —→ cancer?

Endorphins (natural painkillers) increase w/ exer

Shift to rt-brain dom. may cause runner's high

After completing this chapter, you will be able to

● Recognize the differences between literary reading and technical reading

● Determine the characteristics of technical reading

● Use strategies for reading technical passages

Technical readings are distinguished by technical subject matter, an emphasis on precision, and a description of mechanisms and processes. The vocabulary is highly specialized, and visual aids are common. Technical reading covers readings in science, business, and/or technology. The biology course, marketing course, accounting course, and computer course you take all involve technical reading.

Technical reading differs from **literary reading**. Reading literature requires you to make associations and draw inferences—to interpret and read between the lines. The reading is expansive; you are asked to add your imagination to what you read. Technical readings do not ask you to make emotional associations, to draw inferences, or to interpret symbolic language. They require you to understand what is on the page, to take the time to understand the logic presented to you. The reading is dense, packed with detailed and precise information.

Because technical reading is different from other kinds of reading, it helps to approach technical reading with a plan. When reading technical documents,

● preview the material

● take notes

● repeat difficult notes aloud

● make sure you understand the vocabulary

● anticipate the line of reasoning

● learn how to read visual aids

● pay close attention to numerical data

● pace yourself

● read more in the subject area

Preview the Material

Skim the introduction for an idea of the subject matter. Turn headings into questions; anticipate the information to follow. Previewing warms up the mind for reading just as stretching warms up the body for exercise. You will read with greater efficiency and retention because you'll be more interested in the reading and you'll know what to expect.

While previewing, make sure you understand the layout of the passage. Look at headings to see where information is placed. In a manual, for example, thumb through the pages to see where the schematics are, where the description of parts is, where the glossary is. Also, use the **preview** to activate your background knowledge of the subject. The more background knowledge you can activate, the more meaningful the passage will be.

The opening model shows a technical passage on exercise. Figure 18.1 is how one student previewed the passage on exercise. The student first determined the subject—exercise—and then turned the headings into questions.

Figure 18.1 Sample Preview

Subject: The first heading "Exercise" and the first sentence suggest that the passage will be about how exercise can control stress.

Questions: 1) How can exercise help me cope with stress?
2) What is the connection between stress and illness?
3) What does brain function have to do with exercise?

Take Notes on the Reading Passage

> *If you would be a reader, read; if a writer, write.*
>
> EPICTETUS

It's important to *write* about what you read. As you write, you will activate more brain centers and will, therefore, understand and retain more of the information. When taking notes, use abbreviations, note what is significant, consider outlining the passage, consider using graphic aids, and answer questions.

Use Abbreviations

To help you write about what you read, devise or borrow a system of abbreviations for marking important information. Here are a few examples:

IMPT or **!**	important information	**b/c**	because
EX	example	**?**	questions
∴	math symbol for therefore	**w/**	with

Note What is Significant

When you take notes, take notes on the following:

- summary of information, especially by sections
- main ideas
- definitions
- lists and series
- answers to the questions you posed during the preview
- description of a process
- sections you don't understand and need to go back over or ask questions about

If you own your book, you can mark important information with **margin notes**. If you prefer to take notes in a notebook, write the same information in your notebook. The opening model shows a technical passage with margin notes. Notice how the student has devised symbols and abbreviations for faster writing. The notes summarize, list information, define new terms, and mark information not understood.

Consider an Outline

Figure 18.2 shows two outlines on the exercise passage. Such outlines help you to see where major divisions are and are effective summaries for the passage. The outline can be formal, as illustrated in the first outline; or the outline could be informal, as illustrated by the second outline.

Figure 18.2 Sample Formal and Informal Outline

Formal Outline: Exercise

I. Exercise can help people cope with stress, improve cardiovascular and metabolic capacity, and improve mood.
II. Exercise can prevent illness.
    A. Exercise can lower levels of epinephrine and norepinephrine in bloodstream.
    B. Exercise causes adrenal glands to handle emergency stress more efficiently.
    C. People who exercise have fewer heart attacks and other diseases.
    D. Studies show possible link b/t cancer and stress.

Informal Outline: Exercise

Exercise affects the brain.
    — Vigorous exercise increases endorphins in nervous system.
    — Endorphins are the body's natural painkillers.
    — "Runner's high" may be caused by shift to right-brain dominance.

Consider Graphic Aids

Some students prefer to "draw" notes that map the relationship between ideas with circles, blocks, and lines. A circle or block represents the central idea. Lines drawn to other circles or blocks show how smaller parts of the topic relate to the central idea. Figure 18.3 shows the ideas in the exercise passage illustrated graphically in two ways.

Figure 18.3 Graphic Aids

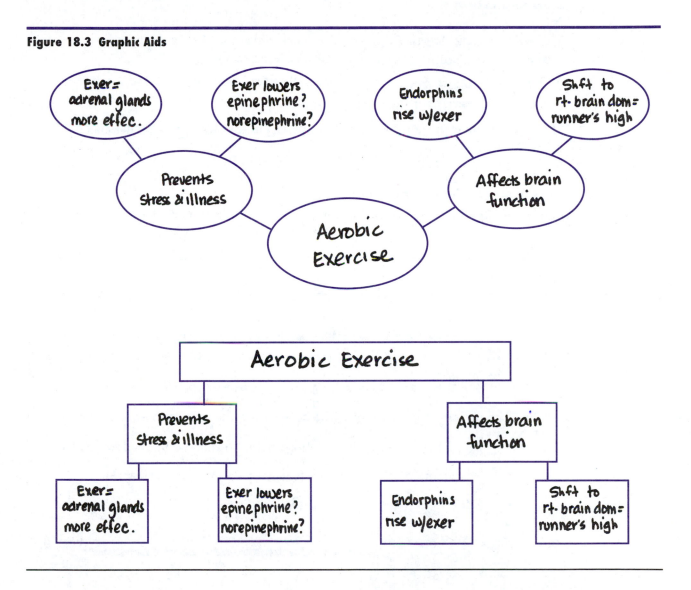

Answer Questions

In addition to previewing, taking notes, and outlining, answering questions is also a helpful note-taking tool. The questions could be your own, your teacher's, or a textbook's end-of-chapter exercises.

In Figure 18.4, one student answers in a notebook the questions posed during the preview in Figure 18.1. Also in Figure 18.4, another student begins to answer the questions at the end of the chapter.

Figure 18.4 Sample Answers to Questions

Answers to preview:

1) Exercise lowers levels of epinephrine and norepinephrine (adrenalin and noradrenalin produced by adrenal glands).
2) Too much stress can lead to stress illnesses like heart attacks — even cancer. Exercise reduces stress levels.
3) Exercise increases endorphins (responsible for feeling of well-being) in brain.

Answers to end-of-chapter questions:

How does exercise affect levels of epinephrine and norepinephrine in the bloodstream?

Exercise lowers levels of epinephrine and norepinephrine in the bloodstream.

WRITERS ON THE JOB

Rosa Tyson is pursuing a career as a teller for First Citizens Bank. Developing positive customer relations and communicating effectively with a variety of people are essential aspects of her job, she says. She also notes that she continues to enhance communication skills she learned as a student so that she can do a better job.

Repeat More Difficult Notes Aloud

Hearing what you have written and read in silence may help you retain difficult information. Try repeating the notes aloud several times:

> Promotion is affected by three types of distribution decisions: the intensity of the distribution, the length of the channel, and the type of intermediary. Promotion is affected by three types of distribution decisions: the intensity of the distribution, the length of the channel, and the type of intermediary. Promotion is affected by . . . .

Make Sure You Understand the Vocabulary

When reading in humanities subject areas, you can often determine vocabulary in context. In technical reading, however, everyday words can be used in unusual or limited ways. Technical reading also uses specialized words.

When a technical term is not defined in the text, look it up. Textbooks often have glossaries that define technical terms. You may have to ask an expert in the field to define the word for you.

When vocabulary is defined in the text, the definition is given in parentheses or in an appositive immediately following the term. In Figure 18.5 some terms are defined in the text, but the writer assumes the reader will know many of the terms already. Notice the use of acronyms (letters to stand for a long or complicated term or series of terms).

In 1963, Soviet Valentina Tereshkova was the first woman in space.

Figure 18.5 Sample 1: Technical Vocabulary

Scientists have identified two very important types of cholesterol packaging: low-density lipoproteins and high-density lipoproteins. Low-density lipoproteins, or LDLs, are considered to be "bad" cholesterol. About 70% of cholesterol intake is in the form of LDLs. High levels of LDLs have been associated with the clogging of arteries—LDL particles bind to receptor sites on cell membranes and are removed from the blood (principally by the liver). However, as the levels of LDLs increase and exceed the number of receptor sites, excess LDL-cholesterol begins to form deposits on the walls of arteries. The accumulation of cholesterol and other lipids on the artery walls, is known as *plaque*.

The number of Americans living under the poverty level increased from 26.1 million (11.7% of the population) in 1979 to 35.7 million (14.2% of the population) in 1991.

Some definitions need more than a phrase or sentence and extend to a paragraph or more. Figure 18.6 illustrates an extended definition of the word *path.* Notice that this definition is not what people generally associate with the word *path.*

Figure 18.6 Sample 2: Technical Vocabulary

What is a Path?

Suppose you had to tell a colleague how to find the 1992 Annual Sales Report . . . . You'd say, "Open drawer C, get out the hanging folder named REPORTS, remove the manila folder named SALES from the REPORTS hanging folder. There you'll find the Annual Sales Report."

Similarly, when you want to access a file on a disk—so you can copy the file, delete it, rename it, or do something else with it—you have to tell DOS where the file is located. The complete specification of a file—including disk, directories (if any), and filename—is called the complete **path** to the file. For example, the complete path to the file SALES92.REP . . . is C:\REPORTS\SALES\SALES92.REP. In this path, "C:\" is the root directory on drive C, "REPORTS" is the directory REPORTS within the root directory, "SALES" is the subdirectory SALES within REPORTS, and "SALES92.REP" is the file that contains the annual sales report. Backslashes separate directories and subdirectories within a path.

Besides complete paths, you can use partial paths. For example, if the default drive were C, you could leave off the C: and just use the path \REPORTS\SALES\SALES92.REP to access the file SALES92.REP. In this case the initial backslash takes the place of "C:\."

You can also specify paths to directories and subdirectories. For example, if you wanted to get a directory listing of the files within the directory REPORTS, you would type the DIR command and then use the path A:\REPORTS (or just \REPORTS if A were the default drive) to indicate the directory you wanted to list.

SOURCE: Roy Ageloff, Scott Zimmerman, and Beverly Zimmerman. *Micro Computer Applications for Business.* Cambridge: Course Technology, Inc., 1993. 44.

Anticipate the Line of Reasoning

Knowing the typical lines of reasoning in technical reading will help you anticipate how to read. Most technical reading calls on the reader to understand

- a process or procedure (steps; how something works),
- a cause/effect relationship (what makes something happen), or
- a mechanism (what something looks like and what it's supposed to do).

Figure 18.7 shows a process description of photosynthesis. In this description of process, however, are also several cause/effect relationships. One action causes another action. As a result, this chain reaction is also responsible for the process. Notice, too, the importance of knowing the vocabulary.

Figure 18.7 Process Description of Photosynthesis

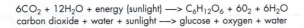

$$6CO_2 + 12H_2O + energy\ (sunlight) \longrightarrow C_6H_{12}O_6 + 6O_2 + 6H_2O$$
$$carbon\ dioxide + water + sunlight \longrightarrow glucose + oxygen + water$$

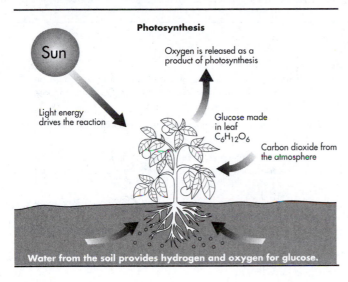

Photosynthesis

Sun

Oxygen is released as a
product of photosynthesis

Light energy
drives the reaction

Glucose made
in leaf
$C_6H_{12}O_6$

Carbon dioxide from
the atmosphere

Water from the soil provides hydrogen and oxygen for glucose.

Figure 3.19
Plants utilize light
energy to form
glucose from water
and carbon dioxide.

PHOTOSYNTHESIS AND ENERGY

The extent to which our planet relies on plants can be demonstrated by a study of photosynthesis. The word is a composite of *photo*, meaning "light," and *synthesis* meaning "to make or build." In photosynthesis, carbon dioxide from the air and water from the soil are combined to form glucose, a carbohydrate. Light energy is used to convert the low-energy reactants, carbon dioxide and water, into a complex, high-energy product. Although animals rely on glucose to fuel the cells of their bodies, they cannot produce it themselves—they must rely on plants for their food. The chemical reaction for photosynthesis is shown in Figure 3.19.

During photosynthesis, plants convert light energy into chemical energy. However, the conversion is not a single-step process. Photosynthesis can be broken down into two components: the light-dependent reactions and the carbon-fixation reactions. During the light-dependent reactions, light energy is converted into chemical energy and temporarily stored in ATP. The absorption of light energy also causes the loss of electrons by pigments involved in photosynthesis. The pigments replace their electrons by taking them from water molecules, and in the process, water molecules are split into two component parts: hydrogen and oxygen. The oxygen is released into the atmosphere. The hydrogen proton and its electron temporarily combine with the coenzyme $NADP^+$. During the oxidation-reduction reaction, the $NADP^+$ accepts a hydrogen proton and its electron to become NADPH, the reduced form of $NADP^+$. As in all oxidation-reduction reactions, energy is released. This energy is then stored in ATP.

During the carbon-fixation phase, hydrogen atoms extracted from water molecules are joined with carbon dioxide molecules to make glucose. The energy required to make glucose comes from the NADPH and ATP made during the light reaction.

Figure 18.8 shows another process, a set of instructions, the first steps involved in setting up a directory. The reasoning here is linear, a chronologically organized sequence of events.

Figure 18.8 Step-by-Step Process

To make a new directory:

❶ If you have a *two-diskette system,* insert the Systems Disk into drive A, turn on your computer, and get to the DOS prompt A>. After the DOS prompt appears on the screen, remove the Systems Disk from the drive.

If you have a *hard-disk system,* turn on your computer and get to the DOS prompt C>.

If you're using a computer on a network, make sure the computer is on, that you are logged into the network, and that the DOS prompt (for example, F>) is on the screen.

❷ Insert the work diskette, the diskette you formatted in DOS Tutorial 1 or some other newly formatted diskette, into drive A.

❸ Make sure drive A is the default drive.

If necessary type **a:** and press **[Enter]** to make A the default drive.

❹ Type **md reports** and press **[Enter]**.

The DOS command MD requires one parameter, the name of the new directory you want to create. DOS makes the new directory REPORTS, which in this case is a subdirectory of the root directory.

❺ Type **md corresp** and press **[Enter]** to create a directory for holding letters and other correspondence.

DOS creates a second directory within the root directory.

❻ Type **md memos** and press **[Enter]** to create a directory for holding memo files.

DOS creates a third subdirectory of the root directory. Now REPORTS, CORRESP, and MEMOS are all subdirectories within the root directory (Figure 2-3).

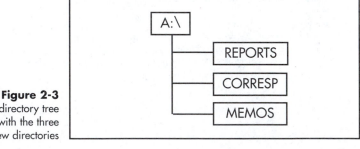

Figure 2-3
a directory tree
with the three
new directories

SOURCE: Roy Ageloff, Scott Zimmerman, and Beverly Zimmerman. *Micro Computer Applications for Business.* Cambridge: Course Technology, Inc., 1993. 45.

Figure 18.9 shows a mechanism description that describes the function of each part of a computer toolbar.

Figure 18.9 Mechanism Description of Computer Toolbar

 FILL Fills the highlighted range with a sequence of values.

 CALC Recalculates all formulas in the worksheet.

 DATE Enters a number that corresponds to the current date and time in the current cell. If the cell is formatted with a date format, the date appears in the cell in that format. If the cell is not formatted with a date format, the date appears in the cell in the default date format. If the cell is formatted with a time format, the time appears in the cell in that format.

 CRCL This icon can only be used with WYSIWYG attached. Circles the data in the highlighted range. 1-2-3 creates the circle by adding a graphic to the highlighted range.

SOURCE: Roy Ageloff, Scott Zimmerman, and Beverly Zimmerman. *Micro Computer Applications for Business.* Cambridge: Course Technology, Inc., 1993. L365.

Learn How to Read Visuals

Be prepared to think visually when reading a technical passage. Notice the diagrams. Draw a picture of what you're reading—on paper or in your mind.

Most technical reading places information in visual form to help you see what is happening. To read visuals, make sure you understand the purpose of each type of visual. Then study the visual closely as well as the author's explanation of the visual.

Understand the Purpose of Each Type of Visual

Figure 18.10 shows the purpose of the most often used visual aids. When you see a diagram, for example, you should know the purpose of the diagram is to help you see what something looks like. You can then read the visual specifically with that purpose in mind.

Figure 18.10 Purposes of Common Visual Aids

TYPE OF VISUAL	PURPOSE
simple line drawing or diagram	to show a mechanism or part of a mechanism
pie graph	to show how the whole is divided into parts, to show how the parts relate to the whole
informal table	to present a small amount of data (especially numbers) in an easy-to-read format
bar graph	to compare several sets of data; to present differences in a dramatic way; sometimes to depict a trend
double bar graph	to compare several sets of data; sometimes to depict a trend
line graph	to show a trend; to show how data is related
multiple line graph	to show several trends; to compare trends; to show how data is related
formal table	to present information, especially lots of numbers, in an easy-to-read format
flowchart	to present a process
organizational chart	to present the structure of an organization

Read the Visual Aid Closely

After you have noted what kind of visual you are reading and what its purpose is, then read the visual aid closely, noticing everything about it:

- Read the title to find out the visual's subject matter.
- Look for keys to understanding the visual aid.

> Read the legend.
>
> Read the call outs.
>
> Read the Y-axis and X-axis information.

Next, relate the information in the visual aid to the author's discussion of the visual aid. Use your fingers to trace the visual while you read the explanation. Compare the author's discussion to the visual. The discussion should point out what information in the visual is important. You can then take notes on the important aspects of the visual. If you will be asked to remember a diagram, you may wish to draw the diagram yourself.

A number of the technical reading passages presented thus far illustrate the importance of visual aids. Figure 18.7 on page 375 uses a picture and arrows to represent the process of photosynthesis. Figure 18.8 on page 376 uses a flow chart to make clearer the steps of setting up a directory. Figure 18.9 on page 377 includes pictures of icons to make the description easier to follow. Each visual presents technical information quickly and clarifies the explanation given in words.

Pay Close Attention to Numerical Data

Resist the temptation to read too quickly through discussions using numbers. Note that the number $1,245, while only four digits long, actually stands for six words—*one thousand two hundred forty-five dollars*. Figure 18.11 shows a process description of a capital statement. Even though the digits save space on the page, remember to take time to process the digits *as words* in your mind.

Figure 18.11 Technical Reading Using Numbers

The capital statement is prepared by listing the beginning capital balance of $6,490, adding the net income of $1,245 for the month, and subtracting withdrawals for the month, $200. The formal capital statement is presented in Illustration 4-6.

Illustration 4-6
Capital
Statement

George Delivery Service		
Capital Statement		
For Month Ended December 31, 19--		
Capital, December 1, 19--		$6,490.00
Net income for the month	$1,245.00	
Less withdrawals	200.00	
Change in capital		1045.00
Capital, December 31, 19--		$7,535.00

SOURCE: L. Paden Neeley and Frank J. Imke. *Accounting Principles and Practices.* Cincinnati: South-Western Publishing Co., 1991. 109.

Pace Yourself

Runners pace themselves in order to expend their energy evenly throughout a race. You, too, should pace yourself when you read. Follow these suggestions:

● Read slowly. Technical reading is packed with details. Often the details include numbers that can be misread if you are not careful. Because

the reading is dense, you should read slowly, making sure you take in all the details.

- Read small amounts of information for short periods of time (maybe 10–15 minutes). Then take a brief break and summarize or take notes on what you have read.

- Read the selection twice. The first time you read anything, there will be parts you do not read as carefully. A second reading will enable you to see what you missed the first time. Also, a second reading will allow you to see how the parts of the passage fit together. You will notice transitions and see relationships.

Read More in Your Technical Subject

The more that you read in a certain subject area, the better reader you will be in that subject area. For example, if you are used to reading car magazines, you will read a new article about cars better than someone who is used to reading computer magazines. You build a knowledge base in the subject and get used to vocabulary typically used in the subject. Additional readings build on that knowledge base and vocabulary. Thus, if you want to be a good technical reader, you should read more in your technical reading subject. You can also expand your knowledge base by reading in less familiar subject areas. The more background knowledge you bring to a subject, the better reader you will be.

SUMMARY

1. Technical reading differs from literary reading. Technical reading does not require readers to make emotional associations, draw inferences, or interpret symbolic language.

2. Technical reading includes densely packed precise details. The reading depends on frequent use of specialized vocabulary, a description of processes and mechanisms, cause-to-effect reasoning, and visual aids.

3. Strategies for becoming a proficient technical reader include the following: previewing the material, taking notes (in the margins or a notebook), repeating difficult notes aloud, making sure you understand the vocabulary, anticipating the line of reasoning, learning how to read visual aids, paying attention to numerical data, pacing yourself, and reading more in the subject area.

4. Take good notes by summarizing information (especially by sections), identifying main ideas, defining words, writing lists and series, answering the questions you posed during the preview, describing a process, noting what you don't understand and need to go back over or ask questions about.

BUILD ON WHAT YOU KNOW

1. How did you read technical passages before you read this chapter? Will you change anything about how you read technical passages now? If so, what?

2. List vocabulary in a technical field you are familiar with. Ask your classmates if they understand the vocabulary.

3. In your own words, list the characteristics of technical reading.

4. In your own words describe the difference between reading something technical and reading something literary.

5. Tell how to read something technical. Tell which suggestions for technical reading appeal to you.

CONDUCT YOUR OWN RESEARCH

1. Interview people who work in technical fields. Find out how much reading they do on the job. Do they have any suggestions for reading technical information?

2. Take a poll of 20 people you know. What kind of reading do they prefer—technical reading or literary reading? What kind of technical reading do they prefer?

3. Analyze your textbooks or technical magazines. Isolate one chapter or one article. How much of the vocabulary is new to you? How much technical vocabulary is in the passage? How many visual aids are there? Do some of the passages use numbers? How are numbers used?

4. Look back at the chapter or article you used in question **#3**. How would you chunk (divide up) some of this information? Which parts would be clearer to you if repeated aloud?

5. Read these sentences. Underline the technical word and the part of the sentence that defines that word.

   a. "Impulses originating from these cells [hairlike cells in the inner ear] provide an awareness of body position or balance, called equilibrium, which makes it possible to maintain an upright posture" (Parham 160).

   b. "Sort keys can be unique or non-unique. Sort keys are unique if the value of the sort key field for each record is different. Sort keys are non-unique if more than one record can have the same value in the sort key field" (Ageloff 137).

   c. "Auditing is a field of activity involving an independent review of the accounting records. In conducting an audit, CPA's examine the records supporting the financial reports of an enterprise" (Warren 11).

   d. "The adrenal glands release epinephrine (adrenalin) and norepinephrine (noradrenalin) into the bloodstream, resulting in a number of important changes in the body, all of which prepare it for action" (Parham 60).

e. "Hyperinflation is said to exist when an abrupt and substantial rise in prices of 50 percent or more per month causes the value of the currency to deteriorate so quickly that people become reluctant to accept and hold money" (Kamerschen 11).

APPLY WHAT YOU HAVE LEARNED

1. Preview the reading in Passages **1** and **2** below. Write your preview and then read it to your classmates.

2. Read the passages you just previewed. Pick out the technical reading elements. First, describe the thought processes. Which parts would you describe as process description? In which parts do you see cause/effect reasoning? Which words represent the specialized vocabulary of the subject area? Are they defined in the text?

3. Practice taking a variety of notes—margin notes (only if your teacher provides a copy you can take notes on) and notebook notes. In your notes, be sure to summarize, define, list, and mark what you have questions about.

4. Would you benefit from repeating parts of your notes aloud? Which parts?

5. Read the passages again. Which parts do you understand more clearly because you read them twice?

6. Describe what you thought about as you read the visual. Was the visual aid immediately clear to you? What is significant about the visual? Does the technical passage adequately explain the visual? Explain the visual to your classmates.

7. Which note-taking procedure do you prefer? Why?

Passage 1

Discovery

Ivan Pavlov (1927), a Russian physiologist, . . . inserted tubes into the salivary glands [of dogs] to measure the amount of saliva produced when he fed the dogs. He became perplexed when, after being in the laboratory for a while, the dogs would salivate before they were given food . . . .

Pavlov's Demonstration. Pavlov demonstrated classical conditioning by immediately following the ringing of a bell with the presentation of food to the dogs. Initially, the dogs did not salivate when the bell rang. After following the bell with food several times, Pavlov rang the bell without presenting food. He discovered that the bell alone now produced salivation in the dogs. A form of learning currently referred to as classical (earliest model) conditioning had occurred (see Figure 6-1). The dogs responded differently to an environmental event (bell) as a result of an environmental experience (pairing of bell with food). Originally the bell was neutral; it did not bring forth a specific response in the dog. After the bell became associated with food, it came to signal presence of food in the mouth—salivation. Classical conditioning had occurred by associating a neutral stimulus with an unconditioned stimulus.

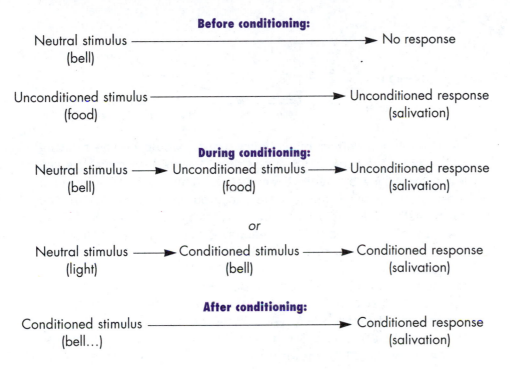

Before conditioning:

Neutral stimulus ————————————————————► No response
(bell)

Unconditioned stimulus ——————————————► Unconditioned response
(food)   (salivation)

During conditioning:

Neutral stimulus ——► Unconditioned stimulus ——► Unconditioned response
(bell)   (food)   (salivation)

or

Neutral stimulus ——► Conditioned stimulus ——► Conditioned response
(light)   (bell)   (salivation)

After conditioning:

Conditioned stimulus ————————————————► Conditioned response
(bell...)   (salivation)

Figure 6-1. Diagram of classical conditioning.

SOURCE: A. Christine Parham. *Psychology: Studying the Behavior of People*. 2nd ed. Cincinnati: South-Western Publishing Co., 1988. 192.

A **neutral stimulus** is a person, place, event or object that does not bring forth a specific response from the organism. An **unconditioned stimulus** is some phenomenon that brings forth a specific response, even the first time it is presented—a reflex response. A reflex response is referred to as an unlearned or **unconditioned response**.

Passage 2

. . . Worldwide estimates indicate that nearly five billion tons [of carbon dioxide] are being added to the atmosphere each year. Because of this massive increase in carbon dioxide levels, some scientists have predicted an increase in global temperatures of 2 to 5°C by the end of the next century (see Figure 14.17). This may not sound like much of a change, but on a global scale it is enormous. Mathematical computer models have been developed using available data on warming and climate to predict future events. At best these models can only show a trend, since they cannot account for all of the variables involved in both climate changes and potential warming. However, many of the models to date support the prediction of increasing world temperatures.

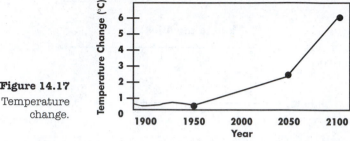

Figure 14.17
Temperature change.

One obvious effect of global warming would be the melting of the polar ice caps. If all of the polar ice were to melt, the sea level could rise by over three meters. This could totally flood most of the world's major cities, located as they are along the sea coasts. The various climate patterns of the world would also undergo change. Some regions of the earth would receive an increase in rainfall, while others would experience a decrease. These factors would have an impact on agriculture and food production and alter natural vegetation patterns.

The first regions to feel the effect would be the north—the **tundra** and the **boreal** forest. Winter temperatures over the Hudson Bay, the Davis Strait, and the Arctic Ocean might rise by as much as 11°C, making these bodies of water ice free in the winter. Precipitation patterns would also be disrupted. Since ocean water can modify the climate of land, the tundra conditions of the far north could disappear. This may seem potentially beneficial since it would increase the area of land suitable for agriculture. Whether the vegetation could tolerate such a sudden transition or whether soil could form normally or rapidly enough are some of the questions that remain unanswered . . . .

WORKS CITED

Ageloff, Roy, Scott Zimmerman, and Beverly Zimmerman. *Micro Computer Applications for Business.* Cambridge: Course Technology, Inc., 1993.

Kamerschen, David R. *Money and Banking.* 10th ed. Cincinnati: South-Western Publishing Co., 1992.

Parham, Christine A. *Psychology: Studying the Behavior of People.* 2nd ed. Cincinnati: South-Western Publishing Co., 1988.

Warren, Carl S., James Reeve, and Philip E. Fess. *Financial and Managerial Accounting.* 4th ed. Cincinnati: South-Western Publishing Co., 1994.

Appendix

Internet@a.glance

E-mail pals from across the globe "chat" while experiencing virtually no delay in transmission. A student in Australia researching archaeology locates and transfers files from a remote computer in Iceland. A business executive in Paris obtains the most recent stock market values in Tokyo as the changes occur. These examples are made reality through using the Internet.

This Appendix provides an overview of the Internet. It introduces terms and navigational tools that lend themselves to specific business applications. A glossary of basic Internet terms that expands on the material covered in this Appendix is included at the end of this Appendix.

What is the Internet?

The information "superhighway" is probably the best analogy for the Internet. The information system is named the "Internet" because of the connection, not only between computers, but also among computer networks. A network is two or more computers connected to each other with the capability of exchanging information.

Currently, the Internet is the world's largest computer network. Composed of smaller networks linked together, the Internet has become a community of people using computers to interact with each other. In addition to being a communication tool, the Internet also provides a method for obtaining information from a variety of sources worldwide. This information covers a multitude of topics from governments to academic research to businesses and corporations.

Where Did the Internet Originate?

The Internet started as a network for the Defense Department. The Defense Department utilized a language to transfer data in information packets from one computer system to another. This language is known as TCP/IP (Transmission Control Protocol/Internet Protocol). The Internet still uses TCP/IP as a standard method for information transfer.

Both NASA and NSF developed their own computer networks in the 1980s. This development provided easier information access for research scientists.

Then, universities and academic institutions expanded their own networks. The academic links included both intrastate and interstate computers for larger data sources.

During the late 1980s, a tremendous growth occurred in the number of networked computers. The most recent development in the Internet system is the expanded access available to the general public. This access is provided through commercial carriers (America Online, Prodigy, Delphi, CompuServe, and others) and through direct access. The Internet seems destined to continue expanding as more and more people use the system.

What Can You Do With the Internet?

You can use the Internet to perform three basic functions. You can communicate (primarily through E-mail), research information, and transfer information files.

All communication modes allow you to correspond in real time, without any delay in sending or receiving. Electronic mail or E-mail is probably the most utilized feature of the Internet. In order to use E-mail, you must know (or be able to find) the receiver's address.

E-mail addresses will always have two parts—the name and the location of the user. An example of an address is

cpbrantley@aol.com

This means that the username is *cpbrantley*, who is located at America Online (*aol*), which is a commercial carrier (*com*). The location part of the address is known as the domain.

Seven different organizational domains exist as shown in Figure 1.

Figure 1 Organizational Domains

Domain	Purpose
com	Commercial entities
edu	Educational institutions
gov	Non-military US government institutions
int	International institutions
mil	US military institutions
net	Network resources
org	Non-profit organizations

Another address example is

tclesc32@mail.firn.edu

In this address, the *tclesc32* is a username assigned by the carrier. The domains (to the right of the @ symbol) indicate this is an educational carrier (*edu*) through the Florida Information Resource Network (*firn*) routed to the mail program (*mail*).

Geographic domains represent addresses outside the United States. Some examples are: *au* (Australia), *jp* (Japan), *es* (Spain), and *fr* (France).

You may use a number of tools to search for information on any topic imaginable from computers around the world. Some of these tools include GOPHER, ARCHIE, WAIS, VERONICA, WWW, and JUGHEAD.

Once the desired information has been located, another tool transfers the data you have located from the host computer to your location. FTP (File Transfer Protocol) is the primary program that retrieves information from global sources.

How Do You Get Connected?

You must have one of two systems to connect into the Internet. The first system is from your personal computer via a modem. The second system is through direct wiring to larger computers, which are usually available on academic campuses or in large businesses. Internet connections may be complete service (able to access worldwide databases) or may be limited to electronic mail functions.

In order to connect, you need a computer, a modem, communications software with proper settings or parameters, a login/user name, a password, and an Internet account. An Internet account may be provided through one of several carriers. The following are frequently used carriers:

1. Commercial carriers such as America Online, CompuServe, Delphi, and Prodigy (require a monthly fee)

2. Universities and other educational institutions (usually free to staff and students)

3. Statewide networks, which may also connect academic institutions (CORE in California, PEN in Virginia, FIRN in Florida)

4. Governmental agencies

5. Internet access sites (require a monthly fee)

How Can You Use the Internet?

When you use the Internet, you select appropriate navigation tools, follow navigation basics, and observe Internet etiquette.

Navigation Tools

Navigation tools enhance your ability to communicate, research information, and transfer files.

Communication Tools. Communication tools include the following:

1. *Electronic mail* (E-mail) has many advantages over standard postal service or "snail-mail." E-mail is paperless, instantaneous, private, and requires no postage.

2. *TALK* (chat mode) allows real-time dialogue between users.

3. *TELNET* connects you to other host computers; then, you proceed as if you were at that site. One example of TELNET use is to access the National Weather Service weather report through a computer at the University of Michigan.

4. *USENET* is a group of users who share information on a central theme. People contributing to this "net" may be located anywhere in the world.

5. *IRC* (Internet Relay Chat) enables many users to communicate simultaneously.

6. The *FINGER* command allows you to find information on other users. Another feature of this command enables you to list everyone logged on at a specific site. If you are trying to send a message to someone and are unsure of the address, the finger command may be used.

Research Tools. Research tools include the following:

1. *ARCHIE* electronically searches directories of other computers and gives you the location or FTP site of the desired information. You may access ARCHIE directly; or you may go through a GOPHER command, through a TELNET command, or through E-mail.

2. *GOPHER* (named after a human "go-fer" and after the University of Minnesota mascot where the program was developed) also searches by keyword or topic. In addition to finding matching files, GOPHER also displays the files in a menu format. You can access GOPHER directly or TELNET to a public GOPHER client.

3. *WAIS* (Wide Area Information Server) does keyword searches and lists files containing keywords. WAIS provides a slightly broader source of information than GOPHER because WAIS includes indexes from a number of databases rather than just one or a few.

4. *WWW* (World Wide Web) searches a larger number of databases using "hypertext" links. Hypertext simply means that certain words or graphics are highlighted on the screen. Clicking these highlighted areas automatically sends you into another set of files with further information on that topic.

5. *VERONICA* acts as an index for GOPHER menus. While GOPHER may only access the information in one particular database, VERONICA searches all the titles in GOPHER sites and then displays a menu.

6. *JUGHEAD* operates as a limiting factor for the number of articles listed. In conjunction with the GOPHER command, JUGHEAD allows you to narrow a data search to finer parameters.

Many of these tools simply give a listing of sites where files of interest are found. If you want to read the file, you may then TELNET to that site. If you want to transfer the file to your computer, you use a transfer tool.

Transfer Tool. The primary file transfer tool is FTP, a program that sends and receives information between computers. Using FTP, you can transfer text as well as graphics from anywhere in the world to your computer. When transferring any files, you must include both the address where the file is coming from and the address where the file is going.

Navigation Basics

The UNIX operating system is the language of the Internet, just as DOS is the operating language for many computer systems. In order to "surf" the Internet, you do not need to know UNIX—commercial carriers provide a user interface that will execute the UNIX commands for you.

The first step in using the Internet is to **login** or **logon** to a host computer. This procedure varies depending on the type of carrier used. A sample logon screen is shown in Figure 2.

The screen may then include a menu or may show only a command prompt (similar to a DOS prompt). From this beginning screen, you may enter into a variety of programs.

Communicate. When you send an E-mail message, the procedure is relatively the same, no matter what system you use. Basically, the message needs an **address** (where the message will be sent) and a command to **send**. You may send messages to anyone on the Internet. The receiver does not have to be on the same carrier as you are.

When receiving a message, the screen may appear as shown in Figure 3.

Figure 2 America Online logon screen

Figure 3 An E-mail message using America Online

Subject: Word Usage

Date: 95-06-07 20:07:52 EDT

From: millermg@aol.com (Miller, Michele)

To: cpbrantley@aol.com

Clarice,

You are right. Midwesterners use some unique words. A water fountain is called a "bubbler." I'm not sure where this name originated, but I have not heard anyone from a different part of the country use the same term. Please share some of the unique terms used by Southerners.

Michele

If you had actually received this message from America Online, additional "header" information would appear below the signature. This information tells the computer pathways that the message traveled.

Research. Of the many research tools listed, you will probably use GOPHER and WWW the most. You may use WWW to "browse" many different systems simply by clicking on the highlighted text or graphics. If you are using a GOPHER command, you need to know which GOPHER site to select. If you are unsure of the site, you may use one of the additional research tools, such as VERONICA, to search more than one site.

Transfer. When using FTP, you must first login to the system or host holding the desired files. In most systems, you may login as a guest by using "anonymous" at the login prompt. When asked for a password, you may respond with your E-mail address. Although some systems may allow you in without your address, supplying the address is an Internet courtesy.

If you use FTP without the aid of a commercial carrier, you'll need to know some FTP commands. The major commands needed to use FTP are **get** and **put**. As these commands imply, **get** retrieves a file from the host and brings the file to the local host. Sometimes the local host is not your personal computer. Further transferring may be required; follow the guidelines given to you by your local provider. **Put** takes a file from your computer to another host.

When you are finished, you must break the connection. This is accomplished by using either the **close** command or the **quit** command. Both will break the connection; however, **quit** will also end the FTP program.

The methods of proceeding from the original login may vary, but one aspect is constant—etiquette.

Navigation Etiquette or "Netiquette"

Even though you send messages electronically, the communication rules still hold true. Be sure your messages are courteous, clear, concise, concrete, correct, and complete. If you communicate in a USENET, listen (or lurk) before you talk. Many of the frequently asked questions (FAQs) for a specific newsgroup are posted in that newsgroup. Many newsgroups or USENETs have particular interests. If you disagree with any statement expressed in a newsgroup, simply get out of that net. Also, you must be very careful when using sarcasm or humor. Without the benefit of facial expressions, many statements may be misinterpreted.

Additional guidelines include the following:
1. Do not give your password to anyone.
2. Do not use all capital letters in E-mail. Using all caps is comparable to shouting. Also, use limited exclamation marks. These marks also indicate excessive volume.
3. Comply with the system's "Acceptable Use Policy" that is available online.
4. Make sure the address is properly designated with the username correctly spelled and separated from the domain by an @ symbol.
5. Include a signature line on all messages.
7. Limit the use of graphics. Some people have to pay for downloading messages; graphics require extended downloading time.

May You Communicate With the Authors Through E-mail?

Yes, you may. Please communicate with the textbook authors. Use whatever system you have available; send your messages to any of the following addresses.

Sue Mehlich   *mehlich.sue@lrc.pitt.cc.nc.us*

Darlene Smith-Worthington   *pidsmith@eastnet.educ.ecu.edu*

Internet Glossary

A

Address The number sequence that identifies a unique user or computer on a network. Every computer and user on the Internet must have a different address for the system to know where to send E-mail and other computer data. (See Names.)

Archie A tool (software) for finding files stored on anonymous FTP sites. You need to know the exact file name or a sub-string of it.

Articles Information, ideas, and comments posted on USENET and E-mail lists.

B

BBS Bulletin Board System. A computerized meeting and announcement system that allows people to carry on discussions, upload and download files, and make announcements without the people being connected to the computer at the same time.

Backbone The Internet backbone was created by the National Science Foundation. The backbone links major computer centers together with a high-speed telecommunication connection. Subnetworks attach to the backbone.

BITNET Because It's Time Network. A network of educational sites separate from the Internet, but E-mail is freely exchanged between BITNET and the Internet. Listservs, the most popular form of E-mail discussion groups, originated on BITNET. BITNET machines are IBM VMS machines, and the network is probably the only international network that is getting smaller.

Bits Per Second A measurement of speed for network telecommunications systems. A bit is the smallest piece of information communicated by computers. The number of bits that pass through a modem determines the speed of a modem.

Bookmark A means of collecting favorite Home Pages and addresses in Netscape and in other Gopher and Internet Clients for future reference.

bps See Bits Per Second.

Browsers Browsers are the newest and most significant new software tools on the Internet. Browsers, like Netscape and Mosaic, are user-friendly viewers and are required to navigate the World Wide Web and to manipulate hypertext documents. Well-designed Browsers have the other major Internet software tools built right into their software.

C

Category Collection of related Newsgroups.

Client The term given to any computer that is connected to the Internet and has the software it needs to share information over the Internet.

Client Software Software that allows your computer to talk, communicate, and share information with Internet host computers and Internet servers.

com Indicates a commercial domain.

Connections The software and hardware links between computers are called connections. The speed and compatibility of your computer's connection to your Internet host computer will determine the efficiency with which you can access Internet resources. (See SLIP and PPP)

Cybernetics The science that compares the functions of the brain with the functions of a computer.

Cyberspace A term given to the electronic, computerized world of the Internet. Often called virtual reality. When you are on the Internet or the World Wide Web, you are in Cyberspace.

D

Directory A storage location, like a file folder, where related data and files are stored.

Distributed Network The Internet is a distributed network, meaning that there is not one central authority or group guiding its growth, use, and development. If one part of the Internet goes down, as in a natural disaster like an earthquake, Internet communications can be transferred to other lines of communication, and the downed portion of the network can be bypassed until repairs are made.

Domain Name System A system of computers and software that allows Internet names like karl@dixon.edu to be converted into a number like 158.90.62.25 and back again.

Domains A division or section of the Internet. For example, the military is one domain, education is another. Service providers like America Online and Prodigy have their own domains. Domains can be divided geographically by country, region, or state, or by other similarities such as business, commerce, government agencies, or private organizations.

Download To copy files, data, information, and software from a remote host computer to your computer or to another computer.

DNS See Domain Name System.

Dumb Terminal A dumb terminal is attached to a mainframe or minicomputer. The terminal does not do any of the computer processing. Dumb terminals allow input from the user and display the processing taking place on a host computer.

Dynamic Constantly changing.

E

edu Indicates an educational domain.

E-Mail E-mail is short for electronic mail. Electronic mail is the most widely used feature of the Internet. Mail is written in an E-mail program and transmitted over networks to other users with compatible E-mail software.

Emulate To imitate. (See Dumb Terminal.)

Etiquette Rules of conduct and behavior. (See Netiquette.)

F

FAQs Frequently Asked Questions. Hosts will post answers to their most frequently asked questions.

Finger An Internet software tool for locating people (via E-mail addresses) on other Internet sites.

Flamers Newsgroup or E-mail users who send flames or written rebukes.

Flames Rebukes sent by agitated Internet users to people who violate rules of Internet "netiquette," or who "spam" the Internet.

FTP File Transfer Protocol. FTP software transfers files, information, and data from one computer to another.

G

Gateways Tools that allow commercial E-mail software to communicate with each other.

Gopher A system of menus that allow users with Gopher Client software to access information on computers called Gopher Servers.

Gopher Client Software that allows users access to Gopher Servers.

Gopher Servers Software that allows Gopher Clients access to Gopher files, directories, and menus.

Gopherspace The Internet pathways available from a Gopher Client.

gov Indicates a governmental domain.

Groups USENET Newsgroups.

GUI Graphical User Interface. GUI, pronounced gooie, replaces commands with pictures, or icons, in software usually associated with Windows or Macintosh computers.

H

Hits A hit is recorded anytime someone connects to a remote computer, site, or Home Page.

Home Page A Home Page is like an index that contains related information on a single topic in a hypertext WWW environment.

Host

Host Any computer providing network services and resources to other computers is called a host. Host computers are also called servers. Servers are the key computers in networks.

Hotlist A catalog or list of Home Pages in Mosaic.

HTML (See Hypertext Markup Language.)

HTTP (See Hypertext Transfer Protocol.)

Hypermedia Computer data that creates hypertext links between more than one kind of media. Types of media include video, pictures, graphics, animation, and text. (See Multimedia.)

Hypertext A system of information retrieval, where selected keywords are linked to text and other information in the same document or in another document. Clicking on a hypertext word will execute a command to find the text you have selected. Hypertext links are not limited to the local computer network. Hypertext links can take you to information located on another computer in another part of the world.

Hypertext Markup Language (HTML) A set of commands that describe a file to a GUI Browser.

Hypertext Transfer Protocol (HTTP) Protocols are instructions that tell computers how to handle and send hypertext documents and data from one computer to another.

I

Icon A picture or graphic that represents something. For example, an icon of a printer may represent the Print command. (See GUI.)

Incompatability When software from a client computer does not communicate with the software on an Internet host, there is an incompatibility. Incompatibilities exist with different versions of software, when internal software settings do not correspond, or for a variety of other reasons. Hardware may also be incompatible, limiting Internet access.

Internet The name given to the current telecommunications system between networks of computers. The Internet is often called a "network of networks." The Internet will grow into the electronic superhighway of the future. The Internet is often called the Net because it is the largest computer network in the world.

IP Internet Protocol, an address label for Internet packages called packets. IP makes sure the packets arrive at the correct destination.

L

Links Hypertext Words that jump automatically to another selection of text.

Listserv The most common kind of maillist, Listervs originated on BITNET, but they are now common on the Internet.

Lurkers Newsgroup or E-mail users who read groups but don't post their own articles.

M

Maillist (or Mailing List) A (usually automated) system that allows people to send E-mail to one address, whereupon their message is copied and sent to all of the other subscribers to the maillist.

Menu A menu is a list of choices.

mil Indicates a military domain.

Modem A simple communications tool that converts computer signals into signals that can travel over telephone lines.

Moderated Screened by a person or group for anything going into a Newsgroup for distribution to its readers. Moderators cut out unnecessary postings and articles that do not fit the topic of the group.

Mosaic The popular and widespread WWW browser or client software. The source-code to Mosaic has been licensed by several companies.

Multimedia Systems that use more than one medium. A multimedia computer can utilize various types of media including video, sound, pictures, graphics, animation, and text.

N

Names A unique or different name is required for Internet users. In common speech, the words "name" and "address" are often used interchangeably. Technically speaking, a name involves the use of words (eugene@dixon.edu), and an address is a number like 158.95.6.2.

net Indicates a network provider domain.

Net Short for Network.

Netiquette Internet rules of behavior and conduct.

Network Two or more computers linked together to share information and data.

Network Administrators The most important person on a network is the Network Administrator. These people manage all the hardware and software issues on a network and keep things running. They manage the security of the network and grant network rights to users. Network Administrators are often overworked and underpaid, but they usually have some really cool computers.

Newbies New members of discussion groups.

Newsgroup Participants who follow threads of a particular topic with the help of a USENET newsreader.

Newsreader Software tool required to read and participate in USENET Newsgroups.

NIC Network Information Center. Generally, any office that handles information for a network. The most famous of these on the Internet is the InterNIC, which is where new domain names are registered.

O

On-line Using computer connections to networks.

org Indicates an organizational domain.

P

Packets The bundles of data that can be transmitted over the Internet.

Password A special word used to secure computer systems. Passwords are usually created by authorized users under the directions of a Network Administrator. Hosts use passwords to distinguish users that are allowed on a computer network from those that are trying to gain illegal or unauthorized entry.

Platforms There are many different and sometimes incompatible computer hardware and software systems, called platforms.

Post To send articles to Newsgroups or to electronic bulletin board systems.

PPP Point-to-Point Protocol. One of the types of connections that allow Internet communications over a modem. PPP allows your computer to act like you have a direct connection to the Internet. (See SLIP.)

R

Resources Anything you can find on the Internet is a resource, including software, files, data, information, services, and people.

S

Saints People who provide help to new members of discussion groups.

Server Any computer providing network services and resources to other computers. Server computers are also called "hosts." Servers are the key computers in networks.

Service Providers Companies that provide Internet connections.

Site A computer connected to the Internet that contains information that can be accessed using a navigation tool such as gopher or FTP.

SLIP Serial Line Internet Protocol. One of the types of connections that allow Internet communications over a modem. SLIP allows your computer to act like you have a direct connection to the Internet. (See PPP.)

Spam Unwanted Internet garbage, particularly advertising on the public Internet.

Subject Line The title of a Newsgroup posting or article.

Subscribers Participants in a Newsgroup or E-mail discussion list.

Superhighway Another name for Cyberspace. Also, the name given to the Internet of the future.

Surf Exploring the Internet. When you surf, you are looking for interesting information.

T

TCP Transmission Control Protocol. TCP keeps track of every item in a packet or package that is transmitted over the Internet. If an item arrives broken or incomplete, TCP asks the host computer to send the packet over again.

Telnet Telnet provides the ability to log in to remote servers or host computers and to use its resources as if you were a computer terminal on that particular host computer.

Telnet Session Anytime you log in to a Telnet computer, you start a Telnet session. When you log out of Telnet, you end the session.

Text-Based Internet systems that rely on words rather than on graphics and pictures.

Thread A series of messages on the same theme or topic.

Title The particular name of a Newsgroup within its category.

Transfer Rate The speed at which data is exchanged between computers.

U

Uniform Resource Locator An address or reference code that makes it possible for a GUI Browser like Mosaic or Netscape to locate hypertext and hypermedia documents on any WWW host server in the world.

Unique Different, individualized.

Unmoderated Not screened for anything going into a Newsgroup for distribution to its readers. Therefore, group members must be more aware of what is and is not appropriate for the group.

URL See Uniform Resource Locator.

USENET A huge collection of computers that allow you to post, distribute, or publish Newsgroup articles. USENET is one of the most widely used Internet services.

User-Friendly Easy-to-use software. User-friendly software is intuitive; in other words, people are able to figure out by the name, icon, or location of a command what a particular software command will do.

V

Veronica Very Easy Rodent Oriented Net-wide Index to Computerized Archives. Developed at the University of Nevada, Veronica is a constantly updated database of the names of almost every menu item on thousands of gopher servers. The Veronica database can be searched from most major gopher menus.

W

WAIS Wide Area Information Servers. A commercial software package that allows the indexing of huge quantities of information, and then making those indexes searchable across networks such as the Internet. A prominent feature of WAIS is that the search results are ranked according to how relevant the "hits" are, and that subsequent searches can find similar topics and thus refine the search process. WAIS database searches take you inside the documents or files you're interested in; whereas Gopher and Archie searches only look at key words in the file title and description.

WAN Wide Area Network. Any internet or network that covers an area larger than a single building or campus.

Wizards Newsgroup experts.

WWW The World Wide Web, or W3. WWW is a system of computers that can share information by means of hypertext links.

Index

Key in visual aid, 143, 156
Key words, repeated, 330
Knowledge index, 288
Knowledge level of audience, 20, 25, 26

Letter/memo of transmittal for formal proposal, 353, 357
Letter of application, 76, 92, 96
    follow-up letter to, 96
    parts of, 92
    sample of, 93
    sentence structure of, 93
Letter of transmittal, 333
Library catalog, 286–287
Limitations, 270
Line graph, 143, 156–157
    multiple, 157
List of illustrations for formal proposal, 353
Literary reading, 366
    comparison of technical reading and, 368
Literary writing, 2, 8
Lotus 1-2-3, 159

Main idea for clarity, 188
Margin notes, 366, 370
Maslow's hierarchy of needs, 52, 64–65
Mechanism description, 190, 194
Media, 120, 122
Memorandums (memo), 32
    audience for, 35–36
    characteristics of, 34
    composing message for, 40–44
    definition of, 34
    editing and revision checklist for, 46
    formatting, 37–39
    humor in, 44
    model for, 33
    prewriting in, 36–37
    template for, 35
    tone in, 44
    of transmittal, 333
Message
    composing for memos, 40–44
    in professional letters
        negative, 61–64
        persuasive, 64–68
        positive, 59–61
Microsoft Works, 159
Mixed punctuation, 58
Modern Language Association (MLA)
    documentation style, 289, 291

Modified block style, 52, 57
Modifiers, deleting unnecessary, 137
Motivate, 52
Multiple audience, 18
    meeting needs of, 22–24
Multiple bar graph, 143, 155
Multiple line graph, 143, 157

Narrative, 190, 195
NewsBank, 287
News directors as audience for news release, 123
News releases, 120, 122–123
    audience for, 123–124
    body in, 127
    editing and revision checklist for, 133
    formatting, 125–128
    introduction in, 126–127
    model of, 121
    organizing and composing, 128–131
    prewriting, 124–125
News writer's approach to news release, 130–131
Notecards for oral presentation, 111
Note taking
    from secondary sources, 294–297
    in technical reading, 369–372
Novell PerfectWorks, 159
Numbers, using, 168-169
Numerical data in technical reading, 379

Objectivity, 204, 207, 213
Observation, 304
On-line catalog, 284, 286–287
Online Computer Library Center, Inc. (OCLC), 287
Open-ended questions, 284
Open punctuation, 57–58
Oral presentation, 105
    audience for, 106–107
    body in, 109–110
    conclusion in, 109–110
    ethics for, 117
    introduction in, 109
    notecards for, 111
    organizing and composing, 108–110
    personal appearance in, 112–113
    planning, 106–107
    preparing, 110–113
    presenting, 114–116
    rehearsing, 113–114
    stage fright in, 107

topic and message in, 107
    visual aids for, 112
Organization
    direct approach in, 50–51
    of formal proposal, 355–358
    of informal proposals, 318–319
    of instructions, 174–177
    of news release, 128–131
    of oral presentation, 108–110
    of periodic report, 237–238
    of progress reports, 233-237
    of recommendation reports, 255–258
    of resumes, 83–89
    of science lab reports, 209–210
    in technical writing, 9
Organizational chart, 142, 160
Outline
    for recommendation report, 256
    in technical reading, 370

Pagination
    for formal proposal, 333, 354–355
    for news releases, 128
Parallelism, 102–104
Parallel lists, 103
Parallel order, 103
Parallel structure, 76, 89
    in clarity, 189
    as transitions, 330–331
Paraphrase, 284, 296
Passive voice, 170, 204
    versus active voice, 213–214, 223-225
Periodicals, 284, 287
Periodic report, 226, 229, 232–233, 242
    audience for, 229–230
    composing, 237–240
    editing and revision checklist for, 241
    ethics for, 234
    formatting, 232–233
    model for, 239–240
    prewriting, 231–232
Personal appearance in oral presentation, 112–113
Personal essay, excerpt from, 4
Personality
    of audience, 21–22, 25, 26
    format of, 22, 25, 26
Persuasive writing, 2, 8, 42, 253
    planning for, 351
Phrases, reducing needless, 137
Pie graph, 143, 158
Plagiarism, 284, 296

Photo Credits